Tha

DREA

ANDREW SPOONER

CONTENTS

PLANNING YOUR TRIP	04
This is Thailand	04
Putting it all together	06
Bangkok	08
Bangkok-Chiang Mai-Golden Triangle	12
Bangkok-Koh Chang-Mekong	18
Bangkok-Gulf Islands-Nakhon Si Thammarat	22
Bangkok-Phuket-Andaman Coast and Islands	26

BANGKOK	33
Old City	39
Banglamphu and Khaosan Road	45
Golden Mount and around	46
Chinatown	48
Thonburi, Wat Arun and the khlongs	49
Siam Square area	52
Silom area	54
Sukhumvit Road	55
Bangkok suburbs	55
Around Bangkok	56

BANGKOK → CHIANG MAI → GOLDEN TRIANGLE			63
Kanchanaburi (above)	65	Tha Ton (opposite page, bottom)	131
Ayutthaya	72	Mae Salong	131
Phitsanulok	83	Mae Sai	133
Chiang Mai (top)	100	Sop Ruak and the Golden Triangle	134
Western loop from Chiang Mai	119	Chiang Saen	134
Chiang Rai	125	Chiang Khong	136

BANGKOK → KOH CHANG → MEKONG			139
Koh Si Chang	141	Khon Kaen	156
Pattaya	141	Udon Thani	156
Koh Samet	143	Nong Khai	157
Chantaburi	144	Nakhon Phanom	158
Koh Chang (below)	148	Ubon Ratchathani	158
Nakhon Ratchasima (Korat)	154		

BANGKOK → GULF ISLANDS → NAKHON SI THAMMARAT   163

Phetburi (right)	165
Hua Hin	165
Prachuap Khiri Khan	167
Chumphon and around (above)	167
Koh Tao	172
Koh Phangan	174
Koh Samui	181
Nakhon Si Thammarat	190

BANGKOK → PHUKET → ANDAMAN COAST AND ISLANDS   197

Ranong and around	199
Phuket	208
Phangnga Bay	222
Krabi	227
Koh Phi Phi and Lanta	239, 243
Trang	250
Taratao National Park	256
Satun	261

PRACTICALITIES   265

Ins and outs	266
Best time to visit Thailand	266
Getting to Thailand	266
Transport in Thailand	267
Where to stay in Thailand	270
Food and drink in Thailand	271
Essentials A-Z	274
Index	281
Credits	288

If you're planning a trip to Thailand the first thing to do is put your expectations to one side. Sure, you'll be able to find the kind of remote and exotic tropical beach where you'll be alone with a choice of languid sunset or sunrise. Then there's the unparalleled luxury of Thailand's numerous and excellent resorts to indulge yourself as you forget the vagaries and stresses of life back home. There's no doubt you can absorb yourself in the variety of culinary delights and yummy food encounters that have seduced travellers for decades. The capital, Bangkok, is where chaotic and beguiling post-modernity might sweep you off your feet in an energetic rush of excitement, shopping and eating. Conversely, the tranquil charms of Isaan and the communities along the Mekong River may make you want to stay a while and experience a quieter moment. If you have the energy the northern hills, filled with diverse peoples, switchback roads and endless verdant vistas could induce you to put on your hiking boots and explore close-up. There are islands that run the gamut from wild, brash party zones to far-flung, peaceful, almost uninhabited exotica, all of which always offer opportunities to feel like you're entering another world. Finally, you might consider contemplating the divine in any one of Thailand's endless supply of temples, improving and meditating on your karma.

Such expectations of Thailand are not unrealistic and are normally fulfilled for most travellers. Yet, put them aside, and you'll start to notice the details. The soft-drink bottle left at a tiny roadside shine to quench the thirst of the ancestral spirits. The dignity and resourcefulness of ordinary working folk as they struggle to establish democracy in a country battered by coups and violence. A friendly giggling smile as your mangled attempts at ordering food in Thai let you know even when you're getting things wrong you'll be looked after. That moment when a complete stranger offers to share their snack with you, as though they've know you your whole life.

Cherish those moments when your expectations disappear and you'll enjoy your trip to Thailand in a way you never thought was possible.

Andrew Spooner

FIRST STEPS
PUTTING IT ALL TOGETHER

Thailand is one of those countries whose languid charms often waylay travellers.

Thailand is one of those countries whose languid charms often waylay travellers. White sand beaches on tropical beaches can disrupt the best-laid travel plans and that friendly town and guesthouse by the Mekong or up in the hills of the North might seduce you into changing your itinerary at a stroke. So, whilst we've suggested our itineraries here we'd also recommend, if possible, you keep an open-mind en route.

Of course each of these three-week itineraries are just a taste of what the areas of Thailand we've picked have to offer. The more time you have the more you'll get out of them and, of course, given Thailand's excellent network of cheap, budget airlines, you can combine elements and mix and match, taking the bits you like from each one to create your own itinerary.

Most visitors start with at least a few days in Bangkok with the cooler months of November to February making the Thai capital far more bearable as a destination. This time frame is one of the best to visit much of the rest of the country. Bangkok is also the Thai kingdom's premier transport hub, with buses, trains and flights to all corners of the country. For that reason all our suggested routes start in Bangkok. Having said that you can easily forego a stay in Bangkok and fly into Chiang Mai or Phuket, both of which make for excellent regional transport hubs.

→ DOING IT ALL

The northern circuit Bangkok → Kanchanaburi → Ayutthaya → Phitsanulok → Sukhothai → Chiang Mai → Western loop from Chiang Mai → Chiang Rai → Tha Ton → Mae Salong → Mae Sai → Sop Ruak and the Golden Triangle → Chiang Saen → Chiang Khong → Phrae → Nan → Phitsanulok → Loei → Nong Khai → Nong Khai → Ban Chiang → Nakhon Phanom → Ubon Ratchatani → Yasothon → Korat → Chantaburi → Koh Chang → Koh Samet → Koh Si Chang
The southern circuit Bangkok → Phetburi → Cha-am → Hua Hin → Prachuap Khiri Khan → Chumphon → Ranong → Khao Lak → Phuket → Phang Nga Bay → Krabi → Koh Lanta → Trang → Koh Tarutao → Nakhon Si Thammarat → Koh Samui-Phangan → Koh Tao.

1 River Kwai 2 Krabi 3 Ang Thong, Koh Samui 4 White-throated kingfisher, Khao Sok 5 Koh Kood pier, Koh Chang National Park
6 The Reclining Buddha, Wat Pho, Bangkok

For those who want to get firmly off the usual traveller route Thailand's northeastern region of Isaan is where you're most likely to spend days rarely meeting other tourists. Parts of the north also maintain this getting-away-from-it-all feeling and, in particular, Nan province. However, the days of finding that secret, secluded beach on a forgotten tropical island are pretty much over in Thailand. There are still a few spots available but all the main island and beach destinations are now well established with the usual run of hotels, fast food joints, bars and clubs. But read any of our three-coast themed itineraries carefully and you should still be able to cherry pick the more tranquil spots.

One of the other highlights of Thailand is the range of excellent accommodation and eating. What makes it stand out is that all budgets are catered for; you'll be able to find fantastic small guest-houses and some of the best luxury resorts on earth a few hundred metres from each other. The same goes for the food, especially in the more upmarket destinations and the cities where yummy cheap street food eats rub shoulders with first-class dining.

BANGKOK

Best time to visit
The heat and humidity in the Thai capital can be awful at any time of year but during March and April it can be unbearable. Monsoon rains start in May and carry on until October, early November with the cooler drier months of December and January being the most comfortable.

You could spend years in the Thai capital, Bangkok, AKA the City of Angels, and still not be able to keep up with its rapidly spreading environs or its chaotically evolving charms. But most visitors can begin to get a sense of the place within a one- to two-week visit or by using it as a hub for their other routes and itineraries around Thailand and there's no doubt that in terms of transport it's the best-connected spot in the country.

Start in the heart of Bangkok in the Old City (page 39) area where you'll find the dramatic splendour of the Grand Palace, the divine Buddhas of Wat Pho, the blood-splattered Democracy Monument and the enthralling National Museum and National Gallery. The Old City is also home to Banglamphu (page 45) – the famous backpackers' district – and Khao San Road (page 45).

Adjacent to the Old City is one of the most engaging areas of the entire Thai capital: Chinatown (page 48). The main thoroughfares are awash with neon signs, gold shops and food, food and more food. The narrow streets that swarm off in every direction are filled with shophouses selling arcane goods and moody Taoist shrines and temples. Come in the evening and the entire ensemble comes alive, resembling a giant enthralling marketplace.

1

You could spend years in the Thai capital, Bangkok, AKA the City of Angels, and still not be able to keep up with its rapidly spreading environs or its chaotically evolving charms.

The vast expanse of the Chao Phraya River skirts both the Old City and Chinatown. It also separates Bangkok from Thonburi (page 49), the home to the former capital city and now a throng of canals and riverside living. Head south down the Chao Phraya from Chinatown and you'll reach the world famous Oriental Hotel – pop in for afternoon tea – and the far end of Silom Road (page 54), the beginning of Bangkok's business district.

1 Bangkok skyline 2 Weathered statue at Wat Pho 3 Bangkok street food 4 Gateway to Chinatown

BANGKOK

There's a Skytrain station at the riverside end of Silom and you could hop on it and head first for Lumphini Park before choosing the shopping mecca surrounding Siam Square or to the upmarket and tourist-dominated Sukhumvit Road (page 55).

Keep going north through Bangkok's grid-locked streets and you'll reach the dagger-like Victory Monument; for many Thais this represents the centre of the city. It's also home to a lot of excellent street food.

The Dusit district is the home of the official royal residence, Chitralada Palace, and also the seat of government. The atmosphere is very different to the frenetic heart of Bangkok, with wide, open boulevard-style, tree-lined roads and large European-style grandeur.

The suburbs (page 55) are home to the Weekend Market. If you have time take a visit to the small riverine island of Koh Kret, the jungle-clad park of Bang Krachao and Bang Pa-In Palace.

1 Bang Pa In Palace **2** Damnoen Saduak floating market **3** Monitor lizard, Lumphini Park **4** Koh Kret pagoda
5 Chatuchak weekend market

→ WISH LIST

1 The splendour of Bangkok's Grand Palace is a must-see and is also home to Wat Phra Kaeo – the Temple of the Emerald Buddha. 2 A huge reclining golden Buddha greets you at Wat Phra Chetuphon, also known as Wat Pho, one of the oldest and biggest in the city. 3 For hundreds of years Bangkok's mighty Chao Phraya River was the city's main entry and exit point; still teeming with life, a trip along it is a must. 4 Chaotic, wild and gaudy, Bangkok's Chinatown is one of those rare places that surpasses all expectations; you could spend a week here just trying to find your favourite spot for *moo daeng* – barbecued red pork. 5 If the heat and cacophony becomes too much make for one of Bangkok's extravagant shopping centres, such as the upmarket Emporium & Paragorn or, for bargain-hunting, the renowned MBK. 6 Bangkok's famous Weekend Market was a raucous gathering of exotic produce and animals before it went more upmarket and boutique in recent years. 7 Whenever you feel hungry in Bangkok keep your eyes peeled for the busiest of any one of its estimated 100,000 street food stalls; popularity is the best marker of good eats for the Bangkok novice. 8 Rightly famous for its many spas, a massage in Bangkok is a sure fire way to relieve those aching muscles and feet. 9 With some of the most affordable luxury hotels on the planet, if you're going to splurge try to track down that bargain hotel suite. 10 Head just over the river to the lungs of Bangkok: the small jungle-clad park and peninsula of Bang Kra Jao.

5

DREAM TRIP 1
BANGKOK → CHIANG MAI → GOLDEN TRIANGLE

Best time to visit
December-February are the best months when it is cooler and drier. In the far north in elevated towns like Mae Salong temperatures can often drop to 10°C and below during this time, attracting a lot of Thai tourists who want to experience the cold. Hot season is March-May when the rains take hold. When the monsoons are bad the flat, river-fed plains of Central Thailand are prone to floods and the North to landslides, road closures and dangerous flash floods.

Our first itinerary takes you not only on a journey northwards from Bangkok over Thailand's central plains to the hills of the north but also back through the kingdom's past. Of course you could spin the entire itinerary around and fly into Chiang Mai or Chiang Rai and work your way southwards back to the Thai capital. Whichever route you do decide to take to get the best out of this itinerary, including side-trips to places like Nan, Umphang and the Mae Hong Son loop, we'd recommend a minimum three to four weeks. For those on a short one- to two-week time frame, a route directly north taking in Ayutthaya, Sukhothai, Chiang Mai and then northwards to Chiang Rai and the surrounding hills will allow the traveller to experience the basics of what is on offer.

But it is those with time to dawdle who'll get the most out of this itinerary. Start with the River Kwai, the brutal history of the Japanese invasion and the gorgeous, lush hills of Western Thailand near Kanchanaburi (page 65). From here travel back east to the romance of Siam's ancient past and the ruined temples and palaces of Ayutthaya (page 72).

The gateway to the north is the city of Phitsanulok (page 83) – home to Wat Yai, one of Thailand's most important living temples.

Further north are the magnificent ruins at the 13th-century city of Sukhothai (page 87), whilst nearby Si Satchanalai and Kamphang Phet provide yet more ruins and even more atmosphere. West of Sukhothai is the Burmese frontier town of **Mae Sot** (page 98) and the hills surrounding the trekking centre of **Umphang** (page 99).

The capital of the north is almost certainly the 900-year-old citadel of **Chiang Mai** (page 100). Surrounded by mountains and festooned with charming streets and temples, Chiang Mai's cooler climate and gentler atmosphere is a big draw for visitors.

Our first itinerary takes you not only on a journey northwards from Bangkok over Thailand's central plains to the hills of the north but also back through the kingdom's past.

1 River Kwai, Kanchanaburi 2 Wat Yai Chai, Ayutthaya 3 Sukhothai 4 Waterfall near Umphang

An equal attraction for this part of Thailand is the opportunity to explore the hills and mountains and the cultures of the various indigenous peoples – Shan, Akha, Lisu, Lahu, Hmong and Karen, among many others – that populate this region. The Mae Hong Son Loop (page 119) via the backpacker resort-town Pai (page 119), the earthier charms of Soppong (page 120) and the laid-back hang-outs of Mae Hong Son (page 120) and Mae Sariang (page 122) make this an excellent side-trip while making your way northwards.

Next stop is Chiang Rai (page 125), another former capital of a northern principality that has given way to a sleepier, less regal atmosphere. There's not much to see in Chiang Rai itself but it is well served by transport and makes for an excellent and friendly hub from which to explore the remote far north of the country.

From Chiang Rai take a boat for the riverside town of Tha Ton (page 131), set amid towering hills and the pressed up close to the Burmese border. The nearby engaging and eccentric hill-top town of Mae Salong (page 131) is one of the highlights of the north and home to the remnants of Chang Kai Shek's Kuomintang army. These days the former KMT grow tea, run guesthouses and sell some of the best noodles in the country.

There's not much to see in Chiang Rai itself but it is well served by transport and makes for an excellent and friendly hub from which to explore the remote far north of the country.

1 Rak Thai village, Pai **2** Chiang Mai **3** Doi Phatung, Chiang Rai **4** Golden Triangle
5 Mae Salong **6** View of Nan from Wat Phra That Khao Noi **7** (See over) Wat Mahathat, Ayutthaya

The absorbing border town of **Mae Sai** (page 133) provides another frontier outpost with Burma and has recently morphed into a giant market place filled with goods passing both south and north. A short hop east of Mae Sai is the infamous **Golden Triangle** (page 134) at the small town of Sop Ruak and the meeting of Laos, Burma and Thailand in the Mekong River.

Flow south with the Mekong from Sop Ruak to the dusty of the small river port town of **Chiang Saen** (page 134) and the entry point to Laos at **Chiang Khong** (page 136), another backpacker's mecca.

The best for this author though, is saved to last: **Nan** (page 115). You'll need to take a side-trip from the main itinerary to reach here but you won't be disappointed. The province itself is home to some of the most spellbinding vistas in Thailand, whilst Nan town is engaging and filled with interest.

The absorbing border town of Mae Sai provides another frontier outpost with Burma and has recently morphed into a giant market place filled with goods passing both south and north.

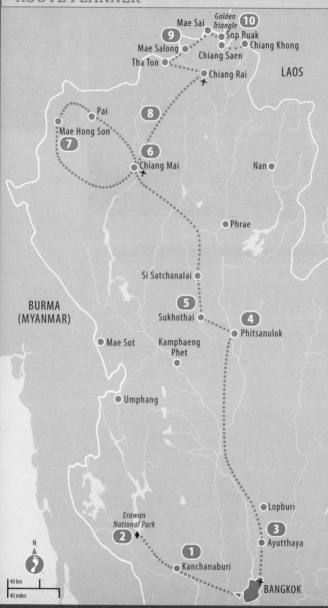

1 Made famous by David Lean's epic film, the Bridge over the River Kwai in Kanchanaburi encapsulates history like few other places in Thailand. 2 A couple of hours west of Kanchanaburi is the verdant Erawan National Park, packed full of fauna, and the impressive seven-tiered Erawan Falls. 3 The one-time capital of ancient Siam, Ayutthaya is home to a diverse range of atmospheric and ruined temples. 4 On the banks of the Nan River is the city of Phitsanulok, home to one of the country's most venerated temples: Wat Phra Sri Ratana Mahathat. 5 The ruins at Sukhothai date back to the 13th century and the giant Buddhas, dreamy landscapes and massive historical park are well worth a couple of days. 6 The one-time capital of its own northern empire, Chiang Mai still retains a modicum of regal import, not least in its walled old town where you'll find creaking temples, flower-bedecked back streets and a soporific charm. 7 The famous Mae Hong Son Loop passes through dramatic mountain scenery, the backpacker mecca of Pai and the sleepy mountain town of Mae Hong Son. 8 Many travellers head to the north for trekking; taking a walk in the northern hills is an excellent way to experience this part of the country. 9 Close to the Burmese border and surrounded by terraced tea plantations, the Chinese-influenced Mae Salong is a good base for trekking. 10 Visit the Golden Triangle on the Mekong, the famous spot where Thailand, Laos and Burma meet.

7

DREAM TRIP 2
BANGKOK → KOH CHANG → MEKONG

Best time to visit
The Eastern Coast and Isaan follow the weather patterns of Bangkok and Central and Northern Thailand with the drier, cooler months at the end and beginning of the year, making December and January the best months to visit. February is also good as the tourist season is ending so prices drop slightly. March to early May is hot with the monsoon and rains lasting until October/November.

The first part of this itinerary, the Eastern Gulf Coast, is home to the most easily accessible beaches and islands from Bangkok. You could just sample this element of the route and flit from beach to beach and island to island, easily using up three weeks on this part of the itinerary alone. Soporific beach-bums could, of course, spend much longer.

If you're planning the suggested three to four weeks first of all plan to spend a couple of days on idiosyncratic Koh Si Chang (page 141) sampling the yummy seafood and eyeballing the troops of monkeys. From there it's a short hop to the notorious fleshpots of Pattaya (page 141).

Whilst cultural delights might not be a big draw in Pattaya – one of Thailand's most infamous sextourism resort towns – there's enough here to draw in the more discerning visitor for a couple of days. Excellent cuisine of almost every stripe along with some surprisingly good diving and a fun-filled night's entertainment at a *katoey* (transsexual) cabaret show make Pattaya as quintessentially Thai as Buddhism and jasmine rice.

Another short hop down the coast is Koh Samet (page 143), a gorgeous splash of green and whitesand cast in azure seas.

1 Koh Si Chang fishing boats 2 Phanom Rung ruins 3 Koh Mak, Trat 4 Cuttlefish, Koh Chang

At weekends Samet becomes a lively party island for young Bangkokians but there are always enough spaces to still get away from it all. Once again a couple of days here is ample but the beaches can entice visitors to stay longer.

Carry on along the coast from Samet to lively Chantaburi (page 144) – the main transport hub to reach Isaan to the north (there are also numerous bus connections from Pattaya) – to experience the gem markets, the riverfront and some delicious *pad thai*. A night or two here is ample.

From there it's an hour or so to Trat and Koh Chang (page 148), the archipelago that offers a smorgasbord of islands, beaches and getaways. Some people are seduced to spend several weeks relaxing and exploring the archipelago on its own although a five-day visit to Koh Chang and/or Koh Kood/Mak/Wai is usually enough.

Chantaburi is also the point to pick up transport to Nakhon Ratchasima, aka Korat (page 154), the entry point to Isaan, Thailand's northeastern, friendliest and least touristy province. The itinerary through Isaan has numerous options and could be completed as a circuitous route starting at Korat, heading north to Khon Kaen, Udon Thani (page 156) and Nong Khai (page 157) on the Mekong and near the Laos border. Then head east to Nakhon Phanom (page 158) and south to Ubon Ratchathani (page 158), and before dropping south to and

At weekends Samet becomes a lively party island for young Bangkokians but there are always enough spaces to still get away from it all.

5 Sunrise over the Mekong River 6 Nakhon Phanom pagoda 7 Udon Thani statue

back to Korat. Each place can be seen in two to three days although you may want to linger a bit longer tasting the delicious Isaan food, sitting by the Mekong or visiting the ancient Khmer ruins.

You could also head directly to Korat from Bangkok and then follow the route through Isaan to Nong Khai and the Mekong, from where you can cross into Laos. Alternatively, if you're overlanding from land-locked Laos you could start this itinerary in Isaan and use it as the quickest route south to the beaches of Samet, Chang and the Eastern Coast. The itinerary could even be used to overland from Cambodia – the border crossing south of Trat at Khlong Yai links directly to Koh Kong and nearby Sihanoukville in Cambodia – and in that instance we'd suggest starting the route at Koh Chang.

If time is short combine a few selected highlights of Isaan – remember you can fly from Bangkok directly into places such as Ubon Ratchatani, Udon Thani and Nakhon Phanom – with a week on the beaches of the Eastern Gulf Coast and you'll have a holiday where you'll experience the rich diversity of Thai culture along with white sand and lazy days.

→ WISH LIST

1 The island of Koh Si Chang is home to a spooky abandoned palace, monkeys, an obscure Chinese temple and incredible seafood. 2 The ultimate Bangkok weekender party spot, the island of Koh Samet still manages to retain plenty of exotic beauty. 3 There's no better place in the country to taste the classic Thai dish, *pad thai*, than Chantaburi and if that doesn't satisfy you try looking for that elusive gem stone in one of the town's famous gem markets. 4 In the last 15 years the island of Koh Chang – or Elephant Island – has become one of Thailand's premier beach destinations. 5 The entry point to Thailand's vast province of Isaan is the large city of Korat, with the spectacular Khmer Angkor era ruins of Phimai and Phnom Rung nearby. 6 The most popular food in Thailand, Isaan food should be the culinary highlight of your trip to Thailand's northeast. Spicy minced meats (*larb*) spicy papaya salad (*som tam*) and sticky rice are the staples in places such as Udon Thani. 7 Tucked away in a remote corner of Isaan is the small, friendly town of Loei, close to the magnificent scenery of the Phu Kradung National Park. 8 Follow one of Asia's most impressive rivers, the Mekong, taking in the interesting towns of Nakhon Phanom, Nong Khai and Chiang Khan. 9 One of the most important archaeological sites in Southeast Asia, Ban Chiang has an excellent museum. 10 Isaan has its fair share of gaudy and wild festivals; the pick of the festivals in this region is Yasothon's extraordinary Rocket Festival.

Mekong

8

Nong Khai

7 Loei

Ban Chiang **9**

Nakhon Phanom

LAOS

Udon Thani

Khon Kaen

ISAAN

6

10

Yasathon

Ubon Ratchatani

Nakhon Ratchasima (Korat)

5

BANGKOK

Koh Si Chang

1

Pattaya

2 Koh Samet

3

Chantaburi

4

Koh Chang

CAMBODIA

N

50 km
50 miles

1 Phu Kradung National Park 2 Koh Chang 3 Tropical beach, Trat 4 Phimai ruins

DREAM TRIP 3
BANGKOK → GULF ISLANDS → NAKHON SI THAMMARAT

Best time to visit
Much like the Andaman Coast one end of the Gulf Coast can be experiencing the beginning of the monsoon and the other the end of the dry season. The driest months in Nakhon Si Thammarat, for example, are February-April whilst in Hua Hin they are December-February, with the monsoon rains moving southwards. This means December is great for Hua Hin but not Koh Samui. Roughly speaking starting in the north in mid-January for a three-week journey south offers the best weather.

Like all itineraries involving numerous stunning beaches and exotic islands, travellers can find themselves seduced by their wily charms and two-day visits can turn into languid weeks of lounging. The route down the Southern Gulf Coast and onto the Gulf islands is no different and while the entire itinerary is easily achievable in three weeks you may find you wished you had more time.

For many a visit to Phetburi (page 165) is just a day trip or a single night stopover when heading south. Given the closeness of the beaches and far superior accommodation at both Cha-am and Hua Hin you don't really need to stay here, although Phetburi is certainly worth exploring even if for a few hours.

Pick either of Cha-am (page 165) or Hua Hin (page 165) for your first proper stop southbound. A couple of days at either should suffice although Cha-am is pure beach resort fare – great for families and topping up suntans – whilst Hua Hin has the splendour of luxury hotels, sumptuous spas and some decent shopping.

For this author Prachuap Khiri Khan (page 167) is the pick of the bunch on this stretch of coast. A mix of fishing industry and the fact that is a provincial capital mean that while tourism is present here it is kept in check. The town itself, set on a lovely arching bay, has no real beach but does have handsome promenades and excellent seafood restaurants. Just outside the town inside a nearby air force base – it's very easy to exit and enter – is the lovely beach at Ao Manao. Once again the trappings of full-blown tourism have been held back and the nearby colony of friendly spectacled langurs with their bright orange babies completes the charm. At least three days here would be recommended.

After Prachuap it's a schlep down the coast to **Chumphon** (page 167), which is mainly used for jump-off point to reach Koh Tao and the islands. The town itself is relatively unremarkable and only worth a stopover to pick up onward transport. The sleepy beaches just to the north though are certainly worth a few days, particularly if you fancy learning to kitesurf; there are a couple of schools there.

With their relatively shallow depths, lack of currents and good visibility, the waters off of **Koh Tao** (page 170) make it a superb spot to learn to scuba dive and the island is home to excellent dive schools. Tao is also a great place to relax for few days, with some neat little beaches and gorgeous coves. A basic PADI Open Water dive course lasts four to five days, so if you've come to learn to dive you might need to factor in a full week on Koh Tao.

A couple more hours' boat ride from Koh Tao is **Phangan** (page 174), the famous home of the full moon party. There's more to do on Phangan than strutting your stuff at a beach party and three or four days here should help reveal the lush, jungle interior and some of the island's quieter and more laid-back beaches.

Koh Samui (page 181) is now pretty much a full-blown resort island and has direct flights from Bangkok, meaning that it could serve as starting point to reverse this entire itinerary and head north back up the coast to Bangkok. If your pockets are deep enough Samui is home to some incredible upmarket resorts and a couple of days in one of them would be memorable.

Finally, back on the mainland is one of Thailand's oldest cities, **Nakhon Si Thammarat** (page 190). It's not much of tourist hub and it retains much local character. The shadow plays are also worth a look as are the nearby beaches and national parks. You can also fly or take the train to/from Bangkok direct from here so Nakhon makes for the perfect end or start point for this itinerary.

1 Khao Luang cave, Phetburi 2 Dusky Leaf Monkey, Ao Manao 3 Wat Mahathat in Nakhon Si Thammarat 4 Koh Nang Yuan
5 (Next page) Hua Hin sunrise

1 The journey south begins at the well-preserved ancient temples of Phetburi, famed for its hitmen, monkeys and *khanoms*, or Thai desserts. 2 The first beaches southbound are found at the friendly, family resort town of Cha-am. 3 More beaches, golf courses, luxury hotels, neat shophouses and a regal atmosphere greet the visitor in Hua Hin. 4 The fishing port of Prachuap Khiri Khan is one of the most authentic spots on this stretch of coast, with a spectacled langur colony and the divine Ao Manao beach. 5 Chumphon offers sea links to Koh Tao and the islands, as well as a string of beaches to the north with excellent windsurfing and awesome sunrises. 6 One of the most popular places in the world to learn to scuba dive Koh Tao is also the one of the least developed islands in this part of the Gulf. 7 The Gulf island of Koh Phangan is now legendary for its full moon parties and wild nightlife, but it also has a verdant interior and some lovely beaches. 8 Once Koh Samui was a sleepy backwater, but now it's the most famous island in Thailand, with its gorgeous beaches filled with some of the most luxurious resorts in the region. 9 Back on the mainland another ancient be-templed town is Nakhon Si Thammarat, well known for its intricate shadow puppets. 10 The Khao Luang National Park is home to Krung Ching, the 'waterfall of a 100,000 rain drops'.

6

BANGKOK

1 ● Phetburi

2 ● Cha-Am

3 ● Hua Hin

4 ● Prachuap
Khiri Khan

5 ● Chumphon

Koh Tao **6**

Koh Phangan **7**

Koh Samui **8**

Surat
Thani

10
*Khao Luang
National Park*

N

20 km
20 miles

✈ Nakhon Si
Thammarat ●
9

DREAM TRIP 4
BANGKOK → PHUKET → ANDAMAN COAST AND ISLANDS

Best time to visit
January-March tend to be reasonably dry along the Andaman Coast with the first serious outbreaks of rain beginning to move north from the far southern corner in early April. It gets increasingly hot and muggy May-June with the start of the monsoon, with rains until late September. By November-December the monsoon has passed and there are clearer skies.

A traveller could spend a lifetime exploring the myriad islands and beaches of Thailand's Andaman Coast. If you have less time then our itinerary down the length of this varied and seductive coastline should still help provide you with a lifetime of memories.

You could, of course, combine this itinerary with the Gulf islands and coast (see itinerary 3: Bangkok-Gulf Islands-Nakhon Si Thammarat, page 22) and if you're heading south from Bangkok jump over the relatively short distance from Chumphon to Ranong and then head south down the Andaman Coast from there. Ranong, unfortunately, is not well served by public transport from Bangkok; there is an overnight bus and sporadic flights – you'll need to check up on the latter on arrival in Thailand as several airlines have tried to establish a profitable Bangkok to Ranong route and failed. You could also take the train direct to Chumphon from Bangkok and then take a bus over to Ranong.

The main transport hub on the Andaman Coast is Phuket with plenty of cheap flights daily from Bangkok and even some international destinations. There are also flights to Trang (to where the convenient sleeper train service from Bangkok runs) and Krabi. Any one of these three towns could be used as a starting point

1 Paddle boarding, Phayam 2 Koh Lak beach 3 Khao Sok National Park

4

for this itinerary as well with Krabi also being a good place to pick up transport to the Gulf Coast and Islands. One suggestion for using this itinerary within the usual three-week time limit is to pick three or four beaches/islands and leave out some of the rest. The distances along this coast are quite long but three or four medium hops are easily enough to cover the whole length.

If you do follow our suggested route then a couple of days sampling the hot springs in Ranong (page 199) should sort out tired limbs induced by a long journey before hopping over to either Koh Chang (page 201) or Phayam (page 202) to get into the beach-life groove. Travel south to either yet more beaches at Khao Lak (page 204) or the treehouses and lake at Khao Sok (page 202). A couple of days at both should suffice although Khao Lak can draw you into its soporific, tropical charms.

One suggestion for using this itinerary within the usual three-week time limit is to pick three or four beaches/islands and leave out some of the rest.

4 Tropical frog, Khao Sok

Phuket (page 208) is next and if you just head away from the main throng of tourist and stay in the main Phuket Town two or three nights taking in the local food, colonial architecture and hip hang-outs will usually be enough. Of course many people choose to spend two or three weeks on Phuket alone and the numerous beaches, resorts and activities can easily eat up your time.

The divine Phangnga Bay (page 222) is next and a few days exploring the islands here is worth a detour and they make an interesting hop, skip and jump route to Krabi from Phuket. Once again Krabi (page 227) is one of those places travellers tend to linger and the beaches at Ao Nang and Rai Leh and the nearby islands are

certainly a draw. However, if you started your itinerary at Ranong and have had beaches, beaches and more beaches already, one or two nights in Krabi town is usually enough.

Koh Lanta (page 243) is next and another place where you'll find people spending weeks at a time languidly lazing along one of its pristine beaches. Trang (page 250), as a town, is less-touristy and more engaging than Krabi although the nearby islands and beaches are not of the same standard as though found to the north.

The best beaches and islands on this entire stretch of coast are, arguably, found right at the end of this itinerary in the Taratao National Park (page 256) and on the islands of Koh Lipe and Koh Taratao. Both are reasonably difficult to reach but the pay-off on arrival is more than worth it. These islands are still the archetype, white-sand crested verdant jewels of the traveller's fantasy.

The best beaches and islands on this entire stretch of coast are, arguably, found right at the end of this itinerary in the Taratao National Park.

1 Phuket town 2 Long tail boats, Krabi 3 Trang at night 4 Koh Lipe 5 Koh Lanta 6 (Next page) Whale Shark, Koh Tao
7 (page 32) Doi Inthanon, Chiang Mai Province

→ ROUTE PLANNER

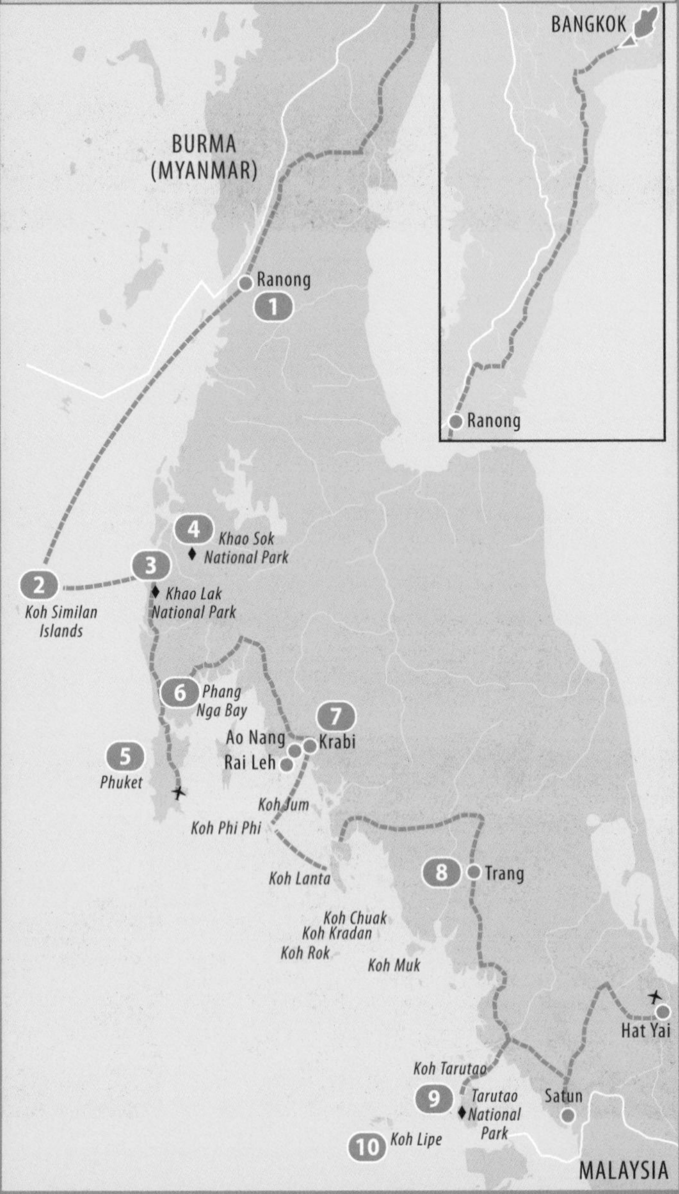

BANGKOK
BURMA
(MYANMAR)
Ranong
1
Ranong
4
Khao Sok
National Park
3
2
Koh Similan
Islands
Khao Lak
National Park
6
Phang
Nga Bay
7
Ao Nang
Krabi
Rai Leh
5
Phuket
Koh Jum
Koh Phi Phi
Koh Lanta
8
Trang
Koh Chuak
Koh Kradan
Koh Rok
Koh Muk
Hat Yai
Koh Tarutao
9
Tarutao
National
Park
Satun
10
Koh Lipe
MALAYSIA

→ WISH LIST

1 Ranong is famed for its hot springs, as a jump-off point for nearby Burma and the hub for the lesser-visited islands of the Laem Son National Park. **2** The diving along the Andaman Coast is easily the best in Thailand with the globally renowned dive-sites near the Koh Similan islands being the pick of the crop. **3** Devastated by the 2004 tsunami the beaches and resorts of the Khao Lak National Park have sprung back to rude health, making it one of the best beach destinations in Thailand. **4** Back inland is the gorgeous Khao Sok National Park with luxury tree-houses, lakes and breathtaking views. **5** The largest island in Thailand, the famous tourist isle of Phuket has a distinct Sino-Thai culture. **6** Limestone karsts, incredible sunsets and a host of islands have made the beauty of Phang Nga Bay world-renowned. **7** The backpacker hub at Krabi provides a friendly link to the islands of Koh Phi Phi, Koh Lanta and Koh Jum. **8** The Sino-Thai town of Trang is famous for its food, including the local speciality, *moo yang* (grilled pork). **9** The one time prison island of Koh Tarutao is one of the few genuinely remote and wild islands left in Thailand. **10** Famed as one of the most beautiful islands in Thailand, Koh Lipe has picture-perfect white sand beaches.

7

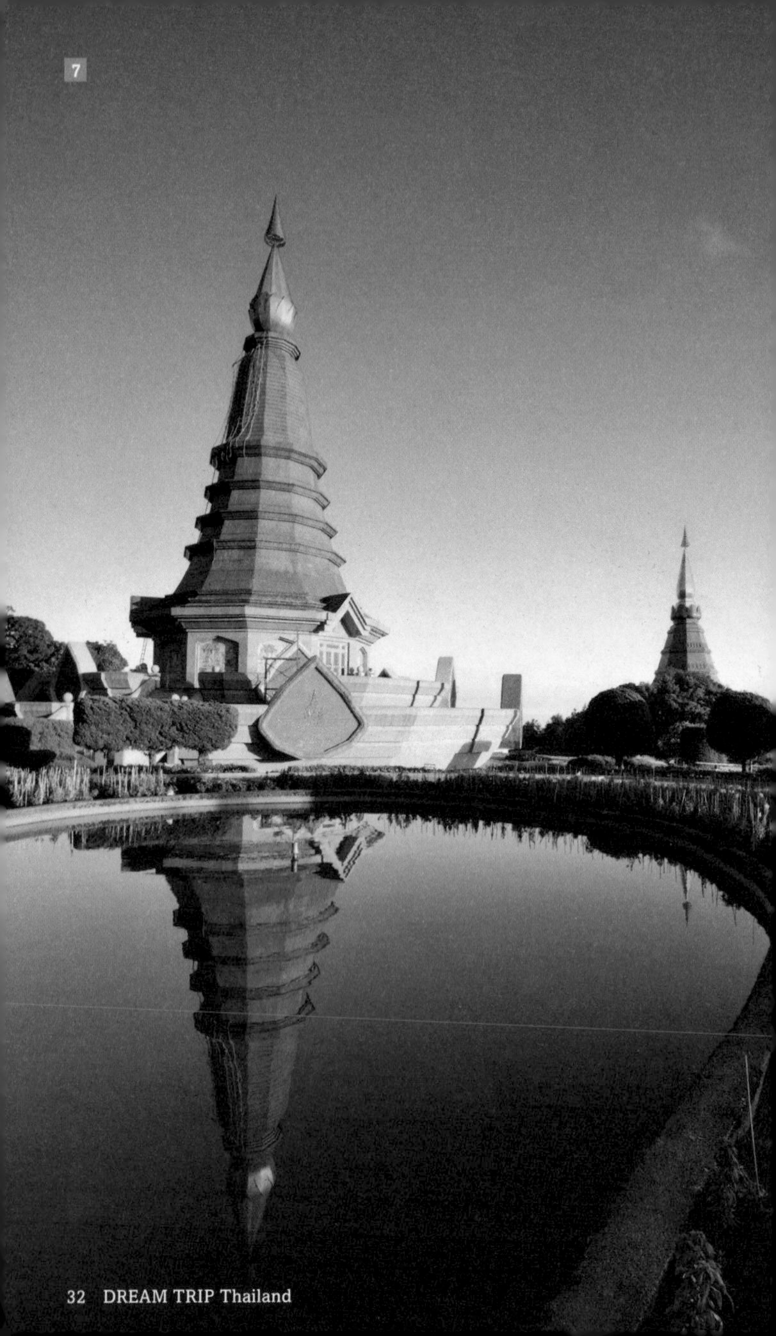

BANGKOK

Arriving in Bangkok page 35

Old City page 39

Banglamphu and Khaosan Road page 45

Golden Mount and around page 46

Chinatown page 48

Thonburi, Wat Arun and the khlongs page 49

Siam Square area page 52

Silom area page 54

Sukhumvit Road page 55

Bangkok suburbs page 55

Around Bangkok page 56

Listings page 61

BANGKOK

Dirty, dynamic, wild and sweaty, Bangkok is a heaving scrum of humanity blended with ancient beauty, booming youth culture and the rituals of a bygone age. The Thais call it the City of Angels but there's nothing angelic about Bangkok. Don't arrive expecting an exotic, languid, dreamy place trapped in some imagined, traditional past. What will hit you is the size, pace, endless olfactory cacophony, friendliness of the locals and interminable gridlocked traffic. The whole place resembles a giant, out-of-control car boot sale whose pavements are humming with open-air kitchens, clothes stalls, hawkers and touts.

Some of the old King and I romanticism does persist, however. There are the khlongs, palaces and temples but ultimately, what marks Bangkok out from the imaginings of its visitors, is its thrusting modernity in open struggle with the ancient, rural traditions of Thai culture. Neon, steel and glass futuristic transport rubs shoulders with blind street bands, alms-collecting monks and crumbling teak villas. It's all here: poverty and wealth, smog-filled thoroughfares and backstreets smothered in alluring exotic aromas, cybercafés and barrows laden with fried bugs.

With your senses fully overloaded don't forget the sheer luxury that's on offer. Bangkok is home to some of the best, and most affordable, hotels in the world. Add the numerous spas, the futuristic super-hip nightlife and the incredibly diverse range of markets and shops selling everything from amulets and sarongs to Prada and hi-tech gadgets – your head will be spinning. And when the urban theatre of Bangkok finally overwhelms, take a day trip to the ancient summer residence of the Thai kings at Bang Pa In or drift upriver to Nonthaburi for its provincial charm.

GETTING THERE

Suvarnabhumi–city transport The city's sleek but troubled Helmut Jahn-designed international airport, **Suvarnabhumi** (pronounced su-wan-na-poom), sits 25 km east of the city. All facilities at Suvarnabhumi Airport are 24 hours so you'll have no problem exchanging money, getting a massage, finding something to eat or taking a taxi or other transport into the city at any time.

Bus: From Suvarnabhumi, an a/c Airport Express bus, T02-134 8030, operates every 15 minutes (0500-2400) and costs a flat fee of ฿150, whether you take the Silom Road service (AE1), Khaosan Road service (AE2), Sukhumvit-Ekkamai service (AE3) or Hualamphong train station service (AE4). Each one stops at between 10 to 12 popular tourist destinations and hotels. The airport offers full details at the stop located outside the Arrivals area on the pavement, and at the Airport Express Counter beside Gate 8. Some of the more popular stops on each line are: **Silom service** (AE1): Central World Plaza, Lumpini Park, Silom Road, Sofitel Silom, BTS Sala Daeng Station. **Khaosan service** (AE2): Pratunam, Democracy Monument, Phra Arthit Road, Khao San Road. **Sukhumvit-Ekkamai service** (AE3): Phra Khanong, Ekkamai Bus Terminal, Sukhumvit Soi 38, 34, 24, 20, 18 and 10. **Hualamphong service** (AE4): Victory Monument, Soi Rangnam, Asia Hotel Ratchathewi, Siam Discovery, MBK, Hualamphong train station.

The public bus station or 'public transportation centre' is linked to the airport by a free shuttle bus service which picks up passengers at the Arrivals area. Public buses are crowded during rush hours and there is little room for luggage. However, the new bus station is well signposted and organized with some English-speaking information services. Local bus services to Pattaya and Nong Khai are also available.

Courtesy car: Many upmarket hotels will meet passengers and provide free transport to town. Check before arrival or contact the **Thai Hotels Association** desk in the terminal.

Taxi: It can take over an hour to get to central Bangkok from either airport, depending on the time of day, the state of the traffic and how insane the driver is. Taking the expressway cuts the journey time significantly and, outside rush-hour, the transit time should be 35-45 minutes.

There are three sets of taxi/limousine services. First, **airport limos** (before exiting from the restricted area), next **airport taxis** (before exiting from the terminal building), and finally, a **public taxi counter** (outside, on the slipway). The latter are the cheapest. Airport flunkies in Suvarnabhumi's Arrival Hall often try to direct passengers to the more expensive 'limousine' service. Unless you fancy entering Bangkok in the back of a BMW 7 series or E-class Benz, and paying ฿1000 or more for the pleasure, ignore them, head down to Level 1 and walk outside to the public taxi desk on the slipway. Tell the booking desk your destination, and you'll be handed a coupon and assigned a taxi driver. Keep hold of the coupon as it details your rights and their obligations.

A public taxi to downtown should cost roughly ฿250-350. Note that tolls on the expressways are paid on top of the fare on the meter and should be no more than ฿45 per toll. There is also a ฿50 airport surcharge on top of the meter cost. If you've picked a hotel in advance, try to print out the map (or, failing that, have the phone number handy) as taxi drivers often do not know where the hotels are, especially the newer or remoter ones.

Suvarnabhumi regulars recommend going up to the Departures floor (Level 4) and flagging down a taxi that has just dropped passengers off. Doing it unofficially like this this will save you around ฿50 and possibly a long wait in a taxi queue. Secure an agreement to use the meter before you get in; many drivers refuse, in which case you'll have to negotiate a fare.

Train: On paper, the 28-km elevated airport rail link is now the cheapest and quickest route into the city. However, bear in mind that even if you're staying centrally, there is still likely to be an inconvenient journey by taxi, tuk-tuk or on foot from the station to your hotel. The **Suvarnabhumi Airport City Line** picks up commuters at four stations in the eastern suburbs before stopping at the inner city stations of Makkasan, Rajprarop and, finally, Phayathai. The whole journey takes about 30 minutes and costs ฿15-45. The **Airport Express** route runs from Suvarnabhumi straight through to Makkasan Station, or from Suvarnabhumi straight through to Phayathai, the only stop that intersects with a Skytrain station. It takes 15-17 mins and costs ฿90 one way, ฿150 return. 2 airlines – **Thai Airways** and **Bangkok Airways** – currently offer an early check-in and baggage-loading service out of Makkasan Station only; see the website for more, http://airportraillink.railway.co.th.

Bus Very few buses arrive in Bangkok at night as nearly all long-distance services are timed to arrive in the morning. Bus stations are well served by meter taxis and if you do arrive late jump into one these. Mo Chit and Ekamai bus stations are also linked to the Skytrain (BTS) which runs from 0600-2400. Mo Chit bus station and Hualamphong train station are linked to the Metro (MBK) which also runs from 0600-2400.

GETTING AROUND

Bangkok has the unenviable reputation for having some of the worst traffic in the world. However, the recently extended **Skytrain** (an elevated railway), along with the newer and still sparkling **Metro** underground system have made travel a lot easier in those areas of the city that they cover. Plentiful **buses** travel to all city sights and offer the cheapest way to get around; the website of the **Bangkok Mass Transit Authority**, www.bmta.co.th/en, has full listings and a route planner. There is an endless supply of metered **taxis**, which should charge ฿50-100 for a trip within the centre of town. All taxis now have meters, although some drivers develop an aversion to using them, the second a foreigner in shorts approaches. If this happens, either insist they turn the meter on or just get out of the car – most drivers will turn the meter on at this point. Alternatively, just wait for another cab. Bangkok's taxi drivers sometimes refuse to pick up fares at all, particularly if they feel your destination is troublesome. This can be frustrating, but try not to get angry with drivers, as aggression towards foreign passengers is not unknown. **Tuk-tuk** (motorized three-wheeled taxi) numbers are dwindling, and the negotiated fares often work out more expensive than a taxi, particularly as tuk-tuk drivers target tourists and have a deserved reputation for rip-offs and scams. What's more, riding in an open-sided tuk-tuk coats you in Bangkok's notorious smog by the time you arrive. **Walking** can be tough in the heat and fumes, although there are some parts of the city where this can be the best way to get around. As Bangkok is a relatively safe city it is usually alright to walk around even the most deserted streets at night. However, be sensible, as you would anywhere else and don't display valuables or appear lost. The best bet late at night, if you're unsure where to go, is to flag down one of the capital's ubiquitous taxis. For an alternative to the smog of Bangkok's streets, you can hop on board one of the express **river taxis** – more like

river buses – which ply the Chao Phraya River (see www.chaophrayaexpressboat.com). Similar services on the city's khlongs (canals) were discontinued years ago, barring one along the putrid Klong Saen Saeb canal, which runs from the Old City's pretty Saphan Phan Fah bridge to the eastern suburbs. If you want to get from modern Bangkok to the Old City, or vice versa, these long-tailed boats are quicker and cheaper than a taxi (but not recommended for those with children). Private ruea hang yao, as they are known in Thai, can also be chartered from many river piers to whisk you along the cleaner khlongs of Thonburi, where glimpses of the fabled 'Venice of the East' survive.

TOURIST INFORMATION

Tourist Authority of Thailand (**TAT**) ⓘ *main office at 1600 New Phetburi Rd, Makkasan, Ratchathewi, T02-250 5500, www.tourismthailand.org; also at 4 Rachdamnern Nok Av (intersection with Chakrapatdipong Rd), Mon-Fri 0830-1630; in addition there are 2 counters at*

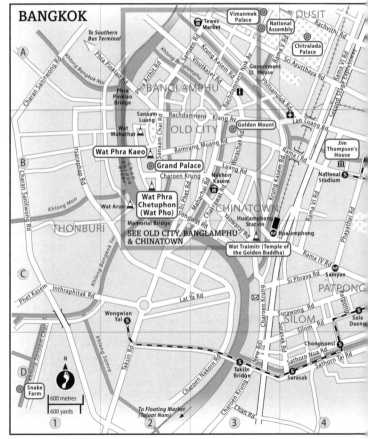

Suvarnabhumi Airport, in the Arrivals halls of Terminals 1 and 2, T02-504 2701, 0800-2400. The two main offices are very helpful and provide a great deal of information for independent travellers – certainly worth a visit. For information, phone T1672 between 0800 and 2000 for the English-speaking **TAT Call Centre**. A number of good, informative English-language magazines provide listings of what to do and where to go in Bangkok. *BK Magazine* is a free weekly publication with good listings for clubs, restaurants and live acts. And, *Bangkok 101* (www.bangkok101.com), ฿100, is a handy monthly city magazine meets travel guide, with a strong focus on eating out, arts and culture.

PLACES IN BANGKOK

Wats and palaces, markets and shopping, traditional dancing and Thai boxing, glorious food, tuk-tuks and water taxis fill Bangkok. Get over the pace and pollution and you'll have a ball

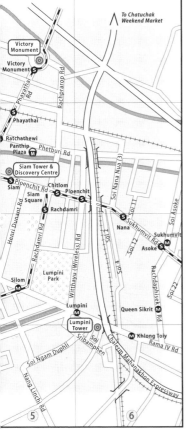

in Bangkok. This is one of the most engaging cities on the planet and its infectious, amiable energy soon wears down even the staunchest tree-hugger. Begin your sojourn in the bejewelled beauty of the **Old City**. Here you'll find the regal heart of Bangkok at the stupendous Grand Palace. The charming **Golden Mount** is a short hop to the east, while to the south are the bewildering alleyways and gaudy temples of Bangkok's frenetic **Chinatown**. Head west over the Chao Phraya River to the magnificent spire of **Wat Arun** and the *khlongs* of **Thonburi**. To the north sits the broad, leafy avenues of **Dusit**, the home of the Thai parliament and the king's residence. Carry on east and south and you'll reach modern Bangkok. A multitude of mini-boutiques forms **Siam Square** and the Thai capital's centre of youth fashion; **Silom** and **Sukhumvit roads** are vibrant runs of shopping centres, restaurants and hotels while the **Chatuchak Weekend Market** (known to locals as JJ), in the northern suburbs, is one of Asia's greatest markets.

→ OLD CITY

Filled with palaces and temples, this is the ancient heart of Bangkok. These days it is the premium destination for visitors and controversial plans are afoot to change it into a 'tourist zone'. This would strip the area

Jetlag pending, head down to the closest park or patch of green around dawn to watch Bangkok rise and shine in typical style. Heading out between 0500 and 0700 you'll find foodstalls firing up their charcoal grills as saffron-clad monks make alms rounds. But it's in parks like Lumpini where Bangkok's day really kicks into action with spandex-clad folk pulling synchronized moves to hi-energy Thai pop. Aside from aerobics, other early morning activities include jogging, tai chi and early morning picnicking/snacking on chickens' feet. Gourmet tourists may want to sample a more farang-friendly bowl of 'jok' or rice porridge flavoured with chicken or pork – the hearty breakfast choice of Bangkok. Swilled down with a cup of bright amber Thai tea packed with caffeine and sugar, you should be ready to face Bangkok's bustling charms.

As the day's heat starts to take hold, jump in an aircon taxi to check out the unmissable opulent splendour of the Grand Palace and Wat Phra Kaew.

The nearby temple of **Wat Pho** and its famous massaging monks is the next stop: have every jetlagged crease and knot pummelled from your limp body. Then, on to nearby Chinatown for lunch. Wander the tiny alleys of the **Thieves' Market**, not forgetting to indulge in the endless throng of tasty street kitchens before walking to the **Chao Phrayo River**.

Climb aboard one of the numerous river taxis and head south to the Saphan Taksin pier where Bangkok's futuristic elevated Skytrain – awaits. Zoom through Silom's glass and concrete to **Siam Square**. Bring a big budget credit card as Siam is now Bangkok's busiest shopping district and is awash with weird fashions and expensive shopping centres.

As the evening kicks in take your pick of the city's endless entertainments. Sample some high-society pre-dinner drinks at Sirocco's Sky Bar at the Dome State Tower for the ultimate in city views and head for dinner at Celadon, in the Sukhothai Hotel, for one of the finest spreads of Thai goodies in the city.

For a more down-to-earth alternative take in a traditional puppet show at Joe Louis Theatre then sample the multiple foodstalls at the Lumpini night bazaar followed by **Lumpini Boxing Stadium** where you'll get a chance to watch the ancient art of Muay Thai (Thai boxing). Finally, join the beautiful people at the **Bed Supper Club** one of Asia's hippest night spots, or head to Silom for some lively street action and a Khatoey cabaret.

of the usual chaotic charm that typifies Bangkok, moving out the remaining poor people who live in the area and creating an ersatz, gentrified feel.

WAT PHRA CHETUPHON (WAT PHO)

ⓘ *The entrance is on the south side of the monastery, www.watpho.com. 0900-2100. ฿100. From Tha Tien pier at the end of Thai Wang Rd, close to Wat Pho, it is possible to get boats to Wat Arun (see page 50).*

Wat Phra Chetuphon, or Wat Pho, is the largest and most famous temple in Bangkok. 'The Temple of the Reclining Buddha' – built in 1781 – houses one of the largest reclining Buddhas in the country; the soles of the Buddha's feet are decorated with mother-of-pearl displaying the 108 auspicious signs of the Buddha.

Now open until 2100 each night, the bustling grounds of the wat display more than 1000 bronze images, mostly rescued from the ruins of Ayutthaya and Sukhothai, while the *bot* contains the ashes of Rama I. The *bot* is enclosed by two galleries, which house 394 seated bronze Buddha images. They were brought from the north during Rama I's reign and are of assorted periods and styles. Around the exterior base of the bot are marble reliefs telling the story of the *Ramakien* as adapted in the Thai poem *Maxims of King Ruang*. They recount only the second section of the *Ramakien*: the abduction and recovery of Ram's wife Seeda.

There are 95 *chedis* of various sizes scattered across the 8-ha complex. To the left of the bot are four large *chedis*, memorials to the first four Bangkok kings. The library nearby is richly decorated with broken pieces of porcelain. The large top-hatted stone figures, the stone animals and the Chinese pagodas scattered throughout the compound came to Bangkok as ballast on the royal rice boats returning from China. Rama III wanted Wat Pho to become known as a place of learning, a kind of exhibition of all the knowledge of the time, and it is regarded as Thailand's first university.

One of Wat Pho's biggest attractions is its role as a respected centre of **traditional Thai massage**. Thousands of tourists, powerful Thai politicians, businessmen and military officers come here to seek relief from the tensions of modern life. The Burmese destroyed most medical texts when they sacked Ayutthaya in 1776. In 1832, to help preserve the ancient medical art, Rama III had what was known about Thai massage inscribed onto a series of stones which were then set into the walls of Wat Pho. If you want to come here for a massage then it is best to arrive in the morning; queues in the afternoon can be long.

GRAND PALACE AND WAT PHRA KAEO

ⓘ *The main entrance is the Viseschaisri Gate on Na Phralan Rd, T02-623 5500, www.palaces. thai.net. Admission to the Grand Palace complex costs ฿400 (ticket office open daily 0830-1530 except Buddhist holidays when Wat Phra Kaeo is free but the rest of the palace is closed). The cost of the admission includes a free guidebook to the palace (with plan) as well as a ticket to the Coin Pavilion, with its collection of medals and 'honours' presented to members of the Royal Family, and to the Vimanmek Palace in the Dusit area. No photography is allowed inside the bot. The Royal Pantheon is only open to the public once a year on Chakri Day, 6 Apr (the anniversary of the founding of the present Royal Dynasty). All labels in Thai. Free guided tours in English throughout the day. There are plenty of touts offering to guide tourists around the palace. Personal audio guides, ฿100 (2 hrs), available in English, French, German and some other languages. Decorum of dress means no shorts, short skirts, no sleeveless shirts, no flip flops or sandals. There are plastic shoes and trousers for hire near the entrance. Close to the Dusit Hall is a small café selling refreshing coconut drinks and other soft drinks.*

The Grand Palace is situated on the banks of the Chao Phraya River and is the most spectacular – some might say 'gaudy' – collection of buildings in Bangkok. The complex covers an area of over 1.5 sq km and the architectural plan is almost identical to that of the Royal Palace in the former capital of Ayutthaya. It began life in 1782.

The buildings of greatest interest are clustered around **Wat Phra Kaeo**, or the **Temple of the Emerald Buddha**. The glittering brilliance of sunlight bouncing off the coloured glass mosaic exterior of Wat Phra Kaeo creates a gobsmacking first impression for visitors to the Grand Palace. Built by Rama I in imitation of the royal chapel in Ayutthaya, Wat Phra Kaeo was the first of the buildings within the Grand Palace complex to be constructed. While it was being erected the king lived in a small wooden building in one corner of the palace compound.

The **ubosoth** is raised on a marble platform with a frieze of gilded *garudas* holding *nagas* running round the base. Mighty, bronze *singhas* (lions) act as door guardians. The inlaid mother-of-pearl door panels date from Rama I's reign (late 18th century) while the

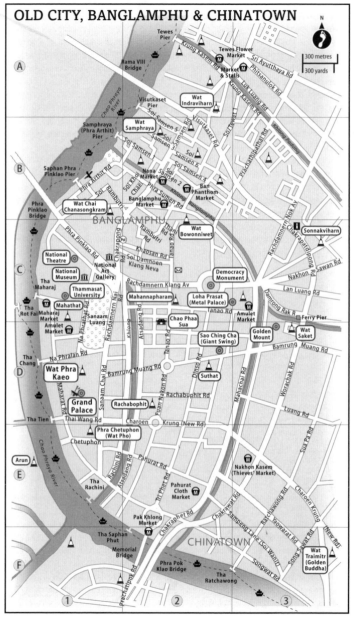

OLD CITY, BANGLAMPHU & CHINATOWN

N

300 metres
300 yards

A

Tewes Pier

Krung Kasem Rd

Tewes Flower Market

Market & Stalls

Sri Ayutthaya Rd

Phitsanulok Rd

Luk Luang Rd

Krung Kasem Rd

Prachathipatai Rd

Khlong Padung

Rama VIII Bridge

Chao Phraya River

Visutkaset Pier

Wat Indraviharn

Visutkaset Rd

B

Samphraya (Phra Arthit) Pier

Wat Samphraya

Soi Samsen 5

Soi Samsen 7

Soi Samsen

Soi Samsen 3

Samsen Rd

Soi Samsen 6

Soi Samsen 4

Soi 2

Saphan Phra Pinklao Pier

Phra Arthit Rd

Soi Rambutri

Soi Khroi

Nana Plaza

Samsen 2

Chakrabongse Rd

Phra Sumen Rd

Khlong Banglamphu

Ban Phanthom Market

Phra Pinklao Bridge

Phra Pinklao Rd

Wat Chai Chanasongkram

Banglamphu Market

Rambutri Rd

Tanel Rd

Wat Bowonniwet

BANGLAMPHU

Sonnakviharn

Rachadamnern Nok Av

Chakrapatdipong Rd

Nakhon Sawan Rd

Phra Pinklao Rd

Chakrapong Rd

Khaosan Rd

Soi Damnoen Klang Neva

C

National Theatre

National Museum

National Art Gallery

Tha Maharaj

Thammasat University

Na Phralan Rd

Rachadamnern Nai Rd

Rachdamnern Klang Av

Mahannapharam

Democracy Monument

Lan Luang Rd

Damrong Rak R

Ferry Pier

Loha Prasat (Metal Palace)

Tha Rot Fai

Mahathat

Maharaj Market

Amulet Market

Sanaam Luang

Khlong

Atsadang Rd

Chao Phaa Sua

Tanao Rd

Amulet Market

Wat Saket

Golden Mount

Tha Chang

Na Phralan Rd

Bamrung Muang Rd

Sao Ching Cha (Giant Swing)

Golden Mount

Bamrung Muang Rd

D

Wat Phra Kaeo

Sanaam Chai Rd

Khlong

Maharat Rd

Fuan Nakon Rd

Dinso Rd

Suthat

Mahachai Rd

Worachak Rd

Luang Rd

Grand Palace

Rachabophit

Rachabuphit Rd

Tha Tien

Thai Wang Rd

Charoen

Krung (New Rd)

E

Arun

Chao Phraya River

Phra Chetuphon (Wat Pho)

Chetuphon

Pahurat Rd

Nakhon Kasem (Thieves' Market)

Sua Pa Rd

Tha Rachini

Rachini Rd

Atsadang Rd

Tri Trit Rd

Pahurat Cloth Market

Chakrawat Rd

Charoen Krung

Pak Khlong Market

Chakraphet Rd

Ratchawong Rd

Yaowarat Rd

F

Tha Saphan Phut

Memorial Bridge

Prachathipok Rd

Phra Pok Klao Bridge

Tha Ratchawong

Sampeng Lane (Soi Wanit)

Song Sawat Rd

Songwat Rd

CHINATOWN

Wat Traimitr (Golden Buddha)

Charoen Krung (New Rd)

1   2   3

42 BANGKOK: Old City

doors are watched over by Chinese door guardians riding on lions. Inside the temple, the Emerald Buddha peers down on the gathered throng from a lofty, illuminated position above a large golden altar. Facing the Buddha on three sides are dozens of other gilded Buddha images, depicting the enlightenment of the Buddha when he subdues the evil demon Mara, the final temptation of the Buddha and the subjugation of evil spirits.

Around the walls of the shaded **cloister**, which encompasses Wat Phra Kaeo, is a continuous mural depicting the *Ramakien* – the Thai version of the Indian *Ramayana*. There are 178 sections in all, which were first painted during the reign of King Rama I but have since been restored on a number of occasions.

To the north of the *ubosoth* on a raised platform are the **Royal Pantheon**, the **Phra Mondop** (the library), two gilt stupas, a **model of Angkor Wat** and the **Golden Stupa**. At the entrance to the Royal Pantheon are gilded *kinarees*. On the same terrace there are two gilt stupas built by King Rama I in commemoration of his parents. The Mondop was also built by Rama I to house the first revised Buddhist scriptural canon. To the west of the Mondop is the large Golden Stupa or *chedi*, with its circular base. To the north of the Mondop is a model of Angkor Wat constructed during the reign of King Mongkut (1851-1868) when Cambodia was under Thai suzerainty.

To the north again from the Royal Pantheon is the **Supplementary Library** and two viharns – **Viharn Yod** and **Phra Nak**. The former is encrusted with pieces of Chinese porcelain.

To the south of Wat Phra Kaeo are the buildings of the **Grand Palace**. These are interesting for the contrast that they make with those of Wat Phra Kaeo. Walk out through the cloisters. On your left is the French-style **Boromabiman Hall**, which was completed during the reign of Rama VI. The **Amarinda Hall** has an impressive, airy interior, with chunky pillars and gilded thrones. The **Chakri Mahaprasart** – the Palace Reception Hall – stands in front of a carefully manicured garden with topiary. It was built and lived in by Rama V shortly after he had returned from a trip to Java and Singapore in 1876, and it shows: the building is a rather unhappy amalgam of colonial and traditional Thai styles of architecture. King Chulalongkorn (Rama V) found the overcrowded Grand Palace oppressive and after a visit to Europe in 1897 built himself a new home at Vimanmek in Dusit where the present king, Bhumibol, lives in the Chitralada Palace. The Grand Palace is now only used for state occasions. Next to the Chakri Mahaprasart is the raised **Dusit Hall**, a cool, airy building containing mother-of-pearl thrones. Near the Dusit Hall is a **museum** ① *0900-1600, ฿50*, which has information on the restoration of the Grand Palace, models of the palace and many more Buddha images. There is a collection of old cannon, mainly supplied by London gun foundries.

Turn left outside the Grand Palace and a five-minute walk leads to **Tha Chang pier and market**. The market sells fruit and food, cold drinks and the like. There is also a small amulet (lucky charm) and second-hand section. From Tha Chang pier it is possible to get a boat to Wat Arun for about ฿150 return; alternatively take a water-taxi.

SANAAM LUANG

To the north of the Grand Palace, across Na Phralan Road, lies the large open space of the Pramane Ground (Royal Cremation Ground), better known as Sanaam Luang. Now open again after a lengthy revamp, this area is historically significant, having originally been used for the cremation of kings, queens and important princes. Later, foreigners began to use it as a race track and as a golf course. Today, Sanaam Luang is used for the annual **Royal Ploughing Ceremony**, held in May. This ancient Brahmanistic ritual, resurrected by Rama

IV, signals the auspicious day on which farmers can begin to prepare their rice paddies, the time and date of the ceremony being set by Royal Astrologers. Bulls decorated with flowers pull a red and gold plough, while the selection of different lengths of cloth by the Ploughing Lord predicts whether the rains will be good or bad.

Sanaam Luang has several other claims to fame. Traditionally, it is also the place in Bangkok to fly kites, eat charcoal-grilled dried squid and have your fortune told. The *mor duu* ('seeing doctors') would sit in the shade of the tamarind trees along the inner ring of the southern footpath. Prior to 1987, the weekend market at Chatuchak was located here. Political protests, some of them bloody, have also been been staged here over the decades, though these, like many of the other activities, have been banned as part of the recent 'improvements'. At the northeast corner of Sanaam Luang, opposite the Royal Hotel, is a statue of the **Goddess of the Earth** erected by King Chulalongkorn to provide drinking water for the public.

LAK MUANG

ⓘ *Open daily, 24 hrs; there is no entrance charge to the compound although touts sometimes insist otherwise; donations can be placed in the boxes within the shrine precincts.*

In the southeast corner of Sanaam Luang, opposite the Grand Palace, is Bangkok's Lak Muang, housing the City Pillar and horoscope, originally placed there by Rama I in 1782. The shrine is believed to grant people's wishes, so it is a hive of activity all day. In a small pavilion to the left of the main entrance, Thai dancers are hired by supplicants to dance for the pleasure of the resident spirits – while providing a free spectacle for everyone else.

WAT MAHATHAT

ⓘ *Daily 0900-1700.*

North along Na Phrathat Road, on the river side of Sanaam Luang, is Wat Mahathat (the Temple of the Great Relic), a temple famous as a meditation centre; walk under the archway marked 'Naradhip Centre for Research in Social Sciences' to reach the wat. For those interested in learning more about Buddhist meditation, contact monks in section five within the compound. The wat is a royal temple of the first grade and a number of Supreme Patriarchs of Bangkok have based themselves here.

On Maharaj Road, a narrow *soi* (lane) leads down towards the river and a large daily **market** selling exotic herbal cures, false teeth, old religious texts, amulets, clothes and food. At weekends, the market spills out onto the surrounding streets (particularly Phra Chan Road) and amulet sellers line the pavement, their magical and holy talismen carefully displayed.

THAMMASAT UNIVERSITY

Further north along Na Phrathat Road is Thammasat University, the site of viciously suppressed student demonstrations in 1973. Sanaam Luang and Thammasat University remain a popular focus of discontent, the last being mass demonstrations in May 1992 demanding the resignation of Prime Minister General Suchinda which led to a military crackdown. In the grounds of Thammasat, there is a new monument to the victims of 1973, 1976 and 1992.

NATIONAL MUSEUM

ⓘ *www.nationalmuseums.finearts.go.th. Wed-Sun 0900-1600 (last tickets sold 1530), ฿200.*

Opposite the northwest rim of Sanam Luang, beside Thammasat University, is the National Museum. Reputedly the largest museum in Southeast Asia, it's an excellent place to visit before exploring the ancient Thai capitals, Ayutthaya and Sukhothai. A palace during the reign of King Rama V, it showcases a vast assortment of Thai Buddhist art and artefacts from all of the country's main historical periods, including the reigning Rattanakosin dynasty.

Each of the complex's buildings exhibits a different kind of relic: weapons, old scriptures, musical instruments, Buddhist sculptures, royal elephant tusks, and more. The **Buddhaisawan Chapel**, to the right of the ticket office, contains some of the finest Bangkok period murals in Thailand. The chapel was built in 1795 to house the famous Phra Sihing Buddha. Legend has it that this image originated in Ceylon and, when the boat carrying it to Thailand sank, it floated off on a plank to be washed ashore in southern Thailand, near the town of Nakhon Si Thammarat. The chapel's magnificent murals were painted between 1795 and 1797 and depict stories from the Buddha's life.

Good information is lacking, so it's recommended that interested visitors join one of the free tours conducted in English, French, German and Japanese by the National Museum Volunteers at 0930 every Wednesday and Thursday (meet at the ticket office). Tailor-made tours in these and other languages can also be arranged by contacting the chairman of this non-profit organization; see www.museumvolunteersbkk.net for details.

NATIONAL THEATRE AND NATIONAL ART GALLERY
ⓘ *National Theatre programmes can be checked by calling T02-224 1342, Mon-Fri 0830-1630. National Art Gallery, T02-281 2224, Wed-Sun 0900-1600, ฿30.*

Next to the National Museum, on the corner of Na Phrathat and Phra Pinklao Bridge roads, is Thailand's National Theatre. Thai classical drama and music are staged here on the last Friday of each month at 1730 as well as periodically on other days.

Opposite the National Theatre is the National Art Gallery on Chao Fa Road. It exhibits traditional and contemporary work by Thai artists in a peeling Italianate mansion.

MUSEUM SIAM
ⓘ *4 Sanaam Chai Rd, T02-622 2599, http://en.museumsiam.com. Tue-Sun 1000-1800. Entry ฿300 for foreigners; free for children under 15. Free entry 1600-1800.*

Just a short walk from Wat Pho, this slick museum is located in a beautifully restored historical building once occupied by the Commerce Ministry. It features a permanent exhibition about Thai identity and its roots. Hands-on activities and games that will appeal to kids – and big kids – include dressing up as an early 20th-century Thai noblemen, or playing a computer game to prevent the fall of Ayutthaya, among many others. Come at 1600 to get in free.

→ BANGLAMPHU AND KHAOSAN ROAD

Northeast of the National Art Gallery is the district of Banglamphu and the legendary Khaosan Road, backpacker haunt and epicentre of Bangkok's travellers' culture. It all began when the **Viengtai Hotel** opened in 1962, giving the area a reputation for budget accommodation and by the mid-1970s the Khaosan Road we love/hate was firmly established. Thai purists look down their noses at it while many locals like the money it brings in but feel threatened by the loose Western culture it brings to the capital. For some younger Thais, it's a hip, liberal hang-out, a space and place apart from the constrictions of traditional Thai culture. The quality of food, accommodation, goods and services are easily surpassed in other parts of the city. So why stay here? If you're travelling on a budget and it's your first time in Asia there are few better places to connect with other travellers. More seasoned travellers may find Khaosan Road a homogeneous spread of tie-dyed, penny-pinching backpackers and every bit as challenging as staying in a packaged resort.

PHRA ARTHIT ROAD

Running north from the National Theatre, following the river upstream, is Phra Arthit Road. The community along this narrow, leafy street is recognised as one of the most cohesive in Bangkok, and a centre for artists and intellectuals as well as traditional shop owners. The nearby addition of a park and Thai *sala* on the river has created a pleasant place to sit and watch the boats. There are interesting shops and restaurants, and the traffic is relatively sedate compared with other parts of the city.

WAT INDRAVIHARN

Wat Indraviharn (see map, page 42) is rather isolated from the other sights, lying just off Visutkaset Road (not too far north of Phra Arthit Road and the traveller nexus of Banglamphu). It contains a 32-m standing Buddha encrusted in gold tiles that can be seen from the entrance to the wat. The image is impressive only for its size.

→ GOLDEN MOUNT AND AROUND

Apart from the obvious sights listed below there's little reason to hang around here but with its history of demonstrations and cries for democracy it beats a defining pulse in the hearts of most Thais. ▸▸ *See Old City map, page 42.*

DEMOCRACY MONUMENT

The Democracy Monument is a 10- to 15-minute walk from the north side of Sanaam Luang, in the middle of Rachdamnern Klang Avenue. Designed by Italian artist and sculptor Corrado Feroci, and completed in 1940 to commemorate the establishment of Siam as a constitutional monarchy, its dimensions signify, in various ways, the date of the 'revolution' – 24 June 1932. For example, the 75 buried cannon which surround the structure denote the Buddhist year (BE – or Buddhist Era) 2475 (AD 1932). In May 1992, the monument was the focus of the anti-Suchinda demonstrations, so brutally suppressed by the army. Scores of Thais died here, many others fleeing into the nearby **Royal Hotel** which also became an impromptu hospital to the many wounded. On the night of 10 April 2010, it witnessed bloodshed again, when government troops dispersed Red Shirt protestors.

GOLDEN MOUNT

From the Democracy Monument, across Mahachai Road, at the point where Rachdamnern Klang Avenue crosses Khlong Banglamphu, the Golden Mount can be seen (also known as the Royal Mount), an impressive artificial hill nearly 80 m high. The climb to the top is exhausting but worth it for the fabulous views of Bangkok. On the way up, the path passes holy trees, memorial plaques and Chinese shrines. The construction of the mount was begun during the reign of Rama III who intended to build the greatest *chedi* in his kingdom. The structure collapsed before completion, and Rama IV decided merely to pile up the rubble in a heap and place a far smaller golden *chedi* on its summit. The *chedi* contains a relic of the Buddha placed there by the present king after repairs in 1966.

WAT SAKET

ⓘ *Daily 0800-1800.*

Wat Saket lies at the bottom of the mount, between it and Damrong Rak Road – the mount actually lies within the wat's compound. Saket means 'washing of hair' and Rama I is reputed to have ceremoniously washed himself before being crowned King in Thonburi. The only building of real note is the *hor trai* (library) which is Ayutthayan in style. The door panels and lower windows are decorated with wood carvings depicting everyday Ayutthayan life, while the window panels show Persian and French soldiers from Louis XIV's reign.

WAT RACHANADA AND LOHA PRASAT

ⓘ *Daily 0900-1700.*

Also in the shadow of the Golden Mount but to the west and on the corner of Rachdamnern Klang Avenue and Mahachai Road, lies Wat Rachanada and the Loha Prasat, a strange-looking 'Metal Palace' with 37 spires. Built by Rama III in 1846 as a memorial to his beloved niece, Princess Soammanas Vadhanavadi, it is said to be modelled on the first Loha Prasat built in India 2500 years ago. The 37 spires represent the 37 Dharma of the Bodhipakya.

Next to the Loha Prasat is the much more traditional Wat Rachanada. The principal Buddha image is made of copper mined in Isaan – the ordination hall also has some fine doors. What makes the wat particularly worth visiting is the **Amulet Market** to be found close by, between the Golden Mount and the wat. The market also contains Buddha images and other religious artefacts.

WAT MAHANNAPHARAM AND CHAO PHAA SUA

West of the Democracy Monument on Tanao Road is Wat Mahannapharam in a large, tree-filled compound. A peaceful place to retreat to, it contains some good examples of high-walled, Bangkok-period architecture decorated with woodcarvings and mother-of-pearl inlay. Just south of here is the bustling Chao Phaa Sua, a Chinese temple with a fine tiled roof surmounted with mythological figures.

GIANT SWING

A five-minute walk south of Wat Rachanada, on Bamrung Muang Road, is the Sao Ching Cha (Giant Swing), consisting of two tall red pillars linked by an elaborate cross piece, set in the centre of a square. A familiar emblem of the city, the Giant Swing was originally the centre for a Brahman festival in honour of Siva. Young men on a giant 'raft' would be swung high into the air to grab pouches of coins, hung from bamboo poles, between their teeth. Because the swinging was from east to west, it has been said that it symbolized the rising and setting of the sun. The festival was banned in the 1930s because of the injuries that occurred; prior to its banning, thousands would congregate around the Giant Swing.

WAT SUTHAT

ⓘ *Bamrung Muang Rd. Daily 0900-1700; viharn only opens on weekends and Buddhist holidays.*

The magnificent Wat Suthat faces the Giant Swing. The wat was begun by Rama I in 1807, and his intention was to build a temple that would equal the most glorious in Ayutthaya. The wat was not finished until the end of the reign of Rama III in 1851. Surrounded by Chinese pagodas, the *viharn*'s six pairs of doors are each made from a single piece of teak, deeply carved with animals and celestial beings. Inside is the bronze Phra Sri Sakyamuni Buddha, while just behind is a very fine gilded stone carving from the Dvaravati period (second-11th centuries AD), 2.5 m in height and showing the miracle at Sravasti and the Buddha preaching in the Tavatimsa heaven. The bot is the tallest in Bangkok and one of the largest in Thailand.

WAT RACHABOPHIT
ⓘ *Atsadang Rd. Daily 0800-1700.*
The little-visited Wat Rachabophit is close to the Ministry of the Interior on Rachabophit Road, a few minutes' walk south of Wat Suthat down Ti Thong Road. It is recognizable by its distinctive doors carved in high relief with jaunty-looking soldiers wearing European-style uniforms and is peculiar in that it follows the ancient temple plan of placing the Phra Chedi in the centre of the complex.

The 43-m-high gilded *chedi*'s most striking feature are the five-coloured Chinese glass tiles which encrust the lower section. The ordination hall has 10 door panels and 28 window panels each decorated with gilded black lacquer on the inside and mother-of-pearl inlay on the outside showing royal insignia.

PAHURAT INDIAN MARKET 'LITTLE INDIA' AND PAK KHLONG MARKET
From Wat Rachabophit, it is only a short distance to the Pahurat Indian textile market on Pahurat Road. Here you'll find a mesmerizing array of spangly fabrics and Indian trinkets as well as plenty of Indian restaurants/foodstalls. Tucked down an alley off Chakraphet Road is **Sri Guru Singh Sabha**, supposedly the second largest Sikh temple outside of India. To get to Pahurat, walk south on Ti Thong Road which quickly becomes Tri Phet Road. After a few blocks, Pahurat Road crosses Tri Phet Road. **Pak Khlong Market** is to be found a little further south on Tri Phet Road at the foot of the Memorial Bridge. A charming, authentic market specializing in fresh flowers, it is best visited between 2200 and dawn for an alternative, but still bedazzling taste of Thai nightlife.

→ CHINATOWN

Chinatown covers the area from Charoen Krung (or New Road) down to the river and leads on from Pahurat market; cross over Chakraphet Road and immediately opposite is the entrance to Sampeng Lane. Few other places in Bangkok match Chinatown for atmosphere. The warren of alleys, lanes and tiny streets are cut through with an industrious hive of shops, temples and restaurants. Weird food, neatly arranged mountains of mechanical parts, gaudy temple architecture, gold, flowers and a constant frenetic bustle will lead to hours of happy wandering. This is an area to explore on foot, getting lost in the miasma of nooks and crannies, and grazing as you go. A trip through Chinatown can start at the Thieves' Market or at Wat Traimitr, the Golden Buddha, to the southeast.

NAKHON KASEM (THIEVES' MARKET)
Nakhon Kasem, strictly speaking Woeng Nakhon Kasem (Thieves' Market), lies between Charoen Krung and Yaowarat Road, to the east of the *khlong* that runs parallel to Mahachai Road. Its boundaries are marked by archways. As its name suggests, this market used to be the centre for the fencing of stolen goods. It is not quite so colourful today, a number of second-hand and antique shops are worth a browse – such as the **Good Luck Antique Shop**.

YAOWARAT ROAD
Just to the southeast of the Thieves' Market are two roads that run parallel with one another: Yaowarat Road and Sampeng Lane. Yaowarat Road, a busy thoroughfare, is the centre of the

country's gold trade. The trade is run by seven shops, the **Gold Traders Association**, and the price is fixed by the government. Sino-Thais often convert their cash into gold jewellery. The jewellery is bought by its 'baht weight' which fluctuates daily with the price of gold. It's at its busiest and best at night, when food stalls abound, and the neon signs flicker to life.

SAMPENG LANE
The narrower Sampeng Lane, also called Soi Wanit, is south of Yaowarat Road. This road's history is shrouded in murder and intrigue. It used to be populated by prostitutes and opium addicts and was fought over by Chinese gangs. Today, it is still an interesting commercial centre, although less illicit. There is not much to buy here – it is primarily a wholesale centre specializing in cloth and textiles although it is good for material, buttons and such like.

WAT TRAIMITR (TEMPLE OF THE GOLDEN BUDDHA)
① *Daily 0900-1700, ฿20.*
The most celebrated example of the goldsmiths' art in Thailand sits within Wat Traimitr (Temple of the Golden Buddha) at the eastern edge of Chinatown, squashed between Charoen Krung, Yaowarat Road and Traimitr Road (just to the south of Bangkok's Hualamphong railway station). The Golden Buddha is housed in a small, rather gaudy and unimpressive room. Although the leaflet offered to visitors says the 3-m-high, 700-year-old image is 'unrivalled in beauty', be prepared for disappointment; it's featureless. What makes it special, drawing large numbers of visitors each day, is that it is made of 5½ tonnes of solid gold. Apparently, when the East Asiatic Company was extending the port of Bangkok, they came across a huge stucco Buddha image, which they obtained permission to move. However, whilst being moved by crane in 1957, it fell and the stucco cracked to reveal a solid gold image within. During the Ayutthayan period it was the custom to cover valuable Buddha images in plaster to protect them from the Burmese, and this particular example stayed that way for several centuries. In the grounds of the wat there is a school, crematorium, foodstalls and the excellent **Yaowarat Chinatown Heritage Centre** (฿100). Entertaining and informative, this museum traces the history of mainland Chinese immigrants in the Kingdom and the rise of Chinatown through their grit and hard work.

Between the river and Soi Wanit 2 is a warren of lanes, too small for traffic – this is the Chinatown of old. From here it is possible to thread your way through to the River City shopping complex, which is air-conditioned and a good place to cool off.

→ THONBURI, WAT ARUN AND THE KHLONGS

Thonburi is Bangkok's little-known alter ego. Few people cross the Chao Phraya to see this side of the city, and if they do it is usually only to catch a glimpse from the seat of a speeding *hang yaaw* (long-tailed boat) and then climb the steps of Wat Arun. But Thonburi, during the reign of King Taksin, was once the capital of ancient Siam. King Rama I believed the other side of the river – present-day Bangkok – would be more easily defended from the Burmese and so, in 1782, he switched river banks.

LONG-TAILED BOAT TOURS, THE FLOATING MARKET AND SNAKE FARM
One of the most enjoyable ways to see Bangkok is by boat – and particularly by the fast and noisy long-tailed boats or *hang yaaws*: powerful, lean machines that roar around the river and the *khlongs* at breakneck speed. There are innumerable tours around the *khlongs* of Thonburi

taking in a number of sights, which include the Floating Market, Snake Farm and Wat Arun. Boats go from the various piers located along the east bank of the Chao Phraya River. The journey begins by travelling downstream along the Chao Phraya, before turning 'inland' after passing beneath Krungthep Bridge. The route skirts past laden rice-barges, squatter communities on public land and houses overhanging the canals. This is a very popular route with tourists, and you may also get caught in a boat jam. Nevertheless, the trip is a fascinating insight into what Bangkok must have been like when it was still the 'Venice of the East'.

On private tours, a common stop at weekends is the **Taling Chan** floating market (Khlong Chak Pra). Don't expect a Damnoen Saduak (see page 57), but the local grub, prepared in boats moored alongside a wooden platform, is superb.

Another popular stop is the **Snake Farm** (Khlong Sanaam Chai) ① ฿70, shows every 20 mins, refreshments available. There is also a zoo with sad-looking animals in small cages. Our advice is to avoid it. The other snake farm in Central Bangkok (see page 55) is cheaper and much more professional. After speeding past the snake farm, boats enter Khlong Bangkok Yai at the site of the large **Wat Paknam**. Just before re-entering the Chao Phraya itself, the route passes the impressive **Wat Kalaya Nimit**. Another popular stop is the Royal Barges Museum, further north, on Khlong Bangkok Noi (see below).

WAT PRAYOON WONG
To the south of Wat Kalaya Nimit, on the Thonburi side of the river, is **Wat Prayoon Wong**, virtually in the shadow of the Saphan Phut bridge. The quirky wat is famous for its **Khao Tao (Turtle Mountain)** ① 0830-1730. This is a concrete fantasy land of grottoes and peaks, with miniature *chedis* and *viharns*, all set around a pond teeming with turtles. This wat, which can be reached by taking a cross-river shuttle boat from Tha Saphan Phut (฿4), is rarely visited by tourists but its imposing white *chedi*, surrounded by 18 satellite *chedis* and a small museum filled with Buddhist statues and amulets, is clearly visible from Bangkok.

SANTA CRUZ CHURCH
A five-minute walk upstream from here is **Santa Cruz Catholic Church**. Cross-river shuttles run between here and Tha Rachini, close to the massive Pak Khlong fresh produce market, facing the river. The church, washed in pastel yellow with a domed tower, was built to serve the Portuguese community and is fully functioning.

WAT ARUN
① 0830-1730, ฿20. Climbing the wat is not permitted. It is possible to get to Wat Arun by water-taxi from Tha Tien pier (at the end of Thai Wang Rd near Wat Pho), or from Tha Chang (at the end of Na Phralan near Wat Phra Kaeo) ฿3.
Facing Wat Pho across the Chao Phraya River is the famous Wat Arun (Temple of the Dawn). Wat Arun stands 81 m high, making it the highest *prang* (tower) in Thailand. It was built in the early 19th century on the site of Wat Chaeng, the Royal Palace complex when Thonburi was briefly the capital of Thailand. The wat housed the Emerald Buddha before the image was transferred to Bangkok and it is said that King Taksin vowed to restore the wat after passing it one dawn. The *prang* is completely covered with fragments of Chinese porcelain and includes some delicate gold and black lacquered doors. The temple is really meant to be viewed from across the river; its scale and beauty can only be appreciated from a distance. The best view of Wat Arun is in the evening from the Bangkok side of the river when the sun sets behind the *prang*.

ROYAL BARGES NATIONAL MUSEUM

ⓘ *0830-1630, ฿30, children free, ฿100 for cameras, ฿200 for video cameras.*

After visiting Wat Arun, some tours then go further upstream to the mouth of Khlong Bangkok Noi where the Royal Barges are housed in a hangar-like boathouse. These ornately carved boats, winched out of the water in cradles, were used by the king at Krathin to present robes to the monks in Wat Arun at the end of the rainy season. The ceremony ceased in 1967 but the Royal Thai Navy restored the barges for the revival of the spectacle, as part of the extensive celebrations for the 60th anniversary of the king's succession to the throne in June 2006. The oldest and most beautiful barge is the *Sri Supannahong*, built during the reign of Rama I (1782-1809) and repaired during that of Rama VI (1910-1925). It measures 45 m long and 3 m wide, weighs 15 tonnes and was created from a single piece of teak. It required a crew of 50 oarsmen and two coxswains, along with such assorted crew members as a flagman, a rhythm-keeper and singer. Its gilded prow was carved in the form of a *hansa* (or goose) and its stern, in the shape of a naga (a mythical serpent-like creature).

WAT RAKHANG

ⓘ *Daily 0500-2100, ฿20. The river ferry stops at the wat.*

Two rarely visited wats are Wat Suwannaram, see below, and Wat Rakhang. The royal Wat Rakhang is located just upstream from Wat Arun, almost opposite Tha Chang landing, and is identifiable from the river by the two plaster sailors standing to attention on either side of the jetty. Dating from the Ayutthaya period, the wat's **Phra Prang** is considered a particularly well proportioned example of early Bangkok architecture (late 18th century). The **Ordination Hall** (not always open – the abbot may oblige if he is available) was built during the reign of Rama III and contains a fine gilded Buddha image. The beautiful red-walled wooden **Tripitaka Hall** (originally a library built in the late 18th century), to the left of the *viharn*, was the residence of Rama I while he was a monk and Thonburi was still the capital of Siam. Consisting of two rooms, it is decorated with faded but nonetheless highly regarded murals of the *Ramakien* (painted by a monk-artist).

WAT SUWANNARAM

Wat Suwannaram is a short distance further on from the Royal Barges National Museum on Khlong Bangkok Noi, on the other side of the canal. The main buildings date from Rama I's reign (late 18th century), although the complex was later extensively renovated by Rama III. There was a wat on this site even prior to Rama I's reign, and the original name, Wat Thong (Golden Wat), remains in popular use. On the right-hand wall, as you enter from the riverside door, is a representation of a boat foundering with the crew being eaten by sharks and sea monsters as they thrash about in the waves. Closer inspection shows that these unfortunates are wearing white skull-caps – presumably they are Muslims returning from the *haj* to Mecca. The principal image in the *bot* is made of bronze and shows the Buddha calling the Earth Goddess to witness. Wat Suwannaram is elegant and rarely visited and is a peaceful place to escape after the bustle of Wat Arun and the Floating Market.

Almost opposite Wat Suwannaram, on the opposite bank of the river, is the home of an unusual occupational group – Chao Phraya's divers. The men use traditional diving gear – heavy bronze helmets, leaden shoes, air pumps and pipes – and search the bed of the murky river for lost precious objects, sunken boats, and the bodies of those who have drowned or been murdered.

Shop, shop and then shop some more. Head for Siam Square if you want to be at the apex of Thai youth culture and the biggest spread of shopping opportunities in the city. From the hi-tech market at Panthip Plaza, the massive MBK complex, the host of upmarket stores at one of Southeast Asia's largest malls, Siam Paragon and neighbour Siam Discovery, pure silk at Jim Thompson's House or the warren of tiny boutiques in Siam Square, you should leave with a big hole in your bank account.

SUAN PAKKARD PALACE (LETTUCE GARDEN PALACE)

ⓘ *352-354 Sri Ayutthaya Rd, south of the Victory Monument, 0900-1600, ฿100 – including a fan to ward off the heat; all profits go to a fund for artists. To get there, take the skytrain to Phaya Thai.* This is a beautiful, relaxing spot. The five raised traditional Thai houses amid lush gardens were built by Princess Chumbhot, a great granddaughter of King Rama IV. They contain her collection of fine, rare but badly labelled antiquities. The rear pavilion is lovely, decorated in black and gold lacquerwork panels. Prince Chumbhot discovered this temple near Ayutthaya and reassembled and restored it here for his wife's 50th birthday.

JIM THOMPSON'S HOUSE

ⓘ *Soi Kasemsan Song (2), opposite the National Stadium, www.jimthompsonhouse.com. Mon-Sat 0900-1700 by compulsory guided tour only, ฿100, concessions ฿50 (profits to charity). Shoes must be removed before entering; no photography allowed. Take the Skytrain to National Stadium; the house is well signposted from here. Alternatively, take a bus, taxi or tuk-tuk along Rama I Rd, or take a public canal boat. To get to the jetty from Jim Thompson's, walk down to the canal, turn right and along to the jetty by the bridge. Boats travelling to the Grand Palace will be coming from the right.*

Jim Thompson's House is an assemblage of traditional teak northern Thai houses, some more than 200 years old (these houses were designed to be transportable, consisting of five parts – the floor, posts, roof, walls and decorative elements constructed without the use of nails). Bustling Bangkok only intrudes in the form of the stench from the *khlong* that runs behind the house. Jim Thompson arrived in Bangkok as an intelligence officer attached to the United States' OSS (Office of Strategic Services) and then made his name by reinvigorating the Thai silk industry after the Second World War. He disappeared mysteriously in the Malaysian jungle on 27 March 1967, but his silk industry continues to thrive. Jim Thompson chose this site for his house partly because a collection of silk weavers lived nearby on Khlong Saensaep. The house contains an eclectic collection of antiques from Thailand and China, with work displayed as though it was still his home. Walking barefoot around the house adds to the appreciation of its cool teak floorboards. There is a little café attached to the museum, as well as a shop and rotating exhibition space upstairs.

The head office of the **Jim Thompson Silk Emporium**, selling fine Thai silk, is at the northeast end of Surawong Road, and there are numerous branches in the top hotels around the city. This shop is a tourist attraction in itself. Shoppers can buy high-quality bolts of silk and silk clothing here (from pocket handkerchiefs to suits). Prices are top of the scale.

SIAM SQUARE

A 10-minute walk east along Rama I Road is the biggest, busiest modern shopping area in the city. Most of it centres on a maze of tiny boutiques and covered market area known

ON THE ROAD
Shopping

After eating, the next big love for many Bangkok residents is shopping. From energetic all-night flower and fruit markets through to original (and fake) Louis Vuitton, Bangkok has the lot, though branded, Western goods are often cheaper back home. It is also wise to do your shopping at the end of your trip rather than the beginning. That way you'll have had a chance to gauge the real value of things and avoid being overcharged. Most street stalls will try and fleece you, so be prepared to shop around and bargain hard. The traditional street market is now supplemented by other types of shopping. Some arcades target the wealthier shopper, and are dominated by brand-name goods and designer wear. Others are not much more than street side stalls transplanted to an arcade environment. Most department stores are fixed price, though you can still ask for a discount. Shops do not generally open until 1000 or 1100.

Sukhumvit Rd and the *sois* to the north are lined with shops and stalls, especially around the **Ambassador** and **Landmark** hotels. Many tailors are to be found in this area. Higher up on Sukhumvit Rd particularly around Soi 49 are various antique and furniture shops.

Nancy Chandler's *Map of Bangkok* is the best shopping guide.

as Siam Square. Thronged with young people, Siam Square plays host to Bangkok's burgeoning youth culture: cutting-edge contemporary and experimental fashions, live music, pavement craft markets, Thai-style fast food, retro cineplexes and dozens of urban stylists keep the kids entertained. Needless to say, it epitomizes older Thais' fears about the direction their country is taking – young people aping East Asian and Western mores and irreverent modern values. Despite this, the area is distinctly Thai, albeit with a contemporary face and the groups of vibrant, self-confidently style-conscious youth will unsettle visitors who'd prefer Bangkok to remain a museum of teak villas and traditional temples. Just across Rama 1 are the shiny bright shopping centres of the enormous Siam Paragon, Siam Centre and Discovery – an elevated walkway connects Siam with Chitlom further down Rama 1. On the corner of Rama 1 and Phayathai Road is **MBK**, Bangkok's largest indoor shopping area. Crammed with bargains and outlets of every description this is one of the Thai capital's most popular shopping spots. Opposite MBK is the 11-storey **Bangkok Art and Culture Centre** ① *939 Rama I Rd, T02-214 6630, T02-214 6631, www.bacc. or.th, Tue-Sun 1000-2100*, worth visiting for contemporary arts and cultural activities.

CHULALONGKORN UNIVERSITY

This is the country's most prestigious university. While Thammasat University on Sanaam Luang is known for its radical politics, Chulalongkorn is more conservative. Just south of Siam Square, on the campus itself (off Soi Chulalongkorn 12, behind the **MBK** shopping centre; ask for *sa-sin*, the houses are nearby) is a collection of **traditional Thai houses**. Also on campus is the **Museum of Imaging Technology** ① *Mon-Fri 1000-1530, ฿100; to get to the museum, enter the campus by the main entrance on the east side of Phaya Thai Rd and walk along the south side of the playing field, turn right after the Chemistry 2 building and then right again at the entrance to the Mathematics Faculty; the museum is at the end of this walkway in the Department of Photographic Science and Printing Technology,* with a few hands-on photographic displays. The Art Centre on the seventh floor of the Centre of Academic Resources (central library) next to the car park, hosts regular exhibitions of contemporary art and discussions in English and Thai.

ERAWAN SHRINE

East of Siam Square is the Erawan Shrine, on the corner of Ploenchit and Rachdamri roads, at the Rachprasong intersection. This is Bangkok's most popular shrine, attracting not just Thais but also large numbers of other Asian visitors. The spirit of the shrine, the Hindu god Thao Maha Brahma, is reputed to grant people's wishes. In thanks, visitors offer three incense sticks, a garland, a candle and a piece of gold leaf to each of its four faces. Some also pay to have dances performed for them accompanied by the resident Thai orchestra. The shrine is a hive of activity at most hours, incongruously set on a noisy, polluted intersection tucked into a corner, and in the shadow of the Zen Department Store.

PANTHIP PLAZA

Sited on Phetburi Road (parallel to Rama I, 800 m to the north), Panthip Plaza, otherwise known as 'geek's paradise', is home to one of the best hi-tech computer markets in Asia. Motherboards, chips, drives and all manner and make of devices are piled high and sold cheap over six floors. You'll be constantly hustled to buy copied software, DVDs, games, most of which make excellent and affordable alternatives to the real thing. There's a great foodhall on the second floor. Many of the named-brand goods are cheaper than back home, but be aware that these are likely to be 'grey market' goods, imported through unofficial channels, and so are unlikely to have the usual manufacturer warranty.

→ SILOM AREA

Hi-tech, high-rise and clad in concrete and glass, Silom is at the centre of booming Bangkok. Banks, international business and many media companies are based in this area as is the heart of Bangkok's gay community on Patpong 2, one of two infamous *sois*. Patpong 1 now houses a famous night market and is largely recognized as the eponymous home of Bangkok's notorious girly shows. Stylish, tacky and sweaty, head down the length of Silom for a slice of contemporary Bangkok life.

PATPONG

ⓘ *Catch the Skytrain to the Sala Daeng station.*

The seedier side of Bangkok life has always been a crowd-puller to the Western tourist. Most people flock to the red-light district of Patpong, which runs along two lanes (Patpong 1 and 2) linking Silom to Surawong. These streets were transformed from a street of 'tea houses' (brothels serving local clients) into a hi-tech lane of go-go bars in 1969 when an American entrepreneur made a major investment. Patpong 1 is the larger and more active of the streets, with a host of stalls down the middle at night; Patpong 2 supports cocktail bars, pharmacies and clinics for STDs, as well as a few go-go bars. There are also restaurants and bars here. Expats and locals (gay and straight) in search of less sleazy surrounds, tend to opt for the middle ground of Patpong 4, still essentially a gay enclave but more sophisticated than seedy. Patpong is also home to a night market infamous for its line in copied designer handbags, some of which are better made than the originals.

LUMPINI PARK

ⓘ *Take a Skytrain to Sala Daeng station or Metro to Lumpini station.*

Lumpini Park, or 'Suan Lum' as it is affectionately known, is Bangkok's oldest, largest and most popular public park. It lies between Wireless Road and Rachdamri Road, just across from the entrance to Silom and Sathorn roads. Activity at the park starts early with large numbers of elderly and not so elderly Thais practising t'ai chi under the trees at dawn and dusk. This is also the time to join in the free en-mass aerobics sessions, jog along with the colourful crowds or lift some weights with the oiled beefcakes at the open-air gyms – all of which make great spectator sports too. Lumpini also has a lap pool, but it's for members only. At the weekend, it is a popular place for family picnics. In the evening, couples stroll along the lake and people jog or work out along the paths. Lumpini is also the site of the Bangkok Symphony Orchestra concerts that run during the cool season (November to February). Check the *Bangkok Post* for performances.

THAI RED CROSS SNAKE FARM
ⓘ *Within the Science Division of the Thai Red Cross Society at the corner of Rama IV and Henri Dunant roads. Mon-Fri 0830-1730 (shows at 1100 and 1430), weekends and holidays 0930-1200 (show at 1100). ฿200.*
The Snake Farm of the Thai Red Cross is very central and easy to reach from Silom or Surawong roads. It was established in 1923 and raises snakes for the production of serum, which is distributed worldwide. The farm also has a collection of non-venomous snakes. During showtime (which lasts a mesmerizing half an hour) various snakes are exhibited, venom extracted and visitors can fondle a python. The farm is well maintained. There is also a small adjoining museum.

→SUKHUMVIT ROAD

With the Skytrain running its length, Sukhumvit Road has developed into Bangkok's most vibrant strip. Shopping centres, girly bars, some of the city's best hotels and awesome places to eat have been joined by futuristic nightclubs. The grid of *sois* that run off the main drag are home to different communities including Arab, African and Korean as well as throngs of pasty Westerners. Sordid and dynamic, there's never a dull moment here.

→BANGKOK SUBURBS

PHAYATHAI PALACE
ⓘ *Phramongkutklao Hospital, 315 Rachawithi Rd, T02-354 7987, www.phyathaipalace.org. Tours in English must be booked at least 7 days in advance; allow 2 hrs, ฿500. Tours in Thai Sat 0930 and 1500, by donation only (if there are enough English speakers, one of the guides will break off from the main group and talk to you in English).*
A 10-minute stroll west of Victory Monument roundabout sits Wang Phayathai, a palace built by King Rama V as a royal retreat back in 1909. After his premature death in 1910, his successor, King Vajiravudh, remodelled it into the palace visitors still enjoy today. An incongruous site, surrounded on both sides by a hulking city hospital, it has a charming Sino-Portugese beige exterior, punctuated by a gothic turret and fringed by a lush lawn. The ground floor's open-sided corridors feature ageing frescoes and original floor tiling and, at the back, there's a neo-classical Roman garden of marble statues and geometric Corinthian columns, and an animist and Buddhist shrine. The lawn here was once home to one of the world's most bizarre manifestations of political thought: a miniature city that served as a fully-functioning model democratic society. You can explore these areas by yourself (and enjoy a cup of coffee in the stunning restaurant, Café de Norasingha) but a guided tour is the only way to see all the

rooms and to learn about the palace's many incarnations (between 1926 and 1932 it served as a luxury hotel) and European-style period motifs.

CHATUCHAK WEEKEND MARKET

ⓘ *At the weekend, the market is officially open from 0800-1800 (although some shops open earlier around 0700, some later around 0900). It's best to go early in the day or after 1500. Beware of pickpockets. Take the Skytrain to Mo Chit station.*

North of Bangkok, the Chatuchak Weekend Market is just off Phahonyothin Road, opposite the Northern bus terminal, near the Mo Chit Skytrain and Chatuchak Park and Kampaeng Phet Metro stations. Until 1982 this market was held at Sanaam Luang in central Bangkok, but was moved after it outgrew its original home. Chatuchak is a huge conglomeration of around 15,000 stallholders spread over an area of 14 ha, selling virtually everything under the sun, and an estimated 200,000 to 300,000 people visit the market each day. There are antique stalls, basket stalls, textile sellers, shirt vendors, carvers and painters along with the usual array of fishmongers, vegetable hawkers and butchers. A huge number of bars and foodstalls have also opened to cater for the crowds, so it is possible to rest and recharge before foraging once more. The head office and information centre, along with the police, first aid, banks and left-baggage facilities, can all be found opposite Gate 1, off Kampaengphet Road. The clock tower serves as a good reference point should visitors become disorientated.

Also here, in the north section of Chatuchak Park adjacent to Kamphaeng Phet Road, is the **Railway Museum** ⓘ *0900-1800, free*, with a small collection of steam locomotives as well as miniature and model trains. Later on, if you still have some energy and money, visit the relatively new **Talad Rot Fai** nearby. Located west of Chatuchak, just off Kampaengphet Road, this excellent night-time flea market is full of antiques, junk and faux-vintage pieces. It takes place on a squalid plot of land owned by the State Railway of Thailand and gets its moniker, the 'train market', from the row of rusting decommissioned rail carriages that flank it. There are also converted warehouses housing antique shops and cool bars, making it a great spot to browse or just hangout. It gets going at sundown every Saturday and Sunday.

MANSION 7

ⓘ *Ratchada Rd (mouth of Ratchada Soi 14), T02-692 6311, www.themansion7.com. Sun-Thu 1200-0000, Fri-Sat 1200-0200. ฿320 for entry to the Dark Mansion.*

Something different: a boutique shopping mall that peddles food, fashion and fear. Owned by the same company behind Hua Hin's faux-vintage market, Plearn Wan (see page 167), this huge, lair-like hangar is just the sort of place you can imagine Tim Burton or The Munsters spending time at the weekend, with restaurants that casually ask for your blood group when you order, eerie (and not-so-eerie) shops and a Victorian Gothic-style haunted house at the back. The latter is called the Dark Mansion and is a real jump-a-minute fright fest, worth the entrance fee, just. It's only a short walk from MRT Huay Kwang station.

→AROUND BANGKOK

If the heat and sprawl becomes too much you don't have to travel far to see ancient palaces, dreamy rivers and bizarre museums. Travel a little further and you'll be taking in sweeping green vistas amid thick forests or dipping your tootsies into warm sand.

BANG KRACHAO

ⓘ *Samut Prakarn; most cycle tour companies go there regularly.*

Peer off the top of one of Bangkok's taller hotels or rooftop bars and, to the south, you should spot a dark mass of land surrounded on three sides by Chao Phraya River and appears to be free of the concrete sprawl. This is Bang Krachao, a peninsula of marshy land that has managed to dodge the development free-for-all. Technically, it's in Samut Prakarn province but it's easily accessible from Bangkok as long as you can find the right ferry pier, which is hidden at the end of Klong Toey port. Alternatively, first-timers are better off taking a cycle tour, since the tour operator will meet you in a downtown location and then ship you, along with your mountain bike, to Bang Krachao. Few regret making the effort: this almost island (considered Bangkok's 'green lung') is criss-crossed with raised concrete paths that cut through the thick palm-studded foliage and are perfect for two wheels. It's also dotted with gorgeously dilapidated temples, friendly locals, a weekend-only floating market (Baan Nam Phung) and a quiet park called Sri Nakhon Keun Kan, among other rustic delights. If you fancy staying, check in at the **Bangkok Treehouse**, a new eco-resort.

MUANG BORAN (ANCIENT CITY)

ⓘ *296/1 Sukhumvit Rd, T02-709 1644, www.ancientcity.com, ฿400, ฿200 children. Take the Skytrain to Bearing station and catch a taxi from there. Alternatively, take city bus No511 to the end of the line, then catch minibus No36, which passes the entrance.*

The Ancient City lies 25 km southeast of Bangkok in the province of Samut Prakarn and is billed as the world's largest outdoor museum. It houses scaled-down constructions of Thailand's most famous wats and palaces (some of which can no longer be visited in their original locations) along with a handful of originals relocated here. Artisans maintain the buildings while helping to keep alive traditional crafts. The 50-ha site corresponds in shape to the map of Thailand, with the wats and palaces appropriately sited. Allocate a full day for a trip out to the Ancient City. Bikes are available for rent for ฿50.

SAMUT PRAKARN CROCODILE FARM AND ZOO

ⓘ *T02-703 4891, www.worldcrocodile.com. 0800-1800, ฿300, ฿200 children. Croc combat and elephant show-time is every hour Mon-Fri 0900-1600 (no show at 1200), Sat, Sun and holidays every hour 0900-1700. Take the Skytrain to Bearing station and catch a taxi from there.*

The Samut Prakarn Crocodile Farm and Zoo claims to be the world's oldest crocodile farm. Founded in 1950 by a certain Mr Utai Young-prapakorn, it contains over 50,000 crocs of 28 species. Thailand has become, in recent years, one of the world's largest exporters of farmed crocodile skins and meat. Never slow in seeing a new market niche, Thai entrepreneurs have invested in the farming of the beasts – in some cases in association with chicken farms (the old battery chickens are simply fed to the crocs – no waste, no trouble). The irony is that the wild crocodile is now, to all intents and purposes, extinct in Thailand. The show includes the 'world famous' crocodile wrestling. The farm also has a small zoo, train and playground.

DAMNOEN SADUAK FLOATING MARKET

ⓘ *Catch an early morning bus (No78) from the Southern bus terminal in Thonburi. Damnoen Saduak opens early, from pre-dawn, aim to get there as early as possible, as the market winds down after 0900, leaving only trinket stalls. The trip takes about 1½ hrs. A/c and non-a/c buses leave every 40 mins from 0600 (a/c ฿80) (T02-435 5031 for booking). The bus travels via Nakhon Pathom (where it is possible to stop on the way back and see the Great Chedi). Ask the conductor to drop you at Thanarat Bridge in Damnoen Saduak. Then either walk down the lane (1.5 km) that leads to the market and follows the canal, or take a river taxi for a small fee. Alternatively, take a taxi: a round trip should cost between ฿1200-1500. Most tour companies also visit the Floating Market.*

Damnoen Saduak Floating Market, in Ratchaburi Province, 109 km west of Bangkok, is an exaggerated and very hokey approximation of the real thing. Still, it is one of the most popular day trips from the capital for a reason, namely the clichéed sight of bamboo-hatted elderly ladies paddling along in their long-tails. Much of it is geared towards tourists these days but, if you take time to explore the further-flung *khlongs*, you should stumble across something more authentic. There are a number of floating markets in the maze of khlongs – Ton Khem, Hia Kui and Khun Phithak – and it is best to hire a long-tailed boat to explore the backwaters and roam around the markets; this should cost about ฿300 per hour (agree the price before setting out).

Most visitors arrive and depart on a tour bus, stopping only for a photo opportunity and the chance to buy overpriced fruit from the canny market sellers. Avoid the crowds and long-tail bottlenecks by arriving around sunrise.

NONTHABURI

ⓘ *Take an express river taxi (45 mins) to Tha Nonthaburi or a Bangkok city bus (Nos 32, 64 and 97). It is also possible to stay here.*

Nonthaburi is both a province and a provincial capital immediately to the north of Bangkok. Accessible by express river taxi from the city, the town has a provincial air that contrasts sharply with the overpowering capital: there are *saamlors* in the streets (now banished from Bangkok), plenty of temples, and the pace of life is tangibly less frenetic. About half an hour's walk away are rice fields and rural Thailand. A street market runs inland from the pier, past the *sala klang* (provincial offices), selling clothes, sarong lengths and dried fish. The buildings of the *sala klang* are early 19th century: wooden and decayed and rather lovely. Note the lamp posts with their durian accessories – Nonthaburi's durians are renowned across the kingdom. Walk through the *sala klang* compound (downriver 100 m) to reach an excellent riverside restaurant, **Rim Fung**. Across the river and upstream (five minutes by long-tailed boat) is **Wat Chalerm Phra Kiat**, a refined wat built by Rama III as a tribute to his mother, who is said to have lived in the vicinity. The gables of the bot are encrusted in ceramic tiles; the *chedi* behind the bot was built during the reign of King Mongkut or Rama IV (1851-1868). It is also possible to take interesting day trips along the canal by boat here and Klong Bang Khu Wiang houses an authentic floating market for early risers. Also see the sweet making demonstrations in traditional houses at Klong Khanom Wan and the large public and botanical park, Suan Somdet Phra Sinakarin, off Nonthaburi Pathum Thani Rd.

KOH KRET

ⓘ *Catch the express river boat to Nonthaburi then get a long-tailed boat to the island. Alternatively, catch a taxi from Nonthaburi to Wat Sanam Neua temple in Pak Kret district. From there you can catch a cross-river ferry for ฿2.*

An island in the middle of the Chao Phraya River, just past Nonthaburi, Koh Kret has a sleepy village that specializes in pottery production. A small meditation centre **Baan Dvara Prateep** ⓘ *T02-373 6457, www.baandvaraprateep.com*, is currently the only place to stay. Often referred to as a 'step back in time', this interesting little island is most famous for its production of traditional earthenware. During the late 16th century, the ancestors of the Mon families who still live here took refuge on the island to escape political instability. More recently it's become a popular weekend destination for Bangkok residents escaping the bustle of city life. Cars are not allowed on the island, only motorbikes and bikes. A walkway rings the island and it is possible to walk around in two or three hours. Old wooden buildings line both sides of the raised walkway and the surrounding forest's verdant foliage provides plenty of shade. Monks in saffron robes stroll in quiet temple courtyards in villages that give way to banana and coconut plantations. It is lined with pottery shops and quaint eateries with small, covered wooden porches jutting over the water.

NATIONAL SCIENCE MUSEUM

① *Ministry of Science and Technology, Klong 5 Klong, T02-577 9999 ext 2102, www.nsm. or.th, Tue-Fri 0930-1600, Sat-Sun 0930-1700 (closed Mon) ฿60, free for children and students. In neighbouring Pathum Thani province, the Thai name for the museum is Ongkaan Phiphitiphan Withayasaat Haeng Chaat (or Or Por Wor Chor), but even if you manage to say that the chances are that the taxi driver will not know where you mean, so get someone from your hotel to make sure. Take the Chaeng Wattana-Bang Pa In expressway north and exit at Chiang Rak (for Thammasat University's new out-of-town campus). Continue west on Khlong Luang Rd, over Phahonyothin Rd, and follow your nose over khlong 1 to khlong 5 (canals) until the road ends at a T-junction. Turn right and the NSM is 4 km or so down here on the left.*
The National Science Museum (NSM), north of town, past the old airport, opened in Pathum Thani province in 2000. It is part of the Technopolis complex which consists of the Science and Natural History Museum as well as an IT museum and Bioworld. The money for the project – a cool one billion baht – was allocated before the economic crisis. Air-conditioned buildings, internet centre, and lots of hands-on exhibits to thrill children (and adults) is the result. The exhibits are labelled in English and Thai and the recorded information is also in both languages. It is very good, well designed and with charming student helpers for that human touch.

BANG PA-IN PALACE

① *www.palaces.thai.net. 0800-1600, ฿100. Regular bus connections from Bangkok's Northern terminal (Mo Chit; journey time: 1 hr) and train connections daily 0420-2340 from Hualamphong station.*
Coach and river day tours to Ayutthaya (see page 72) normally begin at Bang Pa-In, the summer residence of the Ayutthayan kings in the 17th century. King Prasat Thong (1630-1656) started the trend of retiring here during the hot season and he built both a palace and a temple. The palace is located in the middle of a lake that the king had created on the island. It is said that his fondness for Bang Pa-In was because he was born here.

After the Thai capital was moved to Bangkok, Bang Pa-In was abandoned and left to degenerate. It was not until Rama IV stopped here that a restoration programme was begun. The only original buildings that remain are those of Wat Chumphon Nikayaram, outside the palace walls, near the bridge and close to the railway station. Start at the Varophat Phiman Hall, built by Chulalongkorn in 1876 as his private residence, and, from here, take the bridge that leads past the Thewarat Khanlai Gate overlooking the Isawan Thipaya-at Hall in the middle of the lake. Facing the gate and bridge is the Phra Thinang Uthayan Phumisathian; though it was designed to resemble a Swiss chalet, it looks more like a New England country house.

Behind the 'chalet', the Vehat Chamroon Hall, built in 1889, was a gift from Chinese traders to King Chulalongkorn. It is the only building open to the public and contains some interesting Chinese artefacts. In front stands the Hor Vithun Thasna, a tall observation tower. Another bridge leads to a pair of memorials. The second commemorates Queen Sunanda, Rama V's half-sister and favourite wife who drowned here; it is said her servants watched her drown because of the law that forbade a commoner from touching royalty. South of the palace, over the Chao Phraya River, is the Gothic-style Wat Nivet Thamaprawat, built in 1878 and resembling a Christian church.

BANG SAI
① Take a bus from the Northern bus terminal or a boat up the Chao Phraya.
The **Royal Folk Arts and Crafts Centre** ① *T03-536 6666, Tue-Sun 0830-1600, ฿100,* is based north of Bangkok in the riverside workshops of Amphoe (district) Bang Sai, around 24 km from Bang Pa In. Another popular stop for day-trippers heading to or returning from Ayutthaya, it covers an area of nearly 50 ha. Local farmers are trained in traditional arts and crafts such as basketry, weaving and wood carvings. The project is funded by the royal family in an attempt to keep alive Thailand's traditions. Visitors are offered a glimpse of traditional life and technologies. All products – artificial flowers, dolls, silk and cotton cloth, wood carvings, baskets and so on – are for sale. Other attractions at Bang Sai include a freshwater aquarium and a bird park.

CHACHOENGSAO
① Trains leaves from Hualamphong station 0555-1825 (journey time 1 hr 40 mins). The train station is to the north of the fruit market, an easy walk to/from the chedi. Buses depart from both the Mo Chit and Ekkamai terminals but it is quickest from Ekkamai – about 2 hrs, depending on the traffic. A/c buses also stop to the north of the fruit market.
Chachoengsao lies just 1½ hours from Bangkok by train or bus making it a nifty day excursion from the capital – and offering an insight into 'traditional' Thailand. This is the country's mango capital, with thousands of hectares of plantations (March being the best month for mango fans to visit). It is also famous for Irrawaddy and Indo-Pacific dolphin watching, possible between November and February. Two- to three-hour trips are available from Tha Kham, or call the district office for details T038-573 411.

Chachoengsao lies on the Bang Pakong River, to the east of the capital, and has almost been engulfed by fast-expanding Bangkok. Nonetheless, old-style shophouses and restaurants, as well as some evidence of a much more rustic past, remain. The old heart of the town is near the confluence of the Bang Pakong River and Khlong Ban Mai, on Supakit Road. **Ban Mai market** is worth exploring not so much for its wares – the main market has moved into the centre of the new town – as for its traditional wooden shophouse architecture. A concrete footbridge over Khlong Ban Mai links the two halves of the century-old market. A Chinese clan house reveals the largely Chinese origin of the population of the market area; most arrived before the outbreak of the Second World War. **Wat Sothorn Woramahavihan** is the town's best-known monastery and it contains one of the country's most revered images of the Buddha, Luang Por Sothorn. The monastery is a little over 2 km south of Sala Changwat (the Provincial Hall), on the banks of the Bang Prakong. A public park opposite Chach aengsao Fortress on Maruphong Road offers good floating restaurants along the river bank.

BANGKOK LISTINGS

WHERE TO STAY

From humble backstreet digs through to opulent extravagance, Bangkok has an incredibly diverse range of hotels, guesthouses and serviced apartments. The best-value bargains are often to be had in the luxury sector; you'll find some of the best hotels in the world here, many of which offer rooms at knock-down prices. The boutique boom has also seen an explosion of stylish independent guesthouses which often offer exceptional style and comfort at reasonable prices. The guesthouses of Khaosan are cheapish but often more expensive than those in many other parts of the country. Possibly the biggest bargains to be had are with long-stay options or serviced apartments. These are lavish flats, most of which come with all the amenities (pool, gym, maid and room service) you'd expect from a 4- or 5-star hotel, but at half the price. Officially, apartments are required to demand a minimum stay of a week; however, many allow nightly stays.

Old City and Chinatown

$$$$-$$$ Phranakorn Nornlen Hotel, 46 Tewes Soi 1, T02-628 8188, www. phranakorn-nornlen.com. A little gem of an independent hotel with incredible attention to detail. Airy Thai-style rooms with artistic design are as homely as an artfully crafted doll's house. Wooden shutters, a garden café, beautiful rooftop views and an intimate, relaxed atmosphere. Recommended.

$$$$-$$ Loy la Long, Wat Patumkongka, 1620/2 Song Wat Rd, T026-391-390, www.loylalong.com. The quirkiest guesthouse in town: a converted 2-storey teak structure perched over the river. 7 a/c rooms (including 1 dorm) feature recycled wood, gorgeous bathrooms, bold colour schemes, TV and DVD players. There's also a decent breakfast and Wi-Fi. Wake to the sound of waves sloshing beneath the

structure, as commuter boats whizz past. The highlight is the communal living room with terrace – a chill-out spot where guests lean back on flowery cushions, eyes glued to the wide-screen river views. Great Chinatown location. Recommended.

$$-$ Lamphu House, 75 Soi Rambutri, T02-629 5861, www.lamphuhouse.com. Undoubtedly one of the best budget options on offer. Situated down a very quiet *soi*. Clean, modern, pleasantly decorated rooms with a/c and very comfy beds, the superior rooms have a large balcony and are the best value. Great restaurant downstairs and an extremely professional spa on the roof terrace. Highly recommended.

Siam Sq and Sukhumvit Rd

$$$$ Four Seasons Bangkok, 155 Rachdamri Rd, T02-126-8866, www.four seasons.com. Show-stoppingly stylish and post-modern in atmosphere, with arguably the best range of cuisine (and Sun brunch) in Bangkok, as well as a lavish spa. The restaurants have excellent reputations and ambience. Recommended.

$$$ Baan Sukhumvit, 392/38-39 Soi 20, T02-258 5622, www.baansukhumvit.com. Small rooms with good facilities including a/c, TVs and DVD players in all the rooms. Free Wi-Fi and breakfast for 2. Restaurant downstairs. Weekly rates available. Friendly staff. Recommended.

$$-$ The Atlanta, 78 Sukhumvit Soi 2, T02-252 1650, www.theatlantahotelbangkok. com. With personality in abundance the **Atlanta**'s rooms are at best basic, although a/c and family rooms are available. The amazing art deco interior is often used by Thai filmmakers and there's a large pool surrounded by hammocks and sunbeds – a real treat for this price range. A sign above the door requests that "Oiks, lager louts and sex tourists" go elsewhere and staff can be sniffy with late-nighters and rule breakers (there is a long list at reception). Excellent restaurant. Book early. Recommended.

Silom
$$$$ Mandarin Oriental, 48 Soi Oriental, Charoen Krung, T02-659 9000, www. mandarinoriental.com. At over 100 years old and host to some of history's most infamous literary figures, the **Oriental** is both a Bangkok legend and one of the finest hotels in the world. A fairy-tale like interior of grandiose proportions,

beautiful position overlooking the river and incomparable individual service (despite its 400 rooms). Recommended.

$$-$ Charlie's House, 1034/36-37 Soi Saphan Khu, T02-679 8330, www.charlie housethailand.com. Helpful owners create a friendly atmosphere, and the rooms are carpeted and very clean, with a/c and TV. This is probably the best of the area's budget bunch. There is a restaurant and coffee corner downstairs, with good food at reasonable prices. Recommended.

RESTAURANTS

Bangkok is one of the greatest food cities on earth. You could spend an entire lifetime finding the best places to eat in this city that seems totally obsessed with its tastebuds. Streetfood can be found across the city and a rice or noodle dish will cost ฿25-40 instead of a minimum of ฿50 in the restaurants. Judge quality by popularity and don't be afraid to point out what you want if your Thai is lacking.

Old City and Chinatown
$$ Ban Khun Mae, 458/6-9 Siam Sq Soi 8, T02-658 4112. Good Thai food and friendly service in quaint, faux-vintage Thai surroundings that are slightly at odds with this funky shopping area.

$ The Canton House, 530 Yaowarat Rd, T02-221 3335. Hugely popular dim sum canteen set on the main drag. The prices – ฿15 – for a plate of dim sum are legendary and this has to be one of the best value places to eat in town. The food is OK but nothing exceptional while the frenetic, friendly atmosphere is 100% Chinatown. Recommended.

$ Mont Nom Sod, 160/1-3 Dinsor Rd (near Giant Swing), T02-224 1147. Legendary for its fresh sweet milk and thick hot toast slathered in sankaya (Thai-style custard). A delicious late-morning or early evening pitstop.

Sukhumvit Rd
$$$ Bo.lan, 42 Soi Pichai Ronnarong, Sukhumvit Soi 26, T02-260 2962, www.

bolan.co.th. Chefs Bo and Dylan trained with David Thompson, the chef behind **Nahm** but their Thai restaurant has arguably been a bigger success. Like Thompson, they pluck forgotten recipes from old cookbooks, recreate them using local products and serve them in fine-dining surrounds. Some complain about the prices (the set menu costs a whopping ฿1,680) but on the flip side, some of these dishes are likely to be the most unusual you'll ever taste.

$$ Baan Khanittha, 36/1 Sukhumvit Soi 23, T02-258 4181, www.baan-khanitha. com. The original branch of this popular Thai restaurant is a rambling house with tastefully decorated rooms. Recently renovated, it attracts clients of all nationalities – the food is of a consistently high standard and service is excellent.

Silom and Lumpini Park area
$$$ Nahm, Metropolitan, 27 South Sathorn Rd, T02-625-3388, www.metropolitan. bangkok.como.bz. Some locals won't dine at this upscale Thai restaurant on principle – an Australian claiming to cook authentic Thai is anathema. But they're missing out: Nahm is the most exciting Thai fine-dining experience headed by David Thompson, the chef behind London's formerly Michelin-starred restaurant of the same name. Spicings can be fierce, and it's not cheap, but ultimately it's worth the splurge. Recommended.

DREAM TRIP 1:
Bangkok→Chiang Mai→Golden Triangle 21 days

Bangkok and around 3 nights, page 33

Kanchanaburi 2 nights, page 65
Bus or train from Bangkok (2-2½ hrs)

Ayutthaya 1 night, page 72
Bus from Kanchanaburi , via
Suphanburi (2 hrs) and then bus to
Ayutthaya (1 hr); there's no direct
Kanchanaburi-Ayutthaya bus

Phitsanulok 1 night, page 83
Bus from Ayutthaya (5 hrs)

Sukhothai 2 nights, page 83
Bus from Phitsanulok (1 hr)

Chiang Mai 3 nights, page 100
Bus (5 hrs) from Sukhothai or fly from
Phitsanulok (1 hr)

Western loop from Chiang Mai
2 nights, page 119
Bus to Pai (4 hrs from Chiang Mai),
Mae Hong Son (2 hrs from Pai) and
Mae Sariang (4 hrs from Mae Hong Son)

Chiang Rai and around 1 night,
page 125
Bus from Chiang Mai, 3 hrs

Tha Ton 1 night, page 131
Boat (3-4 hrs) from Chiang Rai or take a bus
from Chiang Rai to Mae Chan (30-45 mins)
and then songthaew to Tha Ton (2 hrs)

Mae Salong 1 night, page 131
Songthaews from Tha Ton (1½-2 hrs)

Mae Sai 1 night, page 133
Bus to Mae Chan (90 mins) from Mae
Salong then bus to Mae Sai (30-45 mins)

Sop Ruak and the Golden Triangle
1 night, page 134
Songthaew from Mae Sai (40 mins)

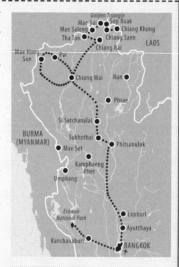

Chiang Saen 1 night, page 134
Songthaew from Sop Ruak (10 mins) or
charter a boat down the river (30 mins)

Chiang Kong 1 night, page 136
Bus from Chiang Saen (2 hrs)

Bangkok page 33
Bus from Chiang Kong to Bangkok (12 hrs)
or bus from Chiang Kong to Chiang Rai
(3 hrs) and then fly back to Bangkok (1¼ hrs)

GOING FURTHER

Lopburi page 81

Kamphaeng Phet page 84

Si Satchanalai page 94

**Mae Sot, the Burmese border and
Umphang** pages 98 and 99

**Phrae, Nan and the Eastern
Highlands** page 116

DREAM TRIP 1
Bangkok→Chiang Mai→Golden Triangle

The entire central plain forms the cradle of Thai civilization. There are ruined cities, temples and fortresses and museums filled with antiquities. The abandoned capital of Ayutthaya is here, as is Sukhothai – the ancient city the Thais consider represents their 'Golden Age' – while the exquisite ruins of Si Satchanalai nestle nearby. Don't forget the diamond citadel of Kamphaeng Phet, the monkey-colonized ruins of Lopburi and the spiritually uplifting, living temple of Wat Phra Sri Ratana Mahathat in Phitsanulok.

Head north and west from Bangkok to the frontier with Burma and Thailand's history takes on a different complexion. It was through this thin slice of western Thailand that the Japanese built their infamous 'death railway'. It's not only this dramatic history that attracts visitors to the region and its hub, Kanchanaburi, but also wonderful cave complexes, jungle trekking, waterfalls, river trips, elephant rides, raft houses and a host of national parks.

Heading even further north, there are limestone hills draped with calming verdant forest, roads and rivers twisting into endless switchbacks. The north feels like another country; factor in the diverse array of the tribal hill peoples, and in many respects it is. Chiang Mai is a magnet for tourists. With its walled centre, serene and ancient temples, bustling markets and excellent hotels it's easy to understand why.

Travel to the west of Chiang Mai and you'll find beautiful Mae Hong Son, encircled by hills and often cloaked in mist. En route take in Pai set in a stunning location. The venerable city of Chiang Rai is an important trekking centre, while further north is Mae Sai, with opportunities for trips into Burma and Chiang Khong, on the Mekong, is a crossing point into Laos. To the northeast is Chiang Saen, an early 14th-century fortified *wiang* (walled city), and the infamous Golden Triangle, where Laos, Burma and Thailand meet.

KANCHANABURI AND AROUND

The wonderful forests, hills and melange of different peoples of this western tract of Thailand are overshadowed by a terrible history – during the Second World War thousands of prisoners of war and local labourers died at the hands of their Japanese captors building a railway line through almost impassable terrain. This piece of history was made famous in David Lean's 1957 Oscar-winning epic, Bridge on the River Kwai. *Today, the bridge, sited at the town of Kanchanaburi, and the war museums and memorials associated with it, has helped turn the region into a tourist mecca. Most come not only to visit the famous bridge but also to relax by Kanchanaburi's elegant Kwai Noi River. As a side-note, Westerners and tourists have long mispronounced 'kwai'; it actually sounds more like 'kwair'.*

The more adventurous head into the national parks and hills further west. Awaiting here are the evocatively named Three Pagodas Pass (Saam Ong), miscellaneous indigenous groups, the resort town of Sangkhlaburi and the Burmese border.

→ KANCHANABURI AND AROUND

Famous for the *Bridge on the River Kwai*, Kanchanaburi is surrounded by a vast area of great natural beauty making it a good base to visit national parks, sail down the Kwai River or travel to one of a number of waterfalls and caves. Over the years, with the languid river providing a charming backdrop, the town has become one of Thailand's biggest tourist destinations, for both foreigners and Thais. The main run of Kanchanaburi's backpacker hang-outs, internet cafés and insipid food, along Mae Nam Kwai Road, is reminiscent of Khao San in Bangkok – there's very little local flavour left here. Head out of the backpacker ghetto and large parts of the rest of the town are filled with markets, shophouses and memorials to those who died in the Second World War. Apart from tourism, the province's wealth is derived from gems mined at the Bo-Phloi mines, teak trading with Burma and sugar cane plantations. It was from here that the Japanese set Allied prisoners of war to work on the construction of the notorious 'death railway', linking Thailand with Burma during the Second World War.

ARRIVING IN KANCHANABURI

Getting there There are regular connections by train and bus with Bangkok. The journey from Bangkok takes around 2½ hours by train while any of the numerous buses take two hours.

Non-air-conditioned buses arrive at the station in the market area, behind Saengchuto Road. Air-conditioned buses run to the corner of Saengchuto Road, opposite Lak Muang Road. The train station is 2 km northwest of town on Saengchuto Road, not far from the cemetery, T034-511285. Many guesthouses will offer to pick you up from either the train or bus station. Also beware of the usual scams from tuk-tuk drivers telling you that your guesthouse of choice is 'closed'.

Getting around Bicycles, motorbikes and jeeps can all be hired in Kanchanaburi and offer the most flexible way to explore the surrounding countryside. Alternatively, *saamlors* provide short-distance trips around town while tuk-tuks are handy for longer journeys. Rafts and long-tailed boats are available for charter on the river.

KANCHANABURI

To Bridge over the River Kwai, Muang Singh
Historical Park, Sai Yok National Park,
Sangkhlaburi & Saam Ong

To Death Railway
& Hellfire Pass

Ponthochan Rd

Saengchuto Rd

Kwai Yai River

Thailand-Burma Railway Centre

Saengchuto Rd

Mae Nam Kwai Rd

Thailand-Burma
Railway Centre

Rt 323

Water Tower

War Cemetery

Soi Rong Heeb Oil

N

200 metres

200 yards

Kwai Yai River

Ban Nue Rd

Motorbike Hire

Thetsaban Bamrung Rd

Saengchuto Rd

Kratai Thong Rd

Baak Phraek Rd

To Erawan
& Bo Phloi

Uthong Rd

To Suphanburi

Bovon Rd

Night Foodstalls

Song Kwai Rd
Restaurants & Night Foodstalls

Prasit Rd

Khumuang Rd

Bus Station

Motorbike Taxis

Lak Muang

Lak Muang Rd

A/C Bus Stop

Rt 323

To Post Office & Bangkok

Town Gate

Governor's House

Kamphaeng Muang Rd

JEATH War Museum

Wisuttharangsi Rd

Mae Klong River

Chungkai War Cemetery

Kwai Noi River

To Wat Tham Kao Poon

Chukkadon Pier

Moving on Unfortunately, there are no direct bus connections with Ayutthaya – you must connect with a slow local service at Suphanburi (two hours, and then another bus from Suphanburi to Ayutthaya, one hour). This is something local tour operators in Kanchanaburi have taken advantage of, cramming rickety minibuses with backpackers willing to pay inflated prices; you're better advised to travel via Bangkok.

Tourist information TAT ① *Saengchuto Rd, T034-511200, daily 0830-1630,* is a good first stop and can supply up-to-date information on accommodation in Kanchanaburi, Nakhon Pathom, Samut Sakhon and Samut Songkhram. It is a short walk from the bus station. Most tour operators offer similar excursions: jungle trekking, elephant rides, bamboo rafting, visits to Hellfire Pass and various waterfalls. In Bangkok, virtually every hotel or tour office will be able to offer a day tour (or longer) to Kanchanaburi and the surrounding sights.

BACKGROUND

Kanchanaburi was established in the 1830s, although the ruins of Muang Singh (see page 69) to the west date from the Khmer period. On entering the town (called Muang Kan by most locals), visitors may notice the fish-shaped street signs. The fish in question is the yisok, a small freshwater fish and the symbol of Kanchanaburi. Another slice of Thai fauna for which this area of Thailand is known is Kitti's hog-nosed bat. As with so many tourist success stories, Kanchanaburi has its downside. In this case, it is pollution from the 900-odd raft-based guesthouse and restaurant operations. Almost none of the rafts has water treatment or waste disposal systems. This was fine when there were just a handful of rafts and a few thousand tourists a year. Now the numbers are far greater and public health officials have detected a significant rise in water pollution.

PLACES IN KANCHANABURI

The **JEATH War Museum** ① *0830-1800, ฿30 (no photographs),* whose name denotes the countries involved – Japan, England, America, Australia, Thailand and Holland – can be found by the river, at the end of Wisuttharangsi Road. The museum, which holds an interesting and harrowing display of prisoners working on the railway, was established in 1977 by the monks of Wat Chanasongkhram.

The **Kanchanaburi War Cemetery (Don Rak)** ① *Saengchuto Rd, 1.5 km out of town, daily 0800-1700 (or you can always look over the gates),* is immaculately maintained by the Commonwealth Cemeteries Commission. Some 6982 Allied servicemen are buried here, most of whom died as prisoners of war while they built the Burma railway. Beside it, the indoor **Thailand-Burma Railway Centre** ① *Jaokannun Rd, T034-512721, www.tbrconline. com, daily 0900-1700, ฿100 adults,* is the definitive World War Two museum in town, captivatingly recounting every aspect of the Death Railway's construction and the Allied bombing missions that attempted to obliterate it. Upstairs are items belonging to former prisoners, including mess tins with crude drawings and poignant messages etched into them. To get there, walk, hire a bicycle (฿20 a day) or take a saamlor.

Situated 2 km south of town, the **Chungkai (UK) War Cemetery** is small, peaceful and well kept, with the graves of 1750 prisoners of war. To get there, take a boat from in front of the town gates, or go by tuk-tuk or bicycle.

Kanchanaburi's **lak muang** (city pillar), encrusted in gold leaf and draped with flowers, can be seen in the middle of Lak Muang Road. Close by are the gates to Kanchanaburi town. Walk through the gates and turn right (north) for the old and most attractive part of town with wooden shops and houses.

BRIDGE OVER THE RIVER KWAI

ⓘ *3-4 km north of town, just off Saengchuto Rd. Take a saamlor, hire a bicycle, catch a songthaew or board the train, which travels from the town's station to the bridge. Boats can be rented at the bridge.*

The bridge over the Kwai River (pronounced 'Kway' in Thai, not 'Kwai') is architecturally unexciting and is of purely historical interest. The central span was destroyed by Allied bombing towards the end of the war, and has been rebuilt in a different style. Visitors can walk across the bridge, visit the **Second World War Museum and Art Gallery** ⓘ *0900-1630, ฿30*, or browse in the many souvenir stalls. The museum is an odd affair with some displays relating to the bridge and the prisoners of war who worked and died here, along with a collection of Thai weaponry and amulets, and some astonishingly bad portraits of Thai kings.

DEATH RAILWAY AND HELLFIRE PASS

ⓘ *No admission fee, but donations requested (most visitors leave ฿100). Two trains leave Kanchanaburi daily at 1045 and 1637, with return trains at 0525 and 1300, approximately 2 hrs. From the Nam Tok station, it is another 14 km to the Hellfire Pass and Museum, for which you need a songthaew (฿400 return, 20 mins one way). To reach the pass by road take a northbound bus about 80 km on Route 323 to a Royal Thai Army farm at the Km 66 marker. A track here leads through the farm to a steep path to the pass. There are numerous organized tours to Hellfire Pass.*

Only 130 km of the Death Railway remain, passing through what is known as Hellfire Pass to reach the small town of Nam Tok. From Kanchanaburi to Nam Tok the railway sweeps through a tranche of dramatic scenery, stopping at the ancient Khmer site of **Muang Singh** en route (see below). The name of the pass was bestowed by one of the prisoners of war who, looking down on his comrades working below at night by the glow of numerous open fires, bamboo torches and carbide lamps, remarked that the sight was like "the jaws of hell". The Office of Australian War Graves, with the support of the Australian government and the Royal Thai Armed Forces, has developed the pass as a memorial, cutting two paths through to it and building a modern museum. Clear, well-written wall panels surrounded by photographs, along with some reproduction objects, provide a very moving account of the cutting of the pass. There is also an impressive viewpoint perched high over the valley below.

WAT THAM KAO POON

ⓘ *5 km southwest of town, a few kilometres on from the Chungkai Cemetery. No entrance fee to the caves, but visitors are encouraged to make a contribution to the maintenance of the monastery (฿10-20). Hire a bicycle or tuk-tuk or charter a boat from in front of the town gates.*

Wat Tham Kao Poon is a rather gaudy temple with caves attached. Follow the arrows through the cave system. There is a large Buddha image at the bottom of the system (and smaller ones elsewhere), as well as *kutis* (cells) in which monks can meditate. Intrepid explorers will find they emerge at the back of the hill. Early in 1996 this cave wat was the site of the murder of British tourist, Johanne Masheder (the cave where the murder took place is permanently closed), by a drug-addicted Thai monk. The crime shook Thailand's religious establishment and the abbot of the monastery was suspended for neglect.

PHU PHRA CAVES, WAT THAM KUN PHAEN AND KANCHANABURI CULTURAL CENTRE

ⓘ *20 km north of town, just off Route 323 to Sangkhlaburi. Take bus 8203 or hire a motorbike or songthaew/tuk-tuk.*

The wat and its associated caves nestle in foothills which rise up towards Burma. Back on Route 323 is the Kanchanaburi Cultural Centre, with a collection of handicrafts, artefacts and historical exhibits.

MUANG SINGH HISTORICAL PARK

ⓘ *45 km west of Kanchanaburi, open 0800-1700, ฿4. Hire a tuk-tuk/songthaew or motorbike, or take the train to Thakilen station – it is about a 1.5-km walk.*

This ancient Khmer town, the 'city of lions', is situated on the banks of the Kwai Noi River. Built of deep red laterite, Muang Singh reached its apogee during the 12th-13th centuries when it flourished as a trading post linking Siam with the Indian Ocean. The city represents an artistic and strategic outlier of the great Cambodian Empire, and it is mentioned in inscriptions from the reign of the Khmer King Jayavarman VII.

SAI YOK NATIONAL PARK

ⓘ *104 km northwest of Kanchanaburi. Boats can be hired from Pak Saeng pier in Tambon Tha Saaw, 50 km north of Kanchanaburi town. A boat (10-12 people) to the park (including the Lawa caves and Sai Yok Yai waterfall), should cost ฿1200 per boat (or go on a tour); the trip will take 2½ hrs upstream and 1½ hrs down. There are also buses from Kanchanaburi to the park, 1 hr. The best time of year to visit is May-Dec.*

The main attraction of Sai Yok National Park is the **Sai Yok Yai Waterfall**. Also near Sai Yok Yai are the **Daowadung Caves** (30 minutes north by boat from the falls and then a 3-km walk). Tigers and elephants still inhabit this wild region of stunning scenery, stretching to the Burmese border.

ERAWAN NATIONAL PARK

ⓘ *65 km north of Kanchanaburi, open 0600-1800, ฿200 entrance fee to the park. Regular buses (No 8170) every 50 mins from 0800 onwards from Kanchanaburi (1½-2 hrs, ฿26). The last bus back to Kanchanaburi leaves Erawan at 1600. The best time to visit the falls is during the rainy season. It is a 35-min walk from the bus station to the first of the series of 7 falls. There are also plenty of places to eat Thai food next to the bus stop. If you want to make like the locals it is considered the done thing to combine ahan Isaan (Isaan food), such as som tam (spicy papaya salad), kai yang (grilled chicken) and khao niaow (sticky rice) with nam tok (waterfall).*

This is an area of great natural beauty, covering 550 sq km and containing the impressive and fun Erawan Falls, which are split into seven unique levels. The first is popular with swimmers and picnickers. As you head further up, towards the source of this naturally occuring waterpark, food and plastic water bottles must be deposited at the park ranger office. Level three is very beautiful and good for swimming, but it is teeming with fish who enjoy gently sucking on your skin (which is off-putting to some); level four features a bulbous rock slide, and level seven is well worth the steep climb, with refreshing pools awaiting any intrepid trekker. The impressive **Phrathat Caves**, with huge and stupendous stalactites and stalagmites, are located about 10 km northwest of headquarters, a good hike or easy drive.

Arguably the most striking waterfalls are those at **Huay Khamin**, some 108 km northwest of town. The falls are awkward to reach independently but tour companies will provide arranged trips. The **Thung Yai** and **Huai Kha Khaeng wildlife sanctuaries**, where the falls are based, were once threatened by a proposed dam that would have destroyed rare stands of riverine tropical forest that exist here. Public pressure ensured that the plans were shelved, representing the first significant victory for environmentalists in Thailand. In 1992 the two sanctuaries were declared Southeast Asia's first Natural World Heritage Site by UNESCO, vindicating the environmentalists' stand.

THAM THAN LOT NATIONAL PARK

ⓘ *There are regular connections between Kanchanaburi and Nong Pru. The road to the park cuts off left from Route 3086 shortly before entering Nong Pru; the park entrance is 22 km from this turn-off. During the week it is usually necessary to charter a motorcycle or songthaew to the park, but at weekends there is a public service from Nong Pru.*

The park encompasses a portion of the Tenasserim range of mountains that form the border between Thailand and Burma and includes small populations of Asiatic black bear, white-handed gibbon and elephant. There is even talk that there may be tigers here. The highest peak is Khao Khampaeng, which rises to 1260 m. Within easy walking of park headquarters (where there is a visitor centre) is **Than Lot Noi Cave**, after which the park was named. The cave reaches around 300 m into the mountain side. A trail leads from here for around 2 km to another cave, **Than Lot Yai**, where there is a small Buddhist shrine.

KANCHANABURI AND AROUND LISTINGS

WHERE TO STAY

Most of the budget accommodation is lined up along busy Mae Nam Kwai Rd. There are also a few raft-type places along the quieter Ron Heeb Oil Rd. Disco boats on the river can cause noise pollution but they are only really active at weekends and usually stop at 2000. Most places will pick you up from the bus/ train stations if you book in advance. Rates vary according to season.

$$$$-$$ Sabai@Kan Restort, 317/4 Mae Nam Kwai Rd, T034-625544, www.sabaiatkan.com. This new resort on the main tourist drag is a decent addition. Most of the simple and stylish rooms (all a/c, ensuite) look out onto a small, well-tended and relaxing garden area, with pool. This latter feature gives it the edge over most of its competitors. The friendly welcome and free Wi-Fi help too. Recommended.

$$-$ Apple's Retreat, 153/4 Moo 4 Sutjai Bridge, T034-512017, www.applenoi-kanchanaburi.com. A quiet option on the other side of the river, with 16 very clean a/c or fan rooms and private showers. Run by the friendly female couple who founded the original Apple's Guesthouse (which no longer exists), this is one of the few locally owned businesses in the area and offers free pickup from bus/train station. Many come solely for the awesome Thai restaurant (see Restaurants, below) and cooking classes. Some of the touts might tell you it is closed – ignore them. Also don't confuse the recommended Retreat with the place calling itself 'Apple Guesthouse' in town, which is not recommendable.

$$-$ Ploy River Kwai Resort, Mae Nam Kwai Rd, T034-515804, www.ploygh.com. Central guesthouse in good location next to the river. Rooms have outdoor showers. Friendly. Excellent value. Free bus/train station pick-up. Recommended.

$$-$ Tamarind Guesthouse, 29/1 Mae Nam Kwai Rd, T034-518790. Probably the best value on the river front – you can get a spotless a/c river-view room with balcony for less than ฿550 here. There are plenty of terraces and a decent little bar. Owners are friendly. Also have raft rooms.

RESTAURANTS

Numerous stalls set up along the river in the afternoon and evening – the best spot is by Song Kwai Rd – and there is also an excellent night market in the vicinity of the bus station. Recommended.

$ Apple's Restaurant, 153/4 Moo 4, Sutjai Bridge (opposite **Apple's Retreat**). Excellent Thai food – the banana flower fritters and grilled pork salad are delicious – in a garden on the other side of the river. Very friendly English-speaking staff. They also run a good cookery school and cater for vegetarians.

WHAT TO DO

State Railways of Thailand, Railway Advance Booking Office, Hualamphong Station in Bangkok, T02-2256964, or Kanchanaburi Train Station, T034-511285 or State Railway of Thailand call centre, T1690, www.railway.co.th. Thailand's **State Railways** offers an all-day tour from Bangkok to Kanchanaburi on weekends and holidays leaving Thonburi station at 0630, stopping at Nakhon Pathom, the River Kwai Bridge, arriving at Nam Tok at 1130. A minibus connects Khao Pang/Sai Yok Noi waterfall and the train leaves Nam Tok at 1430, arriving in Kanchanaburi at 1605 for a brief stop, arriving in Bangkok at 1930. There are also a number of other tours, with overnight stays, rafting and fishing. Advance booking recommended.

AYUTTHAYA AND AROUND

The ancient, venerable capital of the Kingdom of Siam, Ayutthaya, had a population of 150,000 during its heyday and was the equal of any city in Europe. It was at the epicentre of an empire that controlled more than 500,000 sq km and all the wealth of this great kingdom gravitated to the capital city. In late 2011 Ayutthaya was at the epicentre of some of the worst flooding in living memory and, for a while, the entire city was shut down and the future of the antiquities was unknown. By February 2012 the high water mark line was still clearly visible along many buildings and city walls. Things are slowly returning to normal and the damage seems to be less than was originally feared, yet the flooding was a traumatic episode for the city. Floods notwithstanding, a large portion of the city remains a bustling modern Thai conurbation with little to remind the visitor of its halcyon days; in typical Thai fashion, traffic is heavy and city-planning chaotic, though the wider avenues in the old city do provide relief from the usual tumult. Amid all this concrete are several ancient sites; you may find yourself walking past them without even realizing they are there.

If you head west from this urban setting you will soon begin to pick up more traces of the old city of Ayutthaya, until it opens up into a series of broad spaces, littered with atmospheric ruins. Arrive when the setting sun illuminates the deep red-brick ruins and it is not hard to imagine the grandeur of this place which so amazed early European visitors. Here is a stunning complex of palaces, shrines, monasteries and chedis. The historical park, which was made a UNESCO World Heritage Site in 1991, covers some 3 sq km. Rama V (1868-1910) was the first person to appreciate the value of the site, both in terms of Thailand's national identity and in terms of its artistic merit. The historic city of Lopburi, known for its kleptomaniac monkeys, lies to the north.

→ ARRIVING IN AYUTTHAYA

GETTING THERE
Most people get here by bus from Bangkok's Northern bus terminal. It is an easy 1½-hour journey, making a day trip from Bangkok possible. The local bus station in Ayutthaya is centrally located on Naresuan Road, whilst the air-con and long-distance bus-station is a couple of kilometres east of the city centre near the main highway. Another option is to arrive by ferry, which takes a leisurely three hours from Tha Tien pier in Bangkok. You can also take the train from Bangkok's Hualomphong station; it takes about 1½ hours. Local trains leave regularly and charge a fraction of the cost of the express services, yet don't take much longer. The train station in Ayutthaya is just off Rojana Road, across the Pasak River. A songthaew to the old city costs around ฿7. Alternatively, take the small track facing the station down to the river; from the jetty here ferries cross over to the other side every five minutes or so (฿2), just off Uthong Road. Most of the guesthouses are a short walk from here.

GETTING AROUND
The wats are spread over a considerable area, too large to walk around comfortably, so the best way to cover quite a bit of ground is to hire a saamlor by the hour. That way, you can decide your route and instruct accordingly. Long-tailed boats are available to transport people around the perimeter of the town, in order to visit the outlying sites. These can

ON THE ROAD
King Naresuan the Great of Ayutthaya

King Naresuan of Ayutthaya (1590-1605) was one of only five of Thailand's great kings to have posthumously been awarded the sobriquet 'the Great'. In 1569 the Burmese had taken Ayutthaya and placed a puppet monarch on the throne. The great kingdom appeared to be on the wane. But Naresuan, who in American historian David Wyatt's words was "one of those rare figures in Siamese history who, by virtue of dynamic leadership, personal courage, and decisive character, succeed in Herculean tasks that have daunted others before them", proceeded to challenge the Burmese. He confronted their forces in 1585, 1585-1586 and in 1586-1587, defeating armies that grew larger by turn. Finally, at the beginning of 1593, the decisive battle occurred at Nong Sarai, to the northwest of Suphanburi. The Burmese had assembled an army of monumental proportions. During the initial skirmish, Naresuan saw the Burmese crown prince mounted on his war elephant and, according to the chronicles, shouted across the battle field: "Come forth and let us fight an elephant duel for the honour of our kingdoms." When the Burmese prince lunged with his lance, Naresuan ducked beneath the blow to rake, and kill, his opponent with his sword. The battle was won and Ayutthaya was once again in a position to flourish.

be arranged through various guesthouses. A tuk-tuk across town costs ฿50-60 or about ฿200 an hour. *Songthaews* charge about ฿10 along set routes around town and can also be chartered by negotiation. Given that Ayutthaya is flat, bicycles are also a great way to see the ruins. Many guesthouses rent them out, or look for rental shops near the railway station: ฿30-40 a day.

MOVING ON
There are regular buses from Ayutthaya to Phitsanulok (five hours).

TOURIST INFORMATION
TAT ① *Si Sanphet Rd, opposite Chao Sam Phraya Museum, T035-246 076, daily 0830-1630*, offers information on Ayutthaya, Ang Thong, Suphanburi and Nonthaburi. Just behind the TAT office, in the old city hall, is the recently opened **Ayutthaya Tourism Centre** ① *T035-246067, Thu-Tue, 0830-1630, free*, where you'll find exhibitions, information and video presentations about Thailand's former capital.

Ayutthaya is one of the most popular day tours from Bangkok, but for those with an interest in ruins or Thai history, there is more than enough to occupy a couple of days. The average day trip only allows about two hours. Ignore tour operators who maintain there is no accommodation here; it is perfectly adequate.

→ BACKGROUND

"In 712, a Year of the Tiger, second of the decade, on Friday, the sixth day of the waxing moon of the fifth month, at three nalika and nine bat after the break of dawn, the capital city of Ayutthaya was first established." So recorded the Royal Chronicles of Ayutthaya. In translation this is widely accepted to mean Friday 4 March 1351, at about 0900. It is said that Prince Uthong (later King Ramathibodi I) and his court were forced here following an outbreak of cholera and, after a brief interlude at the nearby Wat Panancherng, founded the city. Ayutthaya's name derives from 'Ayodhya', the sacred town in the Indian epic, the *Ramayana*. It became one of the most prosperous kingdoms in the Southeast Asian region, and by 1378 the King of Sukhothai had been forced to swear his allegiance. Ultimately, the kingdom stretched from Angkor (Cambodia) in the east, to Pegu (Burma) in the west. In 1500 it was reported that the kingdom was exporting 30 junk loads (10,000 tonnes) of rice to Malacca (Malaysia), each year while also being an important source of animal skins and ivory.The city is situated on an island at the confluence of three rivers: the Chao Phraya, Pasak and Lopburi. Ayutthaya's strong defensive position proved to be valuable as it was attacked by the Burmese on no less than 24 occasions. Recent research on changes in sea level indicates that in 1351 the coastline was much further north and so the city was considerably closer to the sea. Ayutthaya, therefore, would have been able to develop as a trading port unlike the previous Thai capitals of Sukhothai and Si Satchanalai.

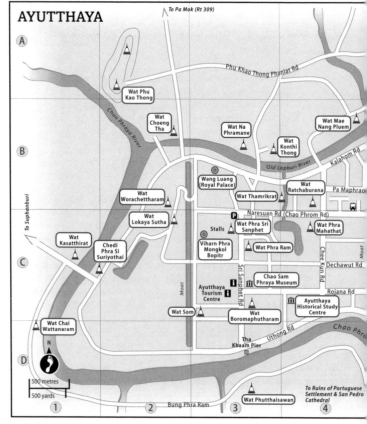

One of Ayutthaya's most famous kings was Boromtrailokant (1448-1488), a model of the benevolent monarch. He is best known for his love of justice and his administrative and legislative reforms. This may seem surprising in view of some of the less than enlightened legal practices employed later in the Ayutthaya period. A plaintiff and defendant might, for example, have had to plunge their hands into molten tin, or their heads into water, to see which party was the guilty one.

A succession struggle in the mid-16th century led to 20 years of warfare with the Burmese, who managed to seize and occupy Ayutthaya. It wasn't long before the hero-king, Naresuan (1590-1605), recaptured the city and led his country back to independence. Under King Narai (1656-1688), Ayutthaya became a rich, cosmopolitan trading post. Merchants came to the city from Portugal, Spain, Holland, China, Arabia, Persia, Malaya, India and Japan. In the 16th century Ayutthaya was said to have 40 different nationalities living in and around the city walls, and supported a population larger than London's.

The city was strongly fortified, with ramparts 20 m high and 5 m thick, and was protected on all sides by waterways: rivers on three sides and a linking canal on the fourth creating an oriental Venice. The cosmopolitan atmosphere was evident on the waterways where royal barges rubbed shoulders with Chinese junks, Arab dhows and ocean-going schooners. Visitors found endless sources of amusement in the city. There were elephant jousts, tiger fights, Muay Thai (Thai boxing), masked plays and puppet theatre.

It was said that the King of Ayutthaya was so wealthy that the elephants were fed from gold vessels. Indeed, early Western visitors to Ayutthaya often commented on the king's elephants and the treatment they received. One of the earliest accounts is by Jacques de Countres, a merchant from Bruges who resided in the city for eight months in 1596 (during Naresuan's reign). His son later recorded his father's experiences: "The palace is surrounded by stables where live the favourite elephants ridden by the king. Each one had its silk cushion, and they slept on it as if they were small dogs. Each one of them had six very large bowls of gold. Some contained oil to grease their skins; others were filled with water for sprinkling; others served for eating; others for drinking; others for urinating and defecating. The elephants were indeed so well trained that they got up from their beds when they felt the urge to urinate or defecate. Their attendants understood at once and handed them the bowls. And they kept their lodges always very sweet-smelling and fumigated with benzoin and other fragrant substances. I would not have believed it if I had not actually seen it." (Smithies, Michael *Descriptions of Old Siam*, Kuala Lumpur, 1995, OUP.)

One European became particularly influential: King Narai's Greek foreign affairs officer (and later prime minister), Constantine Phaulcon. It was at this time the word *'farang'* – to describe any white foreigner – entered the Thai vocabulary, derived from 'ferenghi', the Indian for 'French'. In 1688, Narai was taken ill and at the same time the French, who Phaulcon had been encouraging, became a serious threat, gaining control of a fortress in Bangkok. An anti-French lobby arrested the by now very unpopular Phaulcon and had him executed for suspected designs on the throne. The French troops were expelled and for the next century Europeans were kept at arm's length. It was not until the 19th century that they regained influence in the Thai court.

In 1767 the kingdom was again invaded, by the Burmese, who, at the 24th attempt, were finally successful in vanquishing the defenders. The city was sacked and its defences destroyed, but, unable to consolidate their position, the Burmese left for home, taking with them large numbers of prisoners and leaving the city in ruins. The population was reduced from one million to 10,000. Ayutthaya never recovered from this final attack, and the magnificent temples were left to deteriorate.

→ PLACES IN AYUTTHAYA

The modern town of Ayutthaya is concentrated in the eastern quarter of the old walled city, and beyond the walls to the east. Much of the rest of the old city is green and open, interspersed with abandoned wats and new government buildings.

The sights described below take in the most important wats. Ayutthaya's other fine ruins are described in the second half of this section. The sheer size of the site means that the considerable numbers of tourists are easily dispersed among the ruins, leaving the visitor to wander in complete tranquillity among the walkways, *chedis* and trees.

WAT RATCHABURANA
① *Daily 0800-1700, ฿50.*

This wat was built by King Boromraja II in 1424 on the cremation site of his two brothers (princes Ai and Yo), who were killed while contesting the throne. The Khmer-style *prang* (which has been partially restored) still stands amidst the ruins of the wat. Some of the most important treasures found in Ayutthaya were discovered here in 1958: bronze Buddha images, precious stones and golden royal regalia, belonging, it is assumed, to the two brothers.

WAT PHRA MAHATHAT
① *Daily 0800-1700, ฿50.*

Across the road from Wat Ratchaburana sits the Monastery of the Great Relic. It was founded in 1384, making it one of the earliest *prangs* in Ayutthaya, and was the largest of all Ayutthaya's monasteries, built to house holy relics of the Buddha (hence its name). It is said that King Boromraja I (1370-1388) was meditating one dawn when he saw a glow emanating from the earth; he took this to mean that a relic of the Buddha lay under the soil and ordered a wat to be founded. Only the large base remains of the original Khmer-style *prang*, which collapsed during the reign of King Song Tham (1610-1628). When the Fine Arts Department excavated the site in 1956, it found a number of gold Buddha images as well as relics of the Buddha inside a gold casket, now exhibited in the National Museum, Bangkok.

AYUTTHAYA HISTORICAL STUDY CENTRE
ⓘ *Daily 0900-1700, ฿100.*

Further south, on Rojana Road, this museum and research centre is housed in a surprisingly sensitively designed modern building, proving there are some creative architects in the country. The museum tries to recreate Ayutthaya life and does so with some excellent models.

CHAO SAM PHRAYA MUSEUM
ⓘ *Wed-Sun 0900-1600 (except public holidays), ฿150.*

Located on Rojana Road, this museum was opened in 1961. Votive tablets excavated from Wat Ratchaburana were auctioned off to raise funds for its construction. It houses many of Ayutthaya's relics, in particular the Mongkol Buddha.

WAT PHRA SRI SANPHET
ⓘ *Daily 0800-1700, ฿50.*

Within the extensive grounds of Wang Luang (Royal Palace), this was the largest and most beautiful wat in Ayutthaya – the equivalent of Wat Phra Kaeo in Bangkok. Three restored Ceylonese-style *chedis* dominate the compound. They contain the ashes of King Boromtrailokant (1448-1488) and his two sons (who were also kings of Ayutthaya). There are no *prangs* here; the three central *chedis* are surrounded by alternate smaller *chedis* and *viharns*. Remains of walls and leaning pillars give an impression of the vastness of the wat. In 1500 it is alleged that a 16-m standing Buddha was cast by King Ramathipodi II (1491-1529), using a staggering 5,500,000 kg of bronze and covered in 340 kg of gold leaf. The image's name, Phra Sri Sanphet, later became the name of the wat. When the Burmese invaded the city in 1767 the image was set on fire in order to release the gold, in the process destroying both it and the temple.

VIHARN PHRA MONGKOL BOPITR
ⓘ *Mon-Fri 0830-1630, free.*

South of Wat Phra Sri Sanphet stands this 'new' *viharn*, built in 1956 and modelled on the 15th-century original which was razed by the Burmese. It houses one of the largest bronze Buddhas in the world, at 12.5 m high. This black image, which is made of sheets of copper-bronze fastened onto a core of brick and plaster, probably dates from the 16th century.

WAT NA PHRAMANE
ⓘ *Daily 0800-1800, ฿20. Note the image cannot always be viewed.*

Travel back past Wang Luang to the main road, turn east and after 250 m the road crosses the Old Lopburi River. From the bridge one can see Wat Na Phramane, which dates from 1503 and is one of the most complete examples of Ayutthayan architecture. It is reputed to have been built by one of King Ramathibodi's concubines, Pra Ong, at which time it was known as Wat Pramerurachikaram. A treaty to end one of the many wars with Burma was signed here in 1549. More than two centuries later in 1767, the Burmese used the position to attack the city once again, and it is said that the King of Burma suffered a mortal blow from a cannon which backfired during the initial bombardment. Perhaps because of this, the Burmese – unusually – left the wat intact. Even without the helping hands of the Burmese, the wat still fell into disrepair and was not restored until 1838. The lovely early Ayutthayan *bot* is the largest in the city and contains an impressive crowned bronze Buddha image.

WAT THAMRIKRAT

South over the bridge that crosses a small tributary of the Old Lopburi River, again, a short distance east along Kalahom Road, is Wat Thamrikrat (Monastery of the Pious Monarch), with *singha* (stucco lions) surrounding an overgrown *chedi*. Scholars are not sure exactly when it was built, but they are largely agreed that it predates the reign of King Boromtrailokant (1448-1488).

WAT CHOENG THA

Also on the north bank of the river, not far from the confluence of the Chao Phraya and Old Lopburi rivers, is this wat. It is not known when it was originally built – it has been restored on a number of occasions – but it is said to have been constructed by a man whose daughter ran away with her lover and never returned; it was known as Wat Koy Tha (Monastery of Waiting). The Ayutthaya-style *prang* is in reasonable condition, as is the *sala kan parian*, although the *bot* and *viharn* are both in poor condition.

WAT YAI CHAI MONGKOL

① *Daily 0800-1700, ฿20.*

Southeast of the town is Wat Yai Chai Mongkol, or simply Wat Yai (Big Wat), built by King Uthong, also known as King Ramathibodi I, in 1357, for a group of monks who had studied and been ordained in Ceylon. The imposing 72-m-high *chedi* was built in the Ceylonese style (now with a rather alarming tilt) to celebrate the victory of King Naresuan over the Prince of Burma in 1592, in single-handed elephant combat. The *viharn* contains a massive reclining Buddha image. It is unusual because its eyes are open; reclining images traditionally symbolize death or sleep, so the eyes are closed.

ELEPHANT KRAALS

① *Take a saamlor from Chee Kun Rd northwards over the Old Lopburi River to reach the kraal. If coming from Wat Phu Kao Thong, cross the Pa Mok Highway and drive for 3.5 km.*

Northeast of the city, on the banks of the Old Lopburi River, are the only remaining elephant kraals in Thailand. The kraals were built in the reign of King Maha Chakrapat in 1580 to capture wild elephants. The kraals are square-shaped enclosures with double walls. The inner walls are made of teak posts fixed to the ground at close intervals. The outer walls are made of earth, faced with brick, and are 3 m high. The kraals have two entrances: one to allow the decoy elephant to lure the herd into the enclosure, and the other to lead them out again. The outer wall on the west side is slightly wider to provide a platform from which the king, seated in a pavilion, could watch the elephant round-up. The last round-up of wild elephants occurred in May 1903, to entertain royal guests during King Chulalongkorn's reign. The kraal has been extensively restored and is rather clinical as a result.

RIVER TOURS OF OUTLYING WATS

The extensive waterways of Ayutthaya (more than 50 km of them) are a pleasant way to see some of the less accessible sights. Long-tailed boats can be taken from the landing pier opposite Chandra Kasem Palace, in the northeast corner of the town. During the dry season, it is not possible to circle the entire island; the Old Lopburi River becomes unnavigable. The usual route runs south down the Pasak River and round as far as Wat Chai Wattanaram on the Chao Phraya River. The following wats can also be visited by road.

Situated close to the junction of the Pasak and Chao Phraya rivers, **Wat Phanan Choeng** is the first wat to be reached by boat, travelling clockwise from the Chandra Kasem pier. The 19-m-high seated Buddha image in the *viharn* (immediately behind the bot) is mentioned in a chronicle as having been made in 1324, some 26 years before Ayutthaya became the capital. It is likely that the wat was founded at the same time, making it the oldest in Ayutthaya. The Buddha is made of brick, plaster and is gilded. This image is said to have wept tears when Ayutthaya was sacked by the Burmese in 1767.

Wat Chai Wattanaram ① *daily 0800-1700, ฿50*, sits on the west bank of the Chao Phraya River, to the west of the city. A decapitated Buddha sits overlooking the river in front of the ruins, while the large central *prang* is surrounded by two rows of smaller *chedis* and *prang*-like *chedis*, arranged on the cardinal and sub-cardinal points of the cloister that surrounds the central structure. The wat was built by King Prasat Thong (1630-1656) in honour of his mother and the complex has a Khmer quality about it. Relatively few tours of Ayutthaya include Wat Chai Wattanaram on their itineraries, which is a great shame as this is a marvellous site. It is also possibly the best restored of all the monasteries, avoiding the rather cack-handed over-restoration that mars some of the other sites.

North of here is **Wat Kasatthirat**. This wat represents the end of a river tour unless the Old Lopburi River is navigable in which case Wat Na Phramane (see page 77) can also be reached, returning, full circle, to the Chandra Kasem pier.

Most of the guesthouses will run river tours on long-tailed boats. You can expect to pay somewhere between ฿200-300 per person for a two-hour tour.

SAN PEDRO CATHEDRAL

Lying 11 km south outside the city, this was the site of the original Portuguese settlement in Ayutthaya, dating from 1511. At one point as many as 3000 Portuguese and their mixed-blood offspring were living here, although with the sacking of Ayutthaya by the Burmese in 1767 the community was abandoned. Since the mid-1980s the Fine Arts Department, with financial support from Portugal, has been excavating the site and the cathedral itself is now fully restored. It was opened to the public in 1995.

GOING FURTHER
Lopburi

To the west of Lopburi is the old city with its historical sights. To the east is the new town with its major military base. Inevitably, most visitors will be attracted to the palace, museum, monasteries and *prangs* of the old city. This part of town is also teeming with Lopburi's famous monkeys, which clamber from one telegraph pole to another, laze around the temples (particularly Sam Phra Karn), feast on the offerings left by worshippers, and grasp playfully at the hair of unwitting tourists. They have a penchant for stealing sunglasses or spectacles: be warned. Don't try and feed them, as you are likely to provoke a monkey riot.

Background

Lopburi has been seemingly caught between competing powers for more than 1000 years. The discovery of Neolithic and Bronze Age remains indicate that the site on the left bank of the Lopburi River was in use in prehistoric times. The town became a major centre during the Dvaravati period (6th-11th century), when it was known as Lavo (the original settlers were the 'Lavah', related to the Mon). In AD 950 Lopburi fell to the expanding Khmers who made it a provincial capital; in Thailand, the Khmer period of art and architecture is known as 'Lopburi' because of their artistic impact evident in the town and surrounding area. By the 14th century, Khmer influence had waned and the Thais reclaimed Lopburi. In 1351 King Uthong of Ayutthaya gave his son – Prince Ramesuan – governorship of the town, indicating its continued importance. It fell into obscurity during the 16th century, but was resuscitated when King Narai (1656-1688) restored the city with the assistance of European architects. With Narai's death in Lopburi, the town entered another period of obscurity but was again restored to glory during Rama IV's reign.

Arriving in Lopburi

There are regular bus connections from Bangkok's Northern bus terminal (2-3 hours) and Ayutthaya (one hour), as well as destinations in the north. The bus station is in the new town, 2 km from the old town, close to the roundabout where Routes 311 and 3016 cross (Wongwian Sra Kaeo). It's also possible to arrive by train from Bangkok's Hualamphong station or Ayutthaya. Frequent buses and *songthaews* ferry passengers between the old and new towns.

Places in Lopburi

The **Narai Ratchaniwet Palace** ① *Wed-Sun 0830-1200, 1300-1630, ฿30*, represents the historical heart of Lopburi, encased by massive walls and bordered to the west by the Lopburi River. King Narai declared Lopburi his second capital in the 17th century, and, between 1665 and 1677, built his palace, which became his 'summer' retreat. The main gate is on Sorasak Road, opposite the **Asia Lopburi Hotel**. The well-kept palace grounds are divided into three sections: an outer, middle and an inner courtyard.

The outer courtyard, now in ruins, contained the 'functional' buildings: a tank to supply water to the palace, transported down terracotta pipes from a lake some distance away;

storage warehouses for hides and spices; and elephant and horse stables. There was also a Banquet Hall for royal visitors, and, on the south wall, an Audience Hall (Tuk Phrachao Hao). The niches that line the inner side of the walls by the main gates would have contained oil lamps, lit during festivals and important functions.

An archway leads to the middle courtyard. On the left are the tall ruins of the Dusitsawan Thanya Mahaprasat Hall, built in 1685 for audiences with visiting dignitaries. Next to this is the Phiman Mongkut Pavilion, now the King Narai Museum, housing a fine collection spanning all periods of Thai art, but concentrating, not surprisingly, on Lopburi period sculpture. To the north, the Chantra Paisan Pavilion, looking like a wat, was one of the first structures built by King Narai and served as his audience hall until the Suttha Sawan Pavilion was completed. Behind these buildings were the Women's Quarters, again built by Rama IV. One of them has been turned into a Farmer's Museum displaying traditional central plains farming technology and other implements used in rural life, for pottery and iron production, weaving and fishing. The other buildings in the women's quarters are in the process of being restored.

The inner courtyard contains the ruins of King Narai's own residence, the Suttha Sawan Pavilion. It is isolated from the rest of the complex and was surrounded by gardens, ponds (where the king took his bath under huge canopies) and fountains. King Narai died in this pavilion on 11 July 1688 while his opponents plotted against him.

North of Vichayen Road, next to the railway line, is **Wat Phra Prang Sam Yod** (Wat of Three Prangs), a laterite and sandstone shrine whose three spires originally represented the three Hindu deities: Brahma, Vishnu and Siva. The south *prang* has remnants of some fine stucco friezes and naga heads; also note how the stone door frames are carved to resemble their wooden antecedents. The temple is also home to a large troupe of cute, vicious monkeys who are best left well alone. It's also here where the locals hold, in late November, an annual feast to honour the monkeys. Tables are laid out with fruit, nuts and various monkey treats; the result is a a giant monkey food-fight with nasty spats breaking out over monkey favourites – thousands of Thais turn out to watch.

West along Vichayen Road is the Khmer **Prang Khaek**. Built in the late eighth century, this, like Prang Sam Yod, was also originally a Hindu shrine. The three brick spires represent the oldest Khmer *prangs* found in the Central region of Thailand. It was restored in the 17th century, but today lies in ruins.

Further along Vichayen Road are the remains of **Vichayen House** ① ฿30, better known as Constantine Phaulcon's House, the influential adviser to King Narai. The house, European in style, was constructed for Chevalier de Chaumont, the first French ambassador to Thailand who lived here in 1685. Later, it was used by the Greek Prime Minister, Phaulcon, as his residence.

Opposite the railway station is the entrance to **Wat Phra Sri Ratana Mahathat** ① ฿30, the oldest and tallest wat in Lopburi. The laterite *prang* is slender and elegant and thought to be contemporary with Angkor Wat in Cambodia (12th century).

AYUTTHAYA AND AROUND LISTINGS

WHERE TO STAY

$$$$-$$$ Baan Thai House, 199/19 Moo 4, Pailing, www.baanthaihouse.com, T035-245555. Very popular and well-run guesthouse set around a small pond. The rooms are a mix of bungalows – some of these are replicas of traditional wooden Thai houses – and more modern rooms. The wooden buildings tend to be fan only, with private outdoor bathrooms, while the more contemporary structures have a/c and typical en-suite facilities. Wi-Fi is available. Only drawback is that Baan Thai is set on the opposite side of the river to the old town.

$$$$-$$$ Kantary Hotel, 168 Moo 1 Rojana Rd, T035-337177, www.kantary collection.com. Excellent suites, serviced apartments and hotel rooms from this well-established Thai-owned mini-chain.

Rooms have a nice modern designer feel, with a/c and Wi-Fi, food and service are spot on, and the ambience is upmarket. Breakfast included.

$ Ayutthaya Youth Hostel, 2 Rojana Rd, T035-210941. Very friendly, well-run hostel with pleasant gardens and clean rooms. All are en suite and are the usual mix of fan, a/c and hot/cold water. No dorms. Rates include breakfast. Recommended.

$ Eve Guesthouse, 11/19 Moo 2, Tambon Morrattanachai, T08-1294 3293 (mob). Very cute and well-maintained guesthouse set in a purpose built brick cottage. Located on a quiet back *soi* this place is also sited in a small garden. Rooms are mix of a/c and fan, hot water and cold. Very friendly owner, Eve, is a local lawyer. Recommended.

RESTAURANTS

$$ Baan Joom Zap (the sign is in Thai), Uthong Rd. Daily 1000-2200. Riverside restaurant, set back from the road near the **Bannkunpra** guesthouse. This great Thai restaurant specializes in excellent Isaan food – it even offers a unique deep-fried *somtam* (spicy papaya salad) and Thai style herbal soups with seafood and glass noodles.

$$ Klok Nai Ban, corner of Chee Kun and Uthong roads. A friendly little Thai restaurant with a homely atmosphere and a/c should the heat be getting to you. The fantastic green curry is a must.

$ Lung Lek, just across from Wat Ratchaburana. This shabby lean-to

serves a time-honoured rendition of a dish traditionally hawked from boats: *kuaytiow rua* (boat noodles) in a dark, fragrant beef stock. Recommended.

Foodstalls

A local delicacy you should snack on is muslim dessert *roti mai sai*, thin strands of cotton candy ensconced in fresh roti bread.

There is a **night market** with cheap foodstalls in the parking area in front of Chandra Kasem Palace; stalls are also concentrated at the west end of Chao Phrom Rd and in the market at the northeast corner of the city on Uthong Rd. The covered **Chao Phrom Market** is also an excellent place for cheap food.

WHAT TO DO

Ayutthaya Boat & Travel, 45/2 Rojana Rd. www.ayutthaya-boat.com, T035-244558. Brilliant tour company that runs

bicycle tours, boat tours and the like through Ayutthaya and the local area. Highly recommended.

PHITSANULOK AND SUKHOTHAI

Phitsanulok houses one of the most striking and most important Buddhist shrines in Thailand – Wat Phra Sri Ratana Mahathat (Wat Yai). Vibrant and stunning, you'll be lighting incense and prostrating yourself in front of Buddha before you leave.

The modern conurbation of Sukhothai reveals little of Thailand's ancient capital. Head west about 12 km, keeping an eye on the surrounding landscape, and the ruined brick foundations of ancient religious structures appear in the rice fields, interspersed between wooden shophouses until the road pierces the ramparts of Old Sukhothai.

Si Satchanalai, north of Sukhothai, now a historical park and once linked to Sukhothai by a 50-km highway, is full of Ceylonese-style bell-shaped chedis, Khmer prangs and Sukhothai-era buildings.

The region to the west of Sukhothai is little visited and all the better for it. Just 80 km southwest of the ancient Thai capital sits Kamphaeng Phet. This antiquated city is also a historical park and UNESCO World Heritage Site.

→ PHITSANULOK AND AROUND

Phitsanulok, attractively positioned on the banks of the River Nan, with houseboats lining the steep banks, is home to one of the most striking and important Buddhist shrines in Thailand: Wat Phra Sri Ratana Mahathat (Wat Yai). The rest of this friendly, bustling city is non-descript with most of its old wooden buildings destroyed in a disastrous fire in the 1960s. Phitsanulok is also an important transport hub, linking the central plains with the north and northeast and it is a convenient base from which to visit nearby Sukhothai and Si Satchanalai.

ARRIVING IN PHITSANULOK

Getting there Nok Air (www.nokair.com) flies to Phitsanulok from Bangkok and Chiang Mai. Kan Air operates a daily flight to Phitsanulok from Chiang Mai (www.kanairlines.com). The bus terminal is not central, it's on the road east to Lom Sak (Route 12), 2 km out of town, T055-242430, but bus No 10 travels between the local bus station and the terminal every 10 minutes (and takes 30 minutes). If you arrive by train and are heading straight to Sukhothai, take a tuk-tuk the 4 km to the bus station. It is possible to fly to Phitsanulok, with plenty of daily connections to Bangkok and also with other northern towns. The airport is just out of town on Sanambin Road, T055-301010, to get to town take *songthaew* or there are regular buses that run to the city bus centre near the railway station.

Getting around Phitsanulok is a good walking city with the main site of interest, Wat Yai, being in the northern part of town while an evening stroll along the river allows you to take in the night market at full swing.

Moving on Buses run every 30 minutes to Sukhothai and take one hour.

Tourist information TAT ① *209/7-8 Surasi Shopping Centre, Boromtrailokant Rd, T055-252742, www.tourismthailand.org/phitsanulok, open 0830-1630.* Helpful and informative, with good maps of the town and surrounding area. There's a municipal tourist information

GOING FURTHER
Kamphaeng Phet

It is possible to wander through the ruined monasteries and forts of Kamphaeng Phet, many overgrown with verdant trees, without meeting a single person. The town was originally built by King Lithai in the 14th century as a garrison to protect and consolidate the power of the Sukhothai Kingdom (Kampheng Phet translates as 'Diamond Wall') at a time when surrounding states were growing in threat. In total, the old city, now a historical park, encompasses an area of more than 400 ha. Modern **Kamphaeng Phet** is sleepy and easygoing with a proportion of its older, wooden, shuttered and tiled buildings still surviving.

Arriving in Kamphaeng Phet
Getting there and around Kamphaeng Phet is three hours by bus from Phitsanulok or can be visited as part of a tour. The bus terminal is 2 km from the bridge, some way out of town. The city is open daily 0800-1630. The ticket office is next to Wat Phra Kaeo and north of the river. It costs ฿100 to visit both the area within the ancient city walls and the forested area to the north, known as Aranyik. It is possible to walk within the city walls, but vehicles are useful for the Aranyik area, for which the following charges are levied: ฿10 for a bike, ฿20 for a motorbike, ฿30 for a tuk-tuk and ฿50 for a car. It's possible to walk around the site though you can charter a *saamlor* or tuk-tuk for roughly ฿250 for one hour.

Tourist information There's a Tourist Information Centre next to Wat Phra Kaeo.

Places in Kamphaeng Phet
The massive 6-m-high defensive walls still stand – earthen ramparts topped with laterite – beyond which is a moat to further deter attackers. Within the walls, encompassing an area of 2.5 km by 500 m, lie two old wats, Wat Phra Kaeo and Wat Phrathat, as well as the **Provincial Museum** ① *Wed-Sun 0900-1600, ฿30*. The museum contains, in the entrance hall, what is commonly regarded as one of the finest bronzes of Siva in Thailand. Cast in 1510, in the Khmer 'Bayon' style, its head and hands were removed by an overzealous German visitor in 1886. Fortunately, he was intercepted, and the limbs and head were reunited with the torso. The museum contains some good examples of Buddha images found in the locality.

From the museum, walk west to **Wat Phrathat** (Monastery of the Great Relic). Not much remains except a *chedi* and a well-weathered seated Buddha (of laterite) sitting in the *viharn*. Immediately north, **Wat Phra Kaeo** was probably the largest and most important wat in Kamphaeng Phet. It was initially built during the Sukhothai period and then extensively remodelled in the Ayutthaya period. Just beyond the ticket office is Kamphaeng Phet's **Lak Muang** (City Pillar Shrine). Many *saamlor* drivers ring their bells when passing the shrine in recognition of the power of the spirits that reside here.

Ruins outside the old city's ramparts
Most of the more interesting ruins lie outside the ramparts, to the north of town. They are best seen in the early morning, when it is cooler and the deep red laterite is bathed in golden light. Start with the outer ruins, returning to view Wat Phra Kaeo, Wat Phrathat and the museum. The first wat of significance to be reached travelling north from the New Town

to the Old City is **Wat Phra Non** which, like many of the structures here, dates from the 15th to 16th centuries. The monastery is surrounded by laterite walls and, walking through the complex from the road the buildings are, in turn, the *bot*, *viharn*, the main *chedi*, and then a secondary *viharn*. There are also the remains of monk's quarters, wells and washing areas.

North from here, there is the slightly better-preserved **Wat Phra Si Iriyaboth**, locally known as Wat Yuen or the Monastery of the Standing Buddha. This wat derives its name from the large Buddha images that were to be found in the *mondop* at the end of the *viharn*. The name of the wat literally means 'four postures' – standing, reclining, sitting and walking. They were all in high stucco relief, one on each side of the *mondop*. The impressive standing image is the only one in reasonable repair and is a good example of Sukhothai sculpture, dating from the 14th to 15th centuries. The remains of the walking image give the impression of grace, so typical of the Sukhothai period. The *viharn* was built on a raised platform so that it is higher than the *bot*. It is thought that this was done to show the greater religious significance of the images in the *viharn*.

Adjacent to Wat Phra Si Iriyaboth is **Wat Singh**, again built in the 15th, possibly the 16th, century. The most important structure here is the stupa at the back of the compound, with porches for Buddha images on each side. In front is the bot, with its *bai sema* (boundary stone) still evident.

Walking through the forest behind Wat Singh is **Wat Chang Rob** (Shrine of the Elephants), probably the most impressive structure outside the city walls. The forested position of this monastery is appropriate for it was built for the use of forest-dwelling monks of a meditation sect. This consists of a huge Ceylonese-style laterite *chedi* with its base surrounded by 68 elephants. Only one row of elephants, on the south side, is preserved. Numerous other minor wats are scattered around the area, some in thick undergrowth, others amidst paddy fields – particularly to the northeast and southwest.

On the right-hand side of the approach road to Kamphaeng Phet (Route 1) are the remains of a laterite fort, **Phom Seti**. This walled and moated settlement had similar dimensions to Khamphaeng Phet. It seems that the location of the city was switched to the other bank of the Ping after successive attacks by Ayutthaya from 1373.

Past the bus terminal and on the left before the bridge is **Wat Phra Boromthat**. Just before the bridge, on the right-hand side, is the unusually shaped, square, restored *chedi* of **Wat Chedi Klang**.

New Town sights

A **ruined bot** in the heart of the city is on Thesa Road between Sois 6 and 8. The abandoned brick structure has fallen into ruin; within the 'building' is a Buddha revered by some local residents.

As with any Thai town, Kamphaeng Phet has its share of markets. On Thesa Road, opposite the tourist information centre, is a small **fresh market**; a little further south, also on Thesa Road, is a **night bazaar**, a good place to eat stall food in the evening (near Soi 13). But the main **day market** occupies a large area sandwiched between Wichit and Charoensuk roads.

centre on Buddha Bucha Road and also a small office next to **Wat Yai** which will furnish you with a photocopied map and little else.

BACKGROUND
Phitsanulok was the birthplace of one of the heroes of Thai history: King Naresuan the Great of Ayutthaya, who reigned 1590-1605 (there is a shrine to the king on the west side of the river facing Wat Mahathat). Shortly after his birth, the young Naresuan was bundled off to Burma as a guarantor of his father's – King Thammaracha – good behaviour. He did not return to Phitsanulok until he was 16, when he was awarded the principality by his father. Here he developed the military and political skills which were to stand him in good stead when he assumed the throne of Ayutthaya 19 years later in 1590. For the short period of 25 years, during the reign of King Boromtrailokant of Ayutthaya (1448-1488), Phitsanulok was actually the capital of Siam, and over the four centuries prior to the fall of Ayutthaya to the Burmese in 1767 it was effectively the kingdom's second city.

WAT PHRA SRI RATANA MAHATHAT
ⓘ *0800-1700, donation of ฿50 recommended.*
One of the most venerated temples in Thailand – this is no musuem-like relic but a thriving place of worship – the Monastery of the Great Relic, known as Wat Yai, 'Big Wat' – is to be found on the east bank of the Nan River, close to the Naresuan Bridge. It was built in the reign of King Lithai (1347-1368) of Sukhothai, in 1357. The *viharn* contains one of the most highly regarded and venerated Buddha images in Thailand – the Phra Buddha Chinaraj. Through the centuries, successive Thai kings have come to Phitsanulok to pay homage to the bronze image and to make offerings of gifts. The Buddha is a superlative example of late Sukhothai style and is said to have wept tears of blood when the city was captured by the Ayutthayan army in the early 14th century. The three-tiered *viharn* was built during the Ayutthaya period and shows a fusion of Ayutthayan and Lanna (northern) Thai architectural styles. The low sweeping roofs, supported by black and gold pillars, accentuate the massive gilded bronze Buddha image seated at the end of the nave. The entrance is through inlaid mother-of-pearl doors, made in 1756 in the reign of King Boromkot to replace the original ones of carved wood. The small *viharn* in front of the main building houses another significant Buddha image, known as the 'Remnant Buddha' because it was cast from the bronze remaining after the main image had been produced. The 36-m-high *prang* in the centre of the complex has stairs leading up to a niche containing relics of the Buddha but access is often locked. Also in the wat compound is the **Buddha Chinnarat National Museum**, with a small collection of Sukhothai Buddhas and assorted ceramics. Wat Yai is a very popular site for Thai tourists/ Buddhists. Most buy lotuses and incense from a stall at the gate to offer to the Buddhas. There's also a large antique, food and trinket market next door to the compound plus rows of lottery ticket sellers; the trick is you gain favour by supplicating yourself to the Buddha and then get lucky.

FOLK MUSEUM AND BUDDHA IMAGE FACTORY
ⓘ *Wisutkaset Rd, Folk Museum Tue-Sun 0830-1200, 1300-1630; factory Mon-Sat 0800-1700.*
The Folk Museum exhibits items from everyday rural life, in particular agricultural implements and tools, children's games, festival and ceremonial items, and other bits and pieces. Across the street, and run by the same man, is a factory (the door is always shut; open it and go in), casting Buddha images. These are produced using the lost wax method

and range in size from diminutive to monstrous. It is usually possible to see at least some of the production process.

→ SUKHOTHAI

Officially, the Old City and its surroundings are a national historical park covering 640 ha, which opened in 1988 after a total of 192 wats were restored. The metal lamp posts, concrete-lined ponds and horrible hedgerows of the central area evince overbearing sterility. Head out beyond the city walls and you'll discover dozens of crumbling wats, Buddhas and chedis among the surrounding woodlands.

If you want to stay amid ancient surroundings there is some excellent accommodation in the Old City but choice is limited. Staying here gives you a chance to explore the atmospheric outer ruins in the fresh early-morning mist. There's more accommodation available in the new town, a pleasant enough spot to stay while exploring the glories of Old Sukhothai. Guesthouses here are generally of a high standard, there is good street food at the night market on Ramkhamhaeng Road, a fresh day market off Charodwithithong Road and a useful range of tourist amenities.

ARRIVING IN SUKHOTHAI
Getting there Sukhothai airport is owned by **Bangkok Airways**, which has flights from Bangkok (twice daily). Many people still arrive by bus and there are regular connections with Bangkok, Chiang Mai, Phitsanulok and Khon Kaen, as well as other major towns in the north and central plains. There are also two buses a day from Bangkok's northern Mo Chit bus terminal direct to Old Sukhothai.

Getting around Most people come to Sukhothai to see the ruins of the former capital. Regular buses (every 10 minutes) and *songthaews* ply the route between old and new cities or it is easy to hire a motorcycle. The ruins themselves are spread over a considerable area. ▶▶ *See page 89 for details on getting around the park.*

Moving on It's five hours by bus to Chiang Mai, or take a bus back to Phitsanulok (one hour) and fly to Chiang Mai (50 minutes).

Best time to visit This part of Thailand is one of the hottest. If visiting Sukhothai Old City during the hot or rainy seasons (roughly March to October), it is best to explore either early in the morning or at the end of the day. The best time to visit is November to February.

Tourist Information There is a friendly and helpful TAT office in the New City on Charodwithithong Rd, just west of the bridge and conveniently close to where buses leave for the Old City, T055-616228, www.tourismthailand.org. Brochures, maps and historical information are available, as well as help and advice with booking accommodation and tours. Maps and information are also available at the ticket office in the Old City.

BACKGROUND
If you ask a Thai about the history of Sukhothai, he or she will say that King Intradit ('Glorious Sun-King') founded the Sukhothai Kingdom in 1240, after driving off the Khmers following a single-handed elephant duel with the Khmer commander. King Intradit then

ON THE ROAD
Sukhothai: a 'Golden Age' or mother of invention?

At the beginning of March 1989, several hundred people assembled at the Bangkok Bank's headquarters on Silom Road to debate an issue that threatened to undermine the very identity of the Thai people. Some archaeologists had begun to argue that famous Inscription No 1, on which the interpretation of King Ramkhamhaeng's reign is based, was a forgery. They maintained that the then Prince Mongkut's remarkably timely 'discovery' of the inscription in 1833 served Siam's political purposes – it showed to the expansionist British and French that the country was a 'civilized' kingdom that could govern itself without outside interference. Along with certain literary and artistic anomalies, this led some commentators to maintain that King Mongkut created King Ramkhamhaeng – or at least his popular image – to protect his kingdom from the colonial powers.

Before Mongkut stumbled upon Inscription No 1, knowledge of Sukhothai's history was based upon myth and legend. The great king Phra Ruang – who was believed to have hatched from the egg of a *naga* (serpent) and to be so powerful that he could make trees flower – was clearly the stuff of imagination. And some scholars also argued the same was true of King Ramkhamhaeng.

Since the meeting of 1989, academic opinion has swung back to viewing Mongkut's discovery as genuine. For most Thais, of course, who have been raised to believe that Sukhothai was Thailand's Golden Age and Ramkhamhaeng its chief architect, this is beyond reproach. However, this does not detract from the fact that Inscription No 1 – and the other inscriptions – are fanciful portrayals of history carved to serve the interests of an elite, not to reflect 'reality'. As Betty Gosling writes in *Sukhothai: its history, culture and art* (1991), "... the controversy emphasizes the need to consider Sukhothai inscriptions ... Not in the golden afterglow of Thai mythology, but in the harsh daylight of objective research".

founded Wat Mahathat, the geographical and symbolic heart of the new kingdom. Revisionist historians and archaeologists reject this view, regarding it as myth-making on a grand scale. They maintain that Sukhothai evolved into a great kingdom over a long period and find the big bang theory ultimately unconvincing.

Like Angkor Wat in Cambodia, until comparatively recently Sukhothai was a 'lost city in the jungle'. It was only in 1833 that the future King Mongkut discovered the famous Inscription No 1 and not until 1895 that the French scholar Lucien Fournereau published an incomplete description of the site. The key date, though, is 1907 when crown Prince Maha Vajiravudh made an eight-day visit to Sukhothai. It was his account that laid the foundations for the Sukhothai 'myth': a proud, glorious and civilized past for a country that was on the verge of being submerged by an alien culture. What is remarkable is that Prince Vajiravudh's account, based on a cursory visit, was accepted for so long and by so many. It has only been since the mid-1980s that people have begun to question the conventional history.

Sukhothai became the first capital of Siam and the following 200 years (until the early 15th century) are considered the pinnacle of Thai civilization. There were nine kings during the Sukhothai Dynasty, the most famous being Ramkhamhaeng, whose reign is believed to have been 1275-1317. He was the first ruler to leave accounts of the state inscribed in stone (now displayed in the National Museum in Bangkok). These provide a wealth of information on conquests, taxation and political philosophy. Ramkhamhaeng created the

Thai script, derived from Mon and Khmer, and the Inscription No 1 of 1292 is regarded by many as the first work of Thai literature.

At its peak Ramkhamhaeng's kingdom encompassed much of present-day Thailand, south down the Malay Peninsula and west into Lower Burma, though the northern kingdom of Lanna Thai, Lopburi and the Khorat Plateau were still controlled by the waning Khmer Empire.

Ramkhamhaeng was an absolute monarch, but one who governed his people with justice and magnanimity. If anyone wanted to lodge a complaint, he or she would ring a bell at the gate and the king would grant them an audience. King Ramkhamhaeng was responsible for the introduction of Theravada Buddhism, when he brought Ceylonese monks to his kingdom – partly intended to displace the influence of the Khmers. He displayed considerable diplomatic powers and cultivated good relations with his northern neighbours in order to form an alliance against the Khmers. In addition, he opened relations with China, establishing both economic and cultural links. The fine pottery produced at Sukhothai and Si Satchanalai is thought by some scholars to have developed only after the arrival of expert Chinese potters, with their knowledge of advanced glazing techniques.

The Sukhothai period saw a flowering not just of ceramic arts, but of art in general. The Buddha images are regarded as the most beautiful and original to have ever been created in Thailand, with the walking Buddha image being the first free-standing Buddha the country produced.

King Ramkhamhaeng's son, Lo Thai (1327-1346), was an ineffectual leader, over-shadowed even in death by his father, and much of the territory gained by the previous reign was lost. By the sixth reign of the Sukhothai Dynasty, the kingdom was in decline, and by the seventh, Sukhothai paid homage to Ayutthaya. In 1438 Ayutthaya officially incorporated Sukhothai into its realm; the first Thai kingdom had succumbed to its younger and more vigorous neighbour.

OLD CITY

The Old City is 1800 m long and 1400 m wide, and was originally encompassed by triple earthen ramparts and two moats, punctuated by four gates. Within the city there are 21 historical sites; outside the walls are another 70 or so places of historical interest. At one time the city may have been home to as many as 300,000 people, with an efficient tunnel system to bring water from the mountains and a network of roads. It was an urban centre to rival any in Europe. Within the city are monuments of many different styles – as if the architects were attempting to imbue the centre with the magical power of other Buddhist sites: there are Mon *chedis*, Khmer *prangs* and Ceylonese *chedis*, as well as monuments of clearly Sukhothai inspiration.

Park essentials The park is open daily 0600-1800. A new entrance has also been created about 250 m from its original location towards Namo Gate. It is divided into three zones, each with an admission charge: ฿100 for the central section, and ฿100 for each of the north and east sections. There are additional charges: ฿50 per car, ฿10 per bike, ฿20 per motorcycle. If you want to explore the outer ruins, such as Wat Chetuphon and Wat Saphan Hin no ticket is needed and entrance is free.

Getting around Travelling the 12 km between the new and old cities is easy enough; the open-sided buses leave every 10 minutes (0600-1730, ฿30) from Charodwithithong Road just east of the bridge or from the main bus station (buses from the Old City to Sukhothai stop operating at 1800). Tuk-tuks cost about ฿200 (they congregate on Nikhon Kasem Road). Alternatively, go on a tour, hire a motorbike (฿250) or charter a tuk-tuk for the trip there and back, along with trips around the site (about ฿400 for three hours). When you arrive in the Old City hire a bicycle (฿30 per day) or moped (฿250 per day) from the entrance gate close to the museum, or take the little yellow trolley bus that tours the major sights (฿50). Don't forget a bottle of water if you're cycling.

Places in the Old City Note: letters in brackets refer to the map below. Situated just inside the **Kamphanghek** ('broken wall') **Gate (a)** entrance is the **Ramkhamhaeng National Museum (b)** ⓘ *T055-612167, 0900-1600, ฿100*, a good place to begin a tour. The museum contains a copy of some wonderful Buddha images, along with explanatory information. It also houses a range of household goods giving an indication of the sophistication of Sukhothai society.

The centre of the Sukhothai Kingdom was **Wat Mahathat (c)** and the royal palace – the earliest example in Thailand. This was both the religious and the political centre of the kingdom and is usually regarded as the first truly 'Sukhothai' monument. The complex was begun by King Intradit, expanded by King Ramkhamhaeng and finally completed by King Lo Thai in 1345, or thereabouts.

SUKHOTHAI OLD CITY

Old City ○
Kamphanghek Gate **a**
Ramkhamhaeng
  Museum **b**
Wat Mahathat **c**

Royal Palace **d**
San Da Pa Deng **e**
Wat Trapang Ngoen **f**
Wat Trapang Thong **g**
Wat Sra Sri **h**

King Ramkhamhaeng's
  statue **i**
Wat Sri Sawai **j**

The principal building is the central sanctuary, which King Lo Thai is said to have rebuilt in the 1340s to house the hair and neckbone relics of the Buddha which had been brought back from Ceylon. The central tower is surrounded by four smaller *chedis* in Srivijaya-Ceylonese style, alternating with four Khmer *prangs*. The entire ensemble is raised up on a two-tiered base with a stucco frieze of walking monks in relief.

Some original Buddha images still sit among the ruins. Particularly unusual are the two monumental standing Buddhas, in an attitude of forgiveness, on either side of the central sanctuary, enclosed by brick walls, with their heads protruding over the top.

Little remains of the original **Royal Palace (Phra Ruang Palace) (d)**. It was here that King Mongkut, while he was still the Crown Prince, found the famous Inscription No 1 of King Ramkhamhaeng, the Manangsilabat stone throne, and the stone inscription of King Lithai in 1833. All three objects – which became talismans for the Thai people – were carted off to Bangkok. Whether the Royal Palace really was a palace is a subject for conjecture. The site appears rather too small and, although it has revealed a mass of objects, some scholars believe it was the site of a royal pavilion rather than a royal palace. To the north of Wat Mahathat is **San Da Pa Deng (e)**, the oldest existing structure from the Sukhothai era. It is a small Khmer laterite *prang* built during the first half of the 12th century.

Wat Trapang Ngoen (f) – Temple of the Silver Pond – contains a large lotus-bud *chedi*, similar to that at Wat Mahathat. One passage from Inscription No 1 refers to this wat: "In the middle of this city of Sukhothai the water of the Pho Si Pond is as clear and as good to drink as the river of the Khong [Mekong] in the dry season". **Wat Trapang Thong (g)** sits on an island, after which the monastery is named. It is approached along a rickety bridge. Particularly fine are the stucco reliefs, of which perhaps the most beautiful is that on the south side of the *mondop*. It shows the Buddha descending from the Tavatimsa Heaven with the attendant Brahma on his left and Indra on his right and is considered the finest piece of stucco work from the Sukhothai period.

Wat Sra Sri (h), to the north of Wat Trapang Ngoen, is a popular photo-spot, as the *bot* is reflected in a pond. A Ceylonese-style *chedi* dominates the complex, which also contains a fine, large, seated Buddha image enclosed by columns. To the east of here is **King Ramkhamhaeng's statue (i)**, seated on a copy of the stone throne (the Phra Thaen Manang Silabat) that was found on the site of the Royal Palace and which is now in the Wat Phra Kaeo Museum in Bangkok. The statue was erected in 1969 and the high-relief carvings depict famous episodes from the life of the illustrious king.

To the southwest of Wat Mahathat is **Wat Sri Sawai (j)**, enclosed within laterite walls. It was built during the time that Sukhothai was under Khmer domination. The *prang* is in the three-tower style, with the largest central *prang* (rather badly restored) being 20 m tall. The stucco decoration was added to the towers in the 15th century, as were their upper brick portions. The lower laterite levels are the original sections, built under Khmer influence. It must originally have been a Hindu shrine, as carvings of Vishnu and other Hindu divinities have been found on the site.

WATS OUTSIDE THE OLD CITY WALLS

The main reason to see the monasteries outside the Old City walls is to get a better idea of what Sukhothai was like before it became a historical park and was cleared of undergrowth. Some of the lesser-known monasteries are still in the forest. **Note** Try cycling to these wats during the morning when it is cooler as they are far apart. Alternatively, hire a tuk-tuk.

FESTIVALS
Sukhothai

October/November Loi Krathong is very special and Sukhothai is reputed to be the 'home' of this most beautiful of Thai festivals. It is said that one of the king's mistresses carved the first *krathong* from a piece of fruit and floated it down the river to her king. Today, the festival symbolizes the floating away of the previous year's sins, although traditionally it was linked to the gift of water. The Thai word for irrigation, *chonprathaan*, literally means the 'gift of water', and the festival comes at the end of the rainy season when the rice is maturing in the paddy fields.

Take the northwest gate out of the city to visit the impressive **Wat Sri Chum**. A large *mondop*, with a narrow vaulted entrance, encloses an enormous brick and stucco seated Buddha image. The temple was probably built during the seventh reign of the Sukhothai Kingdom (mid-14th century) and is said to have caused a Burmese army to flee in terror, such is the power of its withering gaze. The large Buddha seems almost suffocated by the surrounding walls, which must have been added at a later stage. There is a stairway in the *mondop* which leads up to a space behind the head of the image (closed since 1988). Here, there are line carvings recounting the Jataka tales, covering the slate slab ceiling. Each slab depicts one story, skilfully carved with free-flowing lines – which originally would have been enlivened with paint. These are the finest and earliest (circa 1350) to be found in Thailand (there are examples from Wat Sri Chum in the National Museum, Bangkok). The image here is said to have talked on a number of occasions – although the back stairs provide a useful hiding place for someone to play a practical joke.

East of Wat Sri Chum is **Wat Phra Pai Luang**, the Monastery of the Great Wind, interesting for the remains of three laterite *prangs*. Built during the reign of King Jayavarman VII (a Khmer king who ruled 1181-1217) it dates from the Khmer period that preceded the rise of Sukhothai. Its Khmer inspiration is clearly evident in the square base and indented tiers. To the east of the *prang* is a later stupa, with niches on all four sides containing damaged Buddha images. Further east still is a ruined *mondop* with the remains of large stucco Buddha images, standing, walking and reclining. In total, Wat Phra Pai Luang contains over 30 stupas of assorted styles. It is thought that not only was it originally a Hindu shrine, but that it was also the site of an earlier Khmer town.

Take the northwest road 3 km beyond the city walls where a large, standing Buddha image is located at the top of an ancient staircase. Sited at the top of a hill amid languorous woodlands **Wat Saphan Hin** has one of the most beautiful locations in Sukhothai. Many Thais still come here, offering prayers and incense. It is also a perfect spot to watch a tropical sunrise, though you'll need to get up early if you want to reach here in time.

Not far away from Wat Saphan Hin are the remains of two other monasteries. **Wat Khao Phrabat Noi** lies about 2.5 km northwest of the city walls and it is approached along a stone-lined footpath. The *chedi* here is unusual in that it is not really Sukhothai in style and it is presumed that it was remodelled during the Ayutthaya period. Four Buddha footprints were found here, but these have been removed to the National Museum in Bangkok.

South from this group of three monasteries is the better-known **Wat Chang Rob** (Monastery Encircled by Elephants). In Buddhist mythology, elephants – the holiest of beasts – support Mount Meru, the centre of the universe.

Continuing south to Route 12 is the impressive, at least in size, **Wat Chedi Ngam** (Monastery of the Beautiful Chedi). The large *chedi*, pure and simple in its form, has been well preserved. Also here are the remains of a large viharn with some standing columns, and what is thought to have been a *kuti* (monks' quarters) or place for bathing.

On the north side of Route 12 is **Wat Mangkon** (Dragon Monastery). A relatively large complex, the *bot*, surrounded by large leaf-shaped boundary stones, has an unusual slate-tiled brick base. To the west of the *bot* is the base of a pavilion or *sala*, and to the north the remains of a Ceylonese-style bell-shaped *phra chedi*. **Wat Phra Yuen** is around 200 m from Wat Mangkon and 1500 m from the city walls, just to the south of Route 12. The remains of a *bot* can be identified by the *bai sema* (boundary stones) that surround it and a *mondop* houses a large standing Buddha image.

There are also a series of monasteries to the south and east of the city. Travel 1 km from the city by the south gate and you'll find **Wat Ton Chan** (Sandalwood Tree Monastery). Although large, the monastery is nothing special, although it is moated and has a bathing pool along with the usual array of *viharn* and *chedi*. Far more impressive is **Wat Chetuphon**, one of Sukhothai's more important monasteries. The building materials are more varied than the usual brick and stucco; stone, slate and brick have also been used in its construction. However, archaeologists and art historians suspect that the monastery was renovated and expanded on a number of occasions, so how much of the structure is Sukhothai, is a source of conjecture.

About 500 m from Wat Chetuphon is **Wat Chedi Si Hong**. The most notable feature of this wat is the fine stucco work depicting *devas* (heavenly beings), humans and *garudas* riding elephants on the base of the *viharn* and *chedi*.

→ AROUND SUKHOTHAI

RAMKHAMHAENG NATIONAL PARK
ⓘ *Public transport is limited – take a local bus along Route 101 towards Kamphaeng Phet, getting off at the road to the national park (Uthayaan Haeng Chart Ramkhamhaeng); it's 16 km from here. Motorcycle taxis are sometimes available at the turn-off.*
Ramkhamhaeng National Park, 30 km southwest of New Sukhothai in Amphoe Khiri Mat, covers 341 sq km. The highest peak here, **Khao Luang** – after which the park is also sometimes known – rises to nearly 1200 m. Highlights of the park include the 100-m-high **Sai Rung Waterfall**, several caves, and an ancient dam which fed the canals of Sukhothai city.

GOING FURTHER
Si Satchanalai and around

Si Sat nestles languidly on the west bank of the Yom River about 50 km to the north of Sukhothai one hour by bus or visit as part of a tour. It remained undiscovered by tourists until 1987, when a grant was provided to prepare the town for 'Visit Thailand Year'. The site has been 'cleaned up', though not to the extent of Sukhothai and still retains a lot of charm. Si Satchanalai makes a fascinating side trip from Sukhothai with examples of Ceylonese-style bell-shaped *chedis*, Khmer *prangs* and Sukhothai-era buildings. There is no modern town here; the whole area has become a 'historical park' and is littered with monuments. Si Satchanalai is compact and the main monuments can be seen on foot. To reach Chaliang and the sights outside the city walls it is best to hire a bicycle (฿35 per day) at the admission gate.

The Si Satchanalai Historical Park Information Centre is just outside Ram Narong Gate, to the southeast. There's not much information here, just a scale model and map of the park and a few books for sale. Admission fee to Si Satchanalai: ฿100, ฿50 for a car.

Background
During the fourth reign of Sukhothai, Si Sat became the seat of the king's son and the two cities were linked by a 50-km-long road, the Phra Ruang Highway. Bounded by a moat 10 m wide and by thick town walls, during its heyday it was the equal of Sukhothai in splendour, and probably superior in terms of its defences. Protected by rapids, swamp and mountains, not to mention a triple moat filled with barbed spikes, Si Sat must have seemed immensely daunting to any prospective attacker.

Critical to Si Sat's vitality was the ceramic industry based at Ban Pha Yang and Ban Ko-noi, to the north of the city. With the technical assistance of Chinese potters these villages produced probably the finest of all Thai ceramics. These were not just for local consumption; Sangkhalok ware has been found as far afield as Java, Borneo and the Philippines.

Places in Si Satchanalai
Wat Chang Lom lies in the heart of the old city and is the most sacred wat in Si Satchanalai. The principal *chedi* was built between 1285 and 1291 to contain sacred relics of the Buddha, which King Ramkhamhaeng dug up, worshipped for a month and six days and buried; he then had a *chedi* built over them, which took three years to complete. The Ceylonese-style *chedi* is the earliest example of its kind in Thailand and became the prototype for many others. Stairs take the pilgrim from the lower, earthly levels, upwards towards the more spiritual realm of the Buddha. The *chedi* is enclosed by 50-m-long laterite walls, and in front of it are the ruins of a large *viharn*, together with another smaller stupa and *viharn*.

Wat Chedi Jet Thaew (30 m south of Wat Chang Lom) stands within a ditch and two rows of laterite walls pierced by four gates. The wat contains the remnants of seven rows of lotus-bud *chedis*, some 34 in total, which house the ashes of members of the Si Satchanalai ruling family.

South of here is **Wat Suan Kaeo Utthayanyai** and the southernmost wat within the walls, **Wat Nang Phaya** (Monastery of the Queen). The latter is enclosed by single walls of laterite, with four gateways. A Ceylonese-style *chedi* dominates the compound. The fine stucco floral motifs (now protected by a shed) on the west wall of the large laterite *viharn* are early Ayutthayan in style (15th century), and are the best preserved of any such decoration in either Sukhothai or Si Sat.

Wat Khao Phanom Phloeng lies on a 20-m-high hillock on the north side of the town and is reached by a laterite staircase of 144 steps. It comprises a Ceylonese-style *chedi*, a large seated Buddha and some stone columns. Recent excavations at this site have revealed an early animist shrine, the **Sala Chao Mae Laong Samli**, which pre-dates both the Khmer and Tai periods, showing that Si Sat was occupied – and of significant importance – long before the rise of the Sukhothai Kingdom. To the west of Wat Khao Phanom Phloeng and linked by a path and staircase, on a higher hillock, are the remains of **Wat Khao Suwan Khiri**.

Chaliang
① *Get off at the pink archway on Route 101, 2 km before Route 1201, which leads to a suspension footbridge crossing the Yom River to Chaliang.*
To the southeast, 2 km outside the Si Satchanalai city walls, is the area known as Chaliang. The first wat you come to along the road to Chaliang is **Wat Kok Singh Karam**, on the right-hand side, which includes three *chedis* on the same base. In front of these stupas are a *viharn* and *bot*.

Wat Chom Chuen (Monastery of Prince Chan) contains a *prang* built in the time of the Khmer King Jayavarman VII (1181-1217). It seems that Chaliang was chosen by the Khmer as the site for one of its outposts at the far extremity of the Khmer Empire because of its defensive position. Next to this wat is an **Archaeological Site Museum** ① *free*, a great building set into the riverbank with a grass roof. The excavations revealed 15 inhumation burials. The bodies were buried during the Dvaravati period (sixth to 11th centuries). Grave goods devoted to the dead comprise glass beads, iron tools and clay paddles. Head orientation is to the west.

Positioned on the banks of the Yom River is **Wat Phra Sri Ratana Mahathat Chaliang** (or Wat Phra Prang), an impressive laterite *prang* originally built in the mid-15th century. Its origins are older still, as the *prang* is thought to have been built on top of an earlier Khmer *prasat*. In front of the *prang* are the ruins of a *viharn* which houses a large seated Sukhothai Buddha image, with long, graceful fingers 'touching ground'. Even more beautiful is the smaller walking Buddha of brick and stucco to the left. It is thought to be one of the finest from the Sukhothai period displaying that enigmatic 'Sukhothai smile'. The wat also contains a number of other interesting Buddha images.

PHITSANULOK AND SUKHOTHAI LISTINGS

WHERE TO STAY

Phitsanulok

$$$ The Grand Riverside, 59 Praroung Rd, 055-248333, www.tgrhotel.com. This large hotel in the centre of town overlooks the river and offers superior and deluxe rooms and suites. Rooms are large and clean, and those on the riverside offer excellent views. Price includes breakfast. Free Wi-Fi.

$$ Nanchao, 242 Boromtrailokant Rd, T055-244702. A/c, modern hotel with views from the upper floors, good value. Wi-Fi and breakfast included. Recommended.

Sukhothai New City

$$ Sukhothai Lotus Village, 170 Rachthani Rd, T055-621484, www.lotus-village.com. The large, leafy compound is scattered with several ponds, has a number of attractive teak houses and several spotless bungalows, some with a/c. Tastefully decorated, clean, peaceful, and managed by an informative Thai/French couple. It also serves tasty Western breakfasts of toast, yoghurt, fresh juice and fresh coffee. Beds are very hard. Highly recommended.

$ Sukhothai Guesthouse, 68 Wichien Chamnong Rd, T055-610453, www.sukhothaiguesthouse.com. Some a/c rooms, hot water showers, restaurant. A well-maintained establishment, with attractive teak balconies. Friendly and informative owners. Also runs informal cookery classes and offers a range of tours, free bikes, free pick-up at the bus station and internet. Highly recommended.

Sukhothai Old City

$$$$ Tharaburi Resort, 321/3 Muangkao-Napoh Rd, T055-697132, www.tharaburiresort.com. Attractive boutique resort located just outside the moat. Comfortable and beautifully appointed suites and rooms are set in a large garden with swimming pool. Free Wi-Fi; tours and cookery courses available.

$$$ Orchid Hibiscus, 407 Old City, T055-633284, www.orchidhibiscus-guesthouse.com. Run by the engaging Paolo – an Italian from Rome – and his Thai wife, Pinthong, this is one of the nicest guesthouses in Thailand. Rates may be a little high for the average backpacker accommodation but the gorgeous en suite a/c bungalows, swimming pool, gardens, tropical birds and wonderful breakfasts (beware of the highly addictive coconut pudding smothered in fresh, wild honey) certainly make it excellent value. Paolo is a font of local knowledge and knows the outer temples so well he can even tell you the best spots for sunrise and sunset. Rate includes breakfast. Highly recommended.

$$ Pin Pao Guesthouse, 723 Old City, just before moat into the Old City on road from New City, T055-633284, www.pinpaoguesthouse.com. Opened in late 2008 by Paolo from **Orchid Hibiscus**, this place offers stylish budget rooms, all with a/c and hot-water showers. The back overlooks a stream and there's a pleasant veranda. Recommended.

RESTAURANTS

Phitsanulok

There is a good choice of excellent restaurants, mostly concentrated in the centre of town around Naresuan, Sairuthai and Phaya Lithai roads. Check out Phitsanulok's 2 famed specialities: *kluay thaak* (sweet bananas) and *thao mai luai* (morning glory). This vegetable is flash-fried in a wok with a great burst of flame and then tossed onto the plate (the dish is usually known as *pad phak boong fai daeng*). 'Flying vegetable' artistes can be seen at work in the night market and at a few restaurants. Not to be missed! Several houseboat restaurants are to be found along the western bank of the river. The houseboats have been known to move, but you shouldn't have to look too far!

$$ Sabai Boat, Wanchan Rd. 1000-2100. Friendly houseboat restaurant serving up tasty Thai food. Excellent spot for a relaxing lunch while taking in the river views.

Foodstalls

The **riverside night market** is open from 1800-2400, selling Thai and Chinese food. Thai desserts such as *khao niaw sangkayaa* (sticky rice and custard) can be bought from the foodstalls on Phaya Lithai Rd in the evening. **Basement of Topland Arcade**, Boromtrailokant Rd, has a good selection of clean, well-presented foodstalls.

Sukhothai New City

$ Dream Café, 86/1 Singhawat Rd, near Sawatdipong Hotel, T055-612081. Tasty Thai and international dishes in a woody, old-world interior, with a great collection of bric-a-brac and antiques. Good for breakfasts.

Foodstalls

Night market (*talaat to rung*), on Ramkhamhaeng Rd, off Nikhon Kasem Rd, opposite the cinema, for good stalls. Open 1800-0600. Other stalls open up at about the same time along the walls of Wat Rachthani.

Sukhothai Old City

A number of stalls and small restaurants sell simple Thai dishes in the Old City. There's a collection of good Thai eateries in the compound just outside the new main entrance and, during the evening, dozens of stalls spring up along the main road selling everything from spicy papaya salad to freshly roasted chicken.

$$ Coffee House, next to the gate into the Old City from new Sukhothai. Snacks, breakfast, overpriced internet, Thai food and excellent range of coffee/tea served from this new, wooden construction.

GOING FURTHER
Mae Sot

Mae Sot lies 5 km from the Burmese border, near the end of Route 105, which swoops its way through hills and forest from Tak to Mae Sot and the Moei River Valley. The town has developed into an important trading centre and just about every ethnic group can be seen wandering the streets: Thais, Chinese, Burmese, Karen, Hmong and other mountain peoples. Although Mae Sot has quietened down over the last few years, it still has a reputation as being one of the more lawless towns in Thailand. With a flourishing, and sometimes illicit, trade in teak and gems and drugs – this is perhaps unsurprising.

The importance of teak has grown since the Thai government imposed a ban on all logging in Thailand, and companies have turned instead to concessions just across the border in Burma to secure their wood. Whether the army and police force are protecting the forests or are making a tidy profit out of the industry is never quite clear. Over the last few years the Burmese army have made intermittent incursions into Thailand near Mae Sot pursuing Karen rebels. There have also been several assassinations of high-profile anti-Burmese rebels – Mae Sot's reputation as a slightly 'dangerous' frontier town is still well deserved. The Thai-Burmese border in this area is strewn with anti-personnel mines and many local people refuse to graze their cattle because of the danger.

Wat Moni Phraison, on Intharakit Road, has an unusual *chedi* in which a golden central spire is surrounded by numerous smaller *chedis* rising in tiers, behind each of which is a small image of the Buddha. **Wat Chumphon**, also on Intharakit Road but on the western side of town, is worth visiting. Many of Mae Sot's older wooden shophouses are still standing, especially on Intharakit Road. There is a busy morning market between Prasat Withi and Intharakit roads in the town centre that attracts many Burmese eager to sell their produce. Burmese day migrants can be identified by their dress (many wear *longyis*, Burmese-style sarongs), their language and the pearl-coloured powder called *tanaka*, which often covers the faces of women and children.

Mae Sot offers some of the best trekking in northern and western Thailand and its popularity is increasing. It's also possible to cross the border into Burma, for an immigration fee of ฿500 (which goes straight to the Burmese government). Treks tend to either go south to Umphang or north towards Mae Sariang, and incorporate visits to caves, waterfalls and mountain villages.

There is a choice of places to stay; we recommend **Irawadee Resort** (Intharakit Road, www.irawadee.com, **$$**) and **Baan Thai Guesthouse** (on the same road, T055-531590, book in advance, **$**). The ethnic mix ensures that the food here is probably the most diverse in the north, with restaurants and food stalls that serve international food, as well as obscure dishes from across the region, especially Burma.

Towards the Burmese border

A visit to the border makes for an interesting day trip, even if you don't actually cross into Burma. There is a modern, covered market at the border selling Burmese goods (hats, blankets, gems, silver, baskets and agricultural produce like dried mushrooms), with gun-toting Thai rangers, powder-covered Burmese girls and a few restaurants.

Around 1 km from the bridge, back along the road to Mae Sot, is **Wat Thai Wattanaram**. This monastery is notable mainly for the massive, recently built, Burmese-style reclining Buddha in the rear courtyard. Also here is a gallery of over 25 smaller sitting Buddhas.

GOING FURTHER
Umphang and around

The 164 km of road that twists and turns its way from Mae Sot to Umphang is one of the most dramatic in the country with vast, jaw-dropping views across into the ranges of hills that lie along the Burmese border. Along this route are also several Karen refugee communities – vast holding pens with the inhabitants not allowed beyond the surrounding area. The Karen, who fought the Burmese dictatorship for decades and held most of the border region until the late 1990s, have also been, in many cases, ruthlessly exploited by their Thai hosts. Mae Sot town is filled with sweatshops staffed by Karen refugees. The struggle by the Karen to secure a decent life is ongoing and a visit to one of the local Karen villages can certainly put paid to the lie that Thailand is the 'Land of Smiles'.

Umphang is one of the least developed regions in western Thailand, its rugged terrain and large expanses of forest, including the Khlong Lan National Park, making it ideal for trekking. Although an organized trek is the best way to see and experience the area's beauty (you can arrange a trek through one of the Umphang guest houses), it is possible to explore the area on one's own. Umphang town is not much more than an oversized village and the majority of its population are Karen.

Many of the trekking companies in Mae Sot head this way, with the guesthouses, tour companies and resorts in Umphang offering similar packages, but only a handful offer English-speaking guides. (Treks arranged from Umphang rather than Mae Sot usually work out considerably cheaper, although you'll have to suffer the five-hour journey from Mae Sot in a *songthaew* rather than a comfortable 4WD.) On Palata Road is **Tu Ka Su Cottage ($)**.

Another reason to visit Umphang is to see the Thi Lo Su waterfall – widely recognized as the most beautiful in the country. Set on a massive limestone escarpment in the middle of the jungle, the 500-m-wide fall drops almost 250 m through a series of pools. To reach the waterfall is difficult and you'll probably need to hire a car or *songthaew* from Umphang as it's a 45-km journey along dirt tracks requiring a 3-km walk at the end to reach the falls. Its remoteness also means that it is not overrun with tourists. Set off early from Umphang and don't forget to pack your swimming kit. The road here is often closed during the wetter months and visit here is best planned from November to May.

If travelling to Umphang in your own transport, leave early in the morning as there are quite a number of worthwhile stops en route, including waterfalls and Karen villages. The **Thara Rak waterfall** is 25 km from Mae Sot. Turn off the road after the Km 24 marker.

Khlong Lan National Park

The park covers around 300 sq km with its highest point at 1440-m-high Khun Klong Lan. Wildlife includes sambar deer, wild pig and macaques. There are also a number of waterfalls, including the **Khlong Lan Waterfall** which cascades over a 100-m-high rock face. Khlong Nam Lai Waterfall is good for swimming.

CHIANG MAI AND AROUND

When Reginald Le May wrote about Chiang Mai back in 1938, this was, in his view, one of the loveliest cities imaginable. Life, as they say, has moved on since then. But while old Thailand hands may worry about lost innocence, Chiang Mai is still worth visiting.

While in Chiang Mai don't forget to climb Doi Suthep, the city's revered mountain, which rises 1000 m above the city and is crowned with an important temple. While this temple has succumbed to money-grabbing practices, it is still a beautiful setting and worth the effort. A visit to the tribal museum, just to the north of the city centre, is essential to understanding the region's indigenous peoples while to the south rests the handsome remains of a ruined city, Wiang Kum Kam.

The city's monasteries are the most beautiful in the north; there is a rich tradition of arts and crafts, and the moated old city still gives a flavour of the past. It is the unofficial 'capital of the north', there are also some good practical reasons to base yourself here. It is an important transport hub, there is an excellent range of hotels and restaurants, the shopping is the best in the north, and there are also scores of trekking and other companies offering everything from whitewater rafting to elephant treks.

The nearby historical towns of Lamphun and Lampang provide handsome, striking temples – some say they are the best in the whole country. Both can be reached as day excursions from Chiang Mai though Lampang, with its laid-back riverside vibe, warrants a little more attention.

→ ARRIVING IN CHIANG MAI

GETTING THERE

The quickest way of getting to Chiang Mai is by air. A number of airlines offer flights from Bangkok as well as links to other provincial centres. The airport, www.chiangmaiairportonline.com, is 3 km southwest of town, call T053-270222 for airport information. Banks, currency exchange, hotel booking counters, car rental counters and airport information are all at hand in the arrivals area. Taxis into town cost about ฿100-150 and can be arranged at the taxi booking counter.

There are several trains a day from Bangkok (12 hours) including the splendid sleeper service. 'Special Express' trains with first class and second class sleeper berths depart Bangkok at 1810 and 1935 and arrive in Chiang mai at 0745 and 0945 respectively. The later 'Express', departing Bangkok at 2200 and arriving in Chiang Mai at 1245, offers second class berths. For more information on trains from Bangkok, see www.railway.co.th. The station is in the east of the town, on Charoen Muang Road, across the Ping River. To get to town, there are frequent *songthaews* and tuk-tuks.

Scores of buses arrive from all over Thailand – from super-luxury VIP buses through to the bone-shaking ordinary variety. The long-distance bus station is at the Chiang Mai Arcade, on the corner of the super highway and Kaew Nawarat Road, northeast of town, T053-242664. Tuk-tuks and *songthaews* wait at the station to take passengers into town.

GETTING AROUND

Much of the central part of the city can be easily covered on foot. *Songthaews* (converted pick-ups) operate as the main mode of public transport, ferrying people around for ฿20 per person. They do not operate set routes so before boarding tell the driver where you

FESTIVALS
Chiang Mai

1st weekend in February Flower Festival. This is a great festival and is centred on the inner moat road, at the southwest corner of the Old City, where small displays of flowers and plants are arranged by schools, colleges and professional gardeners and garden shops from across the north. There are also, as you would expect in Thailand, lots of foodstalls as well as handicrafts. If you have ever felt the urge to grow a papaya tree, then this is the place to get your seeds. The highlight is a parade of floral floats along with the requisite beauty contest. If you want to avoid the crowds, come on the Fri evening.

13-16 April Songkran, traditional Thai New Year (public holiday) celebrated with more gusto in Chiang Mai than elsewhere. Boisterous water-throwing, particularly directed at *farangs*; expect to be soaked to the skin for the entire four days.

want to go. *Songthaews* can also be used for longer journeys and day trips. The price is negotiable. Use landmarks (such as hotels, bridges, gates, etc) rather than street names as a guide for where you want to go. There are also tuk-tuks, some taxis, and a good number of car, motorbike and bicycle hire companies. Tuk-tuks charge a minimum of ฿40 per trip, ฿60-120 for longer journeys. *Saamlors* charge ฿20 within city, more for longer distances.

MOVING ON
For the Western Loop from Chiang Mai (see page 119), take a bus to Pai, four hours. Once you've done the Western Loop and are back in Chiang Mai, head north to Chiang Rai by bus, three to four hours.

TOURIST INFORMATION
TAT ① 105/1 Chiang Mai-Lamphun Rd, T053-248607, http://www.tourismthailand.org/chiangmai, daily 0830-1630, is very helpful and informative with good English spoken and a good range of maps and leaflets, including information on guesthouses and guidelines for trekking. In addition, there are also various free, tourist-oriented magazines. Chiang Mai Citylife (www.chiangmainews.com) is useful and the pick of the bunch.

→ BACKGROUND

Around 1290 King Mengrai annexed the last of the Mon kingdoms at Lamphun and moved his capital from Chiang Rai to a site on the banks of the Ping River called Nopburi Sri Nakawan Ping Chiang Mai. It is said he chose the site after seeing a big mouse accompanied by four smaller mice scurry down a hole beneath a holy Bodhi tree. He made this site the heart of his Lanna kingdom.

Mengrai was a great patron of Theravada Buddhism and he brought monks from Ceylon to unify the country. Up until the 15th century, Chiang Mai flourished. As this century ended, relations with up-and-coming Ayutthaya became strained and the two kingdoms engaged in a series of wars with few gains on either side.

While Chiang Mai and Ayutthaya were busy fighting, the Burmese eventually captured the city of Chiang Mai in 1556. King Bayinnaung, who had unified Burma, took Chiang Mai after a three-day battle and the city remained a Burmese regency for 220 years. There was constant conflict during these years and by the time the Burmese succeeded in overthrowing Ayutthaya in 1767, the city of Chiang Mai was decimated and depopulated. In 1775, General Taksin united the kingdom of Thailand and a semi-autonomous prince of the Lampang Dynasty was appointed to rule the north. Chiang Mai lost its semi-independence in 1938 and came under direct rule from Bangkok.

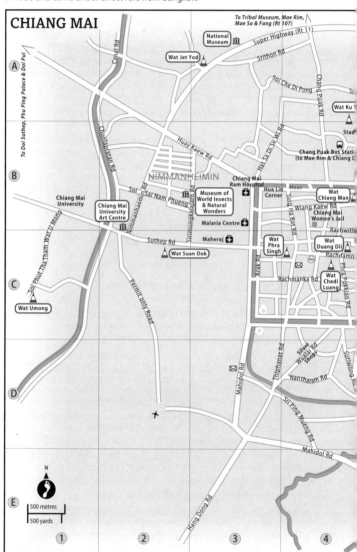

MODERN CHIANG MAI

Today, Chiang Mai is the second largest city in Thailand, with a population of roughly 500,000; a thriving commercial centre as well as a favourite tourist destination. TAT estimates that 12% of Thailand's tourists travel to Chiang Mai. Its attractions to the visitor are obvious: the

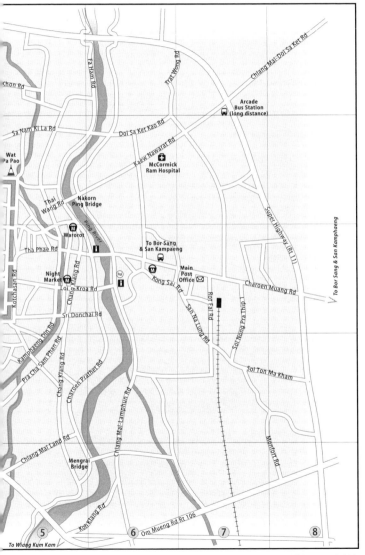

city has a rich and colourful history, still evident in the architecture of the city, which includes more than 300 wats; it is manageable and still relatively 'user friendly' (unlike Bangkok); it has perhaps the greatest concentration of handicraft industries in the country; and it is also an excellent base from which to go trekking and visit the famous hilltribe villages in the surrounding highlands. Chiang Mai has developed into a major tourist centre with a good infrastructure, including excellent hotels and restaurants in all price categories. Some long-term visitors argue that the city has lost some of its charm in the process: traffic congestion, pollution and frantic property development are now much in evidence.

On a clear day at the start of the cold season, or after the rains have begun towards the end of the hot season, Chiang Mai's strategic location becomes clear. Mountains surround the city to the north, west and east, enclosing a large and rich bowl of rice fields drained by the Ping River. With Doi Suthep to the west clothed in trees and the golden *chedi* of Wat Phrathat Doi Suthep glittering on its slopes, it is a magical place.

→ PLACES IN CHIANG MAI

Chiang Mai is centred on a square moat and defensive wall built during the 19th century. The four corner bastions are reasonably well preserved and are a useful reference point when roaming the city. Much of the rest of the town's walls were demolished during the Second World War and the bricks used for road construction. Not surprisingly, given Chiang Mai's turbulent history, many of the more important and interesting wats are within the city walls which is – surprisingly – the least built-up part. Modern commercial development has been concentrated to the east of the city and now well beyond the Ping River.

WAT CHIANG MAN
Situated in the northeast of the walled town, Wat Chiang Man is on Rachpakinai Road within a peaceful compound. The wat is the oldest in the city and was built by King Mengrai soon after he had chosen the site for his new capital in 1296. It is said that he resided here while waiting for his new city to be constructed and also spent the last years of his life at the monastery. The gold-topped *chedi* Chang Lom is supported by rows of elephants, similar to those of the two *chedis* of the same name at Si Satchanalai and Sukhothai. Two ancient Buddha images are contained behind bars within the *viharn*, on the right-hand side as you enter the compound. One is the crystal Buddha, Phra Sae Tang Tamani (standing 10 cm high). The second is the Phra Sila (literally, 'Stone Buddha'), believed to have originated in India or Ceylon about 2500 years ago. Wat Chiang Man is an excellent place to see how wat architecture has evolved.

WAT PA PAO
To the northeast of Wat Chiang Man, just outside the city walls, is the unique Burmese Shan, Wat Pa Pao, which was founded more than 400 years ago by a Shan monk. A narrow *soi* leads off the busy road through an archway and into the wat's peaceful and rather ramshackle compound. The *chedi* is a melange of stuccoed animals from *singhas* to *nagas*, while the flat-roofed *viharn*, with its dark and atmospheric interior, contains three Buddha images. The monks at the wat are Shan – most having come here from Burma over the last few years – and it continues to serve Chiang Mai's Shan community.

WAT PHRA SINGH

Wat Phra Singh (Temple of the Lion Buddha) is situated in the west quarter of the **old city** and is impressively positioned at the end of Phra Singh Road (see map, page 102). The wat was founded in 1345 and contains a number of beautiful buildings decorated with fine woodcarving. Towards the back of the compound is the intimate Lai Kham Viharn, which houses the venerated Phra Buddha Singh image. It was built between 1385 and 1400 and the walls are decorated with early 18th-century murals. The **Phra Buddha Sihing** is said to have come from Ceylon by a rather roundabout route (see page 193) but, as art historians point out, is Sukhothai in style. The head, which was stolen in 1922, is a copy. Among the other buildings in the wat is an attractive raised *hor trai* (library), with intricate carved wood decorations, inset with mother-of-pearl.

WAT CHEDI LUANG AND CITY PILLAR

On Phra Pokklao Road, to the east of Wat Phra Singh, is the 500-year-old ruined *chedi* of Wat Chedi Luang. It's a charming place to wander around, set in a sizeable compound with huge trees at the boundaries. Judging by the remains, it must have once been an impressive monument. Only the Buddha in the northern niche is original; the others are reproductions. To the west of the *chedi* is a reclining Buddha in an open pavilion.

Chiang Mai's rather dull city pillar is found in a small shrine close to the large *viharn*, at the western side of the monastery compound. This is the foundation stone of the city and home to Chiang Mai's guardian spirits. These must be periodically appeased if the city is to prosper.

WAT DUANG DII

Just north of the intersection of Rachdamnern and Phra Pokklao roads, is peaceful Wat Duang Dii. The compound contains three northern Thai wooden temple buildings, with fine woodcarving and attractively weathered doors; note the small, almost Chinese, pagoda-roofed structure to the left of the gate with its meticulous stucco work. Behind the *viharn* and *bot* is a *chedi* with elephants at each corner, topped with copper plate.

WAT SUAN DOK

Outside the walls, Wat Suan Dok lies to the west of town on Suthep Road (Chiang Mai map, page 102). Originally built in 1371 but subsequently restored and enlarged, the wat contains the ashes of Chiang Mai's royal family, housed in white, variously shaped, mini-*chedis* Much of the monastery was erected during the reign of King Kawila (1782-1813). The large central *chedi* is said to house eight relics of the Lord Buddha.

The *bot* is usually open to the public and has a large, brightly lit, gilded bronze Buddha image in the Chiang Saen style. The walls are decorated with lively, rather gaudy, scenes from the Jataka stories. Above the entrance is a mural showing the Buddha's mother being impregnated by a white elephant (highly auspicious), while on the left-hand wall is depicted (along with several other episodes from the Buddha's life) the moment when, as a prince (note the fine clothes and jewellery), he renounces his wealth and position and symbolically cuts his hair.

WAT UMONG

① Take a songthaew along Suthep Rd and ask to be let off at the turning for Wat Umong. It is about a 1-km walk from here (turn left almost opposite the gates to Chiang Mai University, just past a market travelling west).

The wat was founded in 1371 by King Ku Na (1355-1385) who promoted the establishment of a new, ascetic school of forest-dwelling monks. In 1369 he brought a leading Sukhothai monk to Chiang Mai – the Venerable Sumana – and built Wat Umong for him and his followers. Sumana studied here until his death in 1389. Although the wat is at the edge of the city, set in areas of woodland, it feels much more distant. There are tunnels which house several Buddha images. The wat was abandoned in the 19th century and the *chedi* pillaged for its treasures some years later. It became a functioning wat again in 1948. From the trees hang Thai proverbs and sayings from the Buddhist texts, extolling pilgrims to lead good and productive lives.

CHIANG MAI UNIVERSITY ART CENTER

ⓘ *239 Nimmanhaemin Rd, corner of Nimmanhaemin and Suthep roads, T053-944833, www. cmumuseum.org, Tue-Sun 0900-1700.*

Chiang Mai University Art Center (see map, page 102) in a large modern structure, displays modern fine art including paintings, sculpture, installation works and prints by mostly Thai artists. There are occasional temporary exhibitions of work by non-Thais. Other activities include concerts and puppet shows. It is interesting for displaying the progress of Thai fine art, but hardly world class. The small but chic attached **Art Café** and shop (selling books and ceramics) is classier than the works displayed.

WAT JET YOD

The beautiful Wat Jet Yod (literally, 'seven spires') is just off the Superhighway at the intersection with Ladda Land Road, northwest of the city and close to the National Museum (see map, page 102). It was founded in 1453 and contains a highly unusual square *chedi* with seven spires. These represent the seven weeks the Buddha resided in the gardens at Bodhgaya, after his enlightenment under the Bodhi tree. According to the chronicles the structure is a copy of the 13th-century Mahabodhi temple in Pagan, Burma, which itself was a copy of the famous temple at Bodhgaya in Bihar (although it is hard to see the resemblance). On the faces of the *chedi* are an assortment of superbly modelled stucco figures in bas-relief, while at one end is a niche containing a large Buddha image – dating from 1455 – in an attitude of subduing Mara (now protected behind steel bars). The stucco work represents the 70 celestial deities and are among the finest works from the Lanna School of Art.

NATIONAL MUSEUM

ⓘ *T053-221308, www.thailandmuseum.com, Wed-Sun 0900-1600, ฿100.*

The National Museum (see map, page 102) lies just to the east of Wat Jet Yod on Highway 11 and has a fine collection of Buddha images and Sawankhalok china downstairs, as well as some impressive ethnological exhibits upstairs.

OTHER WATS

Wat Ku Tao (see map, page 102), to the north of the city off Chotana Road, dates from 1613. It is situated in a leafy compound and has an unusual *chedi*, shaped like a pile of inverted alms bowls. Others worth a fleeting visit for those not yet 'watted out' include: **Wat Chetawan**, **Wat Mahawan**, **Wat Saen Fang** and **Wat Bupharam** – all on Tha Phae Road – between the east walls of the city and the Ping River. Wat Mahawan displays some accomplished woodcarving on its *viharn*, washed in a delicate yellow, while the stupa is guarded by an array of *singhas* (mythical lions) – some with bodies hanging from their gaping jaws. Wat Bupharam has two old *viharns* a small *bot* and a stupa.

MARKETS AND CHINATOWN

The night market dominates the west side of Chang Klang Road (see map, page 102). It comprises a number of purpose-built buildings with hundreds of stalls, selling a huge array of tribal goods as well as clothing, jewellery and other tourist goodies. For a completely different atmosphere, walk through Chiang Mai's Chinatown which lies to the north of Tha Phae Road, between the moat and the river. Small workshops run by entrepreneurial Sino-Thais jostle between excellent small restaurants serving reasonably priced Thai and Chinese food. Near the river, and running two or three streets in from the river, is the **Warorot Market**, the city's largest. It starts on Praisani Road, close to the river, as a flower market, but transforms into a mixed market with fruit, vegetables, dried fish, pigs' heads and trotters, great dollops of buffalo flesh, crabs, dried beans and deep-fried pork skin. There are several large covered market areas with clothes, textiles, shoes, leather goods, Chinese funeral accessories, stationery and baskets.

MUSEUM OF WORLD INSECTS AND NATURAL WONDERS

ⓘ *72 Nimmanhaemin Soi 13, T053-211891, www.insectmuseumthailand.multiply.com, open 0900-1700, ฿300, ฿100 children.*

Established in 1999 by Manop and Rampa Rattanarithikul, this likeable and very knowledgeable couple take pleasure in showing you around their house which has become a mausoleum for thousands of insectoid beasties (see map, page 102). Rampa's specialism is mosquitoes; there are 420 species of mosquito in Thailand, 18 of which she personally identified and categorized, travelling to London to check the type specimens in the Natural History Museum. There are interesting collections of shells, fossils, petrified wood and, of course, case after case of bugs including beetles, moths, roaches and butterflies. The same family owns a smaller insect museum on Rachdamern Rd in the Old City. Recommended.

→ AROUND CHIANG MAI

DOI SUTHEP

ⓘ *Take a songthaew from town to the zoo (฿20) and switch to a shared songthaew there (฿40). A taxi should cost about ฿300 return. The temple is closed after 1630 and charges a ฿20 entry fee – to foreigners only.*

Overlooking Chiang Mai, 16 km to the northwest, is Doi Suthep (Suthep Mountain) a very popular pilgrimage spot for Thais, perched on the hillside and offering spectacular views of the city and plain below. A steep, winding road climbs 1000 m to the base of a 300-step *naga* staircase, which in turn leads up to **Wat Phrathat**. Initially, you'd be forgiven for thinking you'd arrived at a tacky theme park rather than a revered site, such is the proliferation of overpriced souvenir stalls. And, where foreign tourists are concerned, everybody seems to be on the make, from the tuk-tuk drivers through to the surly temple staff who make sure no foreigner enters without their ฿30 ticket. Some Thais have complained that Doi Suthep is becoming degraded by the influence of tourism, yet the same critics have failed to address the fact that the temple guardians themselves have adopted commercial practices.

If you don't fancy the climb take the cable car (฿20). A white elephant is alleged to have collapsed here, after King Ku Na (1355-1385) gave it the task of finding an auspicious site for a shrine to house a holy relic of the Lord Buddha.

The 24-m-high *chedi* has a number of Buddha images in both Sukhothai and Chiang Saen styles, arrayed in the gallery surrounding it. The whole compound is surrounded by bells (which visitors can no longer ring).

If you're brave enough, this trip is best done by motorbike, which will allow you to take in the waterfalls and viewing points en route. The road is bendy but in good condition, and it's a beautiful drive.

PHU PING PALACE
ⓘ *Fri-Sun and public holidays 0830-1630 when the royal family is not in residence. Songthaews from Doi Suthep to Phu Ping, ฿50.*
The winter residence of the King, Phu Ping Palace, is 5 km past Wat Phrathat. The immaculate gardens are open to the public when the family is not in residence.

DOI PUI
ⓘ *Charter a songthaew; alternatively take a songthaew from the zoo, Doi Suthep or Phu Ping Palace.*
Rather commercialized, Meo village, 4 km past Phu Ping Palace, is only worth a visit for those unable to get to other villages. There are two second-rate museum huts, one focusing on opium production, the other on the different hilltribes. On the hillside above the village is an English flower garden, which is in full bloom in January.

TRIBAL MUSEUM
ⓘ *T053-210872, Mon-Fri 0900-1600. Take a songthaew from the city ฿50. It takes about 15-20 mins to walk to the museum.*
The Tribal Museum, attached to the Tribal Research Institute, overlooks a lake in Rachamankha Park, 5 km north of town off Chotana Road. The building itself looks like a cross between a rocket and a *chedi* and it houses the fine collection of tribal pieces that were formerly held at Chiang Mai University's Tribal Research Centre. Carefully and professionally presented, the pieces on show include textiles, agricultural implements, musical instruments, jewellery and weapons. The museum is particularly worth visiting for those intending to go trekking.

WIANG KUM KAM
ⓘ *Accessible by bicycle, motorbike or tuk-tuk. Take Route 106 south towards Lamphun; the ruins are signposted off to the right about 5 km from Chiang Mai – but only in Thai – from where it is another 2 km. Look out for a ruined chedi on the right and ask along the way for confirmation. To get to Wat Kan Thom, take the yellow sign to the left about 800 m from the main road. It's about a 10- to 15-min walk from the main road. For Wat Chedi Liam, follow the land all the way to the river road (Koh Klang Rd), about 2 km or so, and turn left. The Wat is about 200 m down here, on the left – impossible to miss.*
Wiang Kum Kam is a ruined city, 5 km south of Chiang Mai, which was established by the Mon in the 12th or 13th centuries and abandoned in the 18th century. The gardens and ruins are beautiful and peaceful, dotted with bodhi trees. Today, archaeologists are beginning to uncover a site of about 9 sq km which contains the remains of at least 20 wats. It was discovered in 1984 when rumours surfaced that a hoard of valuable amulets were found. Treasure seekers began to dig up the grounds of the Wat Chang Kham monastery until the Fine Arts Department intervened and began a systematic survey of the site to reveal Wiang Kum Kam. The most complete monument is Wat Chang Kham, which has a marvellous bronze *naga* outside. In front of the wat is the spirit chamber of Chiang Mai's founder, King Mengrai. Nearby are the ruins of Wat Noi and two dilapidated *chedis*. Perhaps the most impressive single structure is the renovated *chedi* at Wat Chedi Liam.

This takes the form of a stepped pyramid – a unique Mon architectural style of which there are only a handful of examples in Thailand.

BOR SANG AND SAN KAMPHAENG CIRCUIT

A pleasant 75-km day trip takes you east of the city, visiting craft centres a couple of interesting wats, some incredible caves and a hot spring. Almost immediately after leaving the city along Route 1006 (Charoen Muang Road), kilns, paper factories and lacquerware stalls start to appear, and continue for a full 15 km all the way to Bor Sang.

Bor Sang is famous for its handmade, painted paper umbrellas. The shaft is crafted from local softwood, the ribs from bamboo, and the covering from oiled rice paper. The **Umbrella Festival** in January is a colourful affair. Beyond Bor Sang is San Kamphaeng, another craft village, which has expanded and diversified so that it has effectively merged with Bor Sang – at least in terms of shopping. If you make it as far as San Kamphaeng, there is a good Muslim restaurant at the intersection with the main road (left hand, near side) serving chicken biryani, other Indian dishes, ice creams and cappuccino.

For **Wat Pa Tung**, which is 10 km on from San Kamphaeng, take a right-hand fork onto Route 1147. At the junction with Route 1317, cross over the road (signposted towards the Chiang Mai-Lamphun Golf Club). Where the road takes a sharp right (with another signpost for the golf club), continue straight ahead on the minor road. About 3 km on is Wat Pa Tung. This wat is a lively and popular modern wat, set amongst sugar palms and rice fields. Its popularity rests on the fact that the revered Luang Phu La Chaiya Janto (an influential thinker and preacher and highly regarded for his asceticism) lived here to the ripe old age of 96. When he died in 1993 his rather diminutive body was entombed in a sealed glass coffin, which was then placed in a specially built stilted modern *kuti* where it still resides today.

From Wat Pa Tung, return to Route 1317 and turn right. After about 10 km, on the left, you will see a rocky outcrop with flags fluttering from the top; this is the only marker for the **Muang On Caves** ① *open daily during daylight hours, ฿20*; take a left turning (no sign in English) and wind up a lane, past a forest of ordained trees, to the car park. From here there are around 170 steps up a *naga* staircase to the entrance to the caves, with great views over the valley. The entrance to the caves is tricky and the steps very steep, with low overhangs of rock. But it is worth the sweating and bending; the cave opens up into a series of impressive caverns with a large stalagmite wrapped with sacred cloth and a number of images of the Buddha. There are drink stalls at the car park.

At the foot of the hill (before returning to the main road), take a left turn for the back route (2.5 km) to the **Roong Arun Hot Springs** ① *฿30, ฿15 children, public baths ฿60*. Here, sulphur springs bubble up into an artificial pond, where visitors can buy chicken or quail eggs to boil in wicker baskets hung from bamboo rods. The springs reach boiling point; if you want a dip head for the public baths, where the water is cooled. A full range of massages, mud baths, saunas and herbal treatments are also available. Return to Chiang Mai by way of Route 118 – about a 20-minute drive.

MAE SA VALLEY – SAMOENG CIRCUIT

① *Buses and* songthaews *run along this route, but it would be much more convenient to do the round-trip by hire car or motorbike.*

The 100-km loop from Chiang Mai along the Mae Sa Valley to Samoeng and then back along Route 1269 is an attractive drive that can easily be accomplished in a day. Travel north on Route 107 out of town and then turn west onto Route 1096, in the district town of Mae Rim. From here the road follows the course of the Mae Sa River. Just past Mae Rim are a couple of exclusive shops selling 'antiques'. At the Km 5 marker is the sign for the **Tad Mok Waterfalls**, which lie 9 km off the main road to the right. These are less popular than the Mae Sa Falls a couple of kilometres on from here (see below), but still worthwhile.

Continuing west on the main road, there are two more orchid gardens: **Suan Bua Mae Sa Orchid** ① *between the Km 5 and Km 6 markers, 0800-1600*, and **Mae Rim Orchid and Butterfly Farm** ① *at the Km 6 marker, 0800-1600, ฿20*. The orchids are beautiful, the butterflies even more so (watch them emerge from their chrysalises), but the food is average and overpriced.

Mae Sa Waterfall ① *0800-1800, ฿10, ฿30 per car*, is located in the **Doi Suthep-Pui National Park**, 1 km off Route 1096 (to the left) and about 1 km beyond the orchid farm. The waterfall is in fact a succession of mini-falls – relatively peaceful, with a visitor centre and a number of stalls.

But the most popular destination of all in the valley, 3 km further on from the waterfall, is the **Elephant Training Camp** ① *T053-206247, www.maesaelephantcamp.com, 3 shows a day at 0800, 0940 and 1330, ฿200; elephant riding before and after shows, ฿800-1200 for 2 people, mahout training courses also available*. Elephants are well cared for here (with a number of babies, which must be a good indicator of their happiness). Visitors can see the elephants bathing, feed them bananas and sugarcane and then watch an elephant show.

Queen Sirikit Botanical Gardens ① *T053-841333, www.qsbg.org, 0830-1630, ฿100, ฿50 child, ฿100 car*, was established in 1993 on the edge of the Doi Suthep-Pui National Park, 12 km from the Mae Rim turn-off. The great bulk of the gardens was designated a conservation area before 1993, and there are a number of large trees. It is Thailand's first botanical gardens and a truly impressive enterprise. There are three marked trails (rock garden and nursery plus waterfall, arboreta and climber trail), a museum and an information centre. But the highlight of the gardens is the glasshouse complex. The largest features a waterfall and elevated boardwalk, and there are also glasshouses for desert flora, savannah flora and wetland plants.

Mae Sa Craft Village ① *T053-290052*, is a leafy resort spread over a hillside, with immaculately kept gardens of brightly coloured annual flowers. There are dozens of great activities to get involved in.

Continuing further on along Route 1096 there are, in turn, the **Mae Yim Falls** (17 km), **Doi Sang** – a Meo village (25 km) – and the **Nang Koi Falls** (34 km). At the furthest point in this loop is **Samoeng**, the district capital. There's little to do here unless you arrive for Samoeng's annual **strawberry festival** held in January or February.

Continuing on from Samoeng, the road skirts around the heavily forested **Doi Suthep-Pui National Park**. The winding road finally descends from the hills and comes out by the north-south irrigation canal at the village of Ban Ton Khwen. Just before you reach the canal is a turning to the right and, a little further along, the bare brick walls of **Wat Inthrawat**. The entrance at the back is by a cluster of sugar palms. This spectacular *viharn* was built in 1858 in Lanna style. Its graceful roofs and detailed woodcarving are a fine sight. Return to Chiang Mai by way of the canal road (turn left at the junction) or on Route 108 (the Hang Dong road), which is a little further to the east of the canal road.

CHIANG DAO ELEPHANT TRAINING CENTRE

ⓘ *T081-0275009, www.chiangdaoelephantcamp.com, ฿60. Numerous companies offer tours to the centre from Chiang Mai, although it is easy enough to get here by public transport as it is on the main road.*

This elephant training centre at Chiang Dao is 56 km from Chiang Mai on the route north to Fang, about 15 km south of Chiang Dao. Shows (฿100), elephant riding (฿800-1400) and rafting (฿400) is available. There is a second elephant camp 17 km south of Chiang Dao, the **Mae Ping Elephant Camp**, which is not as good.

CHIANG DAO

ⓘ *As Chiang Dao is on the main Chiang Mai–Fang road, there are numerous buses and songthaews from the Chang Puak bus station.*

Chiang Dao, a district town 70 km north of Chiang Mai, is a useful stopping-off point for visitors to the Chiang Dao Caves (see below). The surfaced road running east from the town leads to a series of hilltribe villages: Palong, Mussur, Lahu and Karen. Most of these are situated on public forest reserve land and many of the inhabitants do not have Thai citizenship. They have built simple huts where tourists can stay and a number of trekking companies in Chiang Mai begin or end their treks in the villages here. The town has a number of good restaurants; of particular note is the locally renowned **Bun Thong Phanit** (on the left-hand side, travelling north, in a wooden shophouse), which serves excellent *khao kha muu* (boiled pork leg with rice).

CHIANG DAO CAVES

ⓘ *฿20 to go as far as the electric light system extends; ฿100 to hire a guide with lamp for a 40-min tour deeper into the caves (guides congregate 100 m or so into the caves where a rota system ensures an equal share of business). Catch a bus to Fang from the Chang Puak bus station on Chotana Rd and get off at Chiang Dao. Songthaews take visitors the final 6 km from the main road to the caves. A songthaew directly to the caves and back should cost about ฿1000 each way (1½ hrs). It is also possible to hire motorbikes and bicycles in Chiang Dao itself – from the 'tourist corner' on the left-hand side of the main road, shortly before reaching the turn-off for the caves (turn left in the town of Chiang Dao, just after the Km 72 marker; it is clearly signposted).*

These caves, 78 km north of Chiang Mai on Route 107, penetrate deep into the limestone hills and are associated with Wat Chiang Dao. They are among the most extensive in Thailand and are a popular pilgrimage spot for monks and ordinary Thais. There is a profusion of stalls here, many selling herbal remedies said to cure most ailments. The caverns contain Buddha and hermit images, as well as impressive natural rock formations. Electric lights have been installed, but only as far as the **Tham Phra Non** (Cave of the Reclining Buddha), where a royal coat of arms on the cave wall records Queen Sirikit's visit to the caves. To explore further it is necessary to hire a guide.

LAMPANG

ⓘ *Regular buses from Nawarat Bridge or from the Arcade terminal and trains connect with Chiang Mai (2 hrs) while local transport is provided by the town's horse-drawn carriages and songthaews.*

An atmospheric provincial capital complete with horse-drawn carriages, soothing riverside hang-outs and the sumptuous temple of Wat Phra That Lampang Luang, Lampang makes a great day or overnight trip from Chiang Mai. A tour around town in a horse-drawn carriage costs ฿200-300. They generally take two routes, the cheaper one takes about

30 minutes, the more expensive one an hour or alternatively ฿300 per hour. There's some decent accommodation and a chance to indulge in a leisurely lunch at one of the great riverside restaurants. The airport is on the south edge of town, off Prabhat Road, and the bus station is on Route 1, just east of the railway line (a 15-minute walk to the town centre). The railway station is on the west side of town, at the end of Surain Road. *Songthaews* run routes around town (although these are flexibly interpreted); the *rop muang* or *rop wiang* ('around town') are the most useful (฿15 anywhere in town).

Established in the seventh-century Dvaravati period, Lampang prospered as a trading centre, with a wealth of ornate and well-endowed wats. Re-built in the 19th century as a fortified *wiang* (a walled city), it became an important centre for the teak industry with British loggers making this one of their key centres. The influence of the Burmese is reflected in the architecture of some of the more important wats – a number still have Burmese abbots.

Wat Phra Kaeo Don Tao ① ฿20, and its 'sister' **Wat Chadaram** are to be found on Phra Kaeo Road, north across the Rachada Phisek Bridge. Wat Phra Kaeo housed the renowned Emerald Buddha (the Phra Kaeo – now in Wat Phra Kaeo, Bangkok) for 32 years during the 15th century. This royal temple is said to be imbued with particular spiritual power and significance, largely because of its association with the Phra Kaeo. The ceilings and columns of the 18th-century *viharn* are carved in wood and are intricately inlaid with porcelain and enamel. In the compound, there is also a Burmese-style chapel (probably late 18th century) and a golden *chedi*. Next door, Wat Chadaram contains the most attractive building in the whole complex: a small, intimate, well-proportioned, wooden *viharn*.

WAT PHRA THAT LAMPANG LUANG

① *0900-1200, 1300-1700, donation; there are drinks and foodstalls in the car park area across the road from the wat. Take a songthaew to Ko Kha and then a motorbike taxi the last 2.5 km to the wat. Songthaews for Ko Kha run regularly along Phahonyothin Rd. Alternatively, charter a songthaew from Lampang (฿300-400). If travelling by private transport from Lampang, drive along Route 1 towards Ko Kha. In Ko Kha pass through the town, over the bridge, and then turn right at the T-junction onto Route 1034. The wat is 2.5 km away – just off Route 1034 (the chedi can be seen rising up behind some sugar palms). From Chiang Mai, turn right off Route 11 just past the Km 80 marker, signposted to Ko Kha.*

The monastery stands on a slight hill, surrounded by a brick wall – all that remains of the original fortressed city which was sited here more than 1000 years ago. Sand and tiles, rather than concrete, surround the monuments. While the buildings have been restored on a number of occasions over the years, it remains beautifully complete and authentic.

Originally this wat was a fortified site, protected by walls, moats and ramparts. Approached by a staircase flanked by guardian lions and *nagas*, visitors enter through an archway of intricate 15th-century stone carving. The large, open central *viharn*, **Viharn Luang**, houses a *ku* – a brick, stucco and gilded pyramid peculiar to northern wats – containing a Buddha image (dating from 1563), a collection of thrones and some wall paintings. The building, with its intricate woodcarving and fine pattern work on the pillars and ceiling, is dazzling.

Behind the *viharn* is the principal **chedi**, 45 m high it contains three relics of the Buddha: a hair and the ashes of the Buddha's right forehead and neck bone. Made of beaten copper and brass plates over a brick core, it is typically Lanna Thai in style and was erected in the late 15th century. The **Buddha Viharn** to the left of the *chedi* is thought to date from the 13th century and was restored in 1802. Beautifully carved and painted, it contains a seated Buddha image. Immediately behind this *viharn* is a small, raised building housing a **footprint of the Buddha** (only men are permitted). This building houses a camera obscura; at certain times of day (from late morning through to early afternoon) the sun's rays pass through a small hole in the building's wall, projecting an inverted image of the *chedi* and the surrounding buildings onto a sheet.

To the right of the main *viharn* are two more small, but equally beautiful, *viharn*: the **Viharn Nam Taem** and the **Viharn Ton Kaew**. The former is thought to date from the early 16th century, and may be the oldest wooden building in Thailand. It also contains some old wall paintings, although these are difficult to see in the gloom. Finally within the walls are the **Viharn Phra Chao Sila**, built to enshrine a stone image of the Buddha.

Outside the walls, through the southern doorway, is an enormous and ancient **bodhi tree**, supported by a veritable army of crutches. Close by is a small, musty and rather unexciting **museum**. Next to this is a fine raised scripture library and a *viharn*, within which is another revered **Emerald Buddha** – heavily obscured by two rows of steel bars. It is rumoured to have been made from the same block of jasper as the famous Emerald Buddha in Bangkok.

THAI ELEPHANT CONSERVATION CENTRE
ⓘ *T054-829333, www.thailandelephant.org. Bathing sessions daily at 0945, 'shows' daily at 1000,1100 and 1330, ฿170. Elephant rides ฿500 for 30 mins, ฿1000 for 1 hr. There is also a small restaurant, souvenir shop and toilets. The ECC also runs English-language mahout training courses – contact them directly for details. Take an early morning bus towards Chiang Mai; the elephant centre is about 30km before Lampang, just tell the driver where you're going. From the road it is a 1.8-km walk by road or take a short cut through the forest. Alternatively charter a songthaew from town for about ฿600 return. It is possible to stay at the camp; see the website for further details.*

The recent fate of the Thai elephant has been a slow inexorable decline. Numbers are dwindling and the few that do remain are mainly used as tourist attractions. Many of the places that offer chances to interact with elephants are poorly run, treating their charges with contempt. Not so the excellent Thai Elephant Conservation Centre, northwest of Lampang near Thung Kwian, on the road to Chiang Mai (Highway 11). Here elephants are trained for forest work, others are released back into the wild, there are elephant musicians, elephant artists and elephant dung paper. There's even an elephant hospital and rescue centre. All in all there are about 50 animals here.

PHA THAI CAVES
ⓘ *The first 400 m of the cave is open to the public but the great majority of the system is off-limits. Refreshments are available. Take Route 1 from Lampang towards Ngao and 19 km before Ngao turn left for the caves.*

The Pha Thai caves are some of the most spectacular in Thailand; the cave system is one of the country's deepest too, extending more than 1200 m. The caves are renowned not only for their length but also for the quantity of snakes that have taken up residence here. From the arrival point to the cave entrance visitors have to climb 283 steps. As with many caves, it has acquired religious significance and the cave is associated with a wat. A white *chedi* stands like a sentinel just outside the mouth of the cave and a large gilded Buddha fills the entrance itself.

JAI SORN (CHAE SORN) NATIONAL PARK

ⓘ *Take the road from Lampang towards Wak Nua and then turn left at the Km 58-59 marker. Continue along this road for another 17 km.*

The park, Lampang's only protected area, has hot volcanic springs in the waterfall pools – the Chae Son Waterfall and Chae Son Hot Spa Park, which are just 1 km apart. The waterfall tumbles down seven levels and during the wet season is particularly spectacular. The hot springs bubble out at 75-80°C, are mixed with cold water from the waterfall and are channelled into 11 bathrooms.

DOI INTHANON NATIONAL PARK

ⓘ *0600-1800, ฿400, ฿200 children. ฿50 car, ฿20 motorbike, ฿50 songthaew and minibus. Best time to visit: just after the end of the rainy season, in late Oct or Nov. By Jan and Feb the air becomes hazy, not least because of forest fires. Buses, minibuses and songthaews for Hang Dong and Chom Thong leave from the Chiang Mai Gate. Take a yellow songthaew for the 58 km from Chiang Mai Gate to Chom Thong (฿15). From Chom Thong market, take another yellow songthaew to the Mae Klang Falls (฿10) or the Wachiratan Falls (฿15). To reach Mae Ya Falls and Doi Inthanon summit, a songthaew must be chartered (this will seat 10 people); ฿500 and ฿700 respectively. From Hang Dong there are songthaews to Doi Inthanon.*

Located off Route 108, on Route 1009, Doi Inthanon is Thailand's highest peak at 2595 m. The mountain is a national park and the winding route to the top is stunning, with terraced rice fields, cultivated valleys and a few hilltribe villages. The park covers 482 sq km and is one of the most visited in Thailand. Although the drive to the top is dramatic, the park's flora and fauna can only really be appreciated by taking one of the hiking trails off the main road. The flora ranges from dry deciduous forest on the lower slopes, to moist evergreen between 1000 m and 1800 m, and 'cloud' forest and a sphagnum (moss) bog towards the summit. There are even some relict pines. Once the habitat of bears and tigers, the wildlife has been severely depleted through over-hunting. However, it is still possible to see flying squirrel, red-toothed shrew, Chinese pangolin and Pere David's vole, as well as an abundance of butterflies and moths. Although the mountain, in its entirety, is a national park, there are several thousand Hmong and Karen living here and cultivating the slopes.

Just beneath the summit, in a spectacular position, are a pair of bronze and gold-tiled *chedis*, one dedicated to the king in 1989 and the other dedicated to Queen Sirikit at the end of 1992. Both *chedis* contain intricate symbolism and have been built to reaffirm the unity of the Thai nation. The ashes of Chiang Mai's last king, Inthawichayanon, are contained in a small white *chedi* on the summit – the ultimate reflection of the idea that no one should be higher than the king, in life or in death.

There are a number of waterfalls on the slopes: the **Mae Klang Falls** (near the Km 8 marker and not far from the visitor centre), **Wachiratan Falls** (26 km down from the summit and near the Km 21 marker, restaurant here) and **Siriphum Falls** (3-4 km off the road near the Km 31 marker and not far from the park headquarters), as well as the large **Borichinda Cave** (a 2-km hike off the main road near the visitor centre at the Km 9 marker). Note that it is a tiring climb up steep steps to the Mae Klang and Wachiratan falls. The **Mae Ya Falls** in the south of the park are the most spectacular, plunging more than 250 m (they lie 15 km from park headquarters and are accessible from Chom Thong town). Ask for details at the visitor centre a few kilometres on from the park's entrance.

GOING FURTHER
Phrae, Nan and the Eastern Highlands

The provincial capital, Phrae, is an attractive and friendly town with good accommodation and restaurants, situated in a narrow rice valley on the banks of the Mae Yom River, flanked by mountains to the east and west. The Eastern Highlands, an area of outstanding natural beauty with a relaxed vibe and an intriguing history, is still off the main tourist and backpacker routes. The lack of development adds to its charm: the area's burgeoning tourist industry is easily integrated into a genuine slice of Thai rural life. In the last few years, travel through Phrae and Nan has become an increasingly feasible alternative route to Laos, although, it t is still rarely used because onward travel on the Laos side of the border is not so easy. A through road to Luang Prabang is rumoured to be on the cards but, at the time of writing, this was still on the drawing board.

Phrae

Phrae was founded in the 12th century – when it was known as Wiang Kosai or Silk Cloth City – and is one of the oldest cities in Thailand. It still has its own 'royal' family and was an independent Thai *muang* (city state) until the early 16th century. Phrae's ancient roots can still be seen in the city walls and moat, which separate the old city from the new commercial centre. On Charoen Muang Road, there are a handful of attractive wooden Chinese shophouses, although the scourge of uncontrolled development is gradually gnawing away at the remnants of old Phrae. Phrae is not a large place and the town is pleasant enough to stroll around.

Known as the Seri or 'Free' Thai, the country's Second World War resistance movement had Thammasat University founder and leading Thai social democrat, Pridi Banomyong, as its leader and much of its activity was centred in Phrae. The former Seri Thai HQ is sited in a beautiful old school building just behind the **Paradorn Hotel**. It is now the **Seri Thai Museum** ⓘ *daily 1000-1700, free*, one of the north's best little museums. It charts the Seri Thai's resistance to the Japanese invaders, with plenty of information in English, including a thank you letter from George W Bush.

The Burmese-style **Wat Chom Sawan** ⓘ *on the edge of town, 1 km northeast of the centre, on the road to Nan, admission by donation*, was commissioned by Rama V (1868-1910) and designed by a Burmese architect. Like most Burmese (Thai Yai) wats, the *bot* and *viharn* are consolidated in one elaborate, multi-roofed towering structure, with verandas and side rooms. **Wat Luang** ⓘ *admission by donation*, is a few minutes' walk from Wat Sri Chum, near the city wall and moat. The wat was founded in the 12th century, although continuous renovation and expansion has obscured its ancient origins. The wat also supports an impressive museum which houses valuable Buddha images, swords, coins, burial caskets, Buddhist texts, old photographs (one of a decapitation), betel boxes and jewellery.

Nan

Nan is a province to be explored for its natural beauty. Fertile valleys are chequered with paddy fields, teak plantations, hilltribes and fast-flowing rivers. It was not until 1931 that the central authorities managed to overcome the area's inaccessibility and bring Nan under Bangkok's direct control. Ever since then, there have been periods – most recently in the 1970s when Communist insurgency was a problem – when the army and police have treated the province as a no-go area, and it still exudes an atmosphere of other-worldliness and isolation. The area also boasts rarely visited national parks, some of the finest forest in the country, weaving villages and excellent hill treks.

A charming, friendly town with a historical ambience, Nan occupies a small valley in the far north of the Eastern Highlands – about 50 km from the border with Laos. These days, Nan is having something of a renaissance and has become a popular destination for wealthy Bangkok hipsters.

The **National Museum** ① *Phakong Rd, Wed-Sun 0900-1600, ฿30*, once the home of the Nan royal family, houses an impressive collection, including beautiful wood and bronze Buddha images, ceramics, textiles, jewellery and musical instruments. This is a great little museum and well worth a visit; exhibits are well displayed with English explanations throughout.

Just opposite the National Museum is **Wat Phumin** ① *Phakong Rd*. Built in 1596 it was restored between 1865 and 1873. The cruciform *bot-cum-viharn* is supported by the coils of two magnificent *nagas* (mythical serpents). Inside, there are some of the finest murals to be found in the north, painted at the end of the 19th century. The naive style of the murals – large areas of empty space, figures of various sizes – distinguish them from the sophisticated art of Bangkok.

Wat Chang Kham, on the diagonally opposite corner to Wat Phumin, features a *chedi* supported by elephant buttresses (caryatids), similar to those at Sukhothai. The *viharn* was built in 1547 and contains three Sukhothai-style Buddha images. There's a large seminary here and the temple compound is often filled with dozens of friendly, shaven-headed novices.

Wat Ming Muang ① *Suriyaphong Rd*, contains the city of Nan's **lak muang** (city pillar), liberally draped in garlands. Gaudy **Wat Hua Wiang Tai** ① *Sumonthewarat Rd, just north of Anantavoraritdet Rd*, has *nagas* running along the top of the surrounding wall and bright murals painted on the exterior of the *viharn*.

At the end of the Buddhist Lent, from mid-October to mid-November, boat races are held, which probably started about a century ago, when they were part of the Songkran celebrations. The boats are hollowed-out logs, painted in bright designs. There is a lively fair in the weeks before (and during) the races.

Where to stay
Nan
$$$$-$$$ Pukha Nanfa Hotel, 369 Sumondevaraj Rd, T054-771111, www.pukhananfa hotel.co.th. Nan's most luxurious accommodation, with original teak fittings and several gorgeous and sumptuous rooms. The rooms are on the small side but this is still a fantastic property if you can afford the price tag. Wi-Fi, flat-screen TVs, en suite facilities and a nice relaxing private library complete the appeal.

$$-$ Nan River Guesthouse, 1 Mano Rd, T08-96359375. Friendly little guesthouse run by the same female couple who own **Hot Bread**. Small, basic rooms in a town villa in a very quiet part of Nan, away from the centre. All have shared facilities and are fan-only. There are plenty of communal spaces: garden, living room and even a kitchen. Bicycles available, and owners will collect you from the bus station/airport or transfer you from **Hot Bread**. Recommended.

CHIANG MAI AND AROUND LISTINGS

WHERE TO STAY

Chiang Mai

$$$$ The Chedi, 123 Charoen Prathet Rd, T053-253333, www.ghmhotels.com. A stunningly designed property built around the restored 1920s British consulate – itself a historical treat – has been created here by the river. The rooms are minimalist, with huge tubs and plasma screens while the lobby is spacious with relaxed tones. Pool, sundeck and great food complete the picture. Expensive but almost certainly the best hotel in town. Highly recommended.

$$$ Baan Orapin, 150 Charoenrat Rd, T053-243677, www.baanorapin.com. It is easy to see why this is one of the most popular places in Chiang Mai. A run of well-maintained bungalows surround a central teak house, all set in quiet, gated gardens on a road on the east side of the Ping River. The owner speaks great English and is friendly, though can sometimes be hard to find; it's best to email (see website) or call ahead as **Orapin** is often booked solid. Highly recommended.

$$ Baan Say-La, 4-4/1 Nimmanhaemin Rd, Soi 5, T053-894229, www.baansaylaguest house.com. This cute guesthouse in an old colonial-style house is one of Chiang Mai's best bargains. The tasteful rooms are well designed – some have balconies while everyone has access to the cool air on the roof terrace. The friendly vibe stems from the half-Thai, half-Spanish owner, Rodney. Its location right in the heart of hip Nimmanhaemin means that you can escape most of the other tourists. The only drawback is noisy nightclub next door – bring your earplugs. Recommended.

$$ Lai Thai, 111/4-5 Kotchasan Rd, T053-271725, www.laithai.com. A cross between a north Thai house and a Swiss chalet. Spotless rooms, some with a/c, free baby cots. Popular and professional set-up, good facilities, attractive surroundings, tours, trekking and motorbike rental. Restaurant,

good clean pool. Note that the cheaper rooms at the back are noisy, so expect an early wake-up. Nonetheless, recommended.

$ CM Blue House, 30/1 Moonmuang Rd, Soi 6, T053-418512, www.cmbluehouse.com. Friendly guesthouse with attractive garden area in the laid back northeastern corner of the Old City. A nice budget option with good facilities for the price. Recommended.

$ Kim House, 62 Charoen Prathet Rd, T053-282441, www.kimhousethailand.com. Small hotel in a leafy compound down a secluded soi, with clean rooms (some a/c) and hot showers. Friendly atmosphere, and free Wi-Fi. Breakfast included. Recommended.

$ Sarah Guest House, 20 Tha Phae Soi 4, T053-208271, www.sarahgh.hypermart.net. This well-established guesthouse in the heart of the guesthouse area is run by an English woman married to a Thai and is popular. 12 basic but clean rooms, with attached bathrooms and shared hot-water showers. Trekking, tour services and cookery courses. Free Wi-Fi. Recommended.

$ Western House Hotel, Soi 5 Sripoom Rd, T053-215961, www.chiangmaiwestern house.com. One of the best budget places in the entire city. Nicely decorated, simple, clean rooms come with a/c, small balcony (the ones at the front overlook a temple), cable TV and free Wi-Fi. A real find. Little English spoken but friendly and competent. You might need to pay when you check-in. Highly recommended.

Lampang

$ Riverside Guesthouse, 286 Talad Kao Rd, T054-227005, www.theriverside-lampang. com. Simple fan or a/c rooms are housed in an old teak complex on the river and individually decorated by the very helpful Italian owner. The restaurant and terraced communal garden overlooking the Wang River is a lovely chill-out spot. Highly recommended.

Chiang Dao
$$ Chiang Dao Nest, 144/4 Moo 5
Chiang Dao, T053-456242. www.nest.
chiangdao.com. 20 clean and comfortable
fan bungalows in a beautiful setting about
2 km from the Chiang Dao caves. Beautiful
chill-out gardens, pool. The trip from Chiang
Mai is worth it for the restaurant alone.
Highly recommended.

Doin Inthanon National Park
There is a camping ground at the Km 31 mark
(฿40 per person). Small tents are available for
hire with sleeping bag (฿250 per night).

$$$ Bungalows, Km 31, out-station
on the route up the mountain. To book,
T02-579 0529 or www.dnp.go.th. Advance
reservation recommended as this is a very
popular park. A relatively new Karen eco-
resort has been set up by 4 villages with
support from the National Parks Authorities.
The bungalows, sleeping 4-30 people, have
been built in the traditional style and the
location is fantastic. The resort organizes
treks, teaches about medicinal plants,
introduces visitors to Karen dance, etc.
The resort is on the road to the summit,
before the 2nd checkpoint.

RESTAURANTS

Chiang Mai
$$$ Palaad Tawanron Restaurant,
Suthep Rd (near university), T053-217 073,
www.palaadtawanron.com. Set on the lower
parts of the Doi Suthep mountain near a
large waterfall and amid thick forest, this is
an award-winning restaurant. Book a terrace
table at the back and you'll also secure an
awesome view to go with your sundowner.
Palaad also offers some of the best Thai food
in Chiang Mai. Highly recommended.
$$$ The Restaurant, The Chedi,
123 Charoen Prathet Rd, T053-253333,
www.ghm hotels.com. You'll find great
traditional northern Thai specialities
and innovative Pacific Rim cuisine
complemented by an extensive wine
list served in what was once the British

consulate – it also serves afternoon tea.
Expensive but recommended.
$$ The Gallery, 25-29 Charoenrat Rd, T053-
248601, www.thegallery-restaurant.com.
Quiet and refined Thai restaurant on the
River Ping, in a century-old traditional Thai
house with art and crafts gallery attached.
Superb food, highly recommended for a
special night out.
$ SP Chicken, Sri Phum Rd, Open 1500-
2200. This local and expat favourite does
a roaring trade and that's no surprise.
Delicious BBQ meats, spicy salads and
surprisingly good thum yam goong (spicy-
sour prawn soup). Can be a little hard to
spot, look out for the chickens barbecuing
outside. Highly recommended.

WHAT TO DO

Chiang Mai
Trekking companies
The city's **TAT office**, 105/1 Chiang Mai-
Lamphun Rd, T053-248604, has information
on trekking in the region, including a list of
licensed agencies. Many of the companies
are concentrated on Tha Phae, Chaiyaphum,
Moon Muang and Kotchasan rds. Standards
change so rapidly that recommending
companies is a dangerous business, but
the safest bet is to find somewhere with
permanent, long-term staff. One such outfit

is **Panda Tour**, 127/5 Rajchapakinai Rd, T053-
418 920, www.pandatourchiangmai.com.
Prices for treks are highly variable with
2-day trips costing somewhere between
฿2000-3000; 3-day treks ฿2500-4000 and
4-day treks ฿3000-5000. Be aware that
the better trips usually cost more, either
because they're more off the beaten track
and therefore further away, or because the
company is paying for one of the better
guides. If you find a trek for a price that
seems too good to be true, it probably is.

WESTERN LOOP

Some of the most spectacular scenery in Thailand lies west of Chiang Mai, where the Tenasserim range divides Burma from Thailand. Northwest from Chiang Mai on Route 107, then Route 108, the road passes through Mae Sa Valley to the popular backpacker town of Pai, a distance of 140 km. From Pai to Soppong is more stunning scenery, then onto the hill town of Mae Hong Son, a centre for trekking and home to fine Burmese-style wats. Due south to Mae Sariang (160 km from Mae Hong Son), close to the Burmese border, there is some more excellent trekking.

→ PAI

The road from Chiang Mai winds its way through scintillating landscapes and thick forest until the view unfolds into a broad valley. In the middle, encircled by handsome, high ridges, sits Pai. Over the last 25 years this small mountain village has transformed itself into one of Northern Thailand's most popular destinations. These days, with its organic eateries and reggae bars Pai could be considered a travellers' oasis. Even hip young city dwellers from Bangkok are catching onto the area's beauty, facilities, hot springs and diversity – Lisu, Karen, Shan, Red Lahu, Kuomintang-Chinese are all represented. But in January 2008 Pai's idyllic charms were somewhat shattered by the shooting of two, young Canadian backpackers by a drunk, off-duty Thai policeman.

However, Pai's tourist trade continues to flourish, and for good reason. There's excellent trekking, superb rafting, a plethora of places to get massaged and pummelled, some great

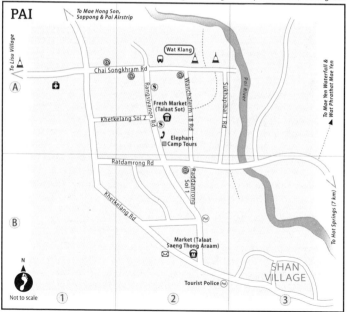

food and the town still manages to retain a sense of charm. The range of accommodation is also huge – everything from boutique spa resorts through to cheap and nasty huts populated with wasted travellers. Don't come here thinking you're going to get an authentic slice of Thai life. This is a generic, contrived Khaosan Road-style experience, though, admittedly, in very pleasant surroundings. Helping to cement Pai's growing status, an airstrip has opened with a few flights a day linking Pai with Chiang Mai.

There are two markets in town – the *talaat sot* (fresh market) on Rangsiyanon Road and the *talaat saeng thong araam* on Khetkelang Road. The finest monastery in town is Thai Yai-style **Wat Klang** near the bus station. There's another monastery, **Wat Phrathat Mae Yen**, about 1.5 km east of town, on a hill. Head a further 3 km east and you'll arrive at Pai's famous **hot springs**. The sulphurous water bubbles up through a systems of streams – bring a towel and jump in. There's also a campsite here.

Lisu, **Shan**, **Red Lahu** and **Kuomintang-Chinese villages** are all in the vicinity. Most guesthouses provide rough maps detailing hilltribe villages, hot springs, caves and waterfalls.

→ SOPPONG

Soppong, or Phang Ma Pha, is a small way station between Pai (one hour by bus) and Mae Hong Son (two hours by bus). It is slowly metamorphosing into an alternative to Pai – there's no real backpacker 'scene' here, though there a few great guesthouses offering trekking services. Many people come here to trek and explore the surrounding countryside. Most guesthouses organize treks and this is one of the best bases hereabouts. Local villages include Lisu, Black and Red Lahu, and Shan. This is also a good place to escape to if what you want to do is nothing. The journey from Pai to Soppong is stunning with magnificent views. The road winds through beautiful cultivated valleys and forest.

Guesthouses provide maps of the surrounding countryside and villages, with tracks marked. The main sight is **Lod Cave (Tham Lod)** ① *0800-1700*, about 10 km from town. The cave (in fact a series of three accessible caves) has been used for habitation since prehistoric times and is a small part of what is presumed to be one of the largest cave systems in northern Thailand. To explore the accessible areas of the cave system takes around two hours; guides hire out their services – and their lamps – to take visitors through the cave, which has a large stream running through it. Rafts are available to traverse the stream. In the nearby village is **Cave Lodge**, an excellent guesthouse, which offers trips through the caves and serves great coffee and food.

Mae Lanna is a quiet, highland Shan village/town 16 km northwest of Soppong, off Route 1095. The area offers limestone caves, good forest walks and stunning limestone scenery. To get there, take a bus towards Mae Hong Song and get off at the turn-off for Mae Lanna, about 10 km west of Soppong. Pick-ups run the steep 6 km up to the village – or walk. Guesthouses in Soppong provide sketch maps of the area, with hiking trails marked.

→ MAE HONG SON

Mae Hong Son lies in a forested valley, surrounded by soaring verdant hills and just about lives up to its claim of being the 'Switzerland of Thailand'. The road from Pai is continuous switchback, cutting through spectacular scenery and communities of diverse ethnicities. On a clear day, the short flight from Chiang Mai is breathtaking – the plane crosses a range of high hills before spiralling down into a tight series of continuous banks.

An excellent centre for trekking, the town is changing rapidly from a backpackers' hideaway to a tour centre, with the construction of two major hotels and some 'resort'-style hotels. Despite this, Mae Hong Son still manages to retain peaceful, upland vibe.

ARRIVING IN MAE HONG SON

Getting there and around   There are regular flights from Chiang Mai. You can easily walk from the airport to the town. The airport is to the north of town on Niveshpishan Road. It has an information counter and currency exchange booth, and *songthaews* are also available for hire. The bus station is at the northern end of town on Khunlum Praphat Road; there are plenty of connections with Chiang Mai. It's a short walk to town and most guesthouses from the bus station. Mae Hong Son is small enough to walk around and tuk-tuk journeys around town cost ฿10-20. It is a friendly, accessible and amenable place.

Moving on   There are buses and minibuses to Mae Sariang (four hours).

Best time to visit   During the cool season (December to February), when the days are warm and clear and the nights are fresh, with evening temperatures as low as 2°C.

Tourist information   TAT, 4 Ratchathumpitak Rd, T053-612982, www.tourismthailand. org/maehongson, provides leaflets and information.

BACKGROUND

Mae Hong Son Province is about as far removed from 'Thailand' as you are likely to get, with only an estimated 2% of the population here being ethnic Thais. The great majority belong to one of the various hilltribes: mostly Karen, but also Lisu, Hmong and Lahu.

Mae Hong Son has always been caught between the competing powers of Burma and Siam/Thailand. For much of recent history the area has been under the (loose) control of various Burmese kingdoms. The influence of Burmese culture is also clearly reflected in the architecture of the town's many monasteries. Mae Hong Son also has a murky reputation for illegal logging; this area has some of the richest forests in the country.

PLACES IN MAE HONG SON

Most postcards of the town picture the lake, with **Wat Jong Klang**, a Burmese wat, in the background. It is particularly beautiful in the early morning, when mist rises off the lake. Wat Jong Klang started life as a rest pavilion for monks on pilgrimage, with a wat being built by the Shans living in the area between 1867 and 1871. The monastery contains some 50 carved Burmese *tukata* (wooden dolls) depicting characters from the Jataka stories, as well as a series of mediocre painted glass panels. In the same compound is **Wat Jong Kham**, which contains a large seated Buddha. **Wat Hua Wiang**, next to the market, contains an important Burmese-style brass Buddha image – the Phra Chao Phla La Khaeng. It is said that the image was cast in nine pieces in Burma and brought to Mae Hong Son along the Pai River.

Doi Kong Mu, the hill overlooking the town, provides superb views of the valley and is home to the Burmese-style **Wat Phrathat Doi Kong Mu**, constructed by the first King of Mae Hong Son in the mid-19th century. At the foot of Doi Kung Mu Hill is **Wat Phra Non**, which contains a 12-m-long Burmese-style reclining Buddha. The main fresh **market** in town is on Phanit Watana Road, next to Wat Hua Wiang. The usual commodities from slippery catfish to synthetic clothing are sold here, together with some produce from Burma.

KHUN YUAM AND MUANG PON

ⓘ *Buses plying the Mae Hong Son to Mae Sariang road will pass through both towns – Khun Yuam is about 90 mins south of Mae Hong Son, Muang Pon is 15 mins further. Homestays at Muang Pon can arrange pick-ups from Khun Yuam, Mae Hong Son and Mae Sariang.*

Roughly halfway between Mae Sariang and Mae Hong Son is the bustling market town of Khun Yuam. The town itself has few attractions yet it is an engaging and friendly place to stop off for a couple of days if you want to make a slow meander through this part of the country. Most of the people who live here are Karen, Shan or Hmong. There is a pretty Hmong/Burmese-style temple 5 km to the west at **Wat To Phae**, which is worth a look; it houses a 150-year-old tapestry just to the side of the main altar. There is also a **War Museum** ⓘ *on the main road near the town centre, Tue-Sat 0930-1200, 1400-1600, ฿90*, which focuses on the plight of Japanese soldiers during World War Two. Thousands died here as Khun Yuam was home to a Japanese army hospital. The museum houses a collection of poignant artefacts left behind by the dying soldiers.

The nearby Shan village of Muang Pon, about 15 km to the south of Khun Yuam on the road to Mae Sariang, hosts an excellent homestay programme that is run, managed and owned by local people. Stay here for a few days and you'll get a chance to engage in a genuine encounter with local people a million miles from the usual intrusions of a 'hilltribe' trek. Nearby you'll find hot springs, mountain walks and a small hilltop temple.

The capital of Amphoe district, Mae Sariang is a small market town on the banks of the Yuam River, and a good departure point for trekking. The road from Chom Thong runs up the Ping Valley, before turning west to follow the Chaem River, climbing steadily through beautiful dipterocarp forest, the Op Luang National Park (17 km from Hod), and into the mountains of western Thailand. There is little to draw people here, except as a stopping-off point for Mae Hong Son or as a starting point for trekking.

The town is small and leafy, with many of the houses still built of wood – a comparative oasis after the dusty urban centres. The bus station is on Mae Sariang Road in the centre of town, five minutes' walk from the Riverside Guesthouse, next to Wat Jong Sung.

There are a handful of unremarkable wats. The town also has a better stock of wooden shophouses than most Thai towns – that is on Laeng Phanit Road (the river road). The morning market operates from a plot on Sathit Phon Road and there is also an evening market – good for stall food – at the end of Wiang Mai Road.

Trekking, rafting, cave and waterfall visits and elephants rides are also possible.

MOVING ON

Kan Airlines (www.kanairlines.com) has one flight daily to Chiang Mai. The airport is located about 3 km from town on Laeng Phanit Road. There are seven buses daily to Chiang Mai (four hours). There are also regular air-conditioned minibus connections daily.

WESTERN LOOP LISTINGS

WHERE TO STAY

Pai

$$$$ Pai River Corner, Chai Shongkhram Rd, T053-699049, www.pairivercorner.com. Gorgeous little resort laid out beside the river around a nicely kept garden of mini-villas. All are a/c, with en suite hot showers and balconies. Stylish and well-kept, the upper rooms come complete with big, breezy balconies. There's also a small pool here. Recommended.

$$ Blue Lagoon, 227 Moo 4 Pai (on main road in centre of town), T053-699998, www.paibluelagoon.com. Well-run and priced. Clean, decent rooms, excellent disabled facilities. Pool.

$ Golden Huts, 107 Moo 3 Wiang Tai, T053-699949. Very quiet, beautiful out-of-the-way location on the riverbank. Quiet and relaxing atmosphere, French owner provides a friendly service. Small but adequate restaurant with good food and great views. Good budget option. Recommended.

Soppong

$$$ Baan Cafe Resort, next to main road, T053-617081. Nicely laid-out rooms and bungalows, some with terraces overlooking a river, which can be used to bathe in. Pleasant gardens, friendly, good food. Small shop selling local produce. Recommended.

$$-$ Cave Lodge, T053-617203, www.cavelodge.com. Cave Lodge is a labour of love for its Aussie owner, John Spies. A cluster of small bungalows cling to a steep rock face, which leads down to a small glade and stream. Facilities are basic but include everything from en suite rooms with hot water to dorms, and even a home-made sauna. Excellent Western, Thai and local cuisine available. The owner has an incredible local knowledge of the nearby cave systems, trekking routes and different ethnic groups. From Soppong, a motorbike taxi costs ฿70, or walk the 6.5 km from the

villlage. One of the best guesthouses in the country, attracting a real cross-section of travellers. Highly recommended.

$ Kemarin Garden, a short way down a lane 200 m up the hill towards Pai. 4 simple A-frame bungalows, peaceful rural position with views over the hills, clean hot-water showers. Friendly management (but no English spoken). Recommended.

Mae Hong Son

$$$$ Mountain Inn, 112/2 Khunlum Praphat Rd, T053-611802, www.mhs mountaininn.com. A/c, well-thought-out rooms surround an atmospheric garden. Friendly management and also serves good food. Recommended.

$$ Sang Tong Huts, 250 Moo 11 T Pangmoo, T053-611680, www.sang tonghuts.com. Secluded spot northwest of town (near Yuk Guesthouse), with great views. Range of huts, dining area with great food and hilltribe coffee. Friendly and helpful owners. Recommended.

$ Prince's Guesthouse, 31 Udomchaonitet Rd, T053-611136, princesguesthouse@gmail. com. A/c and fan, some rooms overlooking the lake. Free Wi-Fi. Rooms are simple but clean. A good-value option in a good location. Recommended.

Khun Yuam/Muang Pon

$ The Muang Pon Homestay, T053-684644, kunlaya_mall@hotmail.com. Several houses in this appealing Shan village take part in a very well-run homestay programme. You'll get treated as one of the family and introduced to the eccentricities of village life and earthy Shan cuisine. Rates includes breakfast and dinner. The villagers run excursions to nearby temples, villages, mountains and hot springs. Call or email to book and you'll be allocated your family. Transfers from

Mae Hong Son and even Chiang Mai can be arranged for a set fee. This is one of the best examples of low-impact, fair trade tourism in Thailand. Highly recommended.

Mae Sariang
$$ Riverside, 85/1 Laeng Phanit Rd, T053-681188. A 5-min stroll from the bus station, this attractive building has large, clean rooms by the river and wonderful views from the breakfast/seating area.

$ See View, 70 Wiang Mai Rd (across the river, and overlooking it, on the edge of town), T053-681556. Good-sized rooms in stone bungalows, smaller wooden rooms available, with shared facilities. Quiet and peaceful. It is a good source of information, the owner speaks English and is very helpful.

RESTAURANTS

Pai
$$ Baan Ben Jarong, edge of town, on the way to Chiang Mai. High-class Thai cuisine – exceptional and one of the best places to eat in the area. Highly recommended.
$ Na's Kitchen, Ratdamrong Rd. A favourite with expat locals, this small restaurant serves up tasty curries, Thai salads and other Thai dishes for bargain prices. Popular, so can be difficult to get a seat some evenings. Recommended.

Mae Hong Son
$ Baan Tua Lek, Chamnansatid Rd, across from Jung Klang Temple, T053-620688. Coffee bar with cosy atmosphere, friendly staff and free Wi-Fi. A popular hangout.

Coffee, smoothies and tea, as well as home-made sandwiches, cakes and cookies. Recommended.
$ Salween River Restaurant, Pradit Jong Klang Rd, www.salweenriver.com. Top-notch budget fare at this small restaurant by the lake. Specializes in authentic Shan and Burmese dishes, but Western food also available. Recommended.

Mae Sariang
$$ Coriander in Redwood, Lang Phanit Rd. Excellent Thai fare and steaks in a beautiful wooden building. Friendly service, good menu and an attractive outside eating area too. Recommended.

TOURS/TREKKING

Pai
Thai Adventure Rafting, just past the bus station, T053-699111, www.thairafting.com. The oldest whitewater rafting company in Thailand. It runs unforgettable, professional 2-day expeditions down the Pai River and beyond. It is run by Guy, a friendly Frenchman who has lived in Pai for 25 years. The river is only high enough Jul to end of Jan, trips start at ฿2500 and include everything from insurance to food/drinks. 1-day rafting trips cost ฿1500. It also offers 1-2 day treks and rock climbing expeditions. There are other companies organizing similar (and cheaper) rafting trips in the area though none are as good.

Mae Hong Son
There are various day tours to sights such as Pha Sua Waterfall, Pang Tong Summer Palace, the KMT village of Mae Aw, Tham Plaa (Fish Cave) and Tham Nam Lot (Water Cave). A number of companies also advertise trips to the 'long-necked' Padaung, which involves a bumpy 1-hr trip to the 2 villages where they live. Many people deplore this type of tourism. Most guesthouses will organize treks ranging from trips down the Salween River to the Burmese border to Mae Sot, elephant treks and rafting on the Pai River.

CHIANG RAI

Given the ancient roots of Chiang Rai, the capital of Thailand's most northerly province, there's little here in the way of historical interest, with modern shophouse architecture predominating. What Chiang Rai lacks in sights it makes up for with a dose of rootsy, friendly charm and some great accommodation. It also makes a perfect base for trekking and to visit the towns further to the north.

West of the city are Ta Thon, a centre for rafting down to Chiang Rai and another good base for trekking. Fang, south of Ta Thon, has some good examples of shophouses, and is an opium trafficking centre.

→ ARRIVING IN CHIANG RAI

GETTING THERE

The international airport is 8 km north of the city, just off the main Chiang Rai–Mae Sai Highway. There's a pre-paid taxi stand in the airport from about ฿200 for a trip to the centre. A tuk-tuk to the airport from town is usually ฿150. The bus station is in the town centre just off Phahonyothin Road, T053-711224. The local *songthaew* stand is near the morning market on Uttarakit Road.

The new road to Chiang Rai from Chiang Mai cuts through forests and is fast and scenic. There are rather novel European-style country cottages along the way and some good resort-style hotels. **Mae Suai**, with a hilltop monastery, is at the junction where roads lead south to Chiang Mai, north to Chiang Rai, west to Fang and southeast to Phayao.

GETTING AROUND

The centre of Chiang Rai is small enough to walk or cycle around but there are tuk tuks available from about ฿40. Most of the area's attractions lie in the surrounding countryside, and there are ample vehicle hire shops offering bicycles, cars, motorbikes and jeeps.

MOVING ON

Daily public scheduled boats for Tha Ton depart daily at 1000 (฿350) and take three-four hours, depending on river conditions. Long-tailed boats can also be chartered for up to six people for ฿2200 to Tha Ton. The pier is open daily 0700-1600. Alternatively, take a bus from Chiang Rai to Mae Chan (30-45 minutes) and then songthaew (two hours) to Tha Ton.

TOURIST INFORMATION

TAT ① *448/16 Singhaklai Rd (near the river, opposite Wat Phra Singh), T053-744674.* Well-run office with useful town maps and information on trekking and accommodation. Areas of responsibility are Chiang Rai, Phayao, Uttaradit, Phrae and Nan.

→BACKGROUND

Chiang Rai was founded in 1268 by King Mengrai, who later moved his capital here. The city became one of the key *muang* (city states), within the Lanna Kingdom's sphere of control – until Lanna began to disintegrate in the 16th century. Although it is now Thailand's most northerly town, at the time of its foundation Chiang Rai represented the

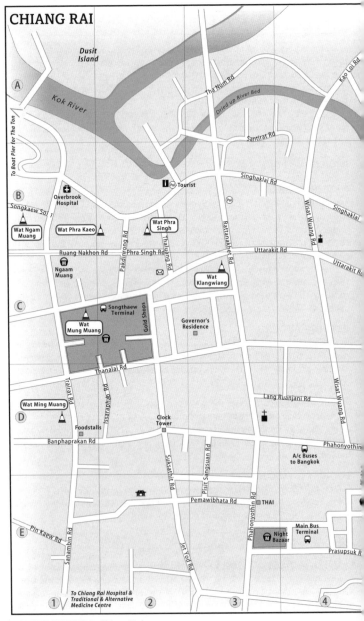

CHIANG RAI

Dusit
Island

Kok River

To Boat Pier for Tha Ton

Tha Num Rd

Dried up River Bed

Santirat Rd

Kao Loi Rd

Singhaklai Rd

Singhaklai

Tourist

Overbrook
Hospital

Songkaew Soi 1

Wat Ngam
Muang

Wat Phra Kaeo

Wat Phra
Singh

Pakdinong Rd

Thalung Rd

Phra Singh Rd

Rattanakhet Rd

Uttarakit Rd

Uttarakit Rd

Wisat Wuang Rd

Ruang Nakhon Rd

Ngaam
Muang

Wat
Klangwiang

Songthaew
Terminal

Wat
Mung Muang

Gold Shops

Governor's
Residence

Thanalai Rd

Trairat Rd

Issaraphab Rd

Wat Ming Muang

Lang Ruanjani Rd

Foodstalls

Clock
Tower

Banphaprakan Rd

Suksathit Rd

Pisit Sangsuan Rd

Phahonyothin Rd

Phahonyothin

A/c Buses
to Bangkok

Pin Kaew Rd

Sanambin Rd

Jet Yod Rd

Pemawibhata Rd

THAI

Night
Bazaar

Main Bus
Terminal

Prasupsuk Rd

Wisat Wuang Rd

To Chiang Rai Hospital &
Traditional & Alternative
Medicine Centre

A   B   C   D   E

1   2   3   4

most southerly bulwark against the Mons. It was later conquered by the Burmese and only became part of Thailand again in 1786.

Today, Chiang Rai has ambitious plans for the future. Lying close to what has been termed the 'Golden Rectangle', linking Thailand with Laos, Burma (Myanmar) and southern China, the city's politicians and businessmen hope to cash in on the opening up of the latter three countries. Always searching for catchy phrases to talk up a nascent idea, they even talk of the 'Five Chiangs strategy' – referring to the five towns of Chiang Tung (or Kengtung in Burma), Chiang Rung (in China), Chiang Thong (in Laos), and Chiang Mai and Chiang Rai (both in Thailand). Roads linking the five are being planned and an EU-style free trade area discussed. Talk, as they say, is cheap; a mini-EU in this peripheral part of Asia seems a distant dream, despite a noticeable increase in cross-border activity.

→ PLACES IN CHIANG RAI

The city's finest monastery is **Wat Phra Kaeo**, at the north end of Trairat Road. The wat is thought to have been founded in the 13th century when it was known as Wat Pa-Year. Its change of name came about following divine intervention in 1434 when, local legend recounts, the stupa was struck by lightning to reveal the famous Emerald Buddha or Phra Kaeo, now in residence in Bangkok's Temple of the Emerald Buddha. With this momentous discovery, the wat was renamed Wat Phra Kaeo and was elevated to the status of a royal wat in 1987.

The finest structure here is the *bot* (straight ahead as you pass through the main gates on Trairat Road) featuring accomplished woodcarving, a pair of fine *nagas* flanking the entrance way and, inside, a 13th-century image of the Buddha calling the earth goddess to witness. Presumably slightly peeved that the Phra Kaeo itself had been carted off to Bangkok, a rich local Chinese businessman – Mr Lo – commissioned a Chinese artist to carve a replica image from Canadian jade. The work was undertaken in Beijing to mark the 90th birthday of the Princess Mother and she gave it the gargantuan name Phraphuttaratanakorn Nawutiwatsanusornmong-khon, or The Lord Buddha is the source of the Three Gems of Buddhism. The image was kept in the monastery's *bot* until a new building, specially designed to house it, had been completed and the image installed in a consecration ceremony held in 1991. The Chiang Rai Phra Kaeo Shrine is behind the *bot*, with two ponds filled with turtles (set free by people to gain merit) in front of it.

Above Wat Phra Kaeo, perched at the top of a small hill, is **Wat Ngam Muang**, unremarkable except for the views it offers of the city and surrounding countryside. However, historically it is important, as the stupa here contains the ashes of the great King Mengrai (1259-1317). The edifice is currently being renovated and will have a statue of the king placed in front of his *ku*.

Further northwest still is **Wat Phrathat Doi Chom Thong**, built at the top of a small hill. The wat contains the *lak muang* (city pillar).

Wat Phra Singh (dating from 1385) is an important teaching monastery on Singhaklai Road, in the north of town. Note the finely wrought animal medallions below the windows of the *bot* – rats, elephants, tigers, snakes and other beasts – and the gaudy but vivacious murals that decorate the interior. Also unusual is the Bodhi tree, surrounded by images of the Buddha in each of the principal *mudras*.

South of Wat Phra Singh is **Wat Mung Muang**, notable for its corpulent image of the Buddha, which projects above the monastery walls. The image is not at all Thai in style, but appears Chinese with its sausage-like fingers spinning the wheel of law. The area around Wat Mung Muang supports a daily **market** and, in the mornings from 0600, vegetable hawkers set up along the monastery walls, providing a wonderful contrast in colour and texture with the golden Buddha image. *Songthaews*, *saamlors* and tuk-tuks wait to transport market-goers back to their houses and villages. In the east of town, at the so-called *haa yaek* (five-way junction) on Phahonyothin Road, is the new statue of King Mengrai, Chiang Rai's most illustrious king.

Building on the success of Chiang Mai's night bazaar or market, Chiang Rai opened its own **night bazaar** off Phahonyothin Road a few years back. It has since expanded tremendously and sells the usual range of hilltribe handicrafts, carvings, china products, wooden boxes, picture frames, the Thai equivalent of beanie babies, catapults and so on. In many ways it is a nicer place to browse than the Chiang Mai night bazaar. It is more open, less frenetic, friendlier, and there is live music and open-air restaurants.

About 10 km south towards Chiang Mai stands one of the north's newest and most popular temples, **Wat Rong Khun** ① *Mon-Fri 0800-1730, Sat and Sun 0800-1800, free*. Crafted by a local artist, this temple looks like it has been frosted white by a freezing Arctic storm – the entire construction is built in concrete, inlaid with mirrors and then whitewashed. Some might think the result is daring beauty – others could come to the conclusion it is kitsch trash dressed up as art. The general populous seems to love the place and at weekends queues of camera-phone-wielding Thais eagerly take snaps of their loved ones in front of this startling structure. If you want to judge for yourself take a *songthaew* (every 30 minutes) from the centre of Chiang Rai to Mae Lao and get off at the temple (฿30). Alternatively hire a tuk-tuk for a half-day excursion (฿300-400).

The **Hilltribe Education Center** ⓘ *620/ 25 Thanalai Rd, 1300-1330, or on request, for a small fee, in English, Thai, French or Japanese*, is one of the more interesting attractions in the town, with a small, informative **hilltribe museum** ⓘ *0830-2000; admission to museum ฿20, CRPDA@hotmail.com*, and an audiovisual presentation on hilltribe life. It is run by the Population and Development Association's (PDA), which is better known for its family planning and AIDS work. With this project, it is attempting to provide hilltribe communities with additional income-earning opportunities, as the pressures of commercial life increase. The museum has recently been expanded and refurbished. Attached to the museum is a branch of the **Cabbages and Condoms** chain of restaurants.

Ban Du is a paper-making village, 8 km north of Chiang Rai off Route 110. Paper is produced from the bark of the sa tree, which is stripped off, air dried, soaked in water, boiled in caustic soda and finally beaten, before being made into paper.

CHIANG RAI LISTINGS

WHERE TO STAY

$$$-$$ Wiang Inn, 893 Phahonyothin Rd, T053-711533. The original 'luxury' hotel in town, renovated in 1992-1993 and still holding its own. Competitively priced, central location but set back from the main road so comparatively peaceful, stylish lobby. Rooms are fairly standard, but perfectly adequate with satellite TV. A/c, restaurant, small pool, The buffet breakfast and lunch (with dim sum) are very good value. Recommended.

$$-$ Baan Rub Aroon Guesthouse, 65 Ngam-muang Rd, T053-711827, www.baanrubaroon.net. An old whitewashed town villa, set in its own private grounds, this charming guesthouse has a variety of airy, well-lit rooms and a friendly, homestay ambience. There's a kitchen for guests' use and Wi-Fi. Bathroom facilities are shared. Lots of communal hang-out spaces. Recommended.

$$-$ Baan Wararbordee, 59/1 Moo 18, Sanpanard Rd, T053-754888. Delightful little guesthouse tucked away on a quiet *soi*. Very friendly, helpful owner, free coffee, tea and internet. Rooms on the upper floors are better lit – all have TV, en suite, hot water and a/c. There's a garden as well. Recommended.

RESTAURANTS

$$ Vietnam Restaurant, Sanpanard Rd. Easy to spot, funky wooden building down this quiet soi. Run by an artist, with slightly random opening hours. The food is excellent and authentic. Recommended.

$ Nakhon Pathom (Thai signage only), 869/25 Phahonyothin Rd, T053-713617, daily 0600-1500. Excellent and popular shophouse-style restaurant selling great noodles, BBQ pork and crispy pork-belly over rice. Gets packed with locals at breakfast time. Recommended.

$ Por Jai, Jed Yod Rd (behind **Wiang Come Hotel**), daily 0600-1700. One of the best khao soy shops in Chiang Rai, popular with locals and highly recommended.

WHAT TO DO

Most treks are cheaper if organized through guesthouses, and they are usually also more adventurous. The usual range of **elephant rides** and **boat trips** as part of a trek are available, too. A 2-day/1-night **raft trip** costs ฿800-1100 per person, 4-day/3-night **trek** about ฿1500-2000. Day tours to visit **hilltribe villages** such as Sop Ruak and the Golden Triangle, Mae Sai, Mae Salong and Chiang Saen, are organized by most of the tour/trekking companies listed below (฿600). Tours that include an elephant ride and boat trip, plus visits to hilltribe villages, cost about ฿700. **Motorcycle tours** are also becoming increasingly popular, and many guesthouses provide rental services and information on routes to take for a day's excursion. Before embarking on a trek, it is worth visiting the **Hilltribe Education Center** (see page 129). Tribes in the area include Karen, Lisu, Lahu and Akha.

There are several trekking companies and tour operators around the **Wangcome Hotel** plaza area, along Phahonyothin and Premwipak rds (a *soi* off Phahonyothin). The **TAT** office produces a list of companies with average prices and other useful advice. **Golden Triangle Tours**, 590 Phahonyothin Rd, T053-711339 (attached to the **Golden Triangle Hotel**). Recommended.

Mae Salong Tour, 882/4 Phahonyothin Rd, T053-712515. Recommended treks, also organizes river cruises on the Mekong including Laos, China and Thailand.

THE FAR NORTH

Chiang Saen, northeast of Chiang Rai on the banks of the mighty Mekong River, was once the evocative capital of an ancient kingdom. Follow the meandering Mekong downstream and the road reaches the small outpost of Chiang Khong, home of the giant catfish and a crossing point into Laos. Meanwhile, 11 km upstream from Chiang Saen, is the infamous Golden Triangle, the meeting point of Laos, Thailand and Burma. This was once a lawless area filled with smugglers and drug lords. These days it's home to the tourist village of Sop Ruak and the compelling Opium Museum. Still further upstream, 61 km north of Chiang Rai, Mae Sai is Thailand's most northerly town and a busy border trading post with Burma. A new road runs off Route 110 to the hill town of Mae Salong, from where a poor track continues west to Tha Ton.

→THA TON

Tha Ton lies on the Mae Kok and is a good starting point for trips on the Kok River to Chiang Rai, and for treks to the various hilltribe villages in the area. It is a pleasant little town with good accommodation and a friendly atmosphere. It also makes a good base for exploring this area of the north.

MOVING ON
Songthaews operate to Mae Salong four to six times a day (90 minutes).

PLACES IN THA TON
Wat Tha Ton overlooks the river, not far from the bridge. A stairway leads up to this schizophrenic monastery. On the hillside is a rather ersatz Chinese grotto, with gods, goddesses and fantastic animals including Kuan Yin, the monkey god and entwined dragons. From this little piece of China, the stairway emerges in the compound of a classic, but rather ugly, modern Theravada Buddhist monastery. There is a restaurant, souvenir stall and more to show that Wat Tha Ton has truly embraced the pilgrim's dollar (or baht).

The regular boat down the Kok River stops at riverside villages, from where it is possible to trek to hilltribe communities. **Louta**, 14 km east of Tha Ton and 1.5 km off the main road between Tha Ton and Doi Mae Salong/Chiang Rai, is a well-off, developed Lisu village. It's also possible to get here by yellow pick-up (14 km), then take a motorbike taxi the remaining 1500 m uphill.

Other nearby villages include: **Tahamakeng**, one hour from Tha Ton (Lahu and Lisu villages within easy reach); **Ban Mai**, 45 minutes on from Tahamakeng (Lahu, Karen and Akha villages); and Mae Salak, further on still (Lahu, Lisu and Yao villages).

→MAE SALONG (SANTIKHIRI)

Mae Salong is situated at an altitude of over 1200 m, close to the border with Burma. It is like a small pocket of China. After the Communist victory in China in 1949, remnants of the nationalist KMT (Kuomintang) sought refuge here and developed it as a base from which they would mount an invasion of China. This wish has long since faded into fantasy and the Thai authorities have attempted to integrate the exiled Chinese into the Thai mainstream. A paved road now leads to the town, which is now so easily accessible it has turned into one of Thailand's most popular weekend destinations, particularly with middle class Bangkokians who pack the place out from December to February. For New Year on 31st December, the place gets completely overrun with Thai tourists, and you'll be hard-pressed to find a room or any space to relax. Mae Salong is also an alternative trekking centre; it's easily possible to do day-hikes into the Lisu and Akha villages from here. However, you should speak to locals about the current security situation before embarking on a trek, as the nearby Burmese border can lead to incursions by the rebel Wa Army, and the area is still a hive of drug-smuggling activity.

Despite the attempts to Thai-ify Mae Salong, it still feels Chinese. The hillsides are scattered with Japanese sakura trees, with beautiful pink blossom, whilst Chinese herbs and vegetables are grown in the surrounding countryside and sold at the morning market. Many of the inhabitants still speak Chinese, Yunnanese food is sold on the streets, and there are glimpses of China everywhere. One of the reasons why Mae Salong has remained so distinctive is because a significant proportion of the KMT refugees who settled here became involved in opium production and trade. This put the inhabitants in conflict with the Thai authorities and created the conditions whereby they were excluded from mainstream Thai society. Mae Salong's remoteness – at least until recently – also isolated the town from intensive interaction with other areas of the country.

Tea growing has now become a massive industry in and around Mae Salong and the hills are filled with endless tea terraces while the village is now home to dozens of tea-houses. The local brew is subtle and tasty – the variety of Oolong is particularly good. Less nuanced and completely tasteless are attempts to build a weird **tea visitor centre** just outside of town. Here massive gold and silver tea pots (soon to have fountains pouring from the spouts) sit beside giant Chinese dragons as surreal, gaudy evidence of someone with too much money and not enough sense.

The **morning market** is worth a visit for early risers (0530-0800), as this is where hilltribe people come to sell their produce. **Wat Santakhiri** is situated in a great position above the town. There's a long steep staircase just past the entrance to the **Mae Salong Resort**. Also worth a visit is the **Chinese Martyrs Memorial Museum** ⓘ *look for the large gate about 1 km towards Tha Ton from the day market, daily 1000-1600, ฿50*, where the history of the KMT fighters who founded Mae Salong is mapped out. One room contains mini-red wooden plinths, each inscribed with the name of a fallen comrade.

The walk up to **General Tuan's tomb** on the road behind the **Khum Nai Phol Resort** is a pleasant diversion as well, with some friendly teashops and exhilarating views when you arrive. Tuan was the KMT leader who brought his men to Mae Salong, and he is still deeply revered locally.

AROUND MAE SALONG

Thord Thai (Toerd Thai) is a small Shan village about 20 km north towards the Burmese border. It was here that Khun Sa, the legendary leader of the Shan state and notorious opium warlord, lived for a while. You can visit the house where he stayed and see a collection of photographs and other artefacts. There are a few signs for **Khun Sa House**, just ask around; there are no fixed opening hours, so aim for early afternoon when it's more likely the family across the road who hold the key will be there. To get to the village, you'll need to arrange your own transport or rent a motorbike. You can also walk there from Mae Salong in about three to four hours; ask at **Little Home** for directions. There is a guesthouse and some good places to eat in Thord Thai.

Trekking to **Akha** and other hilltribe villages is arranged by the **Little Home** or **Sinsane** guesthouses. The latter also organizes pony trekking to local hilltribe villages.

→ MAE SAI

Marking Thailand's northernmost point, Mae Sai is a busy trading centre with Burma and has a rather clandestine and frenetic frontier atmosphere. The area around the bridge is the centre of activity, with stalls and shops selling gems and an array of Burmese and Chinese goods, from knitted hats and Burmese marionettes to antiques and animal skulls. There is also an abundance of Burmese hawkers (selling Burmese coins and postage stamps) and beggars (particularly children) stretching about 1 km down the road, away from the border and towards Mae Chan. The main bus station is 5 km out of town, just off the main road running to Mae Chan and Chiang Rai. *Songthaews* and motorcycle taxis take passengers from town to the terminal and vice versa. *Songthaews* operate from Mae Sai to Sop Ruak (40 minutes).

Wat Phrathat Doi Wao sits on a hill overlooking the town, off Phahonyothin Road, not far from the **Top North Hotel**. The wat is not particularly beautiful and was reputedly built in the mid-1960s in commemoration of a platoon of Burmese soldiers killed in action against a KMT (Kuomintang – the Chinese Republican Army) force.

AROUND MAE SAI
Luang Cave (Tham Luang) is an impressive cave with natural rock formations, 3 km off Route 110 to Chiang Rai, 7 km from town. After the initial large cavern, the passage narrows, over the course of 1 km, to a series of smaller chambers. Guides with lamps wait outside the cave to lead visitors – for a fee – through the system. To get there take a regular *songthaew* to the turn-off; ask for 'Tham loo-ang'.

Doi Tung is a 2000-m-high hill village, almost 50 km south of Mae Sai. The road snakes its way past Akha, Lahu and KMT villages, as well as former poppy fields, before reaching Wat Phrathat Doi Tung, some 24 km from the main road. The road is now surfaced to the summit, although it is still quite a stomach-churning journey and the road can deteriorate after heavy rain. The twin *chedis* on the summit are said to contain the left collarbone of the Buddha and to have been initially built by a king of Chiang Saen in the 10th century. The views from the wat are breathtaking. A few years ago the king's mother built a palace here, a vast Austrian/Thai chalet with fantastic views over what was, at the time of construction, a devastated and deforested landscape. (Depending on who you talk to, the culprits were either shifting cultivators growing opium or big business interests logging protected land.) With the king's mother's influence, the hills around the palace were reforested. These days Doi Tung is very popular with Thai day-trippers and there's an overpriced restaurant, some gardens and a café. To get there, travel south on Route 110 from Mae Sai for 22 km to Huai Klai and then turn off onto Route 1149. Or take a bus heading for Chiang Rai and ask to be let off in Ban Huai Klai, at the turn-off for Doi Tung. From there, *songthaews* run to Doi Tung. Now that the road is upgraded the *songthaew* service is rather more regular – but check on return journeys if you intend to make it back the same day; it is easiest to explore the area by rented motorbike.

→ SOP RUAK

This small 'village', 11 km north of Chiang Saen at the apex of the Golden Triangle, where Burma, Laos and Thailand meet, has become a busy tourist spot on the basis (largely unwarranted) of its association with drugs, intrigue and violence. It's actually rather dull, with rows of tacky stalls selling hilltribe handicrafts and Burmese and Laotian goods, and a succession of maps and marble constructions informing visitors they are at the Golden Triangle. Two first-class hotels have been built to exploit the supposed romance of the place.

For those searching for something else to experience, **Wat Prathat Phukaeo** provides good views of the Golden Triangle. The **Hall of Opium** ① *just outside town opposite the gate to the Anantara, Tue-Sun 0830-1600, ฿300,* charts the rise of the international opium trade – largely put in place by 19th-century British businessmen with the backing of the British government – and the contemporary effects of the narcotics trade.

Wanglao, 4 km west towards Mae Sai, is a rice-farming community. It is sometimes possible to buy handicrafts here. *Songthaews* run through here on the (longer) back route to Mae Sai.

Boats can be chartered from the riverbank for trips downstream to Chiang Saen (฿400 for five people, 30 minutes), or further on still to Chiang Khong (around ฿1500-1700, 1½ hours). Alternatively they can be chartered just to explore the Golden Triangle area. *Songthaews* operate from Sop Ruak to Chiang Saen (10 minutes).

→ CHIANG SAEN

Chiang Saen is an ancient capital on the banks of the Mekong River, the last village before the famed 'Golden Triangle'. Today, with the impressive town ramparts still very much in evidence, it is a charming one-street market town. The city walls run along three sides of the town and are pierced by five gates. The fourth 'wall' is formed by the Mekong River. Quiet, with wooden shophouses and a scattering of ruins lying haphazardly and untended in the undergrowth, it has so far managed to escape the uncontrolled tourist development of other towns in northern Thailand.

ARRIVING IN CHIANG SAEN
Getting around Motorized *saamlors* congregate by the bus stop and offer trips around the sights.

Moving on There are regular buses to Chiang Khong (two hours). Long-tailed boats ply the Mekong River connecting Chiang Saen with Chiang Khong and Jin Hang in China.

Tourist information TAT ① *Phahonyothin Rd, opposite the National Museum, 0830-1630,* is attached to the sensitively designed Bureau for the Restoration and Conservation of the Historic City of Chiang Mai.

BACKGROUND
Chiang Saen was probably established during the early years of the last millennium and became the capital of the Chiang Saen Kingdom, founded in 1328 by King Saen Phu, the grandson of King Mengrai. Captured in the 16th century by the Burmese, the town became a Burmese stronghold in their constant wars with the Thais. It was not recaptured until Rama I sent an army here in 1803. Fearing that the Burmese might use the town

to mount raids against his kingdom in the future, Rama I ordered it to be destroyed. Chiang Saen remained deserted for nearly 100 years. King Mongkut ordered the town to be repopulated, but it still feels as though it is only part-filled, its inhabitants rattling around in the area's illustrious history. The ancient city is a gazetted historic monument managed by the Thai Fine Arts Department, and in total there are 75 monasteries and other monuments inside the city walls and another 66 outside.

In September 1992, a 120-tonne ship, with 60 Chinese delegates aboard, made the 385-km trip down the Mekong from Yunnan. Since then, links with China – as well as Laos – have developed apace. Cargo boats unload apples and other produce from China, and the market in Chiang Saen is stocked with low-quality manufactured goods. Anticipating a trade boom, two new piers were built (one of which was promptly washed away) as well as a luxurious business centre south of town – demonstrating how much money there is around as people try to cash in on the 'Golden Quadrangle' (Thailand, Burma, Laos and China). These days a mini-river port is now developing in Chiang Saen and it is becoming an important hub for the import of Chinese goods. The road to Mae Sai and the Burmese border is being redeveloped into a four-lane highway, and this sleepy corner of Thailand will soon be transformed.

PLACES IN CHIANG SEAN

Entering the town from Chiang Rai, the ruins of **Wat Phrathat Chedi Luang** can be seen on the right-hand side shortly after passing through the city's ancient ramparts. Built by King Saen Phu in 1331, this wat was established as the main monastery in the city. The *chedi*, resting on an octagonal base, is 60 m tall, but has fallen into disrepair over the centuries and is now clothed in long grass. The *viharn* is in a similar state of decrepitude and is protected by a jury-rigged corrugated-iron roof.

Just to the west of Wat Phrathat Chedi Luang is a small branch of the **National Museum** ① *Wed-Sun 0900-1200, 1300-1600, ฿10*. It contains various Buddha images and other artefacts unearthed in the area, as well as a small display of hilltribe handicrafts including clothing and musical instruments. Of the Buddha images, the most significant are those in the so-called Chiang Saen style, with their oval faces and slender bodies. They are regarded by art historians as being among the first true 'Thai' works of art.

West of town, just outside the city ramparts, is the beautiful **Wat Pa Sak** ① *฿30*, or 'Forest of Teak Wat' – so-called because of a wall of 300 teak trees, planted around the wat when it was founded. The monastery was founded in 1295 during the reign of Ramkhamhaeng of Sukhothai and actually predates the town. The unusual pyramid-shaped *chedi*, said to house a bone relic of the Lord Buddha, is the main building of interest here. Art historians see a combination of influences in the *chedi*: Pagan (Burma), Dvaravati, Sukhothai, and even Srivijaya. The niches along the base contain alternating *devatas* (heavenly beings) and standing Buddha images – poorly restored – the latter in the mudra of the Buddha 'Calling for Rain' (an attitude common in Laos but less so in Thailand). Much of the fine stucco work, save for fragments of *nagas* and *garudas*, has disappeared (some can be seen in the Chiang Saen Museum). The Spirit House at the entrance, by the ramparts, is also worth a little more than a glance.

On a hill 2.5 km north of Wat Pa Sak, following the ramparts, is **Wat Phrathat Chom Kitti**, which may date from as early as the 10th century. A golden-topped stupa is being restored, but there is little else save for the views. **Wat Chom Cheung**, a small ruined *chedi*, lies close by on the same hill. If visiting by foot, the stairs start about 150 m from the city walls and come first to Wat Chom Cheung. A highly decorated new wat has recently been completed here.

Strung out along the riverbank, the market sells plenty of unnecessary plastic objects and is a good place to watch hilltribe people (Karen and Lua among others) browsing through the goods. Since trade with China and Laos has expanded, it is also possible to pick up cheap – but poorly made – products from 'across the water'.

Wat Phrathat Pa Ngao, lies 4 km from Chiang Saen, along the road that follows the Mekong downstream. Perched on a hill, it provides views of the river and countryside. For Sop Ruak and the Golden Triangle take the same road upstream, 11 km from town (see below). Take a *songthaew* or long-tailed boat; boats can be hired from the jetty below the **Salathai Restaurant** and will also take passengers to riverside villages (bargain hard).

→ CHIANG KHONG

This border settlement, on the south bank of the Mekong, is really more a collection of villages than a town: Ban Haad Khrai, Ban Sobsom and Ban Hua Wiang were all originally individual communities – and still retain their village monasteries. For such a small town, it has had a relatively high profile in Thai history. In the 1260s, King Mengrai extended control over the area and Chiang Khong became one of the Lanna Thai Kingdom's major principalities. Later, the town was captured by the Burmese.

The area's popularity is due to its proximity to a border crossing into Laos – just the other side of the river. These days large ferries carrying giant trucks cross here and it is strongly rumoured that a bridge will be built here in the near future. Boats from the Laos town of Huay Xai, on the opposite side, travel downriver to the ancient city of Luang Prabang. Aside from that, Chiang Khong has a relaxed atmosphere making it an attractive spot to unwind.

GETTING AROUND
Chiang Khong is small enough to explore on foot. Bicycles and motorbikes are available for hire from guesthouses.

MOVING ON
Take a bus from Chiang Kong to Bangkok (12 hours) or a bus from Chiang Kong to Chiang Rai (three hours) and then fly back to Bangkok (1¼ hours).

PLACES IN CHIANG KHONG
Wat Luang, in the centre of town, dates from the 13th century. An engraved plaque maintains that two hairs of the Buddha were interred in the *chedi* in AD 704 – a date that would seem to owe more to poor maths or over-optimism than to historical veracity. However, it was reputedly restored by the ruler of Chiang Khong in 1881. The *viharn* sports some rather lurid murals. **Wat Phra Kaew**, a little further north, has two fine, red guardian lions at its entrance. Otherwise it is very ordinary, save for the *kutis* (small huts that serve as the monks' quarters) along the inside of the front wall, which look like a row of assorted Wendy houses, and the *nagas* which curl their way up the entrance to the *viharn*, on the far side of the building. Like Nong Khai and the other towns that line the Mekong in the northeastern region, *pla buk* catfish are caught here. It is sometimes possible to watch the fishermen catching a giant catfish on the riverbank to the south of town.

There are **hilltribe villages** within reach of Chiang Khong, but the trekking industry here is relatively undeveloped. Ask at the guesthouses to see if a guide is available. Tour operators cater mainly for those travelling on to Laos.

THE FAR NORTH LISTINGS

WHERE TO STAY

Tha Ton

$$$-$$ Old Trees House, on road to Mae Salong, 1 km before bridge, T08-5722 9002, www.oldtreeshouse.net. Eccentric collection of 4 cute bungalows in this entrancing hill-top resort. There's a small pool, stunning views and great food and wine. Rooms are fairly basic but comfortable. Recommended

$$$-$ Garden Home, T053-373015. Away from the main bustle, this peaceful resort has bungalows set in a large tree-filled orchard garden on the river's edge. Spotlessly clean rooms. Quiet and friendly, no restaurant. Recommended.

Mae Salong

$$-$ Little Home Guesthouse, 31 Moo 1 (next to Shin Sane), T053-765389, www. maesalonglittlehome.com. One of the friendliest and best-run small guesthouses in this part of the north. The owner, Somboon – an ex child soldier with the KMT – and his family really go out of their way to be hospitable. There are basic, spotless rooms in the teak house at the front and a couple of bungalows for rent at the back. They also serve food and drinks, have internet access, motorbikes for hire and arrange tours. Highly recommended.

$ Saeng Aroon Hotel, opposite Little Home, T053-765029. With its eccentric yet captivatingly friendly owners, Saeng Aroon is a small slice of Yunnan China in north Thailand. The rooms have imported chintzy Chinese furniture and tiled floors, but are spotless; those at the back on the upper floors have fine views. A Footprint favourite. Recommended.

Mae Sai

$$$-$$ Afterglow Hostel, 139/5 Moo 4 Wiang Phang Kham, T053-734188, www.afterglowhostel.com. Reminiscent of Bangkok's new wave of flashpacker digs, this spacious hostel has clean, funky rooms. A/c, TV.

$ S House, 384 Sailomjoy Rd, T053-733811, www.s-house-hotel-maesai.com. Set in the middle of the riverside market, S-House has plenty of atmosphere and, with its well-decorated rooms, it's one of the best budget options in town. Get rooms on the top floor for more light/views.

Sop Ruak

$$$$ Anantara Golden Triangle, 1 km north of Sop Ruak, T053-784084. Relatively peaceful location, with wonderful evening views. 'Traditional' architecture has been taken to the limit and it's a bit of a blot on the landscape for this timeless area of Thailand. However, the hotel is very well run with good service and facilities (including pool, tennis and squash courts, gymnasium, pétanque and sauna). It also runs an excellent Elephant Camp in conjunction with the Thai Elephant Conservation Centre near Lampang (see page 113).

$$$-$$ The Mae Khong River Side, 587 Moo 1, T053-784198. Overpriced though decent clean rooms with balconies overlooking the Golden Triangle. Good option if you want a river view.

Chiang Saen

$$$-$$ Pak-Ping-Rim-Khong, 484 Rimkhong Rd, Moo 2, T053-650151. Another new property for Chiang Saen, this time a purpose-built townhouse turned into a guesthouse on the main road by the river. The airy, well-lit rooms are en suite, and have a/c and Wi-Fi. Recommended.

Chiang Khong

$$$-$$ Ruan Thai Sophaphan Resort, Tambon Wiang Rd, T053-791023. Big wooden house with a large raised veranda. Rooms are large and clean with en suite and hot water. The upstairs rooms are better and have more natural light. There are also bungalows for 2-4 people. Good river views, very friendly, restaurant, self-service drinks, price negotiable out of season. Recommended.

$ Green Inn, 89/4 Moo2, T053-791009. With a central location on the main road, this mini-hotel has good, clean rooms, some with a/c, hot water en suite facilities and TVs. The cheaper rooms have shared bathrooms.

RESTAURANTS

Mae Salong

Mae Salong is a good place to eat Yunnanese food, and there are some great noodle shops around the village. Try the one on the T-junction at the end of the morning market, or the one about 100 m down the main road from the **7-11**. The bakery just down the hill from **Sinsane** also serves great Yunnanese fried noodles.

$$ Sweet Mae Salong. An excellent café serving probably the best chocolate brownies in the whole country. The friendly owners speak great English and offer a range of Thai/ Western food and superb coffee. It's a little pricey but the quality/value is very high, and there's free internet. There's a great little balcony overlooking the hills and magazines to browse. Recommended.

$ Salima Restaurant, 300 m past Sinsane guesthouse. This Muslim restaurant is probably the best place to eat in town. The owners are very friendly, speak almost no English and are slightly eccentric. Memorable and recommended.

Mae Sai

Restaurants in Mae Sai tend to be serious eating establishments with little character. The market area is good for cheaper stall food. Most guesthouses have restaurants serving Thai food. You'll find a run of small shophouses selling excellent Chinese-style roast pork and rice on the road to Chiang Rai about 2 km from the border.

$$ Daw Restaurant (Thai sign), Sailomjoy Rd. Serves up delicious Thai grub. Highly recommended.

Chiang Saen

The areas out of town towards Sop Ruak and the Golden Triangle have better riverside restaurants selling good Thai food, eg **Rim Khong** (2 km north of the city walls) and the **Mekong River Banks** (3 km).

Chiang Khong

The more interesting places are along the river road, or down one of the *sois* leading to the Mekong.

WHAT TO DO

Chiang Khong
Tour operators

There are a growing number of tour companies in Chiang Khong. **Ann Tour**, 6/1 Sai Klang Rd, T053-791218, is recommended. **Chiang Khong Tour** and **Nam Khong Travel**, north of town, by the pier, get most of their business arranging visas for Laos. For further information on visas, see page 279.

Mae Salong (Santikhiri)

Somboon at **Little Home Guesthouse** can help arrange tours or put you in contact with the right people. He also has motorbikes for hire and can arrange private transfers to and from Chiang Rai and other destinations. **Sinsane** arranges pony trekking from ฿500 per person.

DREAM TRIP 2:
Bangkok→Koh Chang→Mekong 21 days

Bangkok and around 3 nights, page 33

Koh Si Chang 2 nights, page 141
Bus from Bangkok to Si Racha (2-3 hrs)
then boat (40 mins)

Pattaya 1 night, page 141
Boat from Koh Si Chang (40 mins) then bus
(45 mins)

Koh Samet 2 nights, page 143
Minivan or taxi from Pattaya to Ban Phe
(1 hr) then a boat (40 mins). Or bus from
Pattaya to Rayong and then a songthaew
to Ban Phe (2 hrs in total)

Chantaburi 1 night, page 144
Boat from Koh Samet to Ban Phe (40 mins)
and then a songthaew to Rayong (20 mins)
and a bus to Chantaburi (2 hrs)

Koh Chang 5 nights, page 148
Bus from Chantaburi to Trat (30 mins),
then songthaew to Laem Ngop (30 mins)
and then boat (30-50 mins, depending on
ferry company)

Nakhon Ratchasima (Korat) 1 night,
page 154
Boat from Koh Chang to Laem Ngop
(30-50 mins), then songthaew to
Trat (30 mins) then bus to Chantaburi
(30 mins), and another to Korat (4-5 hrs)

Khon Kaen 1 night, page 156
Bus from Korat (2 hrs)

Udon Thani 1 night, page 156
Bus from Khon Kaen (2 hrs) or train

Nong Khai 1 night, page 157
Bus or train from Udon Thani (1 hr)

Nakhon Phanom 1 night, page 158
Bus from Nong Khai (5 hrs)

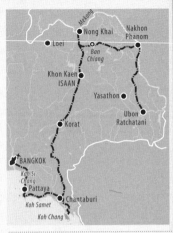

Ubon Ratchathani 1 night, page 158
Bus from Nakhon Phanom (5½-7 hrs)

Bangkok and around 1 night, page 33
Fly from Ubon Ratchathani (1 hr)

GOING FURTHER

Surin and Yasothon
Bus from Ubon Ratchathani to Yasothon
(1 hr) and Surin (4 hrs)

DREAM TRIP 2
Bangkok→Koh Chang→Mekong

Head east from Bangkok into a region that blends trashy gaudiness and gorgeous beaches. Add to the mix some remote forested islands, gem markets and oddball idiosyncrasy and you won't look back.

Koh Si Chang was a long-time haven for smugglers and sailors. Today, awesome seafood, monkeys, ruins and an enigmatic Chinese temple provide the colour. A little further east is Koh Samet, a national marine park. Samet used to be a sleepy island but these days it has been transformed into the weekend destination of choice for Bangkok's younger, trendier and wealthier crowd – at times it can be seem completely overrun with drunk Thai students. Chantaburi is worth a stopover for its gem market, traditional architecture and cathedral. As for Koh Chang: the traveller's idyll of isolated, white-sand beaches has been transformed by the arrival of large hotels and resorts aplenty. However, if you look hard enough, there are still some wonderful spots. Koh Chang's interior is also largely untouched, filled with waterfalls, jungle tracks and a colourful, noisy population of tropical birds and forest beasties.

Northeast from the coast is the friendly Isaan region. At Ban Chiang some of the world's earliest evidence of agriculture has been uncovered, while there are impressive ruins at Phimai, Phnom Rung, Muang Tham and Prasat Khao Phra Viharn. There's a rich, contemporary culture too: check out the exotic temple fairs and wild rocket festivals; the fine handwoven textiles and unique celebrations of Buddhist lent; aromatic *kai yang* (grilled chicken) and fiery *som tam* (papaya salads); while Isaan pop musicians, nasal to the max, are among the highest sellers in the country. And don't forget national parks, mountain walks, elephant treks, tubing on the Mekong and the best bicycling in the country.

EASTERN COAST TO TRAT

Koh Si Chang is home to weird abandoned palaces, sacred Chinese temples and platoons of monkeys. The notorious fleshpots of Pattaya may recommend little to travellers eager to experience local culture, but this place is still distinctively Thai – right the way down to the katoey *(transsexual or 'ladyboy') cabarets. Koh Samet with its beautiful beaches has transformed into an overpriced getaway for wealthy Bangkok students but you can still get away from it all if you pick your spot and moment. Further south, Chantaburi and Trat can provide engaging stop-offs on the way to this coastline's biggest draw – the island of Koh Chang (see page 148).*

→KOH SI CHANG

ARRIVING ON KOH SI CHANG

Getting here is relatively easy – take a half-hourly bus from Bangkok's Eastern Terminal next to Ekkamai Skytrain station to the town of Si Racha, where hourly boats run to Si Chang daily 0700-1900. You'll be greeted on arrival by a host of huge tuk-tuks – it costs ฿50-100 to get to the island though most accommodation is within walking distance. To get to Pattaya, take a boat from Koh Si Chang (40 minutes) to Si Racha then a bus (45 minutes). There are also a couple of places renting bicycles/motorbikes in the town. One of the best sources of information on Koh Si Chang is the excellent www.ko-sichang.com.

PLACES IN KOH SI CHANG

The nearest island getaway to Bangkok, Koh Si Chang has thankfully never made it onto most people's travel itineraries. Koh Si Chang is one of those places that had a moment in the spotlight – King Rama V built a palace here – and then history moved on. It does make for an entertaining, idiosyncratic short break and is a popular spot for weekenders from the capital. At the northern edge of the town, set up on a hill overlooking the town, the **Chaw Por Khaw Yai Chinese temple** is an odd assortment of decorated shrines and caves. There are great views of the island and this is a very important temple for Thailand's Chinese community. On the east coast – you might see monkeys here – are the ruins of **Rama V's palace**. Abandoned in 1893 when the French took control of the island during a confrontation with the Thais, not much remains though what does has a peculiarly eerie quality. The island also has a number of beaches with reasonable swimming and snorkelling. The quietest beach with the best coral and swimming is **Tham Phang** on the western side of the island.

→PATTAYA

Brash, brazen and completely over the top, whatever you feel about Pattaya, it will certainly leave an impression.

GETTING THERE AND AROUND

Getting here from Bangkok is straightforward – almost all tour companies offer mini-buses and private cars and there are plentiful buses from Bangkok's Eastern bus terminal. Most Bangkok taxis will take you here for an agreed fare or on the meter (between ฿1500-2000). There are even a few trains, though the journey time of almost five hours puts off most travellers. In Pattaya itself local transport is abundant with songthaews running between all the tourist centres and scores of people hiring out bikes, motorbikes and jeeps.

MOVING ON

To get to Koh Samet from Pattaya, take a minivan or taxi to Ban Phe (one hour) then a boat (40 minutes). There are no direct buses between Pattaya and Ban Phe; take a bus from Pattaya to Rayong and then a songthaew to Ban Phe (two hours in total).

TOURIST INFORMATION

For tourist information try the helpful TAT office ① *382/1 Beach Rd, T03-842 8750*. There are also several free tourist magazines and maps available in town.

Pattaya began to metamorphose from its sleepy fishing-village origins when the US navy set up at nearby Sattahip (40 km further down the coast). As the war in Vietnam escalated, so the influx of GIs on 'R & R' grew and Pattaya responded enthusiastically. Given these origins, it is hardly surprising that Pattaya's stock in trade is sex tourism and at any one time, about 4000 girls are touting for work around the many bars and restaurants.

The official line on Pattaya is that it is going out of its way to promote itself as a 'family' resort. This emphasis on wholesome family fun is hard to square with reality. The busiest and noisiest area is at the southern end of town along what is now known as 'Walking Street.' It's here you'll find the highest concentration of bars, brothels, pole-dancers, ladyboys, drunken sex-pats, street robberies and bad food. Many people find this tawdry aspect of Pattaya repugnant. However, there is no pretence here – either on the part of the hosts or their guests. Mostly performed by members of Pattaya's legendary *katoey* (transexual) population, the cabaret is an essential night out. The biggest and best are **Alcazar**, www.alcazarpattaya.com, and **Tiffany's**, www.tiffany-show.co.th. Both draw busloads of tourists every night.

As for the beach, it's a pleasant enough spot to chill out in a deckchair but also has its own set of problems. Though cleaner than in the past, in early 2011 the authorities announced that severe sand erosion could result in it disappearing entirely in five years if nothing is done. Then there is the notorious 'Jetski Scam'. This involves a hapless tourist renting a jetski from one of the vendors stationed along the beach and, on returning to shore, the vendor falsely claiming they have damaged it. Demands for compensation – tens of thousands of baht usually – often turn heated, even aggressive, with police officers sometimes showing up announced to help negiotate the amount down (while allegedly getting their cut). Inundated with complaints, the current mayor has promised to stamp it out, but its best to err on the safe side and avoid jetskis here altogether.

Jomtien Beach offers a different face of Pattaya. Some gaudier elements still hold sway closer to Pattaya Bay but the further south you head the more presentable it becomes. Cute, mid-range, boutique hotels appear, each with their own laid-back bar and restaurant. It's also popular with watersports lovers: blustery Jomtien offers some of Thailand's best sailing, parasailing and windsurfing conditions. At the far end – the beach here is about 4 km long – it becomes decidedly tranquil. If you have time in take a trip up the 240-m **Pattaya Park Tower** ① *T038-251201, ฿200*, sited on the Jomtien headland – it provides spectacular views.

AROUND PATTAYA

Trips out of town include the **Siriporn Orchid Farm** ① *235/14 Moo 5, Tambon Nong Prue, T038-429013, daily 0800-1700; Mini Siam, T038-421628, daily 0700-2200*, a cultural and historical park where 80 of Thailand's most famous 'sights' – including Wat Phra Kaeo and the Bridge over the River Kwai – are recreated at a scale of 1:25. The park lies 3 km north of Pattaya Beach, on the Sukhumvit highway (Route 3) at the Km 143 marker and the **Nong Nooch Tropical Garden** ① *T038-429321, daily 0900-1800, ₿20*, is a 200-ha park containing immaculate gardens with lakes (and boating), an orchid farm, family zoo, Thai handicraft demonstrations and a thrice-daily (1015, 1500 and 1545) 'cultural spectacular' with Thai dancing, Thai boxing and an elephant show. In 2000 a British tourist was gored and killed by an enraged elephant. Most people arrive on a tour. The garden is 15 minutes from Pattaya town, 3 km off the main road, at the Km 163 marker.

The island of **Koh Larn**, a short hop from the main Pattaya pier (boats depart at 0930 and 1130, returning at 1600, 45 minutes, ₿250), offers a decent respite from the intense pace of Pattaya. There is a place to stay here and there's some decent snorkelling and scuba-diving.

→KOH SAMET

A 6-km-long, lozenge-shaped island sited in a national park, rimmed with stunning beaches and lapped by azure seas, Koh Samet is just a short boat trip from the mainland. Over the years, much of the island has transformed from the perfect Bangkok getaway into a noisy spot where weekending Bangkok students, office workers and expats come to let off steam. It can still be a charming spot but if you're after quiet, contemplative sunrises/sets then come mid-week. At that time accommodation is cheaper as well, as most resorts hike up their prices on weekends, merely because the increased demand means they can.

These days, like so many other popular islands in Thailand, Koh Samet has evolved into a badly planned place with terrible damage being done to the local environment and unsightly resorts and the odd throbbing disco lining the beach. What's even stranger to outsiders is that Samet's superb beaches are all part of a national park and should be protected. The park rangers who man the entrance points to the island seem more content squeezing cash out of visitors than actually doing their jobs and Samet seems well on its way to eco-meltdown.

VISITING KOH SAMET

To get there take a boat from Ban Phe for 40 minutes or so (₿50 each). All foreign visitors also pay an entrance fee of ₿200 to get into the national park (Thais and foreigners with a Thai driving license or work permit pay ₿40). Speedboats are also available for between ₿800-1,500 (bargain hard). Many visitors arrive at the main Na Dan Pier in the northeast of the island though some bungalow operators will run boats straight onto the beaches – check beforehand.

Samet is one of the driest places in Thailand (1350 mm rain per year) and a good place to pitch up during the rainy season. Between May and October there can be strong winds and rough seas, while heavy rains can be a problem between July and September. During this period rates are cut and the island is less crowded.

Moving on Once back at Ban Phe on the mainland, take a songthaew to Rayong (20 minutes) and a bus to Chantaburi (two hours).

AROUND THE ISLAND

It is possible to explore Koh Samet on foot though take plenty of water – the beach walk from end to end is a good adventure. There is now a Koh Samet taxi union operating a fleet of green songthaews on the island. Their fares – both for rental of the entire vehicle and for one person in a shared vehicle – are posted on a notice board at the main pier. They normally travel when full, though do operate to a rough timetable as well). Tracks are negotiable by motorbike, which are available for about ฿300-400 a day.

There has been a settlement on Koh Samet for many years; junks from China used to anchor here to be checked before the authorities would allow them to sail over the sandbar at the mouth of the Chao Phraya River and north to Bangkok.

The biggest draw these days are, of course, the beaches. The northernmost is **Ao Klong**, a stretch of sand that runs to the west of the Na Dan pier – there are a few 'floating' guesthouses/seafood restaurants built on wooden stilts in the bay. **Hat Sai Kaew** (Diamond or White-Sand Beach) is a 10-minute walk southeast from Na Dan Pier, and remains the most popular place to stay. This is still a beautiful spot, even if it has been disfigured by uncontrolled development. Despite the crowded, bustling atmosphere, the beach remains clean and it has a sandy bottom. Just south along the coast from Hat Sai Kaew is **Ao Hin Khok** while a short distance further south still is **Ao Phai**, which is less developed and more peaceful. About 2 km from Ao Phai, past the smaller **Ao Tubtim**, **Ao Nuan** and **Ao Cho**, is **Ao Vong Duen**. This crescent-shaped bay has a number of more upmarket resort developments. Continuing south is **Ao Thian**, **Ao Wai** and **Ao Kiu Na Nok**. These are the most peaceful and low-key locations on Koh Samet. **Ao Phrao** (Paradise Beach), 2 km from Sai Kaew, is the only beach on the west side of the island.

→CHANTABURI AND AROUND

Head east from Koh Samet and you'll soon reach Chantaburi, famed for its trade in precious stones. Unless you fancy your chances of picking up a bargain in the gemstone market – most *farang* fair badly against the hard-nosed sapphire and ruby traders – many pass Chantaburi by en route to the island of Koh Chang.

Muang Chan – as it is locally known – is an unusual town with its large population of ethnic Vietnamese, a strong Catholic presence, well-preserved traditional shophouses, excellent restaurants, and some of the finest durian in Thailand. Chantaburi has built its wealth on rubies and sapphires with many of the gem mines being developed during the 19th century by Shan people from Burma, who are thought to be among the best miners in the world. While in town take in the French-style Catholic Cathedral of the Immaculate Conception (1880), the largest church in Thailand.

MOVING ON
Regular buses operate from Chantaburi to Trat (30 minutes).

ARANYA PRATHET
Aranya Prathet, a bit more than a day trip from Chantaburi, has gained some measure of notoriety because of its location close to the border with Cambodia and its growing use as an alternative route to Siem Reap. The journey from the border to Siem Reap on the new road now takes 60-90 minutes. The highlight of Aranya Prathet itself is the border market, around 7 km from town (a moto costs around ฿40-50).

The provincial capital and the closest Thai town of any size to Cambodia, Trat is a gem centre that has flourished as a centre of cross-border commerce. Most people visit Trat en route to Koh Chang, not staying any longer than they need to catch a bus or boat out of the place.

MOVING ON

With **Bangkok Airways** flying into the nearby airport, Trat is now the official gateway to nearby Koh Chang for the mass tourism market. To get to Koh Chang, take a songthaew to Laem Ngop (30 minutes) and then a boat (30-50 minutes, depending on the ferry company). See page 148 for more information on boats.

PLACES IN TRAT

If you do decide to stay longer in Trat you'll have the chance to sample the diverse selection of excellent guesthouses. There's also a bustling covered market on Sukhumvit Road offering a good selection of food and drink stalls. On the same road, north of the shopping mall, there is a busy night market. **Wat Buppharam** (Wat Plai Klong), dates from the late Ayutthaya period and is notable for its wooden viharn – it is 2 km west of town.

A great source of local information is the **Tratosphere bookshop** ① *23 Rimklong Soi*, where the French- and English-speaking owner is exceptionally helpful and knowledgeable about everything to do with Trat, Koh Chang and the surrounding islands.

South of Trat is *Khlong Yai*, the southernmost town on this eastern arm of Thailand and an important fishing port. Take a songthaew from the back of the municipal market (฿25) or shared taxi from the front of the market (฿35 each). The journey there is worthwhile for the dramatic scenery with the mountains of Cambodia rising to the east and the sea to the west. There are several Cambodian markets and the seafood is excellent. The border crossing at Hat Lek is a short journey south of Khlong Yai.

There's a **TAT office** ① *T039-597259, Mon-Fri 0830-1630*, by the pier in Laem Ngop. This sleepy fishing village – in fact the district capital – has a long pier lined with boats, along with good seafood and a relaxed atmosphere. As Koh Chang becomes Thailand's next island beach resort to hit the big time, expect things to get busier; at present there's a handful of guesthouses and a few waterside restaurants.

EASTERN COAST TO TRAT LISTINGS

WHERE TO STAY

Pattaya

$$$$ Sheraton Pattaya Resort, 437 Phra Tamnak Rd, T038-259888, www.sheraton.com/pattaya. Superb luxury resort in a great location perched up on the cliffs, with great views to add to the stunning rooms and bungalows. Possibly the best luxury resort in town, with a fantastic spa, restaurants, a huge pool area and all the trimmings you'd expect in such a top-end establishment. Recommended.

$$$-$$ Jomtien Twelve, 240/13 Moo 12, Jomtien Beach Rd, T038-756865, www.jomtientwelve.com. Great little hotel right on the beach road in a very quiet part of Jomtien, perfect for a short weekend break. All rooms are well designed, with pleasing aesthetic touches, en suite facilities, full cable TV and a/c. The ones at the front have decent-sized beach-facing balconies. Breakfast included. Best deal on this stretch of beach. Recommended.

Koh Si Chang

$$$-$$ Rim Talay, 250 m north of entrance to Rama V Palace, T038-216116. Mix of rooms and eccentric bungalow/barge affairs (for up to 7 people) that come complete with sea views. All rooms have TV, a/c and are en suite; the cheapest ones have cold water only. Recommended. Book ahead.

$$$-$ Sichang View Resort, west coast of island, T038-216210. Great location on the Khao Khaad cliffs in a remote corner of the island. Nice gardens make a great spot for sundowners. Huge rooms are well kept with en suite facilities, a/c and TVs. Good food.

Koh Samet

$$$$-$$$ Nimmanoradee, southern end of the island, T038-644 2734, www.nimmanoradee.com. Cute clapboard huts are scattered on rocky outcrops and amid trees, all with sea views, and a private sandy beach is a step away. There are kayaks, a swimming pool, deckchairs everywhere and the rooms are bathed in natural light with neat designer touches. Flat-screen TVs and bathtubs add extra comfort to the natural setting.

$$$$-$ Jep's Bungalow and Restaurant, T038-644112, www.jepbungalow.com. Good-value rooms that come in a range of prices and options (a/c, fan, etc). All are clean and well-tended; some are set directly on the beach. The restaurant has a large range of tasty dishes. Often fully booked. Recommended.

$$$-$$ Samet Villa, T038-644094. This clean and friendly Swiss-run establishment offers some of the best-value accommodation on Samet. All rooms have fans and attached bathrooms, and electricity is on around the clock. It organizes a number of trips and excursions to neighbouring islands and rents out snorkelling equipment. Recommended.

Chantaburi

$$$-$$ Rachan Residence, behind the large Robinson department store, T039-327102, www.rachanresidence.com. A garish pink exterior conceals pleasant, simple rooms with tiled floors, en suite bathrooms, Wi-Fi, a/c and TV. Rooms on top floors at the back overlook at quiet temple and the river.

Trat

$$$-$$ Rimklong Boutique Hotel, 194 Lak Muang Rd, T08-1861 7181. Very popular and friendly small hotel, with pretty white-tiled rooms. Gets full quickly, so book ahead.

$$ Trat Center Hotel, 45/65 Tasaban Rd Soi 5, T039-531234, www.tratcenterhotel.com. New mid-range hotel for 2012 set at the end of a quiet soi about 800 m from town centre. Rooms are basic but more than adequate, with tiled floors, TV, Wi-Fi and en suite. A very simple breakfast of toast and coffee is included.

RESTAURANTS

Pattaya

$$$ Ruen Thai, Pattaya 2 Rd, opposite Soi Post Office. Very good Thai food and not excessively overpriced. Recommended.
$$ Pu Pen Seafood, 62/1 Moo 1, Jomtien Beach (head to far south end and look for the Thai sign with crab icons), T038-231728. Zero-frills joint serving superlative seafood – crab legs, steamed fish, BBQ prawns, etc – for sensible prices, mostly to locals. Recommended.

Koh Si Chang

$$-$ Pan and David, 167 Asdang Rd, 200 m before Rama V Palace, next to Marine Police, T038-216 075. Mon-Fri 1100-2130, Sat and holidays 0830-2200, Sun 0830-2030. Reservations recommended at the weekends. Fantastic place to eat, run by long-term Si Chang residents. Pan cooks up superb steaks, Isaan grub and fresh seafood. David is an American expat who can tell you pretty much anything you need to know about Si Chang. Highly recommended.

Koh Samet

Just about all the resorts and guesthouses on Koh Samet provide the usual Thai dishes and travellers' food. The following places have a particularly good reputation for their food.
$$ Joe Restaurant, Hat Sai Kaew, on the beach. Food and service are passable. Good hang-out spot, with a nice low terrace.
$ Ploy, Hat Sai Kaew on the beach. Popular, lively spot for a BBQ supper while you lie back on a triangle cushion. Talented fire jugglers, too.

WHAT TO DO

Pattaya
Diving

Marine life, after years of degrading, is slowly returning to normal with stunning coral, sea turtles, rays and angelfish all making an appearance. There are even a couple of wrecks within easy reach as well as decent dive schools. This makes Pattaya an excellent place to learn to dive. There are more than 10 dive shops here.

Snorkelling day trips to the offshore islands can be organized through the dive shops.
Seafari, 284/19 Soi 12, opposite **Lek Hotel**, T038-429060, www.seafari.co.th. A 5-star PADI resort. A PADI Open Water course costs ฿16,500, including all equipment (except course manuals), dives and boat fees. Certified divers can do a day's diving (all equipment, 2 dives, boat fees, lunch and soft drinks) to the nearby islands and wrecks for ฿3200.

Koh Samet

The major beaches offer sailing, windsurfing, snorkelling and waterskiing. However, many of the bungalows display notices requesting visitors not to hire jet skis because they are dangerous to swimmers, damage the coral and disrupt the peace. Some of the jet-ski operators are notorious rip-off artists and the whole activity is best avoided. You can also scuba-dive here but the diving isn't great and you'd be better saving your money to dive in other parts of the country.

KOH CHANG NATIONAL PARK

Koh Chang, Thailand's second largest island, is part of a national marine park that includes 50-odd islands and islets covering 650 sq km. Despite the 'protection' that its national park status should offer, Koh Chang is developing rapidly, with resorts and bungalows springing up along its shores. It is Thailand's last tropical island idyll – at least of any size – to be developed and it supports excellent beaches, sea, coral and diving. There are treks, waterfalls, rivers and pools, villages, mangroves, three peaks of over 700 m, and a rich variety of wildlife.

The outlying islands in the national park have developed at a much slower rate than Koh Chang, though the likes of Koh Kood are now figuring in the plans of many travellers.

→KOH CHANG

As you set sail from the mainland across the glittering seas, Koh Chang (Elephant Island), covered in thick, verdant forest and with a vivid, sweeping skyline, rises up to meet you. This 40-km-long and 16-km-wide island is teeming with wildlife, rustic appeal and wonderful beaches that have long attracted the more adventurous traveller.

Things are changing. Koh Chang has now been earmarked as Thailand's next big destination. Hotel chains and tour operators are moving in and the beaches are now almost entirely colonized by Thai and European package tourists. It's not all upmarket; odious 'monkey schools' (where monkey's are forced to perform degrading tricks) and that definitive marker of tourist saturation, the 'girlie bar', have now made their home on Koh Chang. Visitors now have to work harder to find the best parts of the island.

Elephant Island also forms the fulcrum of the Koh Chang National Park – an archipelago of dozens of smaller islands that stretch to the south. Many of these are also being taken over by mass tourism/backpackers and the recently pristine environment is suffering. If you do visit these outlying islands be very aware of your impact – some of them are overwhelmed with mountains of plastic water bottles and other detritus.

VISITING KOH CHANG
With regular flights to nearby Trat (see page 145), Koh Chang is getting easier to reach.

Getting there During the high season (November to May) boats leave every hour from Laem Ngop for Koh Chang. But during the low season departures are much more intermittent.

Getting around Koh Chang's best beaches are on the western side of the island – **Hat Sai Kaew** (White Sand) and **Hat Khlong Phrao** – and, on the southern coast – **Hat Bang Bao**. These can be reached either by jeep taxi from Ao Sapparot (price ranging from ฿50-100, depending upon destination and whether you manage to fill up the taxi) or by boat from Laem Ngop. There is a paved road up the east coast and down the west coast as far south as Bang Bao. If you need to travel later in the day there are pickup trucks you can catch a lift with. However, it is still not possible to travel between Bang Boa and Salak Phet. In addition to songthaews there are also motorbikes (฿200 per day) and mountain bikes for hire. For walkers, there is a path crossing the middle of the island from Ban Khlong Phrao to Than Ma Yom but it is a strenuous day-long hike and locals recommend taking a guide. There are several places claiming to be official tourist information offices – all are agents trying to get you to buy day trips.

Moving on To get to Nakhon Ratchasima (Korat) on the mainland, take a boat from Koh Chang to Laem Ngop (30-50 minutes), then a songthaew to Trat (30 minutes) then bus to Chantaburi (30 minutes). From there, buses run to Korat (four to five hours).

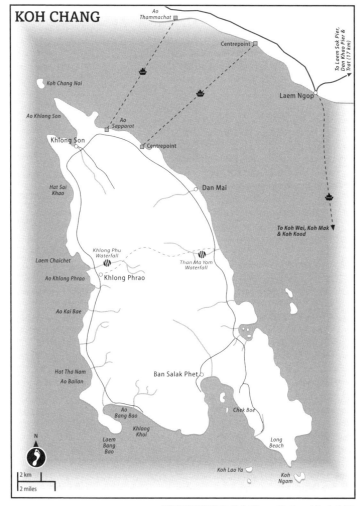

Best time to visit The best time to visit is November to May, when visibility is at its best. This is also the best time to visit from the weather point of view. Koh Chang is a wet island with an annual rainfall of over 3000 mm (the wettest month is August). Mosquitoes (carrying malaria) and sandflies are a problem on Koh Chang and surrounding islands, so repellent and anti-malarials are essential. Take a net if camping.

AROUND THE ISLAND

Khlong Son, near the northern tip, is the island's largest settlement on the island. Even so, there's not much here: a health clinic, a few small noodle shops, a monastery, post office and school. Further south on the western side is **Hat Sai Kaew** (White Sand Beach). Lined with upmarket resorts, **Hat Khlong Phrao**, 5 km south of Hat Sai Kaew, and 2 km long, is spread out each side of the mouth of the Khlong Phrao canal and is a beautiful beach but the water tends to be very shallow. At **Ao Khlong Makok** there is almost no beach at high tide and just a couple of bungalow operations that are virtually deserted in the low season. **Ao Kai Bae** is beautiful but swimming is tricky as the water is very shallow and covered with rocks and dead coral. At low tide you can walk/wade out to the nearest teardrop island.

Haad Tha Nam (Lonely Beach) is an attractive stretch of coastline and much more quiet and relaxed than the more accessible northern stretches. It remains the beach of choice for those looking for basic thatched huts and the cliché backpacker lifestyles that go hand in hand with them (tattoo shops, raging nightly parties fuelled by icy plastic buckets of red bull, coke and Thai rum, etc), but gentrification, spearheaded by a handful of mid-range bungalows and generic resorts, is now well under way.

Popular with longstayers, **Ao Bailan** is a pretty crescent of shallow water and rocks (but home to one of the island's swankiest five-star resorts, the Dusit Princess) and **Ao Bang Bao** is a picturesque bay punctuated by a rickety, 1 km-long wooden fishing pier. Well worth a visit once you tire of the beach, especially just before sunset, it's lined with seafood restaurants, tourist shops, dive shops, and guesthouses and has a pretty lighthouse at the end of it.

Although there is a scattering of bungalow operations on the east coast, very few people choose to stay here even in the high season. The only beach is at **Sai Thong**.

Than Ma Yom Waterfall is on the east side of the island. King Chulalongkorn (Rama V) visited this waterfall on no less than six occasions at the end of the 19th century, so it counts as an impressive one (in fact there are three falls). To prove the point, the king carved his initials (or had them carved), on a stone to mark one of his visits. Rama VI and VII also visited the falls, although it seems that they didn't get quite so far – they left their initials inscribed on stones at the nearest of the falls. The falls are accessible from either Ban Dan Mai or Thaan Ma Yom, both on the east coast. Getting to the first of the cascades involves a walk of around one hour; it is around 4 km to the furthest of the three falls.

Khlong Phu Falls, at Ao Khlong Phrao, are perhaps even more beautiful than Than Ma Yom. There is a good pool here for swimming as well as a restaurant and some bungalows. Because this is a national park it is also possible to camp. To get here, it's a 10-minute taxi or motorbike ride from Hat Sai Kaew; you can also travel to it from the road by elephant for ฿200 or for free by walking just 3 km.

Koh Chang's forest is one of the most species-rich in the country and while the island's coast may be undergoing development, the rugged, mountainous interior is still largely inaccessible and covered with virgin rainforest (around 70% is said to be forested). There is a good population of birds, including parrots, sunbirds, hornbills and trogons, as well as Koh Chang's well-known population of wild boar, although the chances of seeing any are slim. It is advisable, however, to take a guide for exploring – **Jungle Way** bungalows organizes guided hikes for ฿450 including lunch.

While the waters around Koh Chang are clear there have been some reports of a deterioration in water quality connected with coastal gem mining on the mainland. Nonetheless, hard and especially soft corals are abundant. Fish are less numerous and varied than on the other side of the Gulf of Thailand or in the Andaman Sea. During the wet season visibility is very poor, due to high seas, which also makes diving dangerous. The months between November and March are best for diving. Generally, diving is better in the waters to the south of the island. Notable are the wrecks of two Thai warships, the *Thonburi* and *Chonburi*, sunk here in an engagement with seven French ships and the loss of 36 lives on 17 January 1941. There are numerous dive shops on Koh Chang with courses for all levels. Snorkelling off the Koh Chang beaches is poor but is excellent off the smaller islands, which can be reached by boat trips. **Aittipol Tours**, T08-7135 3611, are the best of the bunch.

OUTLYING ISLANDS
On many of the other islands within the national park a fair amount of land, particularly around the coast, has been cleared for agriculture – mostly coconut plantations.

Koh Kood, the next largest island after Koh Chang, has lovely beaches, especially on the west side, and a number of small fishing villages linked by dirt roads. So far it has managed to escape the ravages of development; there aren't any 7-Elevens, banks or girly bars, making this an ideal place to escape and relax. There is an impressive waterfall and the coral is also said to be good. A good source of information is www.kohkood.com.

Much of **Koh Mak**, the third largest island in the archipelago, is privately owned by a few wealthy local families and a little over half of the island has been cleared for coconut plantations. But there is still a reasonable area of forest and the coral is also good. The best beach is on the northwest shore. Many of the prime pieces of shorefront have been sold to developers, and a lot of resorts have sprung up in recent years. See www.kohmak.com, a good insider's resource, with lots of recommendations and a detailed history of the island.

Koh Kham, a tiny island, is well known for its swallows' nests and turtle eggs, as well as good coral and rock formations for divers. Boats leave from Laem Ngop (3½ hours, ฿150).

Koh Ngam, two hours from Laem Ngop by boat, is a very small island with lush vegetation and beautiful beaches. It has two upmarket resorts.

Koh Whai has two resorts but these are better value than those at Koh Ngam. There's a daily ferry from Laem Ngop at 0800, returning at 1500 (฿130).

Many of the more sophisticated bungalow operations on Koh Chang organize day trips to **Koh Lao Ya**, **Koh Phrao**, **Koh Khlum**, **Koh Kra Dad** (which has exceptionally beautiful beaches and lush vegetation) and **Koh Rayang Nok** during the high season, when the seas are calmer, the visibility greater and there is generally more demand. In the low season few boats go to these islands and most of the accommodation closes down.

KOH CHANG NATIONAL PARK LISTINGS

WHERE TO STAY

Koh Chang

$$$$ The Dewa, 24/1 Khlong Prao, Chaichet and Khlong Prao, T039-557339, www.thedewakohchang.com. An ultra-stylish boutique resort, free of the usual generic Thai decor. Spacious deluxe rooms have terraces overlooking a huge pool area, while the pricier villas get the sea views. Facilities include an excellent spa. Great service. Recommended.

$$$$-$$$ Koh Chang Kacha Resort, 88-89 Moo 4, Hat Sai Khao (White Sands Beach), T039-551223, www.kohchang kacha.com. Well-designed villas and bungalows with pools set in a luscious garden. Limited beachfront. Friendly management. Recommended.

$$$-$$ The Mangrove, Ao Bailan (Bailan Bay), T08-1949 7888. Simple and stylish wooden bungalows, hugging the hillside and shaded by trees. They are fan-cooled affairs, with spacious attached bathrooms partly open to the stars. The beach can get a bit narrow at high tide, but the atmosphere of total relaxation and very affordable seclusion more than makes up for that. Recommended.

$$-$ Khlong Koi Cottage, 131 Moo 1, Khlong Koi Beach, Bang Bao and Hat Khlong Koi, T039-558169. Simple, clean fan rooms. Small restaurant serving good food with occasional live music. Friendly management. Recommended.

Koh Kood

$$$$ Soneva Kiri Six Senses, 110 Moo 4, Ao Lak Uan, T039-619 800/08-1345 2791/ 2208 8888, www.sixsenses.com/soneva-kiri. Fly in by Cessna to an airstrip on a nearby tiny uninhabited island and transfer across to a uniquely designed villa with all the facilities you could ever need. Restaurants and pools, cinema on a lake, kids' adventure park, dining pods up in the trees. Not for the budget traveller!

$$-$ Happy Days Guesthouse & Restaurant, next to the post office, Ao Khlong Chao, T08-7144 5945, www. kohkood-happydays.com. Long-established guesthouse within walking distance of the beach. Rooms with fan or a/c; all with bathroom. There are also 2 family bungalows. The owner has a comprehensive local knowledge, and diving courses can be booked here. Highly recommended.

Koh Mak

$$$ Bamboo Hideaway, 55/2 Moo 2, Ao Pai, T039-501085/08-1907 5524, www.bamboohideaway.com. Built inland within a rubber plantation off the beaten track, the resort has 8 bungalows accessed by a raised bamboo walkway. There is a swimming pool, and the nearest beach is a short walk away, with transport provided by the Kiwi owner to Ao Kao if needed.

$$-$ Koh Mak Green View Resort, 45 Moo 2, Ao Ta Lang, T08-1588 1006, www.kohmakgreenview.com. Simple wooden fan and a/c bungalows sit alongside a beachside restaurant on the peaceful northern coast. The water is shallow, so swimming is only possible at high tide. Motorbikes are available for hire.

Koh Wai

$$$$-$$$ Koh Wai Beach Resort, Moo 2, T08-1306 4053/1888 7048, www.kohwai beachresort.com. Open Oct-May. The new resort, the most upmarket on the island, is located on a private beach on the southeastern tip. Accommodation ranges from hillside bungalows to Thai teak houses. Internet and electricity 1500-0900.

RESTAURANTS

Koh Chang

$$$-$$ Saffron by the Sea, Hat Kai Mook (Pearl Beach). The menu is small and often changing, as Ting, the owner and chef, is constantly experimenting. Everything is freshly prepared, so come with plenty of time to relax and enjoy the garden by the sea; the food is worth the wait. Breakfast and lunch are also served here and there are simple bungalows for rent.

$ Krua Sawa's (Sawa's Kitchen), Ao Bailan (Bailan Bay). A very friendly couple serve good Issan and Thai food at very reasonable prices. Their place is in the centre, opposite the no-name village noodle shop – another cheap and tasty option.

Koh Kood

Food and drink tends to revolve around your resort due to the lack of public transport. Khlong Chao is the best area for choice. Prices are a little higher than elsewhere and last orders can be quite early.

Koh Mak

All of the resorts have their own restaurants but there are now plenty of other choices as well, mainly around Ao Kao, in the centre of the island near the school and at Ao Nid. **$$$-$$ Koh Mak Seafood**, Ao Nid. An island institution, with tables and mats scattered over a series of jetties and salas. Live music and even a museum.

WHAT TO DO

Canopying

Tree Top Adventure Park, Ao Bailan (Bailan Bay), T08-4310 7600. Walking, swinging and tight-rope walking high up in the forest canopy, with spectacular views, ฿950.

Diving

BB Divers, T039-558040/08-6155 6212, www.bbdivers.com. Long-established and very professional Belgian-run outfit, with main office in Bang Bao, pool in Lonely Beach (Hat Tha Nam) and smaller office in Hat Sai Khao (White Sands Beach). Offers all courses from DSD (฿4500) to instructor, as well as fun dives (from ฿2700) and snorkelling (from ฿850).
Dolphin Divers, T08-7028 1627 http://www.scubadivingkohchang.com. This Swiss-owned outfit has its main office on Khlong Phrao and an outlet in the Amari Emerald Cove. All courses offered, with some free accommodation thrown in.
Scuba Zone, T08-0094 7222, www.scuba-kohchang.com. Outlets in Hat Sai Khao (White Sands Beach), Kai Bae and Lonely Beach (Hat Tha Nam). All dive trips and courses on offer, with huge array of retail supplies, including equipment for Nitrox/Trimix diving. Specialists in technical diving. Prices similar to above.

Elephant trekking

Ban Kwang Chang elephant camp, inland from the crossroads in Khlong Son, T08-9939 6676. A project set up in conjunction with the Asia Elephant Foundation which offers treks in the valley, ฿500 to ฿900, including transfer.

Kayaking

KayakChang, T08-7673 1923, www.kayakchang.com. This British-run company offers rental and guided half-day, full-day and multi-day excursions off the Koh Chang coast and around the archipelago. Prices start at ฿1500.
Salak Khok Kayak Station, ask in Salak Khok Seafood, T08-1919 3995. An eco-tour programme whereby the locals can make some money from tourism without needing to change their way of life. You can rent kayaks or go with a guide to explore the bay's mangrove swamps.

ISAAN AND THE MEKONG

When compared with the rest of Thailand, there's something very different about travelling in Isaan. For a start there's almost no tourist fatigue, people are friendlier and prices lower. Then comes the food – the earthy, zesty flavours of Isaan food, as exemplified by the famous som tam (spicy papaya salad), larb moo (spicy ground pork) and khao niaow (sticky rice), are some of the most popular in Thailand. The Isaan dialect has far more in common with Laos and for hundreds of years the region was ruled by the Khmers who built a series of extraordinary temples. Isaan people tend to be shorter and darker than the Thais of the Central Plains – a fact the whiter, taller elite of Bangkok never let them forget – Isaan people are often the butt of many Thai jokes. But for Thai aficionados Isaan is one of the most popular places to visit. In many ways Isaan is the soul of Thailand – hardworking, super-friendly, raw and a bit wild. A journey along the banks of the Mekong, a day spent at the Khmer temple of Phnom Rung or just the opportunity to engage with some affable Isaan folk is unlikely to be forgotten.

→NAKHON RATCHASIMA (KORAT) AND AROUND

Most visitors to the northeast only travel as far as Nakhon Ratchasima, more commonly known as Korat, the largest city in the northeast and an important provincial capital. The city has made huge strides to become a pleasant place to visit and there are nice shady parks and promenades circling the city moat. Korat is also a handy base for visiting the magnificent Khmer monuments of Phimai and Phnom Rung and the very popular Khao Yai National Park, just to the south of the city.

ARRIVING IN NAKHON RATCHASIMA

There are three bus terminals serving Bangkok and other destinations around the country, including Khon Kaen (two hours), including Khon Kaen (two hours). The railway station is west of the town centre and provides links with Bangkok and other destinations in the northeast including Khon Kaen including Khon Kaen. A city bus system is provided by a plentiful supply of fixed route songthaews (฿8 per person) while tuk-tuks provide personal transportation. A **tourist information office** ① *2102-2104 Mittraphap Rd, T044-213666, daily 0830-1630*, is a little out of town. Good town maps are available, along with other information on the rest of Isaan.

PLACES IN NAKHON RATCHASIMA

Korat was established when the older settlements of Sema and Khorakpura were merged under King Narai in the 17th century. The older part of the town lies to the west, while the newer section is within the moat, to the east. The remains of the town walls, and the moat that still embraces the city, date from the eighth to 10th centuries. In the centre of town, by the Chumphon Gate, you'll find the Thao Suranari Shrine – a bronze monument erected in 1934 to commemorate the revered wife of a provincial governor, popularly known as Khunying Mo, who in 1826 saved the town from an invading Lao army. In late March and early April a 10-day-long festival honours this heroine. The **night market** ① *Manat Rd, between Chumphon and Mahatthai roads, daily from 1800*, has lots of foodstalls, as well as some clothes and handicraft stalls. The **general market** ① *Suranari Rd*, is opposite Wat Sakae.

ON THE ROAD
Trails in Khao Yai

Trail 1: Kong Kaew to Haew Suwat Starts behind visitors' centre, marked in red, 6 km, 3-4 hours' walking – transport back to headquarters should be arranged. One of the most popular trails, offering opportunities to observe gibbons.

Trail 2: Kong Kaew to Elephant Salt Lick 2 Starts behind visitors' centre, marked in blue, 6 km, 3-4 hours. Not well marked, over grassland to salt lick – guide advisable. Frequented by elephants.

Trail 3: Kong Kaew to Pha Kluai Mai Starts behind visitors' centre, marked in yellow.

Trail 4: Pha Kluai Mai to Haew Suwat Starts on far side of campsite, marked in red, 3 km. Popular trail along Lam Takhong riverbank. Good trail for orchids and birdlife (blue-eared kingfishers, scarlet minivets, cormorant, hornbills – both wreathed and great). Probable sightings of gibbon, macaques and elephants.

Trail 5: Haew Suwat to Khao Laem grassland Starts across the Lam Takhong River from the parking area. Difficult trail to follow, not much wildlife but good views of Khao Laem mountain.

Trail 6: HQ to Nong Phak Chi Watchtower Starts across road from Wang Kong Kaew restaurant, south of Park Office, marked in red, 6-km round-trip. Popular and easy to follow until last 500 m. The tower makes a good viewing spot at dawn or dusk. White-headed gibbon frequently seen. Clouded leopard has been seen occasionally, herds of wild pig, and even tiger.

Trail 7: HQ to Wang Cham Pi Starts in the same place as 6, marked in blue, 4.5-km round-trip, 2-3 hours, good for ornithologists, gibbons and macaques easily seen.

Trail 8: Headquarters Looping Trail Marked in yellow, 2.5 km.

Trail 9: Headquarters to Mo Singto Marked in blue, starts in the same place as 6, ends at a reservoir close to headquarters, 2 km. A favourite haunt for tigers.

AROUND NAKHON RATCHASIMA

The **Khao Yai National Park** ① *south of Korat, ฿400, ฿200 child, 30 car*, has a tourist office and visitor centre, which provide maps and organize guides. The best time to see wildlife is weekday mornings and late afternoons – at weekends the park is busy. There are a few buses a day from Korat to the nearby town of Pak Chong; from here songthaews will take visitors to the park's northern entrance. This fine park covers an area of 2168 sq km, encompassing the limestone Dangrek mountain range, a large area of rainforest, waterfalls and a surprisingly wide selection of wildlife such as Asiatic black bear, Javan mongoose and gibbons, although recent reports have indicated a distinct lack of wildlife. The 50 km of trails are extensive and well marked. **Kong Kaeo Waterfall** is a short walk from the visitor centre and 6 km east is the **Haew Suwat Waterfall** (three to four hours' walk).

A small, ancient town to the north of Korat, **Phimai**, sited on the Mun River, is a charming place that is home to an alluring Khmer temple ruin and a pretty good museum. There are regular bus services to and from Korat (1½ hours), and Phimai town is small enough to walk around. Dating from the reign of the Cambodian King Jayavarman VII (1181-1201), Phimai was built at the western edge of his Khmer Kingdom. The **original complex** ① *daily 0730-1800, ฿40*, houses the central prang, which at the time of construction was a major departure for Khmer architecture and probably became the model for the famous towers at Angkor. Another unusual feature of Phimai is the predominance of carved Buddhist motifs. As Phimai predates Angkor, there is speculation that it served as the prototype for Angkor Wat. The **Phimai open-air museum** ① *0900-1600, ฿60*, on the edge of the town, just before the bridge, displays carved lintels and statues found in the area.

Phnom Rung ① *daily 0730-1800, ฿40, about 100 km east of Korat*, is the finest Khmer temple in Thailand and was built in sandstone and laterite over a period of 200 years between the 10th and early 13th centuries. It stands majestically at the top of Rainbow Hill, an inactive volcano overlooking the Thai–Cambodian border. To get here is tricky – take a Surin-bound bus from Korat and get off at Ban Tako where motorcycle taxis wait at the bus stop and charge ฿250 for a round trip. The best way to visit Phnom Rung is to go on a tour. One of Phnom Rung's most striking features is the monumental staircase which is reached via a five-headed naga bridge. The detail is superb: crowned heads studded with jewels, carefully carved scales and backbones and magnificent rearing bodies. The **Prasat Phnom Rung** (central Hindu sanctuary) was probably built between 1050 and 1150 by the Khmer King Suryavarman II. The outstanding stone carvings on the central prang illustrate scenes from the Hindu epics, the Ramayana and the Mahabharata. The quality of this carving is regarded by some as being the finest of the Angkor period.

→NORTH TO NONG KHAI AND THE MEKONG

The journey north from Korat heads through the hot, flat central plains of Isaan and on to the burgeoning cities of **Khon Kaen** and Udon Thani – both well served by good transport links with numerous bus, train and flights linking to Bangkok and other parts of Thailand.

UDON THANI

At present few visitors stop at sleepy Udon Thani just south of the busy Laos border, preferring to carry on to the frontier town of Nong Khai. If you do find yourself in Udon, don't forget to check out **Precha market** ① *daily 1800-2200ish*, in a huge area just to the west of the railway station. Endless runs of stalls sell awesome Isaan and Thai food – everything from sweet, sticky cakes through to the market's speciality: salted, barbecued fish.

Udon also makes a good base to visit **Ban Chiang** ① *Tue-Sun 0830-1630, ฿150*, one of the most important archaeological sites in Southeast Asia. Buses run direct to the village from the bus stand opposite the Thai-Isaan market on Udon Dutsadee Road every hour from 0600, though the last one back leaves Ban Chiang at 1400 (฿20). Organized excavations only really commenced during the 1970s when a site spanning a time period of over 5000 years was revealed. Perhaps the greatest discovery is the **bronzeware** that has been dated to 3600 BC, thus pre-dating bronzeware found in the Middle East by 500 years. Check out the excellent **museum** where the Ban Chiang story is retold.

NONG KHAI

The last stop before the Friendship Bridge and communist Laos, Nong Khai is a charming laid-back riverside town: the sort of place where jaded travellers get 'stuck' for several days. With good access to Laos and its capital Vientiane, the town has become increasingly popular – it's also, with French-style colonial architecture, one of the most attractive in the region. Situated at the end of Route 2, the Friendship Highway, visitors to Laos cross the Mekong by road-bridge; visas are available on arrival.

Getting there and around The bus station is on the east side of town and there are connections with Bangkok and destinations in the northeast. There's also a train station where trains from Khon Kaen arrive (three hours). Tuk-tuks provide the main means of local transport; the town is strung out along the river, so it is quite a hike getting from one end to the other. Some guesthouses hire out bicycles and motorbikes.

Moving on There are regular bus connections to Nakhon Phanom from Nong Khai via Sakhon Nakhon (five hours).

Places in Nong Khai Nong Khai's riverfront has now been redeveloped into a 'promenade' and it makes for quite a pleasant stroll with the setting sun as a backdrop. The riverside market is now almost fully covered – most of the goods on sale in the market are imported from China and not of particularly good quality. The influence of the French in Indochina is clearly reflected in the architecture along Meechai Road – the most impressive building is the 1920s French colonial style Governor's Mansion. It's now disused but there are plans to open it to the public. Notable among the wats are **Wat Pho Chai** – with its venerated solid gold-headed Buddha (the body is bronze), looted from Vientiane by Rama I – and **Phrathat Nong Khai**, better known as **Phrathat Klang Nam** (Phrathat in the Middle of the River), which is only visible during the dry season when it emerges from the muddy river and is promptly bedecked with pennants. To see it, walk east along Meechai Road for about 2 km from town, and turn left down Soi Paa Phrao 3.

In October Naga Fireballs, glowing orbs of much debated origin, rise from the Mekong River near Nong Khai.

One of the most bizarre sights in the region is found just outside Nong Khai at **Sala Kaew Ku** ① *daily 0830-1800, ฿20, children ฿10.* To get here cycle from town or take a tuk-tuk (including one hour's wait, should cost ฿120). Home to bizarre giant sculptures too weird to miss, Sala Kaew Ku was established in the late 1970s by a Laotian artist named Luang Poo Boun Leua Sourirat, who died in 1996 at the age of 72. Luang Poo saw himself as part holy man, part artist and part sage. Reflecting Luang Poo's beliefs, the wat promotes a strange mixture of Buddhism and Hinduism and is dominated by a vast array of strange brick and cement statues. Enter the surreal domed temple, climb to the top floor and you'll find Luang Poo's mausoleum. At the back, surrounded by a kitsch horde of plastic flowers and fairy lights, lies the shrouded corpse of Luang Poo, his mummified head sticking out of orange sheets.

CHIANG KHAN

If you head east along the Mekong from Nong Khai you'll find the formerly catatonic, but now burgeoning riverside town of Chiang Khan. There's little to do here except laze about – a favourite travellers' past time – and admire all the cutesy cafés, guesthouses and trinket shops that now occupy most of its old woodplank shophouses, many of which back on to the river. Some are calling it the next 'Pai'; others a retro toy town for the snap happy. While not popular with foreigners, yet, young Thai tourists flock here on weekends and long holidays to photograph all the tacked-on nostalgia (vintage Vespas, rickety old bicycles etc), and coo over the mass-made 'Chiang Khan' merchandise. Transport connections are tricky – you'll need to head to Loei first and catch a local bus there.

LOEI

Head south from the Mekong and you'll find the frontier settlement of Loei. Packed with dusty streets and seedy-looking shophouses, most visitors arrive here to sample the remarkable scenery of the area, particularly at the **Phu Kradung National Park** ① *82 km south of Loei, Sep-May 0700-1400 (closed Jun-end Sep), ฿400.* There are regular buses linking Loei with Udon, Khon Kaen and Bangkok. The park station has an information centre, restaurants and porters. Buses from Loei to Phu Kradung town take 1½ hours (the Khon Kaen bus, every 30 minutes); from here there are motorcycles, songthaews and tuk-tuks.

In June/July, in Dansai village, Loei, Phi Ta Khon is celebrated. This is a boisterous festival when villagers parade the streets in colourful, elongated ghost masks.

→SOUTHERN MEKONG TO UBON RATCHATHANI

NAKHON PHANOM

Follow the curve of the Mekong south and you'll reach Nakhon Phanom. There's little to do here except admire the view of the majestic river as it sweeps past the distant mountains of Laos. Like Nong Khai, there are several striking French colonial buildings scattered along the riverfront. Most people only visit Nakhon Phanom en route to **Wat That Phanom** – the northeast's most revered religious shrine – which is 50 km to the south. This impressive temple, set in the small town of **That Phanom**, is dominated by a 52-m white-and-gold Lao-style chedi. During festivals and religious holidays, the wat is seething with people making offerings of flowers and incense. During the full moon in January/February Phra That Phanom Chedi Homage-paying Fair, the northeast's largest temple fair, is held here. Upstream from town, on Mondays and Thursdays from around 0800-1200, an interesting Lao market is held.

Moving on Regular buses link both Nakhon Phanom and That Phanom to Bangkok, Udon and other places in Isaan. Tour buses running south to Ubon Ratchathani leave every two hours during the day from near the Windsor Hotel (4½ hours).

UBON RATCHATHANI

Head into the far southeastern corner of Isaan and you'll find one of the region's most important cities – Ubon Ratchathani. Administrative capital and transport hub, it is a friendly stop-off point while investigating the more impressive sights of this far-flung corner of Thailand. With the border crossing fully open at Chongmek this also now forms an important land route into Laos – there are regular bus connections between Ubon and the Laos city of Pakxe – you'll need a visa before travel. There are plentiful transport links to Ubon with regular flights from Bangkok (one hour), excellent bus connections to destinations throughout the country (such as Bangkok, eight hours) and sleeper trains to and from the capital (10 hours). There are lots of tuk-tuks to get you about town and a TAT office ① *264/1 Khuan Thani Rd (facing the Srikamol Hotel), T045-243770, daily 0830-1630.* In

GOING FURTHER
Surin and Yasothon

Surin

About 100 km west of Ubon is Surin – regular buses link the town to Ubon Ratchathani (four hours) – famous for its annual Elephant Round-up staged by the Suay people, who have a unique relationship with these huge beasts. Held in the third week of November, 40,000 people come to watch the Suay practise their skills with at least 200 elephants; contact **TAT** in Bangkok for details, page 38). The **Surin Museum** ① *Chitbamrung Rd, Wed-Sun*, displays many of the accessories used by the Suay to capture wild elephants, including the magical talismans that are worn to protect men from injury. **Ban Tha Klang** is a Suay settlement, 58 km north of Surin, near the town of Tha Tum. There's an hourly bus from Surin (two hours). It is sometimes possible to see training in progress here, particularly in the weeks just prior to the round-up when the villagers are intensively preparing for the festival.

Yasothon

An hour's bus ride northwest from Ubon is Yasothon, which hosts a yearly skyrocket festival, **Bun bang fai**, in May; see box, page 160.

Where to stay
Surin
$$$-$$ Surin Majestic, 99 Chitbamrung Rd, T044-713980, www.surinmajestic.net. Hotel complex next to the bus station. A well-run, friendly hotel with good, large a/c, en suite rooms complemented by balconies. Free internet for guests, fitness centre, pool and English movie channe ls. Recommended.

Yasothon
$$-$ Yod Nakhon, 143 Uthairamrit Rd, T045-711476. Large, featureless but comfortable enough, with, so it is claimed, a 24-hr coffee shop. A/c rooms have TV but no hot water.

Restaurants
Surin
$ Poom Am, end of Tat Mai Lang Rd. 0600-late. Very authentic shophouse diner with an excellent array of Thai food. Recommended.

Ubon there is a good archaeological, historical and cultural **museum** ① *Khuan Thani Rd, Wed-Sun 0900-1600, ฿30*. Erected in 1918 as a palace for King Vajiravudh (Rama VI), the collection includes prehistoric and Khmer artefacts, local textiles and musical instruments.

Elsewhere, **Phra Viharn** (Preah Vihear In Cambodia), a hop south of Ubon – one of the most spectacular Khmer temples ever built – nestles invitingly just across the Cambodian border. Unfortunately, due to a prolonged and deadly armed stand-off between Thai and Cambodian troops the entire complex is off-limits for the foreseeable future. The situation is incredibly fluid so things can change rapidly and it might re-open at short notice. Ask in local TAT offices for up-to-date information. Also remember that large parts of the area surrounding Preah Viharn are now likely to be mined – our and everyone else's advice is not to visit here unless the local authorities say it is safe to do so.

FESTIVALS

Bun bang fai: the northeast's skyrocket festival

Perhaps the northeast's best-known festival is the bun bang fai or skyrocket festival. This is celebrated across the region between May and June, at the end of the dry season, though most fervently in the town of Yasothon. The festival was originally linked to animist beliefs, but became closely associated with Buddhism. The climax of the festival involves the firing of massive rockets into the air to ensure bountiful rain by invoking the rain god Phya Thaen (or, as some people maintain, Phya Thaen), who also has a penchant for fire.

The rockets can be over 4 m long and contain as much as 500 kg of gunpowder. As well as these bang jut rockets, there are also elaborately constructed bang eh rockets which are just for show. Traditionally, the rockets were made of bamboo; now steel and plastic storm pipes are used while specialist rocket-makers, have taken over from the amateurs of the past.

The rockets are mounted on a bamboo scaffold and fired into the air with much cheering, shouting and exchanging of money. Gambling has become part and parcel of the event with bets laid on which rocket will reach the greatest height. The festival is preceded by a procession of monks, dancing troupes and musicians. There is even a beauty contest, Thida bang fai ko, or the Sparkling daughters of the skyrockets.

In the past, bun bang fai was a lewd and wild festival more akin to Rio de Janeiro than Isaan. Men wearing phallic symbols would parade through the village, drunken groups would dance wildly imitating sexual intercourse. At the same time, young boys would be ordained and monks blessed. The governor of Yasothon has banned the use of phallic symbols, regarding them as unfitting for a national event, although he has had a more difficult time trying to outlaw drunkenness.

The temple is orientated north-south along the escarpment, with a sheer drop on one side of 500 m to the Cambodian jungle below. In total, the walkways, courtyards and gates stretch 850 m along the escarpment, climbing 120 m in the process. In places the stairs are cut from the rock itself; elsewhere, they have been assembled from rock quarried and then carted to the site. In total, there are five *gopuras*, numbered I to V from the sanctuary outwards. Multiple *nagas*, *kalas* and *kirtamukhas* decorate these gateways and the balustrades, pediments and pillars that link them. When Prasat Phra Viharn was built is not certain. Much seems to be linked to King Suryavarman I (1002-1050) but there are also inscriptions from the reign of King Suryavarman II (1113-1150).

ISAAN AND THE MEKONG LISTINGS

WHERE TO STAY

Korat and around

$$$ City Park Hotel, 555/55 Mittraphap Rd, www.cityparkhotel-korat.com. Nicely appointed, recently built hotel, just opposite The Mall shopping centre on the main road into town – a good location for transport. The large stylish rooms are some of the best value in town, with a/c, bathtubs, TV and Wi-Fi. Friendly.

$$$ Eco Valley Lodge, 199/16 Moo 8, Nongnamdaeng, Pakchong, T044-249662, www.ecovalleylodge.com. Secluded resort, with simple bungalows and larger 2-bedroom villas with kitchens and dining area. A/c, gardens, restaurant, pool, cultural and nature tours. Pick up from Pak Chong train or bus station is available but costs extra.

$ San Sabai, 335 Suranaree Rd, T08-1547 3066. This small hotel-cum-guesthouse is a real find amongst the bustle of Korat city centre. The owner, a kindly middle-aged English-speaking Thai woman called Tim, has created the best place by far to stay in Korat. There are spotless budget fan rooms (all with colour TV), some with balconies while the large a/c rooms have wooden floors and are nicely decorated. Every room is en suite with hot water. There's a small courtyard to relax in and free Wi-Fi. Excellent value, great location and highly recommended.

Khon Kaen

$$$-$$ Piman Garden, 6/110 Klangmuang Rd, T043-334111, www.pimangarden.com. Tucked away in between a city block in the centre of Khon Kaen, this resort manages to conjure a very tempting space out of almost nothing. 2 lines of earthy-toned rooms, all with balconies and featuring enough luxuries to make your stay more than comfortable, face onto a lush garden area. The staff/owners are very friendly and every room comes with a/c, TV and en suite facilities. Recommended.

Udon Thani

$$$-$$ Much-che Manta Boutique Hotel, 209-211 Mak Khaeng Rd, T042-245222, www.much-chemanta.com. Neat little city-centre hotel with good restaurant and yummy cake shop. The small rooms are a little overpriced but the larger ones are good value, with tiled floors, dark woods, arty touches, a/c, en suite, free Wi-Fi. There's a small pool as well. Recommended.

Nong Khai

$$$-$ Mut Mee Guesthouse, 1111/4 Kaeo Worawut Rd, F042-460717, mutmee@nk.ksc.co.th. Restaurant, large rooms and bungalows, nice garden by the river, good source of information on Laos, bikes for rent. The rooms are well maintained and mostly en suite, with fan and a/c. Also serves reasonable Thai food, though if you want something more authentic, you'll do better eating on the **Nagarina**. Having said that, the bread, cheese and ham are excellent. Owner can also help set up longer-term rentals. Recommended.

$$-$ Siri, 187/1-3 Tha Reua Hai Sok Rd, T042-460969. This collection of excellent bungalows and rooms sited near the river is often booked out. With a very friendly Thai owner, nicely decorated wooden rooms, all with fan or a/c and en suite hot water showers, it's easy to understand why. Excellent value and recommended.

Loei

$$ Loie Villages, Soi 3 17/52 Nokkeaw Rd, T042-833599, www.loievillages.com. Small hotel complex set down a quiet soi in the centre of Loie. Rooms are tastefully decorated with wooden furniture and silks and come with balconies, a/c, TV, hot water and free Wi-Fi. There are some nice public areas, and the staff are knowledgeable and friendly. Excellent value and recommended.

Chiang Khan

$$$-$$ Poonsawasdi, 251/2 Chai Khong Rd, Soi 9, T042-821114, www.poonsawasdi.com. Attractive wooden hotel near the river with arty touches, clean rooms, friendly management, shared bathrooms and a small book collection to help while away the hours. Recommended.

Nakhon Phanom

$$-$ 777 Hometel, 75/4 Bumrungmuang Rd, www.777hometel.com, T042-514777. Fantastic small and very modern hotel located in the centre of Nakhon Phanom in a private and quiet compound. Rooms are cute, with tiled floors, a/c, flat-screen TVs, hot showers and free Wi-Fi. Recommended.

That Phanom

$$$-$$ That Phanom Riverview Hotel, 258 Moo 2, www.thatphanomriverview.com, T042-541555. New in 2011, this is a welcome addition to That Phanom's riverfront. Friendly and well run, the tasteful rooms with tiled floors and a spacious, well-lit feel are by far the best in town. Some have balconies overlooking the river and there is a great restaurant attached. Recommended.

Ubon Ratchathani

$$-$ Phadang Mansion, 126 Phadaeng Rd, T045-254600. An exterior complete with greco-roman columns belies an interior filled with a bizarre and eclectic art reproductions of everything from tacky paintings of chopper motorbikes to Monets. But this is a very friendly place, and the rooms are an excellent deal. All come with a/c, en suite hot showers, Wi-Fi, flat-screen TVs. Eccentric and recommended.

RESTAURANTS

Korat and around

Good Thai and Chinese food to be found by the west gates, near the **Thao Suranari Shrine**, for example. Good *kwaytio* restaurant, close to the corner of Buarong and Jomsurangyaat roads. The **night market** on Manat Rd, open from 1800, has good cheap Thai/Chinese cafés and excellent foodstalls. Suranaree Rd has a good choice of evening street-food stalls.

Khon Kaen

$$$-$$ Smile, 142/44 Robbueng Rd, T043-320777. Big, very popular, open-air restaurant, set by Bueng Kaen Nakhon. Food is pretty good Isaan and Thai.

Udon Thani

$ Rabeang Pochana, 53 Saphakit Janya Rd, T042-241515 (beside the lake). Locals continue to recommend this restaurant as the best in town. Highly recommended.

Nong Khai

$$ Nem Nuang Deng, Soi Thepbanterng opposite **Thasadej Café**, near the river. Open 1000-2200. Good Vietnamese food, including delicious Vietnamese-style spring rolls. Eat in or takeaway. Recommended.
$ Im Em, Soi Bunternjjit. 0600-1400. Very famous local eatery selling Vietnamese pan-fried eggs with sweet sausage breakfasts. Great coffee too. Recommended but come early.

Chiang Khan

Isaan food is excellent in Chiang Khan; a local speciality is live shrimps, fished straight from the Mekong River, served squirming in a spicy marinade of lemon and chilli (*kung ten*) – not for the faint-hearted. There are several riverside restaurants – the best places to eat – with views over to Laos.

Ubon Ratchathani

$ Sam Chai, Palochai Rd – can't be missed as it has 2 giant concrete chickens outside. Open 0900-1900. Excellent grilled chicken, spicy salads and cat fish curries in this large, popular, down-to-earth establishment. Recommended.

DREAM TRIP 3:
Bangkok→Gulf coast and islands→Nakhon Si Thammarat 21 days

Bangkok and around 3 nights, page 33

Phetburi 1 night, page 165
Bus or train from Bangkok (2 hrs)

Hua Hin 2 nights, page 165
Bus or train from Phetburi (2¼ hrs)

Prachuap Khiri Khan 3 nights, page 167
Bus or train from Hua Hin (1½ hrs)

Chumphon and around 2 nights, page 167
Bus from Prachuap Khiri Khan (3½ hrs)

Koh Tao 2 nights, page 170
Boat from Chumphon (1½-2½ hrs)

Koh Phangan 3 nights, page 174
Boat from Koh Tao (1½ hrs)

Koh Samui 2 nights, page 181
Boat from Koh Phangan (50 mins)

Nakhon Si Thammarat, 2 nights, page 190
Boat from Koh Samui to Surat Thani (2½ hrs) then bus (2½-3 hrs)

Bangkok page 33
Flight from Nakhon Si Thammarat (1½ hrs)

DREAM TRIP 3
Bangkok➔Gulf coast and islands➔Nakhon Si Thammarat

Beaches, resorts, national parks and cultured towns garland the length of the Gulf Coast, with the islands offering unbridled hedonism. Phetburi, south of Bangkok, is peppered with wats and a hilltop royal palace affording sweeping views of the plains, while Khao Sam Roi Yod National Park provides a glimpse of the rare dusky langur. Cha-am, Hua Hin and Prachuap Khiri Khan provide old-world charm, excellent spas, some outstanding resorts and fewer tourists.

The appeal of the northern Gulf Coast towns is eclipsed by the delights of Koh Samui, Koh Phangan and Koh Tao. These islands have it all: there are the pampering palaces, appealing resorts, fine dining, streets of thumping bars, action-packed beaches and quiet bays on Koh Samui; meanwhile, once a month on the smaller Koh Phangan, the world's largest outdoor party spins on the sands at Hat Rin when 10,000 people flock to dance and drink in the glow of the full moon. Around the rest of the island, particularly the east coast, the perfect getaways are waiting in cove after cove with sapphire seas tainted only by a glint of granite.

Further north at Koh Tao, the underwater world is an attraction with so many shallow reefs offshore. Around the island remote bays are guarded by huge granite boulder formations and surrounded by perfect tropical seas. At night Hat Sai Ri is enlivened by funky bars and beachfront dining.

The thriving town of Nakhon Si Thammarat, unmuddied by full-scale tourism, offers an opportunity to see the unusual art of shadow puppetry and savour confectioners' delicate pastries.

GULF COAST TO CHUMPHON

The first notable place heading south from Bangkok is the historic town of Phetburi, home to several Ayutthayan-era temples. Another 70 km south is Hua Hin, one of Thailand's premier beach resorts and the destination of choice for generations of Thai royalty. This resort town manages to maintain slightly more character than its bigger rivals, with a virtually intact waterfront of old wooden fishing houses. Further south is the pleasant resort of Prachuap Khiri Khan, with the stunning beach of Ao Manao, and the long, less-developed coast down to Chumphon. Chumpon offers attractions such as kitesurfing and diving but is mainly the launch pad to the island of Koh Tao.

PHETBURI

Getting there and around The train station is about 1.5 km northeast of the town centre. Trains take two hours from Bangkok. The main bus terminal is about 1.5 km west of town, although air-conditioned buses stop near the town centre. Buses take about two hours from Bangkok. Songthaews meet the buses and take passengers into the town centre. The town itself is small enough to explore on foot.

Moving on There are bus (2¼ hours) and train (one hour) connections south to Hua Hin.

Places in Phetburi Phetburi's initial wealth and influence was based upon the coastal salt pans found in the vicinity, and which Thai chronicles record as being exploited as early as the 12th century. It became particularly important during the Ayutthaya period (14th century) and, because the town wasn't sacked by the Burmese, its fine examples of Ayutthayan art and architecture are in good condition. Today, Phetburi is famous for its paid assassins who usually carry out their work with pistols from the backs of motorcycles – don't worry, they don't target tourists.

Situated in the centre of town on Damnoenkasem Road, **Wat Phra Sri Ratana Mahathat** can be seen from a distance. It is dominated by five much-restored, Khmer-style white prangs, probably dating from the Ayutthaya period (14th century). At the western edge of the city is **Phra Nakhon Khiri**, popularly known as **Khao Wang** (Palace on the Mountain), built in 1858 during the reign of Rama IV. Watch out for the monkeys on the hill – it's best not to feed them as they can become very aggressive.

CHA-AM

Halfway between Phetburi and Hua Hin is Ch-am, a beach resort with some excellent hotels and condominiums for wealthy Bangkokians. The beach is a classic stretch of golden sand and the town has a good reputation for its seafood and grilled pork.

HUA HIN

Getting there and around There is a good network of local public transport: songthaews run along fixed routes, there are taxis, tuks-tuks, bicycles and motorbikes. There is a **tourist office** ① *114 Phetkasem Rd, T032-532433, Mon-Fri 0830-2000 (closed 1200-1300).*

Moving on There are buses to Prachuap Khiri Khan (1½ hours).

Places in Hua Hin Thailand's first beach resort, Hua Hin, has had an almost continuous royal connection since the late 19th century. In 1868, King Mongkut journeyed to Hua Hin to observe a total eclipse of the sun. In 1910, Prince Chakrabongse, brother of Rama VI, visited Hua Hin on a hunting trip and was so enchanted by the area that he built himself a villa. Until his current bout of ill-health, the reigning monarch used to spend most of his time here too. These days, however, the olde-worlde charm that was once Hua Hin's unique selling point is all but lost – it's now a thriving resort town, packed with massage parlours, tourist shops and Western restaurants and bars. The suburbs are filled with condominiums and holiday villas, the sounds of drills and construction work are never far away, and the area is studded with high-end hotels. These luxury places are some of the best in Thailand, if not the world, and are a big draw for many visitors, especially older travellers and families. One of them, the Sofitel Centara hotel, is housed in what used to

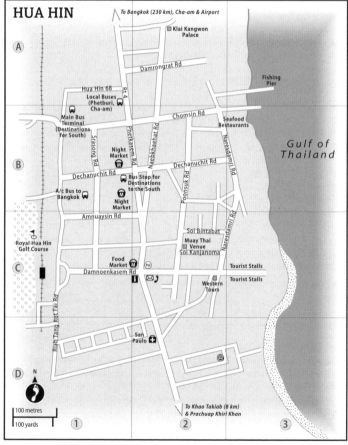

HUA HIN

To Bangkok (230 km), Cha-am & Airport

Klai Kangwon Palace

Damrongrat Rd

Fishing Pier

Hua Hin 68
Local Buses (Phetburi, Cha-am)

Chomsin Rd

Main Bus Terminal (Destinations for South)

Seafood Restaurants

Gulf of Thailand

Phetkasem Rd

Srasong Rd

Naebkhaehat Rd

Night Market

Dechanuchit Rd

Dechanuchit Rd

Naresdamri Rd

Poonsuk Rd

Bus Stop for Destinations to the South

A/c Bus to Bangkok

Night Market

Amnuaysin Rd

Soi Bintabat

Royal Hua Hin Golf Course

Muay Thai Venue
Soi Kanjanoma

Food Market

Tourist Stalls

Damnoenkasem Rd

Tourist Stalls

Western Tours

Rlab Tang Rot Fai Rd

San Paulo

N

To Khao Takiab (8 km) & Prachuap Khiri Khan

100 metres
100 yards

1   2   3

be the **Railway Hotel**. Built in 1923 by a Thai prince, Purachatra, who headed the State Railways of Thailand, it was renovated in 1986. Other spots that hint at Hua Hin's early charm include the railway station, with its quaint Royal Waiting Room, and the waterfront.

As Hua Hin is billed as a beach resort many people come here expecting a beautiful beach, but that isn't quite the case. Many of the nicest stretches of sand are in front of hotels (don't forget that all beaches in Thailand are public), and further south. Away from the shore, there's a popular night market and myriad attractions only a short drive away to explore, including golf courses, temples, wineries and two national parks: Kaeng Kachan to the west, and coastal reserve Sam Roi Yot to the south. The biggest tourist-lurer in town right now is the hokey (but admittedly very photogenic) faux-wooden shophouse village, **Plearn Wan** ① *Phetkasem Rd (between Soi 38 and 40), T032-520311, www.plearnwan.com*. Over on Soi Moobaan Huana, there's now a slick modern arts complex, the **Vic Hua Hin** ① *www.vichuahin.com*. Founded by Miss Patravadi Mejudho, the Thai actress and arts impresario behind Bangkok's Patravadi Theatre, it hosts art classes and weekend shops as well as weekly performances of often quite avant garde contemporary theatre. Hua Hin's staid shopping scene has also been given a bohemian shot in the arm by the Cicada Market, located on the southern outskirts (near the Hyatt Regency Hua Hin hotel). Resembling a public park, this atmospherically lit open-air night market hums with arts and crafts stalls, art galleries and live music every Friday, Saturday and Sunday from 1600 to 2300.

PRACHUAP KHIRI KHAN

This is a small and peaceful resort with a long walled seafront. The town is more popular with Thais than with *farangs* and has a reputation for good seafood. There are buses to Chumphon (3½ hours). At the northern end of town is **Khao Chong Krachok** where an exhausting 20-minute climb – past armies of aggressive, preening monkeys – is rewarded with fine views. **Ao Manao**, 5 km south of town, is one of best beaches on this stretch of coast. A gently sloping slice of sand is fringed by refreshing woodlands and framed by distant islands. Ao Manao is situated in the middle of a military base and development is strictly controlled; you'll find good, cheap Thai food and other facilities. To get there, take a motorbike taxi or tuk-tuk (฿30).

CHUMPHON

Chumphon is considered the 'gateway to the south'. The bus station is 15 km away; it costs ฿200 per person in a taxi to get from there into Chumphon, or take a local bus or songthaew. There isn't much to see in the town itself, but there are good beaches and islands nearby. There are also excellent diving opportunities, with dive sites around the islands of **Koh Ngam Noi** (parcelled out to concessionaires) and **Koh Ngam Yai**. **Hat Thung Wua Laen**, 18 km north of Chumphon, is a beautiful beach that turns into something of a mecca for kite-surfers from November to January. To get to the beach, take a songthaew (฿20) from the market in Chumphon.

Moving on Lomprayah's high-speed catamarans, www.lomprayah.com, use the Thung Makham Noi Pier in Chumphon and offer the quickest connection to Koh Tao (1½ hours), as well as Koh Samui or Koh Phangnan. **Songserm**, www.songserm-expressboat.com, offers a slower (and cheaper) service (2½ hours) that leaves from the nearest pier and carries on to Samui and Phangan. A night boat sails several times a week.

GULF COAST TO CHUMPHON LISTINGS

WHERE TO STAY

Phetburi
$$$-$$ Royal Diamond Hotel, 555 Phetkasem Rd, T032-411061, www.royaldiamond hotel.com. Luxurious hotel compared to most others in Phetburi. The 58 rooms have a/c. The restaurant does a range of international food. There's a beer garden and pleasant, peaceful atmosphere. Internet access.

Cha-am
$$$-$$ Dee-Lek, 225/30-33, Ruamchit Rd, T032-470548. Friendly little guesthouse on the main beach road. The pricier rooms have nice balconies overlooking the beach and all have hot water, TV and a/c. Clean and tidy, if a little dull. Also serve decent food. Recommended.

Hua Hin
$$$$ Evason Hua Hin Resort and Spa, 9 Paknampran Beach, Prachuap Khiri Khan, T032-618200, www.six-senses.com. About 20 km south of Hua Hin (not far from Pranburi) is this stylish resort, set in spacious grounds with a beautiful pool. It is hard to beat for anyone wanting to 'get away from it all'. Light and airy rooms, furnished with contemporary, locally produced furniture. Some more expensive villas have private plunge pools. The groundbreaking Earth Spa, located in conical naturally cooled mud huts, provides the last word in pampering. Other (complimentary) facilities, include watersports (sailing, kayaking), tennis courts, a gym and archery. Low-season prices are good value. Recommended.
$$$-$$ Araya, 15/1 Chomsin Rd, T032-531130, www.araya-residence.com. Officially this is a small apartment block that offers monthly and annual rates, however it also offers rooms by the night and, while it's not the cheapest, it's excellent value. The rooms are comfy and spacious, with contemporary design and art. It's friendly and in a great location. Highly recommended.

Prachuap Khiri Khan
$$$-$$ Sun Beach Guesthouse, 60 Chaitalae Rd, T032-604770, www. sunbeach-guesthouse.com. Brand new property on the seafront with a pool. Each en suite room is comfortably fitted out and has a/c and balcony, though the 'sea view' claim is a bit tenuous. Friendly atmosphere.

Chumphon
$$$-$ Baan Tanaya, 16 Moo 8, T08-9592 7382. A/c, en suite rooms, each with a small balcony, open directly onto a nice stretch of the beach. Run by a friendly family who speak little English, but serve some pretty good Thai food. Recommended.
$$$-$ Chumphon Gardens, 66/1 Tha Tapao Rd, T077-506888. New hotel in central location, but set back a little from the road, so quiet. The cheaper rooms are excellent value: clean, with TV, en suite. Recommended.

RESTAURANTS

Phetburi
Phetburi is well known for its desserts including *khanom mo kaeng* (a hard custard made of mung bean, egg, coconut and sugar, baked over an open fire), *khao kriap* (a pastry with sesame, coconut and sugar) and excellent *kluai khai* (sweet bananas). There are several restaurants along Phetkasem Rd selling Phetburi desserts.

Cha-am
There are plenty of seafood restaurants along Ruamchit Rd. On the road into town from the highway you'll find dozens of places selling excellent grilled pork and Isaan-style food.
$ Moo Hang Nai Wang, almost opposite the KS golf sign on the road in from the highway. This small shack, with Thai

signage only, is arguably the best purveyor of authentic Isaan food on this stretch. Succulent grilled pork and chicken come with superlative, spicy papaya salad and filling sticky rice. It might require a bit of asking but this place is highly recommended.

Hua Hin

Good seafood is widely available, particularly at the northern end of Naresdamri Rd. Most of the fish comes straight from the boats. Try the old central market, Chat Chai, on Petchkasem Rd between Soi 70 and 72, for breakfast. The neighbouring night market is packed full of enticing Thai food, as well as seafood so fresh that they have to tie the crabs' and lobsters' pincers shut. All the top-end hotels have decent restaurants, too.

$$ Chao Lay, 15 Naresdamri Rd, T032-513436. Daily 1000-2200. This stilted building jutting out into the sea has 2 decks and is a great place to watch the sunset. Fruits of the sea, including steamed squid, huge seabass, rock lobster and prawns, are served up with military precision. Hugely popular with Thais.

$ Jeak Peak, on the corner of Naebkhaehat and Dechanuchit rds. This small shophouse is one of Hua Hin's most famous noodle shops. It has been in the same location for 63 years and has lots of old world charm. Renowned for seafood noodles and pork satay, it's often packed, but the queues are worth it. Recommended.

Prachuap Khiri Khan

Prachuap is famous for its seafood and there are excellent restaurants in the centre of town and along the seafront. If you venture to Ao Manao there are plenty of small places selling very good Thai food.

$$-$ Plern Samut, seafront next to the Hadthong Hotel, T032-611115. Daily 0900-2200. The very friendly owner, Khun Narong, and his family have been running this place for over 30 years. It's one of the most famous restaurants in town and serves awesome food, including divine squid and prawn. It's in a great location, too, with outside seating looking over the bay. Highly recommended.

Chumphon

$ Lanna Han Isaan, set near the railway tracks in a cute garden. Delicious, cheap Isaan food that is very popular with locals. The food here is very spicy so ask for *pet nit noi* (a little spicy).

WHAT TO DO

Hua Hin
Kitesurfing

With year round gusts and fairly calm seas, the beach at Hua Hin is fast becoming the premium kitesurfing location in the country; a Kitesurfing World Cup was held here in 2010 and 2011. The organizer, Kiteboarding Asia (T08-1591 4593, www.kiteboardingasia.com), has branches in Hua Hin, as well as further down the Gulf coastline at Pranburi and Chumphon.

Chumphon
Diving

Easy Divers, Ta Taphao Rd, T077-570085, www.chumphoneasydivers.net.

Takes divers to sites around the 41 islands off Chumphon.

Nereides Diving & Sailing Centre, T077-505451, nereidesthailand@yahoo.com. Located on Hat Thung Wua Lean beach, this small, French-run dive shop organize tailor-made trips to most of the nearby dive sites, as well fishing tours and boat rental.

Kitesurfing

Kite Thailand, next to Seabeach Bungalows, Chumphon, T08-1090 3730 (mob), T08-9970 1797 (mob), www.kitethailand.com. At the moment, this friendly Dutch operator is the only place offering classes in this fast-growing sport.

KOH TAO

Koh Tao, the smallest of the three famous islands in the Gulf of Thailand, is a big dive and snorkelling centre with plenty of shallow coral beds and tropical fish. The waters – especially in the south and east – are stunning, a marbling of turquoise blue, sapphire, emerald and seaweed green. For non-divers this small island offers a surprisingly high number of exceptionally well-designed, independent upmarket resorts, with the added bonus of quiet beach life by day and fairly sophisticated nightlife. The name Koh Tao, translated as 'turtle island', relates to the shape of the island.

→ARRIVING ON KOH TAO

GETTING AROUND

There is just one surfaced road on Koh Tao, which runs from the north end of Sai Ri to Chalok Ban Kao, passing through Ban Mae Hat. Motorbike taxis and pickups are the main form of local transport. These can be found just north of the dock next to the exchange booth. They operate from dawn to 2300; rates tend to double after dark. Motorbikes, jeeps and bicycles are available for hire. Long-tailed boats can be chartered to reach more remote beaches and coves, either by the trip, hour or day.

MOVING ON

There are boats of various speeds and sizes connecting Koh Tao with Koh Phangan. **Lomprayah** run boats at 0930 and 1500, one hour, ฿450; **Songserm**, T077-456274, boats leave at 1000, 1½ hours, ฿400; and **Seatran** has services at 0930 and 1500, one hour, ฿400.

TOURIST INFORMATION

The **TAT** office on Koh Samui, see page 183, is responsible for Koh Tao as there is no office on the island. The website, www.kohtao.com, provides lots of information, or see the free quarterly *Koh Tao Info* magazine, www.kohtaoinfo.tv.

Avoid bringing any plastic bottles or tin cans to the island as these are difficult to dispose of. Some environmentalists advise people to drink cans rather than bottles of beer as few businesses find it economically viable to recycle bottles and simply dump them. In addition, due to reduced rainfall in recent years, water is now a great problem on the island, and much of it is imported from the mainland. Visitors should use it sparingly.

→BACKGROUND

The accessibility of interesting marine life at depths available to beginners, the fairly gentle currents and the relatively low costs all contribute to making Koh Tao a particularly good place to learn to dive. The presence of giant manta rays and whale sharks (plankton feeders which can reach 6 m) means that more experienced divers will also find something of interest here. With these attractions in its favour, Koh Tao's reputation as a good, low-cost dive centre has grown rapidly, and in the space of just 10 years the island has made the transition from backwater to mainstream destination. While most people come here for the swimming, snorkelling and diving – as well as beach life – the fact that most paths are not vehicle-friendly makes the island walker-friendly and there are some good trails to explore. Land-based wildlife includes monitor lizards, fruit bats and various non-venomous snakes. For walks it is worth purchasing V Honsombud's *Guide Map of Koh Phangan & Koh Tao*.

The harbour is at the island's main village of **Ban Mae Hat**. On both sides of the harbour there are small beaches with a few resorts. These areas have easy access to the town. There are numerous shops from fashion boutiques to bookstores and supermarkets and some of the best restaurants as well as a burgeoning nightlife, post office, money exchanges, dive shops, tour operators, transport and foodstalls. To the north of Ban Mae Hat on the west coast, is the white-sand curved beach of **Hat Sai Ri**. Stretching to around 2 km, it is the longest beach on the island, the sweep of sand is only interrupted by the occasional large boulder. It has the widest range of accommodation, and many restaurants, shops, dive centres and bars. Although it is a bustling beach with some great bars, the debris – plastic bottles, rotting wood and the like – left by the retreating tide is really unsightly.

The little cove of **Ao Mamuang** on the north coast is only accessible by boat so it remains quiet and unfrequented. It is a great place for solitude and there is some good snorkelling.

Off the northwest coast of Koh Tao is **Koh Nang Yuan**. Once a detention centre for political prisoners, this privately owned island consists of three peaks and three connecting sandbars, making it a mini-archipelago. It's surrounded by crystal-clear water and some wonderful coral. Lomprayah runs boats to the island at 1030, 1500 and 1800, returning at 0830, 1330 and 1630.

Ao Hin Wong is a peaceful bay on the east coast with fantastic views but no beach. However, you can swim off the rocks and boulders and there is some great snorkelling – turtles have been spotted here. The accommodation consists of simple huts tumbling down the steep hillsides.

South of Ao Hin Wong, the bay of **Ao Mao** has just one resort and some great snorkelling, particularly at the **Laem Thian** pinnacle. It is among the more remote and secluded places to stay on Koh Tao. Continuing south, the bay of **Ao Ta Not** is served by a poor road but vehicles brave the conditions to ferry guests. This is one of the more remote bays and it has a good beach. Although it is not as pretty as Hin Wong, it is wider, has boulders, and more facilities, more expensive accommodation, restaurants, watersports and scuba-diving.

Lang Khaai Bay is littered with dozens of boulders which are reached from a steep slope. The bay is good for snorkelling but there is only a tiny slither of beach.

The beach at **Ao Leuk** shelves more steeply than most of the others around Koh Tao and so is good for swimming and has some of the best snorkelling on the island. This is a quiet beach in spite of visiting groups.

Next to Ao Chalok Ban Kao on the south coast, **Ao Thian Ok**, also known as Shark Bay, is a beautiful, privately owned bay with the **Jamahkiri Spa and Resort** set on one hillside. The sea is a stunning mix of blues and greens while the attractive beach is lined with a strip of coconut palms. The bay is known for the black-tip reef sharks that congregate here. The area of **Taa Toh** 'lagoon' is on the south coast and consists of three beaches, the largest of which is **Hat Taa Toh Yai**. There is good snorkelling on the far side of the lagoon from Hat Taa Toh Yai with reef sharks and more. There is easy access from here to Chalok Ban Kao. **Ao Chalok Ban Kao** is a gently shelving beach, enclosed within a horseshoe bay on the south coast capped with weirdly shaped giant boulders. It has a good range of accommodation, restaurants and nightlife. This large bay also has the highest concentration of diving resorts. **Hat Sai Nuan** is a quiet, isolated bay, only accessible by long-tailed boat or by a pleasant 30-minute walk around the hilly headland. There are just a handful of places to stay and a relaxed atmosphere. It is arguably the best spot on the island.

KOH TAO LISTINGS

WHERE TO STAY

$$$$ Sensi Paradise, T077-456244, www.
sensiparadise.com. A great range of rooms.
At the top of the price range the buildings
are sensitively designed wooden affairs
with traditional Thai architectural features
and are incredibly romantic. The garden
is also richly planted and the small bay
behind the resort is truly idyllic. The pretty
beach in front is tiny with several boulders.

$$$$-$$ Koh Tao Royal Resort, T077-
456156, kohtaoroyal@hotmail.com. Smart,
well-maintained wood and bamboo
bungalows. Cheaper rooms climb the hill
behind the beach. Lively restaurant in a great
location. It has a reasonable secluded beach.

$$ Bohemia Resort, T08-7906 5619,
www.bohemia-resort.com. Run by a
friendly Swiss and Italian couple who
speak 6 languages between them, this
intimate resort is a true labour of love.
About 10 mins' walk from the beach, the
4 Thai-style cottages each have a mini
fridge, electric kettle, fan and mosquito
net. Bathrooms are half open air. Stunning
views. Recommended, particularly for the
environmentally conscious.

$$-$ Blue Wind Bakery and Resort, T077-
456116, bluewind_wa@yahoo.com. A small,
friendly and attractive place with excellent
value fan and a/c rooms and a charming
beach restaurant. Pretty wood bungalows
nestled in a beautiful mature garden. Their
bakery serves pastries, pasta and ice cream.
Daily yoga classes. Recommended.

$$-$ Diamond Resort, 40/7 Aow Tanote,
T077-456591. The cheaper rooms are
excellent value; they have cold water
showers and are fan only but are very
comfortable and spacious with plenty
of windows. Homely feel. Next to a very
quiet beach. Restaurant, with others within
walking distance. Recommended.

$$-$ Nice Moon Bungalows, T077-456737,
nicemoon43@hotmail.com. About 200 m
south of the beach on cliffs overlooking the
bay. Free snorkelling equipment, friendly and
informative. Restaurant serves delicious Thai
food. Recommended.

RESTAURANTS

$$$ Thipwimarn Restaurant, on the
northwest headland, T077-456409,
www.thipwimarnresort.com. 0700-2200.
This has become one of the more popular
spots for fashionable dining due to the
stunning views over Sai Ri bay and excellent
Thai food and seafood. Free pickup.

$$ Taraporn Bar & Restaurant, across the
slatted walkway at the west of the beach.
Seating on hammocks, cushions and mats
on the floor. The restaurant itself is on stilts
above the sea. A great venue.

$ Pranee's Kitchen, Mae Hat Sq. 0800-late.
More authentic Thai food than the Koh Tao
norm, served in an open-sided hardwood
sala with cushion or table seating.

WHAT TO DO

Diving

Diving is popular year round here. It is said to be the cheapest place in Thailand to learn to dive, and the shallow waters and plenty of underwater life, make it an easy and interesting place to do so. There's a **recompression chamber** in Ban Mae Hat (**Badalveda**, opposite the main petrol station on the island, north up the main road and turn right, T077-456 661 (main office), T08-1081 9777 (24-hr emergency number), www.sssnetwork.com.

Dive schools have an arrangement where they charge roughly the same for an **Open Water** course (฿9000). Fixed prices also apply to other courses: ฿8500 for **Advanced**, and ฿9500 for rescue. What varies are the sizes of the groups and the additional perks such as a free dive or free/subsidized accommodation. A discover scuba dive is around ฿3000, and a fun-dive for qualified divers is around ฿1800, although the more dives you do the cheaper each dive becomes. All schools accept credit cards. If you are considering diving but want to watch the divers in action before making the investment, many of the dive schools are prepared to take you out to dive sites with their groups. You only pay for the snorkelling equipment.

Asia Divers, Ban Mae Hat, T077-456054, www.asia-divers.com.
Ban's, Hat Sai Ri, T077-456466, www.amazingkohtao.com.
Big Blue, 17/18 Moo 1, Hat Sa Ri, T077-456415, www.bigbluediving.com. Fully-fledged dive resort.
Big Bubble, Chalok Ban Kao, T077-456669, www.tauchen-diving.de.
Buddha View Dive Resort, Chalok Ban Kao, T077-456074, www.buddhaview-diving.com.
Calypso Diving, Ao Ta Not, T077-456745, eugentao@yahoo.de.
Crystal Dive Resort, Ban Mae Hat and Sai Ri, T077-456107, www.crystaldive.com.
Easy Divers, Ban Mae Hat, T077-456010, www.thaidive.com.
Kho Tao Divers, Hat Sai Ri, T08-6069 9244 (mob), kohtaodivers@hotmail.com.
Planet Scuba, Ban Mae Hat, T077-456110, www.planet-scuba.net.
Scuba Junction, Sai Ri Beach, T077-456164, www.scuba-junction.com.
Sunshine Divers, Chalok Ban Kao, T077-456597, www.sunshine-diveresort.com.

KOH PHANGAN

Koh Phangan is Southeast Asia's party island. World renowned for the Full Moon Party, it attracts thousands of young people looking for the night of their life on the sands at Hat Rin, the most developed part of the island. The pace of development on the island has been rapid. Although still unspoilt in part, in the main it is not as beautiful as parts of Koh Samui and Koh Tao, although the beaches at Hat Rin and some along the east coast are attractive and – except for Hat Rin – uncrowded. The water is good for snorkelling, particularly during the dry season when clarity is at its best. Boats leave from Thong Sala, the island's main town, for nearby Ang Thong Marine National Park (see page 184). Between May and September the tide is out all day between Mae Hat and Hat Rin. Fishing and coconut production remain mainstays of the economy, and villages still have a traditional air – although tourism is now by far the largest single industry.

→ARRIVING ON KOH PHANGAN

GETTING THERE

Minibus taxis meet the boats and take people from Thong Sala pier to Hat Rin for ฿150 and to Thong Nai Pan for ฿200.

GETTING AROUND

Koh Phangan stretches 15 km north to south and 10 km east to west. The main settlement is Thong Sala. Thong Sala and Hat Rin are connected by a paved road. Two roads run between Thong Sala and Ao Chao Lok Lum: the west coast route and the one through the centre of the island. Around the remainder of the island there is a limited network of poor roads and tracks, and the stretch from Ban Khai to Hat Rin is steep and treacherous and inadvisable for anything but a 4WD during the rainy season. The number of accidents is huge.

There are some parts of Koh Phangan that are difficult or impossible to access by road, especially during the wet season. It is possible to travel by boat, though this convenience comes at a cost. Longtail boats are the most common way to navigate Koh Phangan's waters, and are available from all main beaches. As a general guide, they leave Hat Rin to: Thong Sala, ฿1500; Hat Thian, ฿600; Thong Nai Pan, ฿1800; Bottle Beach, ฿2000. You can also charter the boats on full day trips starting from around ฿3000, depending on which/how many beaches you would like to visit. Be aware that these prices are for the whole boat, so the larger the group the lower the cost per person. Also note that the prices are only a guide of what is reasonable to pay – be prepared to bargain hard to get these fares. Speed boats are also available to charter, and while significantly faster, will cost about three times as much as a longtail.

Motorbikes and mountain bikes are available for hire, and the most appealing areas to ride are in the north and west of the island, which are flat. *Songthaews* run from the pier to any of the bays served by road. A trip to Hat Rin from Thong Sala is ฿80-100. The cost to the other bays depends on how many people are going with you. At Hat Rin *songthaews* wait close to the **Drop in Club Resort** between Hat Rin East and West. For a few beaches walking is the best option.

MOVING ON

The ferry *Haad Rin Queen*, T077-375113, sails from Hat Rin direct to Big Buddha pier on Koh Samui at 0930, 1140, 1430 and 1730, 50 minutes, ฿200. From Thong Sala there are departures to Koh Samui with **Songserm**, T077-377704, to Nathon pier on Koh Samui at 0700 and 1230, ฿200; with **Lomprayah**, T077-238411, www.lomprayah.com, to Mae Nam beach at 1100 and 1600, and to Nathon at 0715 and 1200, ฿300; with **Seatran**, T077-238679, to Big Buddha pier at 1100 and 1630, ฿250, and with **Speed Boat Line** to Bophut at 0600, 0930, 1300 and 1530, 20 minutes.

TOURIST INFORMATION

There is no official tourist information on the island. The **TAT** on Koh Samui, see page 183, is responsible for the island. See www.kohphangan.com and www.phangan. info, for information.

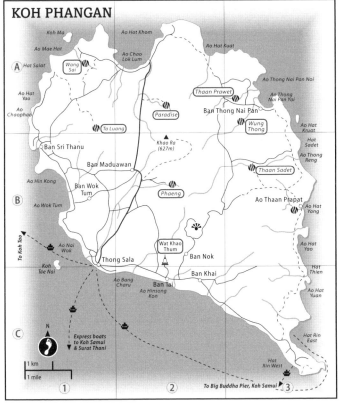

SAFETY

Like other places in Thailand, Koh Phangan has its own annoyances and dangers, particularly from violent crime. On 1 January 2013 a British national was killed here and it's worth checking out the latest advice on www.fco.gov.uk before travelling.

→AROUND THE ISLAND

Koh Phangan offers natural sights such as waterfalls, forests, coral and viewpoints but little of historical or cultural interest. Sometimes the best way to explore the island is on foot, following tracks that link the villages and beaches, which cannot be negotiated by *songthaew* or motorbike. It is possible to walk on a trail from Hat Rin up the east coast to Hat Thien, although other paths are swiftly swallowed up by the forest.

Although it's possible to navigate the roads by motorbike, first-timers should think seriously before heading southeast to Hat Rin, as the roads are often at a 40° gradient which makes them treacherous at best and a death trap when wet. The high number of walking wounded is testimony to the danger of these hilly roads.

THONG SALA AND AROUND

The main town of Koh Phangan is the port of Thong Sala (pronounced Tong-sala) where most boats from Koh Samui, Surat Thani and Koh Tao dock. Thong Sala has banks, ATMs, telephone, internet access, travel agents, a small supermarket, dive shops, motorbike hire and a second-hand bookstore. Humming during the day with all the departures and arrivals, this can be a bit of a ghost town during the evenings, although it's a pleasant place to spend the night, with some good restaurants.

On the coast to the east of Thong Sala, outside Ban Tai, is **Wat Khao Tum** and the **Vipassana Meditation Centre** ① *all-inclusive fees are ฿4500 for 10 days, contact Wat Khao Tum, Koh Phangan, Surat Thani, for more information, or www.watkowtahm.org, where they provide a contact and booking facility*. There are views from the hilltop wat to Samui and the Ang Thong Islands. Ten-day meditation courses are held every month with 20-day courses and three-month retreats also available. All the courses are conducted in English and taught by Australian-US couple Rosemary and Steve Weissman who have been here since 1988.

THE INTERIOR

Phaeng Waterfall is to be found in the interior of the island, about 4.5 km from Thong Sala and 2 km from the village of Maduawan. The walk east to Hat Sadet runs parallel to a river along which are three waterfalls and the carved initials of several Thai kings who visited here, including King Chulalongkorn (Rama V), who was so enamoured that he reportedly came here on 10 occasions between 1888 and 1909, and the present King Bhumibol (Rama IX), who came in 1962. The waterfalls can be reached on foot or on mountain bikes. Other waterfalls include **Ta Luang** and **Wang Sai** in the northwest corner, **Paradise** in the north (near the **Paradise Resort**), and **Thaan Prawet** and **Wung Thong** in the northeast corner. The highest point is **Khao Ra** (627 m). A path runs to the summit although visitors have reported that the trail is indistinct and a guide is necessary.

SOUTH COAST

The stretch of beach from **Ao Bang Charu** to **Ao Hinsong Kon** is unpopular with visitors due to its proximity to Thong Sala and as a result accommodation is good value and bungalows are well spread out and quiet. The beach shelves gently and is good for children, but the water is a little murky.

The beach between **Ban Tai** and **Ban Khai** may not be as good as at Hat Rin and there is a lot of wood debris about, but this is more than made up for by cheaper accommodation and less noise. Some snorkelling and good swimming is possible and it is generally quiet, although on the monthly black moon parties the beach comes alive with techno beats. The area is also well-located for the twice-monthly half moon parties in the nearby jungle and the Wat Po herbal sauna. In July and August the tide is out all day.

HAT RIN

Hat Rin is home to the world-famous Full Moon Parties when thundering bass-lines rock the beach and the streets are awash with alcohol. There are also Half Moon Parties, Black Moon Parties, Pre-Full Moon Parties – in fact any excuse for a party – on the beach so it has become famous for the almighty blow outs.

Hat Rin is at the southeastern tip of Koh Phangan and has the best and most popular beach on the island with some good snorkelling. It also has the greatest concentration of bungalows which are packed close together (except on the hillsides). The 'east' beach, **Hat Rin Nok**, is more attractive and is cleaned every morning. During the day it is packed with sunbathers, coloured blow-up lilos, a small number of hawkers, volleyball nets, and the water is crammed with long-tailed boats. The 'west' beach, **Hat Rin Nai**, is smaller and almost non-existent at high tide; accommodation is slightly cheaper here. The two beaches, less than 10 minutes' walk apart, are both wonderfully quiet until about 1300, as most people are sleeping off the night's excesses. At night the noise from generators and the bars can be overpowering on Hat Rin Nok but a few minutes' walk away from the action towards Hat Rin Nai, the music, incredibly, is inaudible – this applies on full moon nights too. Theft has become a real problem in the area, use safety deposit boxes for valuables and secure bungalows with extra locks wherever possible – especially when sleeping.

EAST COAST

These beaches and coves form **Hat Thien to Hat Sadet** are only accessible by boat. The stretch of stony coastline at Hat Thien doesn't afford much for those hoping to lie and fry, but its rocky, tree-lined character makes it an attractive and rugged area. It's not a bad option at all: there are cheap guesthouses and it's possible to walk over the headland to Hat Yuan where the beautiful and popular white-sand beach is much more palatable to sun worshippers.

Ao Thong Nai Pan Noi and **Ao Thong Nai Pan Yai** is a double bay boasting some of the most beautiful, quiet, white-sand beaches on the island, romantically hemmed in by the mountains and with among the highest recurring visitor rates. The attractive beach is topped by boulders at its northern end, hiding the enormous Santhiya resort spread up the hill beyond. Yai has more palms leaning over the beach and so is slightly more picturesque than Noi, but Noi has a wider beach and is a bit more bustling. There are several shops, ATMs and bars behind Noi beach and bikes can be rented. There's also internet, snorkel gear and kayaks for hire on the beach. It is said to have been Rama V's favourite beach on the island, and it's not hard to see why – plenty of people come here for a short holiday and end up staying for months. It remains fairly off the beaten tourist track and is more a place to relax for those whose main aim is not to party. The journey by truck from Thong Sala takes almost an hour and the road is muddy in the rainy season, but it does take you through untouched jungle and so is quite an experience. It is also possible to get a boat from Hat Rin which is much more comfortable.

NORTH COAST

About 5 km northwest of Thong Nai Pan, **Ao Hat Kuat**, more commonly known by its English translation 'Bottle Beach', is even more isolated, with a beautiful beach. Despite developing a reputation as a bit of a British ghetto and a huge new development here, it retains its escapist appeal.

Along a rutted track, **Ao Hat Khom** is another relaxed place and many stay for weeks. The bay is fringed by a reef offering some of the best snorkelling on Phangan, however, because the seabed shelves gently, swimming is sometimes only really possible at high tide and getting out to the reef can be tricky.

Ao Chao Lok Lum is a deep, sheltered bay on Koh Phangan's north coast. There is now an excellent road from Thong Sala to here and this fishing village is gradually developing into a quiet, comparatively refined resort, with the best part of the beach being to the east. In the village of Ban Chao Lok Lum there are bikes and diving equipment for rent. There's also a 7-11 shop and an ATM.

Hat Salat is one of the most peaceful parts of the island, though due to its picturesque bay it is also one of the fastest-developing spots. **Ao Mae Hat** has a super beach with a sandy bank extending outwards and along which it is possible to walk to Koh Ma when it hasn't rained for some time. There are palm trees, a few bungalows and good snorkelling.

WEST COAST

Ao Hat Yao is an attractive curved, clean beach on the west coast with good swimming and snorkelling, 20 minutes by *songthaew* from Thong Sala. Bungalows are spread out and quiet.

To the south of Ao Hat Yao, **Ao Chaophao** is a relatively quiet and undeveloped bay with just a handful of places to stay. The perfect crescent of sand and sunsets make the bay particularly attractive. There is also good swimming because the seabed shelves steeply before reaching the reef around 100 m offshore where there is good snorkelling. At the southern end is an attractive lagoon and the coast here also has some remnant mangroves.

Ao Sri Thanu is a long but rather narrow beach, 15 minutes by *songthaew* from Thong Sala. It is a peaceful spot to spend a few days and is sparsely settled but is not very attractive. Behind the beach is a freshwater lake fringed by pine trees which is ideal for swimming.

North of Thong Sala and south of Ban Sri Thanu, the beaches at **Ao Wok Tum** are average and the swimming is poor. Accommodation is good value though.

North of Thong Sala and south of Ban Sri Thanu, the beaches between **Ao Hin Kong** and **Ao Nai Wok** aren't particularly striking and swimming is difficult as the seabed shelves so gently. However, it is quite attractive with shallow boulders near **Cookies** and it is not rocky underfoot for the first 10 m or so. Accommodation is good value.

KOH PHANGAN LISTINGS

WHERE TO STAY

$$$$-$$$ Chaloklum Bay T077-374147-8, www.chaloklumbay.com. Attractive beach-front bungalows on stilts with a/c and hot water or fan. There are also a couple of large, attractive beach houses for groups or families.

$$$$-$$$ Tommy Resort, T077-375215, www.phangantommyresort.com. All signs of Tommy's backbacker past have been removed as the resort goes upmarket, now boasting 22 pleasant traditional-style bungalows near the beach that have TV, fridges and hot water. Even the once dingy restaurant has had a facelift, and is now overlooking the water.

$$$-$$ Charm Beach Resort, T077-377165, www.charm-beach-resort-phangan.com. The bungalows are well laid out and the most expensive are a/c. The cheap rooms, which are bamboo and thatch huts, are particularly good value but often full. Also has a tree-house room with beach views. The restaurant serves Thai and European food. Swimming pool.

$$$-$$ Phangnan Rainbow, 25/3 Moo 4, T077-238236, www.rainbowbungalows.com. Very comfortable fan and a/c rooms with high-quality furnishings. The cheapest bungalows have a shared bathroom. Location and size determines the price, some have a sea view. Very friendly family fun resort. Restaurant. Make sure the taxi driver takes you to Bankai Beach and not Hat Hin, where there is another resort of the same name. Recommended.

$$$-$$ Sandy Bay, 54/1 Moo 8, T077-349119, www.sandybaybungalows.com. A good selection of smart spacious a/c and traditional fan bungalows on the beach. All are kept clean and have large verandas with hammocks or varnished wood furniture. This is a popular place with tables and chairs on the sand and the best restaurant on the beach which mainly serves cheap Thai food. Kayaking and island trips offered. Movies shown. Haad Yao Divers attached. Recommended.

$$-$ Cookies, Ao Plaay Laem, T077-377499, cookies_bungalow@hotmail.com. 30 attractive bamboo bungalows, set in a green garden with a small splash pool. Some have shared bathroom, some have a/c and DVD players. The restaurant has a raised platform and the beach is secluded and attractive. Run by the friendly Aom and An. The watersports club offers windsurfing, kayaking and laser boats. Recommended.

$$-$ Lighthouse Bungalows, T077-375075, www.lighthousebungalows.com. This great place is a 20-min walk from Hat Rin on the western side of the headland. It is reached by a long romantic wooden causeway around the rocks to the bungalows. The staff are friendly and helpful and there's a sociable restaurant, which is an excellent place to make friends before the full moon madness. The sunsets are fantastic. Recommended.

$ Dolphin Bungalows, Bar & Restaurant, southern end of the beach, kimgiet@hotmail.com. Enjoys almost legendary status amongst guests that keep returning year after year. Spectacularly and lovingly landscaped jungle-garden houses the beachfront bar and restaurant and further back, hides the wooden fan bungalows, which are all en suite with hammocks on the balcony. Everything here has been designed with genuine care for the environment. Highly recommended.

$ Lee Garden Resort Ban Khai, T077-238150, lees_garden@yahoo.com. A scattering of bungalows set in a garden next to the beach with balconies and hammocks in a quiet location. There are funky tunes, a giant tree swing, good food and great views. Well run.

$ Smile, T08-1956 3133 (mob). Blue-roofed fan bungalows set amongst the boulders and reached by little stone paths; rooms with jungle views are particularly peaceful. It has an attractive restaurant with hanging shell mobiles and newspapers. There's a tree swing and sofa swings on the beach. Recommended.

RESTAURANTS

$$ Fishermen's Restaurant & Bar Ban Tai (near the pier), T08-4454 7240 (mob). Idyllic spot for a memorable seafood supper. The lucky few get to dine in a moored longtail boat. Recommended.
$$ Nic's Restaurant & Bar, Moo 5, T08-0041 8023, heike.heike_64@web.de. 1700-2230. A stylish restaurant/bar/lounge, serving delicious, but very reasonably priced, tapas, pasta, pizza and Thai food.

Chill-out areas and big screen showing major sporting events. Recommended.
$$ Su's Bakery, Thong Nai Pan Yai, 1st shop on the left as you enter the village, www-su-cafe-andhouseforrent.com. Fantastic thin-base pizzas are definitely worth the walk from the beach to the village. Very popular with regulars. Fresh coffees, brownies and banana cake are also a big hit. Recommended.

WHAT TO DO

Diving
For the trained diver, the west coast offers the best diving with hard coral reefs at depths up to about 20 m. There are also some islets which offer small walls, soft coral and filter corals. Dive trips are also available to further sites such as **Koh Wao Yai** in the north of the Ang Thong Marine National Park or **Hin Bai** (Sail Rock). Here the dives are deeper.
Crystal Dive, Hat Rin T077-375535, www.crystaldive.com. This booking branch of the respected dive resort in Koh Tao is run by the good folk at the **Backpackers Information Centre**.
Tropical Dive Club, Thong Nai Pan Noi, T077-445081, www.tropicaldiveclub.com.

Therapies
Chakra, Hat Rin, off the main drag leading up from the pier, T077-375401, www. chakrayoga.com. Open until 2400. Run by a real master, Yan, and his English wife Ella. Whether you're looking for simple relaxation, or you've a specific complaint that needs working on, the staff here dish out any number of good traditional body, face and foot Thai massages, reiki, reflexology and acupressure treatments. For

those looking to learn the art themselves, they also run certificated courses: traditional Thai massage (30 hrs), reiki, levels 1-4; oil massage (30 hrs), foot and head massage (15 hrs), and massage therapy course – similar to acupuncture, but with thumbs instead of needles (30 hrs).
Monte Vista Retreat Centre, 162/1 Nai Wok Beach, T08-9212 9188 (mob), www.montevistathailand.com. This recent addition to the island's holistic vacation scene has won rave reviews. Daily yoga and meditation, cleansing and fasting courses, in-house training for reiki, palm and psychic readings, herbal facials and several types of massage. Basic accommodation also available.

Tour operators
Backpackers Information Centre, Hat Rin, T077-375535, www.backpackersthailand. com. An invaluable source of information and the only TAT-registered independent travel agent on the island. Run by Thai-British couple Rashi and Bambi who are experts on accommodation, tickets, health and safety. The agency also organizes lifeguard and full moon volunteer services on Hat Rin beach.

KOH SAMUI AND SURAT THANI

Koh Samui is the third largest of Thailand's islands, after Phuket and Koh Chang. Over the last decade tourism has exploded and now that it is accessible by air, the palm-studded tropical island is making the transition from a backpackers' haven into a sophisticated beach resort. The most recent development has also seen an identity shift from a simple party and pampering paradise to upmarket spa destination. Unlike Phuket, it still caters for the budget traveller with a variety of bungalows scattered around its shores. Its popularity is deserved, as it boasts some beautiful bays with sandy beaches hemmed by coconut palms seducing many a traveller in search of a paradise beach. But the only area of the island left relatively undeveloped is the southern tip, where the ring-road snakes inland from the coast, leaving a quiet corner away from the thud of dance music. Koh Samui is slowly disappearing under concrete and billboards as the tourism bandwagon continues to gather speed. The two most popular beaches are still Lamai and Chaweng, both on the east side of the island. They are the longest uninterrupted beaches on the island, with good swimming and watersports and busy nightlife. Mae Nam and Bophut, on the north shore, are a little more laid-back and a number of good quality, low-cost accommodation options can still be found there, although expensive resorts rather than backpacker bolt-holes are rapidly taking over.

There are still isolated spots, mainly in the south and west. For a much quieter scene, head for the remote bungalows down the west shore, although it is best to hire a vehicle as many of them are off the main road. An advantage of staying on this side of the island is the sunsets.

Close to Koh Samui are the beautiful islands of Ang Thong, see page 184.

Surat Thani, a proud and friendly town, is home to regular ferries and boats to Koh Samui and Koh Phangan.

→ARRIVING ON KOH SAMUI

GETTING THERE

If you're starting this itinerary with Koh Samui, then flying is the easiest and quickest option to get here. It is relatively expensive but hassle free. The **airport** ① *T077-428500, www.samuiairportonline.com*, in the northeast, is privately owned by **Bangkok Airways**, www.bangkokair.com. There are multiple daily connections with Bangkok, as well as flights from Phuket and Pattaya, and international connections with Singapore and Hong Kong. The airport has an information desk, which deals with hotel reservations (note that this is owned by **Bangkok Airways** and attempts are made to divert clients to **Samui Palm Beach** – also owned by the airline) and reconfirmation of flights. There is also a restaurant, free left luggage and through check-in for international flights for a large number of airlines, **Hertz** and **Budget** car rental, currency exchange and an ATM. Transport to town or the beach is by air-conditioned minibus to Bophut, Mae Nam, Chaweng (฿150), Choeng Mon, Lamai (฿300) and Big Buddha. Prices are inflated. There's a **limousine service** ① *T077-245598, samuiaccom@hotmail.com*, at domestic arrivals. The alternative is to flag down a bus out on the road, but it is a 1-km walk from the terminal and tricky with luggage.

GETTING AROUND

Koh Samui is a large island – well over 20 km both long and wide. Beaches, hotels and guesthouses can be found on most of the coastline, although the two most popular and developed beaches – Chaweng and Lamai – are both on the east coast. The main town of Nathon, where most of the ferries dock, is on the west side of the island. A ring road follows the coast along the north and east sides of the island, but runs inland cutting off the southwestern corner. Many resorts are on small tracks off this main circuit road running down to the beach. The most common form of transport, *songthaews* circulate between the island's northern and eastern beaches during daylight hours. Their final destination is usually written on the front of the vehicle and they stop anywhere when flagged down (prices start at ฿50 per person but are often inflated and some haggling may be required). Occasional nighttime *songthaews* run from 1830 and charge double. From Nathon, *songthaews* travel in a clockwise direction to Chaweng and anti-clockwise to Lamai. There are scores of places renting out motorbikes and jeeps but note that the accident rate on Koh Samui is horrendously high.

MOVING ON

Ferries from Samui depart regularly to one of Surat Thani's piers and take about two hours, costing around ฿200-250 depending on the operator. **Lomprayah**, T077-427765, www. lomprayah.com, operates a daily catamaran service from Nathon pier to Surat Thani (฿450) via Don Sak (which takes longer than the advertised 45 minutes). Prices include transfer to the pier. **Songserm Travel**, on the seafront in Nathon, T077-420157, www.songserm-expressboat.com, office hours 0800-1800, runs express passenger boats departing daily

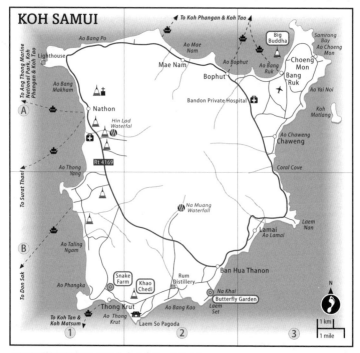

KOH SAMUI

from the southern pier in Nathon to Surat Thani, 0800 and 1300, 2½ hours, ฿300. Be aware that snacks and drinks on board are horribly overpriced, so it is best to come prepared. For the latest schedules call their helpful Bangkok office, T022-808073, daily 0900-2000. **Seatran**, office on pier, T077-426000, www.seatranferry.com, daily 0500-1700, operates large, comfortable a/c boats to Surat Thani from the main northerly pier in Nathon hourly 0500-1800 with the bus arriving in Surat Thani 2½ hours later, ฿240, including bus. The slow overnight boat leaves Surat Thani at 2100, arriving in Nathon at 0300-0400; expect to pay around ฿350. Note that the night boat is not particularly comfortable and, in rough seas, can be thoroughly unpleasant. Get to the pier early during high season as places are limited and demand is high. The boats will not leave in severe weather.

BEST TIME TO VISIT

March to June is hot and fine with a good breeze and only the occasional thunderstorm. At this time of year good discounts are available on accommodation. June to October is also sunny and hot, with short showers. The 'worst' time of year is October to February, when the monsoon breaks and rain is more frequent. However, even during this period daily hours of sunshine average five to seven hours.

TOURIST INFORMATION

The **TAT office** ① *370 Moo 3, T077-420720, daily 0830-1630*, is helpful. Several tourist magazines and maps are distributed free of charge. Be aware that there are agencies advertising themselves as TAT booking offices in Bangkok. Customers book accommodation through them and then on arrival, if they don't like the sleeping choice they have no means to redress it. The official TAT is not a booking office. Companies using its acronym write it as follows: t.a.t. The official **Tourism Authority of Thailand** is just TAT.

→ AROUND THE ISLAND

The island's main attractions are its wonderful beaches; most people head straight to one, where they remain until they leave. However, there are motorbikes or jeeps for hire to explore inland and there are a multitude of activities on offer. Evidence of the immigration of Hainanese can be seen reflected in the traditional architecture of the island. Houses, though they may also incorporate Indian, Thai and Khmer elements, are based on the Hainanese style. The use of fretwork to decorate balconies and windows, the tiled, pitched roofs and the decoration of the eaves make the older houses of Samui distinctive in Thai terms. Sadly, it is unlikely that many will survive the next decade or two. They are being torn down to make way for more modern structures, or renovated and extended in such a way that their origins are obscured.

Two-thirds of the island is forested and hilly with some impressive waterfalls (in the wet season). Hin Lad Waterfall and Wat are 3 km south of Nathon and can be reached from the town on foot, or by road 1 km off Route 4169. It's a 45-minute walk from the car park. Na Muang Waterfall, in the centre of the island, has a 30-m drop and a good pool for swimming. As the only waterfall on the island which is accessible by paved road it is busy at weekends and on holidays.

NATHON

Nathon is Koh Samui's capital and is where the ferry docks. It is a town geared to tourists, with travel agents, exchange booths, clothes stalls, bars and restaurants. Nathon consists of three roads running parallel to the seafront, with two main roads at either end linking them. Although it is used mainly as a transit point, it still has a friendly feel. *Songthaews* travel from Nathon to all the beaches. Motorbikes wait at the end of the pier, *songthaews* wait next to the second southernmost pier.

ANG THONG ('GOLDEN BASIN') MARINE NATIONAL PARK

ⓘ *Daily tours leave from piers around the island. There are no public boats but you can leave the tour, stay on Koh Wua Talap and rejoin it several days later at no extra charge (make sure you tell the ferry driver which day you want to be picked up).*

The park is made up of 40 islands lying northwest of Koh Samui, featuring limestone massifs, tropical rainforests and beaches. Particular features are **Mae Koh** (a beautiful beach) and **Thale Nai** (an emerald saltwater lake), both on **Koh Mae Koh** and **Koh Sam Sao**; the latter has a coral reef and a huge rock arch as well as a hill providing good views of the surrounding islands. The area is the major spawning ground of the short-bodied mackerel, a popular edible fish in Thailand. There is also good snorkelling (the main attraction), swimming and walking. The park's headquarters are on **Koh Wua Talap**. Visibility is at its best between late March and October.

NORTH COAST

Bang Po (Ban Poh) A quiet, secluded and clean beach which is good for swimming. One of the better options for those wanting to escape the buzz of Chaweng and Lamai.

Mae Nam A clean, serene beach with lots of coconut palms and fringed with coral reefs to tempt swimmers and snorkellers. It is a popular spot and a number of new, beautifully designed resorts have opened here.

Bophut Bophut is one of the few places on the island where there are still traditional wooden Samui houses with Chinese lettering above the doors. It has grown increasingly popular in the last few years and there are now currency exchanges, bookshops, yoga schools, bars, restaurants and good watersports facilities, yet these haven't really spoilt the ambience. The beach is straight and narrow and lacks the sweeping expanse of Chaweng, or the quiet intimacy of Laem Set, yet the place maintains a refined and friendly village atmosphere with the string of restaurants making the beachfront a popular evening location. Most hotels offer fishing, snorkelling and sightseeing charters, although there are also plenty of independent outfits. As with most of the more remote beaches on Samui, the *songthaews* that are allotted for the beach run rather infrequently. It is possible to charter them and there are always motorcycle taxis around.

Big Buddha (Bang Ruk) This small bay has typically been a favourite stomping ground with expats although in recent years it has become increasingly popular with travellers. Accommodation is rather cramped and it also tends to be noisy as the bungalows are squashed between the beach and the road. However, the beach is quiet and palm-fringed and the water is always good. During the choppier weather from October to February, this sheltered cove is a popular haven with fishing boats.

The **Temple of the Big Buddha** sits on an island linked to the mainland by a short causeway, near Bophut beach. This unremarkable, rather featureless, modern seated image is 12 m high. In recent years the site has been smartened up and made into a 'proper' tourist attraction; there are now 50 or so trinket stalls at the entrance and several foodstalls.

Samrong Bay Set at the far northeastern corner of the island, this spot is also known as 'Secret Beach'. But it is not a secret any longer as there are two major resorts here. The scenery is more wild and raw.

Choeng Mon At the northeast of the island is arguably the prettiest bay. The crescent of extremely fine white sand has an island at its eastern end, attached to the mainland by a sandbar, traversable at low tide. While in places it is rocky underfoot in the centre of the bay, the sand continues well out to sea. The restaurant scene is pretty lively, particularly in the centre of the beach where bamboo tables with oil lamps reach right down to the water's edge and there are a couple of beach bars at the eastern end. The beach is most popular with couples and families. There is a *songthaew* station at the far eastern side of the area, behind the beach.

South of Choeng Mon, there's good snorkelling at **Yai Noi**, north of Chaweng.

EAST COAST

Chaweng This is the biggest beach on the island, split into three areas – north, central and Chaweng Noi. **Chaweng Noi** is to the south, round a headland, and has three of the most expensive hotels on the island. **Central Chaweng** is an attractive sweep of sand with lovely water for swimming and is lined with resorts, bungalows, restaurants and bars. The town that has grown up here is entirely geared towards tourists and in recent years it has become swamped. Along the road behind the beach there is a further proliferation of bars, clubs, tourist agencies, restaurants, fast-food chains, stalls and watersports facilities. However, the infrastructure has not kept pace with the concrete expansion; the drains stink in the searing heat and flood in the pouring rain. In comparison to the other beaches on the island, it is crowded and getting more resort-ridden by the year, but it's still Samui's most popular and by far the busiest beach. Despite the facilities and energetic activities on offer, most visitors prefer to sunbathe.

Chaweng to Lamai There is not much beach along this stretch of coast but there is some snorkelling off the rocky shore. Snorkelling is best at **Coral Cove**, between Chaweng and Lamai.

Lamai Koh Samui's 'second' beach is 5 km long and has a large assortment of accommodation. The beach is nice but rugged and not as attractive as Chaweng and the sea is rocky underfoot in many places. Cheaper accommodation can be found more readily here than on Chaweng. Just south of Lamai, there is a cultural hall and a group of phallic rock formations known as **Grandmother** and **Grandfather rocks** (*Hinyai* and *Hinta*). There's an array of tourist shops leading up to it. Companies along the main road parallel to the beach offer fishing and snorkelling trips around the islands.

Depending on who you talk to, or who you are, this is either a rather tawdry, down-market Pattaya, or an idiosyncratic, slightly hip and colourful Hua Hin. It is not particularly peaceful or picturesque. It can be fun and some people love it. The original town of Ban Lamai is quiet and separate from the tourist part, which is usually quiet during the day as most of the tourists are on the beach. The sea at Lamai can be wild and challenging during the early months of the year, and suitable only for the most competent of swimmers. Due to the tide there are not as many watersports here and the sea can appear murky, particularly at the northern end. Many hotels and restaurants are geared to the German market.

SOUTH COAST

The small, often stony, beaches that line the south coast from Ban Hua Thanon west to Thong Krut are quieter and less developed with only a handful of hotels and bungalows, although construction continues at a breathless pace and the area is littered with endless 'land for sale' boards. While most tourists head for the white sands and sweeping shores elsewhere, there are some beautiful little coves peppered along this southerly stretch.

Ban Hua Thanon Ban Hua Thanon is an attractive rambling village with wooden shop-houses and *kwaytio* (noodle soup) stalls – and the only Muslim community on Koh Samui. The forebears of the inhabitants come from Pattani in Thailand's far south. With its stony beach being the biggest anchorage for fishing boats on the island, this village is quiet and rarely visited by tourists. North of the village are a couple of restaurants, well situated with cooling sea breezes.

Na Khai Na Khai is a small beach with just a handful of resorts. The swimming can be rocky, but if you are looking for a quiet place to stay and don't require a classic sweep of golden sand, then this is an option.

Laem Set This is not really much of a beach compared with Chaweng and Lamai. However, it is quiet, clean and palm fringed and there is some reasonable snorkelling.

   Samui Butterfly Garden ① *T077-424020, 0830-1730, ฿170*, is set on the side of the hill behind **Laem Set Inn** opposite **Central Samui Village**. It features a screened butterfly garden with a limited collection of butterflies, a display of (dead) insects, moths and butterflies, a few beehives, a hillside observatory, observation platforms for views of the coast, a glass-bottomed boat for viewing a coral reef and a restaurant.

Thong Krut Thong Krut Bay and the hamlet of Ban Thong Krut are at the southern extremity of the island. The stony beach is around a kilometre long and the swimming is average but there are excellent views from here and it is peaceful and undeveloped with just a handful of shops including a little supermarket and **The Beach**, **Java** and **Green Ta'Lay** restaurants. Boat trips to Koh Tan and Koh Matsum or to fish and snorkel can be arranged through various companies in the village.

   Nearby, is the **Samui Snake Farm** ① 88/2 Moo 4, T077-423247. Shows are held at 1100 and 1400. The commentary is hilarious. Not for the squeamish.

Koh Tan and Koh Matsum Koh Tan lies due south of Thong Krut and is about 3 km long and 2 km wide. It was first colonised by Hainanese; the Chinese cemetery on the island has graves from this time. There are three small villages and a few bungalow developments on the island which, although undeveloped, are not blessed with spotless beaches and crystal-clear waters. Still, it is quiet and just about away from it all.

Koh Matsum is a sorry sight – all the coconut trees have been stripped by beetles, leaving a desolate landscape.

WEST COAST

Like the south coast, the western coastline south of Nathon is undeveloped with secluded coves and beautiful sunsets. Phangka, near the southwest tip of the island, has good snorkelling in the quiet waters of a small bay; Thong Yang, further north, is an isolated beach, relatively untouched by frantic development. The vehicle ferry from Don Sak, on the mainland, docks here.

SURAT THANI

Surat Thani, or 'City of the Good People', has an interesting riverfront worth a visit and some fabulously stocked markets, its main purpose is as a transportation hub. The tourist office, TAT ① *5 Talat Mai Rd, T077-288818, daily 0830-1200, 1300-1630*, southwest of the town, is a good source of information. Boats can be hired for trips on the river (฿200 for up to six people). The better journey is upstream.

MOVING ON

From Surat Thani to Nakhon Si Thammarat there are buses and minibuses (2½ to three hours). Or you could fly directly back to Bangkok from here, as there is an airport with several daily flights.

KOH SAMUI AND SURAT THANI LISTINGS

WHERE TO STAY

Koh Samui
Mae Nam
$$$-$$ Maenam Resort, 1/3 Moo 4, T077-247 287, www.maenamresort. com. Alpinesque bungalows with little balconies, wicker furniture, wardrobes, desk and a/c in luscious gardens. Some have wonderful positions set on the gently sloping beach with shallow waters. Popular with young families. Friendly management. Recommended.

Bophut
$$$$-$$ World Resort, 175/Moo 1, T077-425355, www.samuiworldresort.com. Lots of bungalow choice here, from spacious a/c wood-panelled affairs to more modern deluxes with sea views. There are hotel rooms, too, as well as a large pool and a beach restaurant that serves Thai and Western food. Recommended.
$$-$ Oasis Bungalows, opposite Starfish & Coffee, T077-425143. The alleyway beside the restaurant opens onto a beautiful garden with 6 bungalows. All have TV and hot water showers. Good value.

Big Buddha (Bang Ruk)
$$$-$$ Secret Garden, 22/1 Moo 4, T077-245255, www.secretgarden.co.th. Small family-run resort with 9 good-value concrete bungalows, some right by the beach, some slightly back from it. All have a/c, varnished teak floors, TV, fridge and hot water. There are also a few cheaper rooms in a converted building. Clean and comfortable. Friendly British owners. Recommended.

Samrong Bay
$$$$ Six Senses Samui, 9/10 Moo 5, T077-245678, www.sixsenses.com/sixsenses samui. Famous, ultra-chic and exclusive resort and spa with cool, calm and minimalist lines. The 66 hidden villas have rectangular private pools and luxury sun-decks. There are 2 restaurants, a gym, shop and **Six Senses Spa** (1000-2200), with massage rooms that overlook the sea. Recommended.

Choeng Mon
$$$$ Sala Samui, www.salaresorts.com/ samui. Immaculate luxury hotel with 69 villas that enjoy award-winning design and a fresh Mediterranean feel. The beachside pool is surrounded by decking and the hidden private villas have pools, raised platforms and outdoor bathtubs. There are also some cheaper deluxe rooms. 5-star facilities include the **Mandara spa**. Recommended.

Lamai
$$-$ New Hut, next to Beer's House, T077-230437. Simple but good-quality 'A' frame bamboo huts, slap bang on the beach, with mattress on the floor, mosquito net, fan and shared bathroom. There are also bungalows with bathroom inside available. Funky restaurant. Recommended.

Surat Thani
$ Phongkaew Hotel, 126/3 Talat Mai Rd, T077-223410. Small, tidy rooms, complete with a/c, hot water, free Wi-Fi and cable TV, make this one of the best deals in town. Friendly and in a good location near the TAT office. Recommended.

RESTAURANTS

Koh Samui

$$$ Dining on the Rocks, Six Senses Samui. Eating here on a large wood platform is a fine dining experience with some of the most tantalizingly meals on the island. This is a wonderful gourmet experience with great wines on offer.

$$$ Poppies, s119/3 Moo 2, T077-422419, www.poppiessamui.com. An excellent Thai and international restaurant, one of the best on the beach. Live classical guitar accompaniment on Tue, Thu and Fri, and a Thai night on Sat. Booking recommended.

$$$-$$ Karma Sutra, Fisherman's Village, opposite the pier, T077-425198, www.karmasutrasamui.com. 0700-late. French owners Virginie and Laurant have injected plenty of style into this thoroughly chilled out bar/restaurant. Sample the

Mediterranean plate or the Kobe beef carpaccio, but make sure you save room for dessert. Recommended.

$$ Honey Seafood Restaurant, at the most easterly tip of the beach, T077-245032, www.honeyseafood.com. Great seafood. Recommended.

$ Fisherman's Village Night Market, Fri 1700-late. The usually relaxed Fisherman's Village becomes a hive of activity with vendors selling all kinds of wonderful Thai and Western snacks. It's a little more expensive than most walking street markets, but the quality of food is unrivalled. Make sure you bring small money and a big appetite.

$ Nathon Night Market, in front of the pier. Daily 1700-late. Full range of Thai street food at local prices.

WHAT TO DO

Koh Samui
Buffalo fighting

In the stadium at the north end (and several others around the island). Far tamer than it sounds, animals are rarely injured in the 'fights' and it's more a show of tradition than a fierce face-off. Ask at your hotel for date of the next event.

Diving and snorkelling

Easy Divers, Big Buddha, T077-413373, www.easydivers-thailand.com.
One Hundred Degrees East, 23/2 Moo 4 Big Buddha Beach (in front of Ocean's 11 restaurant), T077-245 936, www.100 degreeseast.com. Professional, friendly outfit.
Blue Stars Sea Kayaking, Chaweng Beach Rd, T077-413231, www.bluestars.info.

Therapies

Samui Dharma Healing Centre, 63 Moo Tee 1, Ao Santi Beach, near Nathon, T077-234170, www.dharmahealingintl. com. Alternative health programmes to inspire and rejuvenate. 7- to 21-day fasting courses are directed according to Dharma Buddhist principles in alternative health: fasting, colonic irrigation, yoga, reflexology, iridology and many other therapies. Accommodation is available.

Tamarind Springs, 205/7 Thong Takian, Lamai, T077-230571, www.tamarindsprings. com. 1000-2000. Just up the hill from Spa Samui is possibly the island's most relaxing and authentic spa in a spectacular natural setting. Treatment packages include body scrubs and a variety of massages, which include the divine combination of herbal spa and waterfall dip pool.

NAKHON SI THAMMARAT

Nakhon Si Thammarat ('the Glorious city of the Dead') or Nagara Sri Dhammaraja ('the city of the Sacred Dharma Kings') has masqueraded under many different aliases: Marco Polo referred to it as Lo-Kag, the Portuguese called it Ligor – thought to have been its original name – while to the Chinese it was Tung Ma-ling. Today, it is the second biggest city in the south and most people know it simply as Nakhon or Nakhon Si.

It is not a very popular tourist destination and it has a rather unsavoury reputation as one of the centres of mafia activity in Thailand, but otherwise it is friendly and manageable with a wide range of hotels, some excellent restaurants, a good museum and a fine monastery in Wat Phra Mahathat. It is also famed for its shadow puppetry.

Around Nakhon are the quiet beaches of Khanom and Nai Phlao. The Khao Luang and Khao Nan national parks offer waterfalls, caves, whitewater rafting and homestays.

→NAKHON

ARRIVING IN NAKHON SI THAMMARAT

Getting there and moving on Nakhon is a provincial capital and therefore well connected. There is an airport north of town with daily flights to Bangkok (with Nok Air and Air Asia). Nakhon also lies on the main north–south railway line linking Bangkok with southern Thailand. The station is within easy walking distance of the town centre on Yommarat Road. However, only two southbound trains go into Nakhon itself; most stop instead at the junction of Khao Chum Thong, 30 km west of Nakhon, from where you must take a bus or taxi into town. The main bus station (for non air-conditioned connections) is 1 km out of town over the bridge on Karom Road, west of the mosque. It has connections with Bangkok and most destinations in the south. There are also minibus and shared taxi services to many destinations in the south.

Getting around The centre is comparatively compact and navigable on foot. But for sights on the edge of town – like Wat Phra Mahathat – it is necessary to catch a public *songthaew*, *saamlor* or motorcycle taxi. The *songthaew* is the cheapest option, a trip across town costs ฿10. The old pedal *saamlor* is still in evidence though it is gradually being pushed out by the noisier and more frightening motorcycle taxi, of which there seem to be hundreds.

Tourist information TAT ① *Sanam Na Muang, Rachdamnern Rd, T075-346515-6, www. tat. or.th/south2 (Thai only), daily 0830-1630*, is situated in an old, attractive club building. The staff here produce a helpful pamphlet and hand-out sheets of information on latest bus and taxi prices. It is a useful first stop.

BACKGROUND

Nakhon is surrounded by rich agricultural land and has been a rice exporter for centuries. The city has links with both the Dvaravati and Srivijayan empires. Buddhist monks from Nakhon are thought to have propagated religion throughout the country perhaps even influencing the development of Buddhism in Sukhothai, Thailand's former great kingdom.

Nakhon was at its most powerful and important during King Thammasokarat's reign in the 13th century, when it was busily trading with south India and Ceylon. But as Sukhothai

NAKHON SI THAMMARAT

To Airport, Surat Thani & Khanom

Wat Kit Rd — Chumphon Rd

Chamoen Withi Rd

Neramit Rd

Wat Wang Tawan Tok

Gochart Rd — Bo Ang Rd

Yommarat Rd

Si Prat Rd

Mahayond Rd

Rachdamnern Rd

Karom Rd

Tha Chang Rd

Lak Muang (City Pillar)

Sanam Na Muang

Khlong Na Muang

Old City Wall

Semamuang Temple

Si Thammarat Rd

Si Thammasok Rd

Hor Phra Narai

Hor Phra Isuan

Rachdamnern Rd

Chapel of Phra Buddha Sihing

Clocktower

Saan Chao Mae Thap Thim Chinese Pagoda

Tachee Rd — Phaanyom Rd

Mangkut Rd

Suchart Subsin's Puppet Workshop & Museum

To National Museum, Wat Sa-la Mechai

Wat Phra Mahathat & Phra Viharn Luang

Wat Na Phra Boromthat

Khlong Tung Prong

To Morning Market & Bus Terminal

Khlong Ta Wang

To Pak Nakhon

100 metres
100 yards

and then Ayutthaya grew in influence, the city went into a gradual decline. During the 17th century, King Narai's principal concubine banished the bright young poet Si Phrat to Nakhon. Here he continued to compose risqué rhymes about the women of the governor's court. His youthful impertinence lost him his head.

Nakhon used to have the dubious honour of being regarded as one of the crime capitals of Thailand – a position it had held, apparently, since the 13th century. Locals maintain that the city has now cleaned up its act and Nakhon is probably best known today for its prawn farms and nielloware industry. The shop where the industry started some 50 years ago still stands on Sitama Road and production techniques are demonstrated on Si Thammasok I Road. Elsewhere, other than in a few handicraft shops on Tha Chang Road, nielloware is an elusive commodity, although the National Museum has some examples on display. The art and craft and performance of shadow puppetry is also being kept alive in Nakhon, see box, page 195.

WAT PHRA MAHATHAT

ⓘ *T075-345172, cloisters open daily 0800-1630.*

A 2-km-long wall formerly enclosed the old city and its wats – only a couple of fragments of this remain (the most impressive section is opposite the town jail on Rachdamnern Road). Wat Phra Mahathat, 2 km south of town on Rachdamnern Road, is the oldest temple in town and the biggest in South Thailand – as well as being one of the region's most important. The wat dates

Minibuses 🚐
Minivan to Hat Yai **5**
Minivan to Surat Thani & Khanom **4**
Share taxi terminal to Airport, Trang & Songkhla **2**
To Phuket **3**

from AD 757 and was originally a Srivijayan Mahayana Buddhist shrine. The 77-m high stupa, *Phra Boromathat* – a copy of the Mahathupa in Ceylon – was built early in the 13th century to hold relics of the Buddha from Ceylon. The wat underwent extensive restoration in the Ayutthayan period and endured further alterations in 1990. The *chedi*'s square base, its voluptuous body and towering spire are all Ceylonese-inspired. Below the spire is a small square platform decorated with bas-reliefs in gold of monks circumambulating (*pradaksina*) the monument. The spire itself is said to be topped with 962 kg of gold, while the base is surrounded by small stupas. The covered cloisters at its base contain many beautiful, recently restored Buddha images all in the image of subduing Mara. The base is dotted with attractive elephant heads. Also here is **Vihara Bodhi Langka** ① *0800-1600, entry by donation*, a jumbled treasure trove of a museum. It contains a large collection of archaeological artefacts, donated jewellery, bodhi trees, Buddhas and a collection of sixth- to 13th-century Dvaravati sculpture – some of the latter are particularly fine. The mural at the bottom of the stairs tells the story of the early life of the Buddha, while the doorway at the top is decorated with figures of Vishnu and Phrom dating from the Sukhothai period.

PHRA VIHARN LUANG

The nearby Phra Viharn Luang (to the left of the main entrance to the stupa) is an impressive building, with an intricately painted and decorated ceiling, dating from the 18th century. The best time to visit the monastery is in October during the Tenth Lunar Month Festival when Wat Mahathat becomes a hive of activity. Foodstalls, travelling cinemas, shadow-puppet masters, the local mafia, businessmen in their Mercedes, monks and handicraft sellers all set up shop, making the wat endlessly interesting.

PUPPET WORKSHOP AND MUSEUM

① *110/18 Si Thammasok, Soi 3, T075-346394, daily 0830-1700, 20-min performance, ฿100 for 2; 3 or more ฿50 each.*

Not far from Wat Mahathat is the puppet workshop of Nakhon's most famous *nang thalung* master – Khun Suchart Subsin. His workshop is signposted off the main road near the Chinese temple (hard to miss). As well as giving shows and selling examples of his work starting at ฿200 or so for a simple elephant, the compound itself is interesting and peaceful with craftsmen hammering out puppets under thatched awnings and dozens of buffalo skulls hung everywhere. There is also a small museum exhibiting puppet characters from as far back as the 18th century. See box, page 195.

SAAN CHAO MAE THAP THIM CHINESE PAGODA

① *It's a 2-km hike out to the monastery; blue songthaews constantly ply the road to the monastery and back (฿6).*

Returning to the main road, this Chinese pagoda offers a respite from Theravada Buddhist Thailand. Magnificent dragons claw their way up the pillars and inside, wafted by incense, are various Chinese gods, Bodhisattvas and demons.

NAKHON SI THAMMARAT NATIONAL MUSEUM

① *Rachdamnern Rd, about 700 m beyond Wat Mahathat, Wed-Sun 0830-1630, ฿30. The museum is a 2-km walk from most of the hotels; catch one of the numerous blue songthaews running along Rachdamnern Rd and ask for 'Pipitipan Nakhon Si Thammarat' (฿6).*

The Nakhon branch of the National Museum is one of the town's most worthwhile sights. The impressive collection includes many interesting Indian-influenced pieces as well as rare pieces from the Dvaravati and later Ayutthaya periods. Some exhibits are labelled in English. The section on art in South Thailand explains and charts the development of the unusual local Phra Phutthasihing (or Buddha Sihing) style of Buddha image, which was popular locally in the 16th century. Also in this section is the oldest Vishnu statue in Southeast Asian art (holding a conch shell on his hip), which dates from the fifth century. The museum has sections on folk arts and crafts and local everyday implements. To the right of the entrance hall, in the prehistory section, stand two large Dongson bronze kettle drums – two of only 12 found in the country. The one decorated with four ornamental frogs is the biggest ever found in Thailand.

CHAPEL OF PHRA BUDDHA SIHING

The Chapel of Phra Buddha Sihing, sandwiched between two large provincial office buildings just before Rachdamnern Road splits in two, may contain one of Thailand's most important Buddha images. During the 13th century an image, magically created, was shipped to Thailand from Ceylon (hence the name – Sihing for the Sinhalese people). The Nakhon statue, like the other two images that claim to be the Phra Buddha Sihing (one in Bangkok, see page 44, and one in Chiang Mai, northern Thailand, see page 105), is not Ceylonese in style at all; it conforms with the Thai style of the peninsula.

WAT WANG TAWAN TOK

Back in the centre of town is Wat Wang Tawan Tok, across Rachdamnern Road from the bookshop. It has, at the far side of its sprawling compound, a southern Thai-style wooden house built between 1888 and 1901. Originally the house (which is really three houses in one) was constructed without nails – it has since been poorly repaired using them. The door panels, window frames and gables, all rather weather-beaten now, were once intricately carved but it is still infinitely more appealing than the concrete shophouses going up all over Thailand.

HINDU TEMPLES

There are two 13th- to 14th-century Hindu temples in the city, along Rachdamnern Road. **Hor Phra Isuan**, next to the Semamuang Temple, houses an image of Siva, the destroyer. Opposite is **Hor Phra Narai** which once contained images of Vishnu, now in the city museum.

MORNING MARKET

A worthwhile early-morning walk is west across the bridge along Karom Road to the morning market (about 1 km), which sells fresh food. This gets going early and is feverish with activity from around 0630.

THAI TRADITIONAL MEDICINE CENTRE

ⓘ *Take a local bus, ฿8.*

On the outskirts of the city, after Wat Mahathat is the small **Wat Sa-la Mechai**. While the temple is fairly ordinary, at one end of the temple grounds is a recently established centre for traditional medicine, including massage. If you want a traditional massage, it costs about ฿100 per hour – you pay before you begin. You can also take a course in massage, paying by the hour, and learn more about traditional herbal medicine (there is a small garden of medicinal plants at the front).

KHANOM AND NAI PHLAO BEACHES

ⓘ *Regular buses from Nakhon (฿20), a/c micro buses (฿60) leave from Wat Kit Rd and also from Surat Thani. The beaches are about 8 km off the main road; turn at the Km 80 marker.*

Eighty kilometres north of Nakhon, near Khanom district, there are some secluded stretches of shoreline: Khanom beach (2 km from town), Nai Phlao beach to the south, and a couple of other bays are opening up to development. This area is predominantly visited by Thai tourists. Newer operations seem to be targeting Western tourists who are beginning to look towards the mainland in this area for reasonably priced peace and quiet, and convenience they have failed to find on Samui. There are better beaches in Thailand but you're likely to have most of what you find to yourself – particularly if you come mid-week. Khanom beach is a long run of coconut-grove fringed sand that slopes steeply into the sea. Development is picking up here but it still has a remote feeling. Khanom town is a very lively rough and ready fishing port. There are few facilities aimed at *farang* in this town meaning that it offers a genuine slice of Thai rural life to the more adventurous traveller. Nai Phlao beach offers a much shorter run of beach and has a greater concentration of resorts. That's not saying much though as it still feels like a relatively untouched spot, despite the best efforts of the new development at the **Chada Racha Resort** to introduce an unhealthy dose of concrete to the coastline.

KHAO LUANG NATIONAL PARK

ⓘ *To get to Karom Waterfall take a bus to Lan Saka (then walk 3 km to falls) or charter a minibus direct. To get to Phrom Lok Waterfall take a minibus from Nakhon then hire a motorbike taxi for the last very pleasant 8 km. The villagers at Khiriwong village can organize trips up Khao Luang mountain but do not speak English. Songthaews leave Nakhon for Khiriwong every 15 mins or so (฿15).*

The Khao Luang National Park is named after Khao Luang, a peak of 1835 m – the highest in the south – which lies less than 10 km west of Nakhon. Within the boundaries of the mountainous, 570-sq-km national park are three waterfalls. **Karom Waterfall** lies 30 km from Nakhon, off Route 4015, and has a great location with views over the lowlands. Also here are cool forest trails and fast-flowing streams. The park is said to support small populations of tiger, leopard and elephant, although many naturalists believe they are on the verge of extinction here. **Phrom Lok Waterfall** is about 25 km from Nakhon, off Route 4132. However, the most spectacular of the waterfalls is **Krung Ching** – 'waterfall of a hundred thousand raindrops' – 70 km out of town, and a 4-km walk from the park's accommodation. The 1835-m climb up **Khao Luang** starts from Khiriwong village, 23 km from Nakhon, off Route 4015. The mountain is part of the Nakhon Si Thammarat range, running from Koh Samui south through Surat Thani to Satun. The scenic village, surrounded by forest, was partially destroyed by mudslides in 1988 – an event which led to the introduction of a nationwide logging ban at the beginning of 1989. The climb takes three days and is very steep in parts, with over 60° slopes. If you plan to do this walk on your own, there is no accommodation so it is necessary to carry your own equipment and food.

Most of the plays relate tales from the **Ramakien** and the *Jataka* tales. Narrators sing in ear-piercing falsetto accompanied by a band comprising *tab* (drums), *pi* (flute), *mong* (bass gong), *saw* (fiddle) and *ching* (miniature cymbals). There are two sizes of puppets. *Nang yai* (large puppets) which may be 2 m tall, and *nang lek* (small puppets). Shows and demonstrations of how the puppets are made can be seen at the workshop of **Suchart Subsin**, 110/18 Si Thammasok Soi 3 (take the road opposite Wat Phra Mahathat, turn left – at the top of the *soi* Suchart Subsin's house is signposted – and walk 50 m). This group has undertaken several royal performances.

KHAO WANG THONG CAVE

ⓘ *Charter a songthaew for around ฿800 per day. The entrance is past the cave keeper's house, 15 mins' walk uphill from the village.*

One of the less-publicized sights in the Nakhon area is Khao Wang Thong Cave. The cave is on the south side of the middle peak of three limestone mountains near Ban Khao Wang Thong in Khanom district. It lies 100 km north of Nakhon, 11 km off Route 4142. Villagers and a group of Nakhon conservationists saved the cave from a dolomite mining company in 1990. A few tight squeezes and a short ladder climb are rewarded by some of Thailand's most spectacular cave formations. Its four spacious chambers – one of which has been dubbed 'the throne hall' – are decorated with gleaming white curtain stalactites. It is presently maintained by groups of local villagers and plans are afoot to install a lighting system. Until then, it is advisable that you bring your own torch (flashlight).

KHAO NAN NATIONAL PARK

ⓘ *Take the main route up to Khanom beyond Ta Sala and turn left down the road from where there are signposts to the park.*

Just north of Khao Luang National Park is the new Khao Nan National Park. At 1430 m, Khao Nan Yai is not as high as Khao Luang, but is still tall enough to support cloud forest on its summit. The national park has a beautiful waterfall near its entrance, lush forests, waterfalls and caves. One cave, **Tham Hong**, has a waterfall inside it and is well worth visiting, and fairly easily accessible but you'll need a torch. Treks to the top of Khao Nan Yai taking three to four days are organized by the Forestry Department staff. You should call the Forestry Department in Bangkok at least a couple of days in advance to arrange a guide. The treks go to the top of Khao Nan where you can camp out in cloud forest. Temperatures at the top are always cool and there is a wide variety of ferns and mosses in the understorey of the forest. Khao Nan and Khao Luang are also known for *pa pra* – a deciduous tree which loses its leaves during the dry season (February to April) with the leaves first changing colour to a brilliant red.

NAKHON SI THAMMARAT LISTINGS

WHERE TO STAY

Nakhon

$$$$-$$ Twin Lotus Hotel, 97/8 Hatankarnhukwag Rd, outskirts of town, T075-323777, www.twinlotushotel.com. Nearly 400 a/c rooms, with TV and minibars, and a good-sized swimming pool and fitness centre, plus the usual services expected of a top-end hotel. The reasonable tariff includes a good buffet-style breakfast. A well-run and well-maintained hotel.

$$-$ Thaksin Hotel, 1584/23 Si Prat Rd. T075-342790, www.thaksinhotel. com. Comfortable, good-value rooms, with cable TV, en suite and a/c. Decent location, friendly and some English spoken. Recommended.

Khanom/Nai Phlao

$$$-$$ Ekman Garden Resort, 39/2 Moo 5 Tumble SaoPao, T075-367566, www.ekmangarden.com. About half way between Nakhon and Khanom, this resort, run by extremely friendly Thai and Swedish owners, Ann and Stefan, is designed for those with relaxation in mind. It's about 2 km to the ocean, which may deter some, but the real draw is the stunning flower garden and man-made lakes where you can catch your own dinner. Rooms are very private and homely, though the furniture is a little dated. Also has a pool, putting green and restaurant.

$$$-$$ Khanom Golden Beach Hotel, 59/3 Moo 4, Ban Na Dan, T075-326690, www.khanomgoldenbeach.com. Hotel block with pool, snooker room, children's room, tour desk, restaurant and rental of windsurf boards, sailing dinghies and bicycles. Friendly and professional staff. Rooms are rather characterless but clean and comfortable. The larger more expensive suites are very spacious and well equipped.

Khao Luang National Park

The **$$** bungalows at the park office of the **Karom Waterfall** sleep up to 10 people. Camping is possible if you have your own gear. The 2nd park office at **Krung Ching Waterfall**, T075-309644-5, has 2 guesthouses **$$$$-$$** and a campsite.

RESTAURANTS

Nakhon

$ Krour Nakorn, at the back of Bovorn Bazaar off Rachdamnern Rd next to the massive trunk of an Indian rubber tree. Pleasant eating spot, with open verandas, art work, wicker chairs and a reasonable line in seafood and other spicy dishes. You get given an entire tray of herbs and vegetables to go with your meal. Recommended.

DREAM TRIP 4:
Bangkok→Phuket→Andaman Coast and islands
21 days

Bangkok and around 3 nights, page 33

Ranong and around 3 nights, page 199
Bus from Bangkok (8 hrs) or fly (1½ hrs)

Phuket 3 nights, page 208
Bus from Ranong (6 hrs) or direct flight
from Bangkok (1½ hrs)

Phangnga Bay 2 nights, page 222
Bus from Phuket (2 hrs)

Krabi 2 nights, page 227
Bus from Phangnga Bay (2 hrs)

Koh Phi Phi and Lanta 3 nights,
page 239 and 243
Boat from Krabi (1-2 hrs)

Trang 1 night, page 250
Bus from Koh Lanta (2½ hrs)

Tarutao National Park 3 nights,
page 256
Minivan from Trang to Ban Pak Bara (2 hrs)
and then boat (30 mins-1½ hrs, depending
on which island)

Satun 1 night, page 261
Boat from Tarutao National Park – Koh
Tarutao or Koh Lipe – or take a boat from
the islands to Pak Bara and then catch a
connecting bus to Satun, 60 km south

Bangkok page 33
Train or bus from Trang to Bangkok (15 hrs
and 12 hrs, respectively) or fly (1½ hrs).
Alternatively, from Satun, take a bus to Hat
Yai (2 hrs) and then fly to Bangkok (1½ hrs)

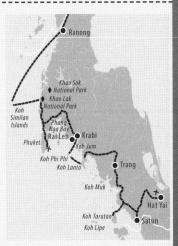

DREAM TRIP 4
Bangkok→Phuket→Andaman Coast and islands

The Andaman coast presents a startling cultural mosaic, from Ranong's cheroot-smoking Burmese in the north to the south's strident Muslims, along with the numerous Chao Le sea gypsies and Chinese traders. On Ranong's rain-drenched islands, bareknuckle boxing matches between Burmese and Thai re-enact an age-old rivalry, while a growing separatist movement continues to spread through the hotly contested deep South, parts of which were Malaysia a little over a century ago. Meanwhile, indigenous sea gypsies persist in animist practices, including offerings of human hair to the spirits of the treacherous Andaman.

Travellers will find many pleasures along this coast, from the Similan islands' world-famous diving sites, including Richelieu Rock, to Phuket's beaches: katoey paradise Patong and jetset Pansea. Further down the coast are Phangnga's sea cave paintings and the magical floating fishing village of Koh Panyi. Off Krabi – where giant prehistoric human skulls were found – are eerie towering limestone karsts revered by climbers.

Further south are Koh Lanta's white-sand, coral-rimmed beaches and the brooding ex-prison island of Tarutao. The latter offers dense and terrifying untouched jungle populated by wild boar, barking deer and poisonous snakes. The Adang-Rawi archipelago's tiny islands – unreachable during the monsoon – provide homes for pythons and hornbills, while, only metres off shore, snorkellers can find untouched sea life, including shoals of barracuda. Finally, the whole of the coast is dotted with island retreats with no electricity or cars, among them Koh Muk, close to the Emerald Cave, and the tropical idyll of Koh Bulon-Leh.

RANONG TO KHAO LAK

A wild, untouched landscape begins to unfold, with waterfalls, lush rainforest and dense mountains all home to fantastical species like the largest flower in the world and insects the size of a man's hand. Ranong, on Route 4, is famous for both its hot springs and visa runs by expats and travellers who can cross the border into Burma by boat to renew their visas in a day. Like Mae Sot, its proximity to Burma fosters a border diaspora as Burmese workers – many illegal – hasten across, desperately searching for work in a country which traditionally has fought bitterly with the their own. In Ranong and the surrounding islands, the tribal Burmese clearly stand out with the men wearing sarongs and the women daubed with clay face paint smoking cheroots. There are often boxing competitions between the two nationalities which dramatically display another difference, between the fighting style of the highly ritualistic Thai muay and compared frenzied freeform Burmese style.

From Prathong Island near Takua Pa (south of Ranong), right down to Phuket, virtually the entire western coast of Phangnga province comprises great long sandy bays with the occasional peninsula or rocky headland. With the Thai Muang National Park to the south, the Khao Lak Lam Ru National Park bordering the Khao Lak area, and the Khao Sok National Park inland to the north, tourism operators along the coast of Phangnga are targeting those interested in 'getaway' and nature tours. Meanwhile Ranong's proximity to the Similan and Surin islands (the western coast resorts in Phangnga are also the closest departure points for the Similan Islands) makes it an ideal stopover for divers. Certainly, as the gateway to Richelieu Rock and the Mergui archipelago, it is hard to beat.

→RANONG

Surrounded by forested mountains, Ranong is a scenic place to stay for a day or two. It is a small and unpretentious provincial capital and an important administrative centre. Increasingly, it is being eyed up as a spa/hot spring location but is currently still more popular with Southeast Asian tourists than those from further afield. The free municipal hot springs just outside the town are a charming spot, where the area's varied population gather day and night to get warm, floppy and relaxed in the ever hot water. It offers an excellent way to watch all levels of Thai society at their most lethargic while warming yourself after one of the town's many thunderstorms. There are waterfalls here, one of which, Punyaban, can be seen from the road as you approach the town. It is also the jumping-off point for a number of beautiful islands in the Andaman Sea. There is a small tourist office on Kamlungsab Road.

ARRIVING IN RANONG

Getting there From Bangkok, there are several bus departures daily, with the best air-conditioned buses departing roughly nine times a day. However, the road journey from the north is arduous (eight hours at least) and the last half is through hills, so is not good for travel-sickness sufferers. Consider taking the train from Bangkok to Chumphon (see page 167) and the bus from there (which takes the same time in total). The bus terminal is on Highway 4 on the edge of town, near the Jansom Thara Hotel; buses also stop in town on Ruangrat Road before the terminal. You can also reach Ranong by bus from Khao Lak, Phuket, Surat Thani and Krabi. There is an airport 20 km south of town; in early 2013, small budget airline **Happy Air** (www.happyair.co.th) was flying six times a week to Bangkok.

Moving on To get to Phuket, take a bus (four hours). Buses go via Kuraburi, from where you can take a detour by boat to Koh Surin (1½ hours on the speedboat, 4½ hours on the slow boat).

PLACES IN RANGONG

The town contains excellent geo-thermal mineral water springs (65°C) at **Wat Tapotharam** ① *2 km east of the town and behind the Jansom Thara Hotel, free*. To get there, walk or take a *songthaew* along Route 2; ask for 'bor nam rawn' (hot water well). Surrounded by dramatic forested hills, the spa water bubbles out of the ground hot enough to boil an egg and cools sufficiently to allow the city's residents to enjoy a free hot bath and take refuge in its cosy depths during Ranong's frequent thunderstorms. The valley also has a luxurious hot spring and health club, offering a jacuzzi, gym, steam room, sauna and massages from ₿300, but it lacks the natural setting and village green feel of the municipal springs across the road. Around the park are several seafood restaurants and food stands. The springs also provide the **Jansom Thara Hotel** with thermal water for hot baths and a giant jacuzzi. There is a small park with a cable bridge over the river, a tiny cave containing a small Buddhist shrine and a number of municipal bathing pools. The wat here contains a footprint of the Buddha. Continuing along Route 2 for another 6 km or so, the road reaches the old tin-mining village of **Hat Som Paen**. **Wat Som Paen** is worth a visit to see the numerous giant carp, protected because of their supposed magical qualities. Deep in the hills, a few kilometres further up the road, is Ranong canyon, where city folk escape to recline in pretty shalas above the water, swim or feed countless hungry catfish.

Port of Ranong lies 3 km from town. Each morning the dock seethes with activity as Thai and Burmese fishing boats unload their catches. Boats can be hired, at a pontoon next to the dock, to tour the bustling harbour and look across the Kra River estuary to the Burmese border (approximately ₿400). Border officials can be touchy so carry your passport. Ranong is an important point of contact between Burma and Thailand. Like Mae Sot, there are more intensive searches and check points as you leave the area. Do not be surprised if the military come onto your bus up to three or four times on the way out to check documents.

→LAEM SON NATIONAL PARK

There are a number of notable beaches and islands in the neighbourhood of Ranong, many within the limits of the Laem Son National Park, such as Hat Bang Baen, Koh Khang Khao, Koh Khao Khwai, Koh Nam Noi, Koh Kam Yai, Koh Kam Tok, Koh Chang and Koh Phayam (pronounced pie-yam). The water here is warm and a pleasure to swim in, especially around the reefs. The park and the islands effectively lie at the outer limits of the Kra River estuary – so don't expect coral on all islands or excellent visibility. Mangroves fringe many of the islands and because of the high rainfall in the area the natural vegetation is tropical rainforest. While the islands may not have the best snorkelling and water, they hide some wonderfully white sand and secluded beaches and they do have good birdlife (there are around 138 bird species in the park). The best birdwatching months are December to February with many migrating birds and optimum weather conditions.

ARRIVING IN LAEM SON NATIONAL PARK

Laem Son National Park is 45 km south of Ranong. The park offices are at Hat Bang Baen (see below). Slow boats leave up to four times a day during high season to Koh Chang and Koh Phayam from the island pier (aka Sapaan Plaa pier) in Ranong at the end of Sapaan Plaa Rd. The cost is ฿150 and the journey takes one to two hours. The schedule in low season is less certain and you may have to wait some time in Ranong for a boat. There are also some speedboat connections in high season; these vary from year to year but there should be up to three departures a day. The price is likely to more than double that of the slow boat, but journey times are only 30 to 40 minutes. Other islands can be accessed via Hat Bang Baen (see below). For trips to Koh Surin, see page 204, and Koh Similan, see page 205.

BEACHES AND ISLANDS

Hat Bang Baen is an enormous, relatively untouched beach lined by forest, with lovely shells and fine sand. You can organize boat trips from here to nearby islands. These include **Koh Khang Khao** (25 minutes from Hat Bang Baen), where you'll find a small white-sand beach for sunbathing and rocks for picnics; **Koh Khao Khwai** (30 minutes from Khang Khao), another beautiful island boasting a long stretch of beach and azure water; **Koh Kam Yai** (15 minutes from Khao Khwai), which is all rocks and mountains, with just one short, quiet beach, and **Koh Kam Noi** (10 minutes from Kam Yai), which has only one small white-sand beach. To reach all these islands you will need to negotiate with the locals for boat transportation; prices fluctuate widely during the seasonal highs and lows. You may have to pay an entry fee here of ฿200. To get there take any bus heading to the south from Ranong and get off on the main route No. 4 road roughly 60 km south at Sam Nak. From there you might be able to find a pick-up, motorcycle or tuk tuk to take you to the beach – you are very likely to be overcharged. Alternatively you can call **Wasana Resort** (**$$-$**, T077-828209) who offer a free pick-up for their guests. Another option is to just rent a motorcycle in Ranong and make your own way.

Koh Chang Unlike the larger Koh Chang on Thailand's east coast, Ranong's tiny Koh Chang has more to offer birdwatchers than beach lovers, but is best known for its distinctly laid-back ambience. Commonly sighted birds are kites, sea eagles and the endearingly clumsy hornbill. And, in the forest along the coast, monkeys and deer can be spied – and heard. The beaches here are mediocre at best and grim at worst, with streaks of black and dubious grey-yellow sand. The island also hibernates from June to mid-October when the monsoon rains lash down with even locals shifting to the mainland, leaving Koh Chang almost empty. But what this island lacks in beach bounty, it makes up for in the chill-out stakes. While there is a burgeoning backpacker tourist industry replete with yoga and dive schools, beach bars and tattooists, the economy still depends on fishing and plantations of rubber, palm and cashew nut. Self-generated electricity remains sporadic and there is no sign of cars, with most people getting around on motorbikes through tracks to the beaches. But, while the beaches are never going to be used in an ice cream advert, the swimmable **Ao Yai** on the west coast is well worth a visit. It's split in two by a strip of a lagoon. From Ao Yai you can see the thuggish silhouette of Burma's mountainous jungle-covered **St Matthew's Island**, which seems to take up most of the horizon. St Matthew's is a massive radar site with a direct satellite link to China. Koh Chang also sports a radar site, for the Thai navy.

Koh Phayam Buffered by Koh Similan, Koh Phayam, along with Koh Chang, were the only inhabited islands on the Ranong coastline not to suffer any deaths from the 2004 tsunami. Only on Koh Phayam would there be both Full Moon Parties – albeit low-key ones – and a Miss Cashew Nut Beauty Competition (held during the Cashew Nut Festival). Koh Phayam has no cars, and boasts only narrow rutted roads, which run through the nut plantations. There are, however, a series of small tracks around the island for walking, cycling or motorbiking to make a change from lounging on the long and curving white-sand beaches at Ao Yai 'Sunset Bay' or Ao Khao Kwai 'Buffalo Bay'. These days, Koh Phayam has become a quiet hit for the laid-back diving and snorkelling set. This is partly because the island, sometimes called the 'muck divers playground,' offers such offshore delights as flat worms, ascidians, sponges, soft corals, nudibranchs and a variety of sea horses. If you are not the diving sort, the island is also home to wonderfully diverse wildlife with hornbills, while further inland away from the white sandy beaches are monitor lizards, boar, deer, monkeys and snakes. There is also a tiny fishing village on the east coast of the island and a sea gypsy settlement to the west. As for locals, Koh Phayam is populated by Burmese and Thai, 200 and 300 respectively, and there are even a handful of full-time *farang* but, come May, this hardy bunch largely dribbles away.

Though still a relatively sleepy island, Koh Phayam's guesthouses, especially on Buffalo Bay, have developed steadily since the tsunami, flourishing as the Koh Surin, which are easily accessible from Phayam, become ever more popular. The effects of this development on the island's idyllic status is a cause of concern; there are already serious problems with sewage and rubbish from the ferries crossing between the islands and the mainland. Ecological awareness is therefore high on the island's agenda; recycling, solar power and conservative use of electricity are encouraged (bring a torch). It is possible to hire motorbikes (฿200 per day) but be warned that the roads are sometimes treacherous, narrow and uneven.

TAKUAPA AND AROUND

Located about 25 km north of Khao Lak, Takuapa is an important transport hub if you are travelling between Khao Lak, Khao Sok, Phuket, Surat Thani and Ranong. There is little to do in the small town itself, apart from wait for a bus, but the nearby small fishing town of **Bang Nam Khem** is worth a visit if you do stop off here. Nam Khem suffered the largest number of Thai-national deaths in the 2004 tsunami, with an unknown total of maybe thousands of illegal Burmese migrants also dying here. A few years ago a **Tsunami Memorial Park** was created here and represents one of the only proper monuments to the tsunami dead anywhere on the Andaman coast. It consists of a large walk-through sculpture and a long black stone wave breaking onto a concrete wall. The inner wall of the wave is inscribed with the names of the lost. Despite its obscure location, the park is a tasteful and relaxing space to spend a couple of hours, located on a promontory with cooling sea breezes, plenty of shade and a decent beach at low tide. You can also find food and drink here. South of Nam Khem are some fantastic and almost completely unspoilt beaches, with at least one excellent place to stay available at the time of publication.

KHAO SOK NATIONAL PARK

ⓘ *www.khaosok.com, entry ฿400.*

Arriving in the park The closest town to Khao Sok National Park is Takua Pa but companies from Phuket, Phangnga, Krabi and Surat Thani operate day and overnight tours. An overnight tour is the best way to explore the park. If you want to get into the forest, take an overnight tour into the park with an experienced guide. Overnight stays by the lake, although spartan, are recommended, as the scenery is spectacular and the early morning calm is hard to beat. Tours are available from virtually all the guesthouses near the park. Park rangers will also act as guides. Have a chat with your guide before you make up your mind to go so you can be sure you feel comfortable about the level of English (or other languages) they speak, familiarity with the park and knowledge of the environment and wildlife. Taking a guide is sensible as the treks take longer than a day and can be daunting, even for the more experienced walkers. Expect to pay from ฿1300 per person for a guide to take you on a day trek, and around ฿2500 per person for an overnight trip to the reservoir (this includes accommodation and all meals), plus the ฿400 to enter the park. Prices vary depending on how many people are in the group. If visiting the park independently, buses from Phuket to Surat Thani stop on the main road a couple of kilometres from the park entrance and hub of guesthouses. When you arrive at the stop, there will usually be a number of bungalow operators waiting to whisk you off to their establishment; you can otherwise walk or take transport into the park. If you decide to walk, take a small pack as it's quite a hike to some bungalows.

Landscape and wildlife Khao Sok National Park has limestone karst mountains (the tallest reaches more than 900 m), low mountains covered with evergreen forest, streams and waterfalls, and a large reservoir and dam. The impressive scenery alone would be a good enough reason to visit, but Khao Sok also has a high degree of endemism and an exceptionally large number of mammals, birds, reptiles and other fauna.

The list of 48 confirmed species of mammals include: wild elephants, tigers, barking deer, langur, macaques, civets, bears, gibbons and cloud leopards. Of the 184 confirmed bird species, perhaps the most dramatic include: the rhinoceros hornbill, great hornbill, Malayan peacock pheasant and crested serpent-eagle. The plants to be found here are also of interest. The orchids are best seen from late February to April. If you visit between December and February, the **rafflesia Kerri Meijer** is in flower. This parasitic flower (it depends on low-lying lianas) has an 80-cm bloom – the largest in the world – with a phenomenally pungent odour so that it can attract the highest number of pollinating insects. It also has no chlorophyll. Besides the astounding rafflesia, there are also at least two palms endemic to the Khao Sok area.

Around the park In the centre of the park is the **Rachabrapah Reservoir**. Near the dam there is a longhouse of sorts, and several houseboats. The best location for animal spotting is near the reservoir where grassland at the edge of the reservoir attracts animals.

In addition to camping, canoeing and walking tours, you can take elephant treks at Khao Sok. The routes taken must be outside the park, however, as elephant trekking is not permitted within the confines of the national park.

Like many of the wonders of nature in Thailand, Khao Sok does not come without a giant technological blot. In this case, it's a hydroelectric dam right next to Khao Sok that has formed a vast artificial lake that now comprises one border of the national park. This dam began in the 1980s and has since become the bane of the park, as it transformed hills and valleys into small islands, trapping the wildlife with rising tides. While there have been attempts to rescue the beleaguered wildlife, nothing has proved successful as yet. But Khao Sok is successfully capitalizing on its assets.

KHAO LAK

A few years ago, before the infamous 2004 tsunami that killed 5000 and before the construction boom that followed it, Khao Lak was a sleepy beach town. Palms swayed, locals served up food and beer, and the almost empty beaches provided an idyllic backdrop. If you look closely enough, Khao Lak's original ambience can still be found, but it is certainly on the endangered list.

Khao Lak encompasses a range of beaches, coves and headlands spread out along a 10- to 15-km stretch of coast. There isn't actually a town officially called Khao Lak, but the main settlement is centred near busy **Nang Thong** beach. Here you'll find a run of generic four- to five-star resorts, with some, illegally, being built directly on the beach. **Bang Niang** is also fairly busy, with a similar run of resorts aimed at package tourists, whilst the beaches to the north (**Khuk Kak**, **Pakweeb** and **Bangsak**) get progressively quieter. It seems that, such was the rush to redevelop Khao Lak after the tsunami, there are now too many resorts competing for a small market share; how many will still be operating in five years' time is debatable. It is also worth noting that the Thai domestic market that existed pre-tsunami has now almost disappeared, because the superstitious Thais refuse to stay somewhere where the potential for malevolent ghosts and spirits is high.

Yet, despite having undergone all these dramatic changes in such a short period, the beaches here are still excellent and, if you find the right spot, you should be able to have an excellent beach holiday or short break here. Given its proximity to the Koh Similans, Khao Lak is now becoming something of a dive mecca, with a few excellent dive operators based here. The best way to get around is to rent a bicycle or small motorbike (฿150-250 per day). There are some songthaews available but they are notorious for fleecing tourists and are best avoided.

→KOH SURIN

Five islands make up this marine national park, just south of the Burmese border, and 53 km off the mainland. The two main islands, **Koh Surin Tai** and **Koh Surin Nua** (South and North Surin respectively), are separated by a narrow strait which can be waded at low tide. Both islands are hilly, with few inhabitants; a small community of Chao Le fishermen live on Koh Surin Tai.

ARRIVING IN KOH SURIN

Boats run by the national park leave from the pier at Ban Hin Lat, 1 km west of Kuraburi (4-5 hours, ฿1500). Kuraburi is two hours by bus south of Ranong. Long-tailed boats can be hired around Koh Surin. Various tour operators, agents, resorts and dive shops from both Phuket and Ranong organize their own speedboats, liveaboards and the like to visit Surin, with prices and travel times varying according to the distance and level of service provided. The national park office is at Ao Mae Yai, on the southwest side of Koh Surin Nua. Best time to visit is December to March. Koh Surin Tai may close to visitors during the full moon each March, when the Chao Le hold a festival.

DIVING

The diving and snorkelling is good here, and the coral reefs are said to be the most diverse in Thailand. However, overfishing has led some people to maintain that diving is now better around the Similan Islands. Novices will still find the experience both exhilarating and enchanting.

There have been concerns expressed regarding the detrimental effects of tourism on several marine national parks, including the Surin Islands Marine National Park and, for a while, parts of the island have been closed to visitors. Everyone visiting the Surin should engage in the best diving/snorkelling practices and not touch or remove any wildlife or coral. A good website for information on snorkelling and diving in and around Surin is www.ko-surin-diving.com.

→KOH SIMILAN

ⓘ *Vessels depart from Thap Lamu pier, 20 km north of Thai Muang (3-5 hrs) to the Similans, 40 km offshore. Boats also leave from Ao Chalong and Patong Beach, Phuket with Songserm Travel (T076-222570), Tue, Thu and Sat from Dec-Apr, 6-10 hrs. Boats also leave from Ranong. The best time to visit is Dec-Apr. The west monsoon makes the islands virtually inaccessible during the rest of the year; be warned that boats have been known to capsize at this time. Also, bear in mind that transport away from the islands is unpredictable and you might find yourself stranded here, rapidly running out of money. At the end of Mar/early Apr underwater visibility is not good, but this is the best time to see manta rays and whale sharks.*

The Similan Islands lying 80 km northwest of Phuket and 65 km west of Khao Lak are some of the most beautiful, unspoilt tropical idylls in Southeast Asia. The national park consists of nine islands (named by Malay fishermen, who referred to them as the 'Nine Islands' – *sembilan* is Malay for nine). The water surrounding the archipelago supports a wealth of marine life and is considered one of the best diving locations in the world, as well as a good place for anglers. A particular feature of the islands is the huge granite boulders. These same boulders litter the seabed and make for interesting peaks and caves for scuba divers. On the west side of the islands the currents have kept the boulders 'clean', while on the east, they have been buried by sand. The contrast between diving on the west and east coasts is defined by the boulders. On the west, currents sweep around these massive granite structures, some as large as houses, which can be swum around and through and many have fantastic colourful soft coral growing on them. A guide is essential on the west, as navigation can be tricky. The east is calmer, with hard coral gardens sloping from the surface down to 30-40 m. Navigation is straightforward here and can be done with a buddy, without the need for a guide.

Koh Miang, named after the king's daughter, houses the park office and some dormitory and camping accommodation. While water did sweep over Koh Miang, it is largely recovered and was the first place that Thailand's navy established a tsunami warning system. **Koh Hu Yong**, the southernmost island, is the most popular diving location.

RANONG TO KHAO LAK LISTINGS

WHERE TO STAY

Ranong

$$$$-$$$ Jansom Hot Spa Hotel, 2/10 Petkasem Rd, T077-811 5103, www.jansomhotsparanong.net. In places, this is a slightly shabby spa hotel with charming pretensions of grandeur. However, there have been some improvements over the years, and the rooms remain a good deal, with bathtubs, linen, fridge and TV. The rooms, pool and a huge jacuzzi are all supplied with mineral water from the nearby hot springs. Breakfast included.

$ Dahla House, 323/5 Ruangrat Rd, T077-812959, dahla.siam2web.com. Nice, clean bungalows set in a private compound within easy walking distance of the town centre. All have en suite facilities with hot water. The owners are friendly and speak good English. They also have an internet café.

Takuapa

$$$$-$$ ThaiLife Homestay, 1/3 Moo 2, Bang Muang, T08-1812 0388, www.thailifehomestay.com. Just south of Baan Nam Khem the beach stretches out into a long slice of unspoilt white sand. Set back some 800 m from the sand, near the village of Bang Muang, is the **ThaiLife Homestay**: a collection of gorgeous, raised wooden villas, set around a pond, all with a/c, TV, hot showers and very comfy interiors. **ThaiLife** is the only resort on this entire stretch of beach, so it has a supremely relaxing vibe. It's also friendly and serves great food. It's slightly tricky to reach; you'll need either your own transport or an arrangement with **ThaiLife** to collect you from Khao Lak (฿400), Phuket town (฿2200) or the airport (฿1800). Recommended.

Khao Sok

$$$-$$ Art's Riverview Lodge, T08-6470 3234 (mob), artsriverviewlodge@yahoo. co.uk. Art's is long-running, stylish and popular, so book ahead. Its 30 rooms include substantial lodges with balconies overlooking the river. There is no hot water. The restaurant is beside the river near a swimming hole with a rope providing endless entertainment. Impertinent monkeys congregate at sunset to be fed bananas by residents.

$$-$ Khao Sok Palmview Resort, 234 Moo 6, T08-6163 5478, www.khaosok-palmview.com. The local family that runs this collection of excellent budget bungalows is wonderfully friendly, and, consequently, this feels more like a homestay than a resort. Rooms are basic – fans and cold water in the cheaper ones – but the atmosphere is pleasingly soporific. The family also serves excellent and authentic Thai food. Recommended.

Khao Lak

$$$-$$ Khao Lak Golden Place, 30/30 Moo 7, Soi Had Nang Thong, T076-485686, www.khaolakgoldenplace.com. Nice small hotel, set a short walk from Nang Thong beach. Contemporary, neat rooms and a/c, en suite, TV, Wi-Fi. One of the cheapest and best options in this part of Khao Lak. Recommended.

$$$-$ Thup Thong Guest House, Bang Niang Beach, 53/1 Moo 5, T076-486722, thupthong@gmail.com. One of the few buildings to survive the 2004 tsunami that obliterated most of Khao Lak, Thup Thong is also one of the only remaining budget, family-run places on a beachfront now dominated by package-tourist resorts. The rooms in the guesthouse are basic, but clean, with a/c and fan and all en suite. The owners have now started to build a few brand-new, more stylish bungalows. There's also a small restaurant/bar plus a friendly welcome. Recommended for those on a budget.

Koh Surin

$$$-$ National Park bungalows are available for ฿2000 a night; camping costs ฿300 in a rented tent. Call the park offices on T076-491378, T076-419028 for bookings, which are advised, or visit www.dnp.go.th for more details.

Koh Similan

$$$-$ Bungalows are now available on Koh Ba Ngu. Reservations can be made at the **Similan National Park Office**, Thai Muang, or at Tap Lamu Pier, T076-411 914. Camping may also be possible on Koh Ba Ngu. Bring your own tent. Visit www.dnp.go.th for more details.

RESTAURANTS

Ranong

The markets on **Ruangrat Rd** offer some of the best eating opportunities in town with specials worth sampling including the roast pork and duck. Also worth seeking out for its famously delicious dahl lunches is the Muslim roti shop (no English sign) on Rungruat Rd, opposite TV Bar and guesthouse. Look for the roti/pancake stand outside.

WHAT TO DO

Ranong

Pon's Place Travel Agency, by the new market on Ruangrat Rd, T077 823344. Run by the affable Mr Pon who is an excellent source of information on the islands and areas surrounding Ranong and can help with tours, travel information, guesthouse/hotel bookings, and car and bike rental.

Khao Sok

Khao Sok Track & Trail Travel, T08-1747 3030, www.khaosoktrackandtrail.info. This very helpful tour operator and travel agency just by the gates of the park can arrange a variety of trekking tours, including canoeing, visits to the lake and overnight trips. They also have currency exchange and internet. Recommended.

Khao Lak
Diving

Diving operations, including live-aboard boats, day trips and courses, are still widely available from various operators. Dive sites along the coast, including the Similan Islands, Koh Bon, Koh Tachai, Koh Surin and Richelieu Rock as well as the Mergui Archipelago, received minimal damage during the tsunami although there have been some changes around Island Number Nine in the Similans that you will need to check. The best way to enjoy the Surin Islands is to join one of the daily dive trips from coastal towns. The dive sites in the Mergui Archipelago were left unscathed while the islands escaped topside damage or destruction. Contrary to reports, there are still Moken sea gypsies living in the Mergui Archipelago. **Khao Lak Scuba Adventures**, 13/47 Moo 7, Khuk Kak, T076-485602, www.khaolakscuba adventures.com. Well-run 5-star PADI dive resort located in central Khao Lak, offering all the usual PADI courses and live-aboard trips to the Koh Similans. **Sea Dragon**, 9/1 Moo 7, T Khuk Kak, T076-420420, www.seadragondivecenter.com. A well-established operation organizing day trips or liveaboards to Richelieu Rock, Similan and Surin Islands. Teaches PADI dive courses. European-managed.

Koh Similan

Hotels and tour operators organize boat and dive trips and most dive companies in Phuket offer tours to the Similan Islands . Although it is possible to visit the Similan Islands independently, it can be an expensive and/or time-consuming business; it is far easier to book onto a tour. See also under Khao Lak, above, for further information.

PHUKET ISLAND

Known as the 'Pearl of the Andaman', Phuket lies on Southern Thailand's west coast on the warm Andaman Sea and is connected to the mainland by a 700-m-long causeway. It is a fully developed resort island, with hundreds of hotels and restaurants, marinas, golf courses and some gorgeous beaches. As Thailand's largest island, about the same size as Singapore, there are still remnants of tropical rainforest and traditional life to be found inland and a few cultural attractions, including the thriving, often-overlooked Phuket City, where there's an emerging arts and dining scene and a push to restore its charming old Sino-Portuguese buildings.

→ARRIVING IN PHUKET

GETTING THERE

Phuket is nearly 900 km south of Bangkok but getting to the island is easy if you're coming direct from the capital rather than Ranong (see page 199). Phuket International Airport is in the north of the island, about 30 km from Phuket City, but rather closer to many of the main beaches and hotels. There are international connections and multiple daily connections with Bangkok and daily connections to Krabi.

The municipal airport bus service to Phuket City (see www.airportbusphuket.com) has 12 departure times 0630-2045 and costs ฿85. It stops at eight destinations along the way and takes about an hour. From Ranong Road in Phuket City you can catch other buses to the main beaches. Alternatively, shared minivans, metered yellow taxis or limousine taxis are available, the latter two options working out a lot more expensive. All have been known to make unscheduled stops at travel agents in the hope that you'll book a hotel or tour – politely decline any sales pitches and you should be on your way again soon.

As you leave the airport, hordes of limousine drivers will try and usher you into their vehicles. To get to the metered taxis, turn right as you exit the airport and walk down to the kiosk. Despite being metered, the taxis will usually insist you agree on the fare beforehand or levy a ฿100 surcharge. A taxi from the airport to Phuket City shouldn't cost more than ฿500, while a minivan service should cost about ฿150. Several resorts offer free transport from the airport; be sure to check when booking. Airport transfers can also be prearranged through most hotels, as well as operators like **Phuket Shuttle** ① *T08-9972 3300 www.phuketshuttle.com*, or **Hello Phuket Co** ① *www.hellophuket.net*.

Cheaper ways into Phuket City are either to walk or catch a *songthaew* the 5 km to the main north–south road, Route 402, and pick up a public bus or alternatively, walk out of the airport gate and wait for a motorcycle taxi dropping someone off (฿30), they cannot pick up fares at the airport itself. Buses take passengers to Patong, Kata and Karon beaches for ฿100, or by private taxi for ฿400.

The main **bus terminal** ① *Phangnga Rd, T076-211480*, is in Phuket City and there are regular connections with Bangkok (14 hours) as well as destinations in the south. In Bangkok, many buses for Phuket leave from Khaosan Rd. Be careful with these and don't economize as thieves have been known to board the Khaosan buses, which have a suspicious habit of 'breaking down'. Much better buses may be booked directly at Bangkok's Southern Bus Terminal. The southern railway line doesn't come to the island. However, it is possible to take a train to Phun Phin near Surat Thani and then catch a connecting bus (six hours).

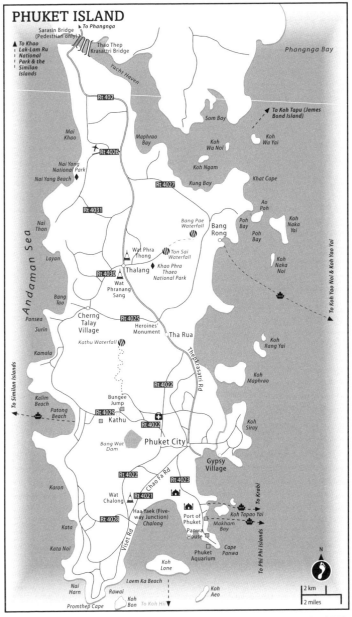

FESTIVALS
Phuket

September to October (movable) **Chinese Vegetarian Festival,** *Tetsakan Kin Jeh*, lasts nine days and marks the beginning of Taoist lent some time between September and October. No meat is eaten, alcohol consumed nor sex indulged in (in order to cleanse the soul). Men pierce their cheeks or tongues with long spears and other sharp objects and walk over hot coals and (supposedly) feel no pain. The festival is celebrated elsewhere, but most enthusiastically in Phuket, especially at Wat Jui Tui on Ranong Road in Phuket City. It's one of Phuket's star attractions; visitors are welcomed and pictures make the international newspapers.

GETTING AROUND

Songthaew buses run from Phuket City to Patong, Kamala, Surin, Makham Bay, Nai Yang, Kata, Karon, Nai Harn, Rawai, Thalang and Chalong about every 30 minutes between 0600 and 1800 from the market on Ranong Road. Fares range from ฿25-35, to whatever the ticket collector thinks he can get away with. There are also numerous places to hire cars/jeeps, for ฿900 a day, and motorbikes, for ฿200 a day, as well as tuk-tuks. Local buses stop around 1800; tuk-tuks take advantage of this so it is essential to know what constitutes a reasonable fare: travel within Phuket City shouldn't be more than about ฿100 and travel to Patong from Phuket City and vice versa should cost you about ฿450. Thanks to the power of the local tuk-tuk operators, metered taxis are not allowed to pick up passengers from anywhere in Phuket except at the airport or unless they are booked privately.

MOVING ON

Buses operate regularly to Phangnga (two hours).

BEST TIME TO VISIT

The driest and sunniest months are November to April. May to October are wetter with more chance of overcast conditions, although daily sunshine still averages five to eight hours. August is when the monsoon begins and red flags appear to warn swimmers not to venture out because of powerful and sometimes fatal currents.

TOURIST INFORMATION

The **TAT** office ① *191 Thalang Rd, T076-212213, tatphket@tat.or.th, daily 0830-1630*, is good for specific local questions. The island's two weekly newspapers, *Phuket Gazette*, www.phuketgazette.net and *The Phuket News*, www.thephuketnews.com, are good sources of information, with quirky local human-interest stories, events calendars and community updates. Two independent expat-run blogs, Jamie's Phuket (www.jamie-monk.blogspot.com) and Phuket 101 (www.phuket101.blogspot.com) offer resort and restaurant reviews and insider's tips on things to do and see.

→PHUKET CITY

Phuket City was given city status in 2004, although most islanders still call it Phuket Town. This upgrade came as a surprise to many who still regard it as a sleepy provincial hub, hardly big or bustling enough to merit the city crown. Treated largely as a stopover by divers en route to the Similan or Surin islands and beach junkies headed further up the coast, Phuket City is now anxious to revamp its image and pull in a more sophisticated crowd. So, in addition to its Sino-Portuguese architectural heritage, which is reminiscent of Georgetown in Malaysian Penang – a leftover of the wealthy Chinese tin barons of the 19th century – there is a burgeoning arts and literary scene. It seems to be working as, increasingly, the city's incomers include weary Bangkok urbanites hankering for a business by the sea and expat foodies attracted by the city's excellent restaurant reputation. But Phuket City is still small enough and swamped enough by the glory of the beaches, to be down the pecking order. Not that this matters to the old-timers who can still remember when the town was surrounded by virgin forest. This is, perhaps, the card up Phuket City's sleeve – a subtle confidence underneath the tourist glitter, especially in the old town, and a feeling that another chapter is unravelling in this prosperous settlement. A cooler, hipper Phuket could easily emerge if the arts scene gets beyond the cottage industry feel and allows itself to be injected by that incoming Bangkok and expat buzz. What will aid Phuket City is that it still has

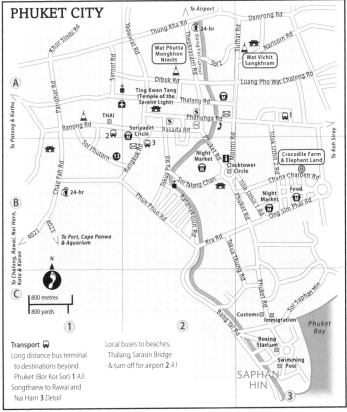

PHUKET CITY

Transport

Long distance bus terminal to destinations beyond Phuket (Bor Kor Sor) 1 A3
Songthaew to Rawai and Nai Harn 3 Detail

Local buses to beaches, Thalang, Sarasin Bridge & turn off for airport 2 A1 some grand old buildings left, which are rare in Thailand and a magnet for those with an eye for architecture. The push in recent years to restore and beautify these historical buildings and streets has certainly helped inject a sense of pride and culture into the Old Town.

At the end of the 19th century, Phuket Town, one of the richest settlements in the country, saw a flowering of Sino-Portuguese mansions built by tin-barons revelling in their wealth. In Old Phuket you'll still find houses and shops in styles similar to that of Penang and Macao and dating back 100 to 130 years. Featuring complex latticework, Mediterranean coloured ceramic tiles, high ceilings and gleaming wooden interiors, these architectural dreams, remain cool in the summer and free of damp during the monsoon. While the style is commonly called Sino-Portuguese, many were actually built by Italian workers who imported materials straight from their homeland. During the Old Phuket Town Festival, held each year after Chinese New Year, some of these houses are open to the public. The best examples are along Thalang, Yaowarat, Ranong, Phangnga, Krabi, Dibuk, Rassada, Soi Romanee and Damrong roads.

A particularly notable example of one of Phuket's finer older buildings is the **Government House**, which stood in as the 'American Embassy' in Phnom Penh in the classic film – *The Killing Fields*. Preservation orders have been placed on all buildings in Old Phuket. Among the finer ones are the **Chartered Bank THAI office** ① *Ranong Rd opposite the market*, and the **Sala Phuket** ① *Damrong Rd*. Less grand, but quietly elegant, are the turn-of-the-20th-century **shophouses** on, for example, Thalang Road. There has been considerable renovation of buildings on Dibuk, Thalang and Krabi roads but nearby there are still side streets with some lovely examples of traditional shophouses. **Soi Romanee**, the island's former red-light district, in particular is such a street with traditional merchant houses on both sides of the road, a few with fading paintwork on the walls. Some of the renovation has introduced smart new restaurants, cafés, art galleries and antique shops. Notably, **The Loft**, which sells expensive Southeast Asian antiques and Chinese porcelains and received an award for its efforts in conserving traditional architecture. At the same time there are still plenty of more traditional hardware stores, small tailors, stationery shops and the like, that clearly cater to the locals. Another sight worth visiting in the old town is the **Temple of the Serene Light** ① *Phangnga Rd, entrance is marked in English and Thai*. The narrow alleyway leading to it has been opened up, making the temple easier to spot from the street but destroying some of its mystery in the process. More than a century old, this is a small Taoist temple, filled with paintings and religious artefacts, that was rebuilt following a fire. It is the oldest Taoist temple in Phuket and is dedicated to the Goddess of Mercy. For more information on Phuket's past, The Old Town Foundation has opened a small museum on Phangnga Road, and a museum for the Baba Perkanen (Straits Chinese) culture is being developed at the former police station on Rassada Rd.

There are **night markets** on Ong Sim Phai and Tilok Uthit 1. These are excellent places to buy spicy rolls and other street foods on a nocturnal prowl through the old town. Khao Rang Viewpoint is a romantic spot atop a large hill in Phuket City. Although the view isn't quite as stunning as at Promthep Cape, Khao Rang is a cool place to watch over the whole of the city. There's also a fitness park up here if you feel like a bit of exercise. There are a few reasonable Thai restaurants around that offer the same great views. To reach Khao Rang, you need to make your way up the hill by either travelling from Yaowarat Road on to Soi Vachira, turning right at the end of the *soi* and following the hill up; or take the turn up to Khao Rang at the point where Thung Kha Road and Mae Luan Road meet.

A few kilometres south of Phuket City is **Phuket Zoo** ① *23/2 Moo 3, Soi Palai, Chao Fa Rd, T076-381227, www.phuketzoo.com*. There are regular elephant, monkey and crocodile shows here but the place screams 'tourist photo opportunity', and foreign visitors are covertly charged about four times the local price. Only recommended if you relish the thought of having your picture taken with a chained-up, heavily sedated white tiger.

→PHUKET'S BEACHES AND SIGHTS

The gorgeous 3-km-long sweep of sand and coconut palms of Patong Beach (see below) that attracted backpackers in the 1970s is now a dim memory. Now the island's party central, Patong has a boisterous nightlife scene and the beach is crammed with speedboats, jet-skis and row upon row of rental sun loungers. For less hedonistic, smaller beaches that still have charm, go south of Patong. Here you will find the twin, horseshoe-shaped Karon and Kata beaches. **Karon Beach** is around half the size of Patong, less densely developed, and with a general atmosphere that is more laid-back and family friendly. **Kata Beach** is also popular with families, but its streets are like a mini-Patong, with hotels, restaurants and shops chaotically jostling for space.

At Phuket's southern end is **Nai Harn**, a pretty white beach favoured by Thais, with a small number of more expensive hotels and limited amenities. In the middle of this charming beach, the **Samnak Song Monastery** acts as an unexpected bodyguard against major developers, but the main road leading here, Sai Yuan, is under furious development.

The east coast of Phuket is only thinly developed from a tourist point of view. Much of it is rocky and the beaches that are to be found here do not compare with those on the west coast. There are some excellent hotels, but these are largely stand-alone establishments; don't expect a great wealth of facilities.

Kamala Beach, north of Patong, was severely affected by the 2004 tsunami, but it has now completely recovered and is one of the fastest-growing resort areas of Phuket. The next beach north is **Surin**, home to Phuket's first golf course more than 60 years ago, during the reign of King Rama VII. The course is now in disuse and serves as a public park and overflow car park. A growing beach club scene is turning Surin into a place to swill cocktails while looking fabulous.

Surin and **Bang Tao**, further north, are similar in that the resorts are widely spaced with no centre for shops. Bang Tao was formerly used for tin mining which turned the landscape into a desert. **Nai Ton** and **Layan** are small bays with exclusive resorts. Finally, at the northern end of the island, is **Nai Yang Beach** and the **Nai Yang National Park**, a 9-km casuarina-lined beach with a few resorts and some park bungalows.

PATONG BEACH

Patong began to metamorphose from a hippy paradise into a commercial centre during the 1970s. It is now a mass of neon signs advertising hotels, massage parlours, restaurants, straight bars, gay bars, nightclubs and the plain peculiar. While families may not be able to avoid vulgarity, they will be able to bypass ladyboys and devious side-street deals by choosing from a range of excellent family hotels. Patong tourists are a mixed lot – a Butlins overspill, shameless beer boys and plump retirees. Increasingly, Russians are also turning up, both for business and revelry.

Take Patong for what it is: an overdeveloped mass of cheap booze, expensive restaurants, mediocre beaches and odd characters. For a night out, it's fun, but otherwise, there's little point in basing your holiday around a stay in Patong. Many visitors to Phuket spend all of their time in Patong and then leave with a negative view of the island as a whole. Don't be one of them, there is so much more to Phuket.

Patong does, however, offer the widest selection of watersports on Phuket and, in spite of hotel development, it is still possible to snorkel on the reef at the southern end of the bay.

Driving towards Karon from Patong you will come to **Tri Trang Beach**, a charming little beach located in front of the Merlin Beach Resort. The area is spotless with very few disturbances but the water is full of rocks and not suitable for swimming during low tide. There is decent snorkelling here and few tourists ever make it out this way. From Tri Trang Beach it's possible to charter a long-tailed boat to picturesque **Freedom Beach**, you can't get to there by road, where the water and sand are beautiful.

KARON AND KATA BEACHES
The horseshoe-shaped Karon and Kata beaches south of Patong are divided by a narrow rocky outcrop. Karon started tourist life as a haven for backpackers; it is now well developed, with a range of hotels and bungalows and a wide selection of restaurants. Though Russian visitors are starting to come here in larger numbers, the Karon scene is dominated by prosperous Scandinavians. Some places bear mini Swedish flags, and it is usually these establishments that are guaranteed to make you feel as if you never left the aeroplane. This can prove tedious and an air of predictability and safety pervades the beach. Karon's major drawback, physically, is the overly exposed beach despite its cosy curve. Nonetheless, there are good mid-range places to stay, and the slower pace of life here will appeal to many.

Kata consists of two beaches: **Kata Yai** (Big) and **Kata Noi** (Little), divided by a cliff. Both bays are picturesque with rocks along the edges and sweeping fine pale yellow sands in the centre. Descending a winding hill, Kata Noi comes as a pleasant surprise, offering an adorable little bay with a small and perfect beach. Although it is dominated by the **Katathani Phuket Beach Resort**, on the whole it feels much like a hidden seaside harbour, and even the tourist infrastructure of souvenir shops, guesthouses, laundries and restaurants are made up of a pleasant jumble of locally owned businesses. There are also cheapish bungalows here. The snorkelling is good at the south end of Kata Noi and around Koh Pu, the island in the middle of the bay that looks like a squashed bowler hat. Kata Yai, just the other side, is a sprawling mass of development: hotels, souvenir shops and roadside restaurants abound. It provides excellent facilities for the holidaymaker. including numerous options for watersports and mostly low-key nightlife choices down the rambling streets running inland from the coast. Despite this, the huge hotels on the beach overwhelm the bay with umbrellas and sunbeds spread across almost the entire beach. The beautifully painted and cared-for tour boats with their smart wooden benches and umbrellas are a far cry from the traditional fisherman's longboats, on which they are obviously modelled.

NAI HARN AND PROMTHEP CAPE
Nai Harn, a small, gently sloping beach – home to the prestigious **Royal Phuket Yacht Club** – is one of the island's most beautiful locations, renowned for its spectacular sunsets. From Nai Harn it is possible to walk to **Promthep Cape**, the best place to view the sunset if you don't mind the crowds. Near the highest point there is a shrine covered in gold leaf and surrounded by wooden elephants.

RAWAI

To the north of Promthep Cape, up the eastern side of the island and 14 km south of Phuket City, the first beach is Rawai, which was 'discovered' by King Rama VII in the 1920s. This crescent-shaped beach is now relatively developed although not to the same degree as Patong or Karon, being more popular with Thai and Southeast Asian tourists, particularly during Chinese New Year and Songkran. Many Thais go to Rawai for the cheap restaurants, although prices are going up. The bay is sheltered and it is safe to swim throughout the year, but the beach, although long and relatively peaceful, is rather dirty and rocky. Rawai is more of a jumping-off point for offshore trips to Koh Hae (Coral Island), Koh Bon and Koh Lone. At Rawai's northern end there is also a sea gypsy village, **Chao Le**.

KOH KAEW PISADARN

ⓘ *Take a long-tailed boat from Rawai Beach; negotiate with one of the boat owners, take a picnic and arrange to be picked up.*

Koh Kaew Pisadarn can be seen from Promthep Cape and is a 15-minute boat ride from Rawai Beach. The island is the site of three footprints of the Buddha. Two are among the boulders and stone on the upper shore; the third is just below the low watermark. For many years important Buddhist festivals were celebrated here because of the island's supposed spiritual power and significance. Then, about 40 years ago, these religious pilgrimages stopped. Sam Fang, who researched a story on the island for the *Bangkok Post*, discovered a tragedy had occurred about that time. Some rowing boats en route to the island had sunk during a storm, which was blamed on a sea serpent that had become enraged by continual trespassing. Between 1952 and 1967, attempts to construct a Buddha on the island were continually thwarted by bad weather and high seas. The island quickly gained the reputation of being cursed. Only in 1994 were attempts at erecting a Buddha image renewed and, defying superstition, a 1.5-m-high concrete statue now stands on the northeastern side of the island, overlooking Promthep Cape. The statue, about a 10-minute walk along a laid path from the boat landing, is surrounded by two protective nagas that slither over the top of the encircling balustrade. Steps lead down to the footprints on the shore beneath the Buddha.

LAEM KA AND CHALONG BEACHES

The next beaches up the east coast and south of Phuket City are Laem Ka and Chalong. Ao Chalong is 1 km off the main road. There is not much here for the sun and sea worshipper: the beach is filthy and full of speedboats. From Chalong's long pier boats can be caught to the offshore islands for game fishing, snorkelling and scuba diving. There are also a few reasonable seafood restaurants from which you can watch the dozens of working and pleasure boats gather off the pier in the harbour. The rest of the east coast is of limited interest for tourists because of a rocky coast.

About 6 km south of Phuket City, just north of Chalong junction, is the ostentatious Wat Chalong, best known for its gold-leaf encrusted statues of the previous abbots, Luang Pho Chaem and Luang Pho Chuang. The former was highly respected for his medical skills, which proved to be particularly valuable when Phuket's Chinese miners revolted in 1876. The halving of the international price of tin coupled with Bangkok's attempt to extract excessive taxes from the province inflamed the Chinese. Some 2000 converged on the governor's house and when they failed to take the building, they rampaged through the less well-defended villages. The spree of killing and looting was only brought to an end at Wat Chalong where the two respected monks talked the mob out of their fury. Visible from almost anywhere around the south of Phuket City is Phuket's own Big Buddha statue. Your reward for scaling the enormous and steep Nakkerd Hill is a sweeping view of the island's southern bays and beaches and an up-close glimpse of a 45-m seated Buddha in white Burmese marble. There is also a smaller golden Buddha statue. To get to the Buddha driving from Phuket City, go past Wat Chalong and look for the sign pointing out the right-hand turn to the statue (Soi Jaofa 51).

CAPE PANWA

South of Phuket City, down Sakdidej Road which becomes Route 4023, in the grounds of the **Cape Panwa Hotel**, is **Panwa House**, one of Phuket's finest examples of Sino-Portuguese architecture. Panwa House was formerly inhabited by a fishing family from Phuket and, later, by the hotel's official coconut catcher. The catcher's job was to remove coconuts from the trees so the guests would not be concussed. However, he was under orders not to take a coconut from the trees on the beach, and in all his years as official coconut catcher, he never disobeyed. The house is now filled with curious artefacts, like the coconut scraper in the shape of an otter. The first floor has attractive views of guests below at their meals, framed by swaying palms and beach and being serenaded by performers At the tip of Panwa Cape is the popular **Phuket Aquarium** ① *T076-391126, www.phuketaquarium.org, daily 0830-1630 (last admission 1600), ฿100, children ฿50.* The air-conditioned aquarium is well laid out with a moderate collection of salt- and freshwater fish, lobsters, molluscs and turtles and some other weird species. There are regular public songthaews every hour (฿20) from the market on Ranong Road to the aquarium. Watching the sun set along the paved seafront is recommended. There are a few café/restaurants, all open to a view which always seems to include imposing Thai naval boats or cruise ships in the distance. It is possible to charter long-tailed boats from Cape Panwa to **Koh Hii** (฿600), and **Koh Mai Ton** (฿1200), or to go fishing (฿1200).

Koh Tapao Yai, a small island off the cape, is home to a few hotels and around 200 hornbills. Baby brother of Koh Tapao Yai, **Koh Tapao Noi** is another small island, secluded and devoid of almost everything except flora, fauna and hornbills. There is also a lighthouse that was built in 1890. Other than that, enjoy the beach and the sea while you can. To get there, take a boat from Ao Makham Pier (6 km from Phuket City).

KOH LONE, KOH MAI TON AND OTHER SOUTHERN ISLANDS

There are places to stay on several of the islands off the east and southeast coasts of Phuket. All the resorts play on the desert island getaway theme. These places are hard to reach in the monsoon season and often shut for up to three months of the year. Koh Mai Ton, for instance, is a private island 9 km southeast of Phuket with little on it except the Honeymoon Island Phuket Resort (formerly the Maithon Resort).

KOH MAPRAO (COCONUT ISLAND)

Coconut Island, up until recently a tourist-free island off the grid, is now home to the sprawling five-star Village Coconut Island Resort on its northern shoreline, with mains electricity coming soon. A luxury villa development is underway, too, on the opposite side. The traditional island life of its few hundred residents is still intact, however, and the village runs agro-tour and homestay programmes. To get there, make your way to Laem Hin Pier (15 minutes north of Phuket City, on the east coast, about ฿150 in a tuk-tuk), take a long-tailed boat (฿15) over to the island and a short motorcycle ride to the beach.

KOH RANG YAI

This small island off the east coast of Phuket has a focus on day trips, so you might feel like you're being herded in and out like cattle. It's a beautiful island, though, and worth a visit. The island has its own pearl farm and demonstrations are given along with a trip to a pearl shop. Bicycles are available, and there's a putting course. The beach is clean, although the water looks a bit murky and if you just fancy loafing about without many people around, this is a good place to do it.

Boats depart from Sapam Bay, which is about 15 km north of Phuket City, on the east coast. Expect to pay up to ฿300 for a tuk-tuk from Phuket City to Sapam Bay. Bungalows can be rented on the island.

KAMALA BEACH

Kamala Beach, was one of the worst hit by the 2004 tsunami, but it's now fully recovered and changing rapidly from a sleepy Muslim fishing village to a bustling resort town. Some of Phuket's priciest hotels and private villas line the rocky cape, known as the 'Millionaire's Mile', at its south end. The beach is sadly under siege by unabated commercial development, its powder-soft sands nearly completely buried under sun loungers and vendor stands in high season. The northern section is quieter, and there's some decent snorkelling among the rocks just offshore.

LAEM SING

Between Kamala and Surin is a tiny beach by the name of Laem Sing. Though it's getting more crowded with each passing year, the sand is clean and the water is clear. The only problem is the onslaught of jet skis that noisily zip around dangerously close to where people are swimming.

SURIN BEACH AND PANSEA BEACH

Surin is developing into something of a 'Tale of Two Beaches'; ritzy beach clubs and cocktail bars visited by the likes of Kate Moss take up ever more beachfront space, while the shrinking public areas, where the locals hang out, appear increasingly neglected and dirty. With numerous private villas and luxury resorts in the surrounding area, Surin's often touted as Phuket's five-star beach, which indeed it is, so long as you avert your eyes from the trash piles. A strong undertow makes swimming at Surin dangerous at times. Pansea Beach has soft sand in a steeply sloping bay just north of Surin, with two exclusive hotels.

BANG TAO BEACH

The **Laguna Phuket** complex at the north of Bang Tao Beach consists of six expensive hotels built around a lagoon. Free tuk-tuks and boats link the hotels, and guests are able to use all the facilities. There is a great range of watersports and good free provision for children. The **Canal Village** offers 40 or so shops and a lagoon-side café serving satay. The adjoining bakery serves good pastries and cakes. To the south of the **Laguna Phuket** are some other places to stay. The southern part of the beach is one of the few areas where you will still see traditional boat builders and the boats themselves in operation, instead of the tourist variety used to take people on island tours.

NAI THON AND LAYAN

Between Bang Tao and Nai Yang are the isolated beaches of Nai Thon and Layan. These beaches have recently been developed with a luxury resort and spa at Layan occupying the whole bay and similarly expensive developments are moving into Nai Thon, which only has a 400-m-long beach. South of Nai Thon is an exquisite cove, most easily accessible by boat.

NAI YANG AND NAI YANG NATIONAL PARK
ⓘ *Entrance to beach ฿200 per person.*

Nai Yang is close to the airport and 37 km from Phuket City. To get there, take a bus from the market on Ranong Road in Phuket City. The attractive and often empty forest-lined beach of Nai Yang lies next to the airport and is part of the Nai Yang National Park. It is the ideal place to pass a few hours before an early evening flight. Further south, there is more activity, with a range of luxury hotels and bungalows. The park encompasses Nai Yang and **Mai Khao** beaches, which together form the longest beach on the island (13 km). The area was declared a national park in 1981 to protect the turtles which lay their eggs here from November to March. Eggs are collected by the Fisheries Department and young turtles are released into the sea around the second week of April (check on the date as it changes), on **Turtle Release Festival Day**. The north end of the beach (where there is good snorkelling on the reef) is peaceful and secluded. There is no accommodation in the national park, although camping is possible.

MAI KHAO
This is Phuket's northernmost and largest beach, now home to a sprinkling of luxury resorts and a gaudy, underused waterpark in the West Sands resort development, founded by Sir Terry Leahy, former CEO of Tesco's hypermarket. It also encompasses the village of Had Mai Khao and the Sirinath National Park. The village is dominated by shrimp nurseries which sell the grown shrimp on to numerous farms throughout the south of Thailand. These discharge waste to the sea off the Mai Khao beach, but not to the same levels as shrimp farms. Again, sea turtles nest on this beach, including the huge leatherbacks; the Turtle Release Festival is in mid-April. The community effort to conserve the turtles involves collecting the eggs and keeping a hatchery. The beach is steeply shelved, so swimming isn't recommended and it is unsuitable for children. The beach is lined with casuarina trees.

HEROINES' MONUMENT AND THALANG NATIONAL MUSEUM
About 12 km north of Phuket City on Route 402, towards the airport, is the village of **Tha Rua**. At the crossroads there is a statue of two female warriors: **Muk** and **Chan**. These are the sisters who repelled an army of Burmese invaders in 1785 by dressing up all the women of the town as men, so fooling the Burmese. Rama I awarded them titles for their deeds and they are celebrated in bronze, swords drawn. The statue was erected in 1966 and Thais rub gold leaf on its base as a sign of respect and to gain merit. The **Thalang National Museum** ⓘ *Wed-Sun 0900-1600 (closed for national holidays), ฿100*, is just east of this crossroads on Route 4027. It has a well-presented collection on Phuket's history and culture.

KHAO PHRA THAEO WILDLIFE PARK
ⓘ *20 km north of Phuket City, T076-311998, 0600-1800, ฿200, half-price for children.*

To get to this wildlife park turn east off the main road in Thalang and follow signs for Ton Sai Waterfall. The beautiful, peaceful road winds through stands of rubber trees and degraded forest. The park supports wild boar and monkeys and represents the last of the island's natural forest ecosystem. During dry season, a walk around the park is a lot of fun and not particularly gruelling. The primary nature trail has 14 stations where you can stop and learn a bit about the park. There isn't much wildlife to be seen, although you may come across a monitor lizard, gibbon or even wild boar. The main trail is about 2 km long. The park's two waterfalls, Bang Pae Waterfall and Ton Sai Waterfall, are not up to much during the dry season when there isn't any water. When there is water, visitors can paddle in the upper pool. There are bungalows, a lakeside restaurant and a number of hiking routes here.

BANG PAE WATERFALL AND GIBBON REHABILITATION PROJECT

The road east from Ton Sai Waterfall becomes rough and can only be negotiated on foot or by motorbike; it leads to **Bang Pae Waterfall** ① *0600-1800*. Alternatively, the falls can be approached from the other direction, by turning off Route 4027 and driving 1 km. There is a beautiful lake, refreshment stands, forest trails, and bathing pools. Just south of the waterfall (follow signs off Route 4027) is a **Gibbon Rehabilitation Project** ① *T076-260492, grp@gibbonproject.org, 0900-1600, free, donations welcome as it is run by volunteers*, funded from the US and apparently the only such initiative in Southeast Asia for these endangered animals.

NAKA NOI PEARL FARM

① *T076-219870, 0900-1530, ฿500. Long-tailed boats can be chartered at any time, ฿700, and the driver will wait for you.*
Also off Route 4027, at Ao Poh, there is a long wooden jetty where boat tours leave for Naka Noi Island and Pearl Farm – Thailand's largest. At the farm, the owner asks you to wait half an hour while they prepare the oysters for the demonstration, which takes around 1½ hours. Ensure your visit is to Naka Noi, rather than Naka Yai, where the 'Pearl Farm' seems to be a fake.

PHUKET ISLAND LISTINGS

WHERE TO STAY

Phuket City

Phuket has hundreds of places to stay, largely at the upper price end. During the low season (Jun-Oct) room rates may be as little as half the high season price. All rates quoted are peak season. Advance booking is recommended during high season (particularly at Christmas and New Year).

$$$ Casa Blanca Boutique Hotel, 26 Phuket Rd, T076-219019, www. casablancaphuket.com. Bright and stylish place with traditional Sino-Portuguese touches in Phuket City centre. Small pool, free Wi-Fi and a cute café tucked away in an indoor garden setting.

$ Thalang Guesthouse, 37 Thalang Rd, T076-214 225, www.thalangguesthouse. com. A pleasant house with old-world charm, large windows, wood floors, double-panelled doors and ceiling fans. This is an excellent base to explore the Old Town. The owner, Mr Tee, has a good reputation with guests, who are encouraged to leave notes and drawings on the landing.

Patong Beach

$$$$ Sunset Beach Resort, 316/2 Phrabarame Rd, T076-342482, www. sunsetphuket.com. What better place to feel safe than a hotel with the tsunami warning tower on the roof? This is another mega-hotel with a double kidney-shaped pool snaking its way between terraced, balconied wings. From the upper floor rooms you can see the sea. There is also a decent spa and good but predictable meals. A 5-min tuk-tuk ride from Bangla Rd. Recommended.

$$-$ Bodega, 189/3 Rat-U-Thit Rd, T076-602191, www.bodegaphuket.com. Fun and friendly spot with a music cafe and art gallery, some dorm rooms, central location. Its travellers' vibe is unusual for Patong. Excellent value.

Karon and Kata beaches

$$$$ Centara Villa Phuket, 701 Patak Rd, T076-286300-9, www.centarahotelsresorts. com/cvp/cvp_default.asp. This luxury resort and spa is perched almost on the highest point overlooking Karon Bay (between Karon and Patong). The 72 villas are set on a steep hill but there are converted tuk-tuks to transport guests. While all villas are ocean-facing, not all have a good view of the beach, although some have a private pool. There's a **Centara Spa** offering a range of services, 2 small pools (can be crowded), a garden and a walkway to the beach. Friendly staff.

$ P&T Kata House 104/1 Koktanod Rd, T076-284203. One of several guesthouses at the southern end of Kata Beach set back from the shore, past a 7-11, offering some of the island's cheapest rooms outside Phuket City. The rooms are clean and many overlook a garden. There is no hot water but a/c rooms are available. Recommended.

Cape Panwa

$$$$ Cape Panwa, 27 Moo 8, Sakdidej Rd, T076-391123, www.capepanwa.com. Beautifully secluded, with a variety of accommodation, including bungalows. There are Italian and Thai fusion restaurants, an excellent cocktail bar and a good breakfast buffet. While you may never wish to leave the hotel, there is also a shuttle service into Phuket Old Town. Recommended.

$$$$ Sri Panwa, 88 Moo 8, Sakdidej Rd, T076-371000, www.sripanwa.com. This resort sets the pace for up-and-coming designer luxury. Each of the enormous pool villas is brilliantly put together and the villas have gorgeous views over the Cape. All the cutting-edge facilities you'd expect, with iPods and players in each room, giant plasma screens, day beds, giant bathtubs and even kitchens in the bigger villas. No beach though. Highly recommended.

Kamala Beach
$$$ Papa Crab Guesthouse, 93/5 Moo 3, Kamala Beach, T076-385315, www.phuket papacrab.com. 10 a/c rooms and 3 bungalows at this unusually named guesthouse. Basic accommodation next to the beach. The rooms are simple, clean and with comfortable beds. Big discounts in low season.

Surin Beach and Pansea Beach
$$$$ Amanpuri Resort, 118/1 Pansea Beach, T076-324333, www.amanresorts. com. This is undoubtedly one of the best resorts on Phuket. The more expensive rooms are beautifully designed Thai pavilions with attention to every detail. Super facilities include private yacht, watersports, tennis and squash courts, fitness centre, private beach and library. Guests include political figures.

Nai Yang and Nai Yang National Park
$$$$ Nai Yang Beach Resort, 65/23-24 Nai Yang Beach Rd, T076-328300, www. naiyangbeachresort.com. Well-built bungalows with good facilities and simple decor. Some a/c. Set in large grounds with plenty of trees for shade. Friendly staff. A bit pricey at the upper end but excellent value at the lower end.

RESTAURANTS

Phuket City
$ Fine Day, Chumphon Rd, finedayphuket. multiply.com. Fine Day is an institution in Phuket. It's a hip hotspot and is always busy. The staff are friendly.

$ Nong Jote Café, 16 Yaowarat Rd. This 100-plus-year-old building looks like a café in Lisbon with high ceilings. Excellent southern Thai food. Try the spicy *yum tour plu*. Recommended.

Foodstalls
There is a late-night *khanom jeen* vendor on Surin Rd (towards Damrong Rd, just up the road from the Shell garage). While usually a breakfast dish, there is no better meal to have late at night when you get a case of the munchies then *khanom jeen*. Choose your curry, throw in a few condiments and enjoy some of the best Thai food on offer. Look for the large brown pots at the side of the road.

The best place to browse on the street is around the market on **Ranong Rd**.

WHAT TO DO

Diving
The greatest concentration of dive companies is to be found along Patong Beach Rd, on Kata and Karon beaches, at Ao Chalong and in Phuket City. Dive centres – over 25 of them – offer a range of courses (introductory to advanced), day trips and liveaboard – leading to one of the internationally recognized certificates such as PADI and NAUI. For an open-water course the cost is about ฿14500. The course stretches over 4 days, beginning in a hotel pool and ending on a reef. An advance open-water diver course costs around ฿13500. A simple introductory dive, fully supervised, will cost about ฿4500-5500 (2 dives). For those with experience, there are a range of tours from single day, 2-dive outings to dive spots like Koh Racha Yai and Koh Racha Noi (south of Phuket), and Shark Point (east of Phuket) which cost ฿3500-5500 depending on the location, to 1-week expeditions to offshore islands such as the Similan and Surin islands. 5 days and 4 nights to the Similans costs around ฿25,000. Other liveaboards, depending on location and length of trip, vary from ฿18,000-30,000.

PHANGNGA BAY

Phangnga Bay is best known as the location for the 1974 James Bond movie The Man with the Golden Gun. *Limestone rocks tower out of the sea (some as high as 100 m); boats can be hired to tour the area from Tha Don, the Phangnga customs pier.*

Travelling from Phuket to Phangnga the road passes through limestone scenery. Much of the land looks scrubby and dry, punctuated by shrimp farms and scrappy farms. But en route, it is possible to watch rubber being processed by smallholders. Not long ago, over-mature rubber trees (those more than 25 years old) were cut down and processed into charcoal. Today, due to the efforts of an enterprising Taiwanese businessman, a rubber-wood furniture industry has developed.

→ARRIVING IN PHANGNGA

GETTING THERE AND AROUND
Phangnga has no train station or airport – the only way here is by bus (or private transport). Phangnga bus station is on Petkasem Road, near the centre of town. Motorcycle taxis will wait at the bus station to take passengers further afield. Cramped but rather extraordinary teak wood *songthaews* with unpadded seats constantly ply the main road, ฿30. They are the main form of transport around town (which is easy to cover on foot) and to surrounding villages.

MOVING ON
There are regular connections by bus to Krabi (two hours).

→PHANGNGA TOWN AND AROUND

The poor relation to its neighbouring tourist hotspots of Phuket and Krabi, Phangnga is often overlooked by visitors. Its relaxed, authentic Thai feel, dramatic setting and interesting daytrips make it an excellent place to pass a few days. There is one main road that goes through the centre of town which nestles narrowly between striking limestone crags. If you want urban sophistication and multiple culinary options, then Phangnga may disappoint. It is a non-tourist Thai experience, and Phangnga folk come across as almost grumpy with tourists – a relief after the feigned jollity of so many Thailand's tourist-drenched resorts.

In the centre of town, behind the **Rattanapong Hotel** is the fresh produce and early morning market while along the main street near the **Thaweesuk Hotel** are some remaining examples of the **Chinese shophouses** that used to line the street.

AROUND PHANGNGA TOWN
Due to the limestone geology, there are a number of caves in the vicinity. The most memorable, and by far the most disgusting, are at **Wat Thomtharpan Amphoe Muang**, the so-called 'Heaven and Hell Caves', around 2 km to the south of town on the road to Phuket. It's hard to see where Heaven is in this Buddhist depiction of Hell, designed to teach youngsters about the consequences of sinning. Cheap plaster models of human are burned on spits, chopped in half, sent through a mangle, torn apart by birds and gutted

by dogs. Hideously distorted demons with metre-long tongues and outsized genitalia glare down on the visitor. Eat before you arrive at this eerily deserted compound. Just on the outskirts of town on Route 4 towards Phuket, on the left-hand side, is the **Somdet Phra Sinakharin Park**, surrounded by limestone mountains; it is visible from the road and opposite the former city hall. Within this park are **Tham Luk Sua** and **Tham Ruesi Sawan**, two adjoining caves with streams, stalactites and stalagmites. These watery, sun-filled caves have rather unsympathic concrete paths. At the entrance to the cave sits Luu Sii, the cave guardian, under an umbrella. **Tham Phung Chang** is a little closer into town on the other side of the road, within the precincts of **Wat Phraphat Phrachim Khet**. To get to the arched entrance to the wat, take a *songthaew* about 300 m past the traffic lights (themselves past the New Lak Muang Hotel). The cave is actually inside the symbol of Phangnga – a huge mountain that apparently looks like a crouched elephant called Khao Chang. It can be found behind Phangnga's former city hall. In this long dark cave, again dripping with stalactites and stalagmites, there is a spring, Buddha images and a small pool where boys swim. The wat is more visually interesting though not as quirky. It enjoys a fine position against the limestone cliff and set within a large compound.

Tham Suwan Kuha ① ฿10, is 12 km from Phangnga on Route 4 to Phuket, take a southwest-bound bus. A turning to the right leads to this cave temple. It is popular with Thais and is full of Buddhas. Stairs lead up to a series of tunnels, containing some natural rock formations. King Chulalongkorn visited the cave in 1890 and his initials are carved into the rock.

Several kilometres out of town, and a right turn off the Krabi road, the **Sra Nang Manora Forest Park** (probably best reached on a scooter) offers a delightful break from the midday heat. The forest is free to enter and offers an easy, shaded 90-minute walk past several caves and sheer limestone cliffs. Thai visitors congregate at the park entrance to picnic next to the gushing stream, but anyone prepared to walk for a few minutes will have the forest to themselves.

Wat Tham Khao Thao is 12 km from Phangnga on Route 4152 to Krabi, on the left-hand side of the road, under a cliff wall (buses travel the route). Views of the surrounding plain can be seen from a stairway up the cliff face. The road here passes through nipa palm which then becomes an area of mangrove. Aquaculture is an important sideline industry, and tiger prawns are raised in the brackish waters of the mangroves and in purpose-built ponds.

→PHANGNGA BAY NATIONAL PARK

① *Park entrance fee, ฿200 (check to make sure it is included in the tour price). To get there take a songthaew to the pier, ฿30, from Phangnga town. 7 km along Route 4 there is a turning to the left (Route 4144 – signposted Phangnga Bay and the Ao Phangnga National Park Headquarters) and the pier is another 3 km down this road.*

Relaxed, excellent-value boat tours of Phangnga Bay can be booked from one of the travel agents in the town's bus station. They cost about ฿1100, and include the park entrance fee, accomodation, meals and a guided canoe tour, where someone does the paddling for you. The trips are just sightseeing tours as the boat drivers speak little English.

The standard tour winds through mangrove swamps, which act as a buffer between land and sea and nipa palm, and past striking limestone cliffs before arriving at **Tham Lod Cave**. This is not really a cave at all, but a tunnel cut into the limestone and dripping with stalagmites that look like petrified chickens hanging upside down. From Tham Lod, the route skirts past **Koh Panyi** – a Muslim fishing village built on stilts which extends out into the bay; its most striking feature being a golden mosque and the sheer peak rearing up behind it. Through the narrow lanes, the main transport is bicycle. There are also overpriced seafood restaurants in this village.

Other sights include **Khao Mah Ju**, a small mountain between Tha Dan and Koh Pnay which resembles a dog. There is also **Khao Khian** or 'Mountain of Writings' with ancient depictions of animals and sea life dating back more than 3000 years. These drawings include a cartoon-like dolphin which looks suspiciously contemporary. It is believed that seamen who used the place to escape from the monsoon, painted these vivid images. While all of these sights may seem highlights in themselves, it is the 'James Bond' island that is touted as the raison d'être for these tours. **James Bond Island** or **Koh Tapu** lies in the little bay of Koh Phing Kan or 'Leaning Mountain' which is a huge rock split into two parts with the smaller part having slid down so that the taller section appears to be leaning. The limestone karst stack that sticks up out from the sea just off this island is called **Koh Tapu** (Nail Island). The 'famous' rock, like a chisel, seems much smaller than it should be, and the tiny beach and cave are littered with trinket-stalls (refreshments available) and other tourists. Endless tour groups are spewed onto the small beach throughout the day to barge into each other as they wander past tatty souvenirs. There are few tackier sights in Asia. For details on the two large islands in the bay, Koh Yao Yai and Koh Yao Noi, see below.

KOH YAO NOI AND KOH YAO YAI

Koh Yao Noi and Koh Yao Yai, equidistant from Krabi mainland and Phuket, are the two most important islands in the 44-strong cluster of islands known as Koh Yao, to the east of Phuket. They are so close to each other that it only takes around eight minutes by long-tailed boat to cross over from Koh Yao Yai to Koh Yao Noi.

There's a strong Muslim and Sea Gypsy community here, and most locals are keen to preserve and promote their traditional way of life. They prefer outsiders to dress modestly and not to drink alcohol outside resorts or restaurants. Traditional handicrafts still persist, such as the inventive 'fish-scale flowers' created by the housewives of Koh Yao. The unusual rural heritage is seen in other ways too, and eco-activities include rubber collecting and fishing demonstrations, kayaking, hiking and snorkelling.

Getting there From Phuket's Bang Rong Pier, eight long-tail and six speedboat ferry trips depart for Koh Yao Noi daily 0730 to 1745, with returns daily 0715 to 1700. A less frequent service is available from Laem Hin Pier and Rassada Port, both on Phuket's east coast. From Krabi's Thalen Pier there are seven trips daily 0900 to 1700, and eight daily return trips 0730 to 1700. From Phangnga there's one boat a day departing 1300 and returning from Yao Noi at 0730. The boats make a brief stop at Koh Yao Yai first, less than 10 minutes away from Yao Noi. Fares are ฿120-200 and the journey takes up to one hour 30 minutes. Private long-tail or speedboat transfers may also be arranged.

Places in Koh Yao Noi and Koh Yao Yai Koh Yao Yai, the larger of the two islands, has better beaches for swimming but fewer places to stay, most of which tend to be overpriced. Although expensive resorts are appearing, there are still wooden houses, rubber plantations and wandering buffalos. There's a spectacular view where the road ends on the west side of the island, overlooking Klong Son Bay. The main attraction is the peace and quiet.

Koh Yao Noi is considerably more advanced than its bigger sister, with better facilities, including a hospital and internet shops but very few restaurants and shops. There is an award-winning homestay programme, the Koh Yao Noi Homestay Club, run by local fishermen and their families, and a few sensitively designed resorts, while most other operations are basic bungalows. A partially paved road encircles Koh Yao Noi, with its village in the middle and huts scattered throughout the island. On the northern tip of this island and best reached by boat, is an enormous tree, the trunk of which takes 23 men to span. Hire a bike for a delightful few hours taking in the beauty of the island while negotiating the (sometimes difficult) roads. Koh Yao Noi has become a bit of a hotspot for alternative traveller groups, who have bagged the place as good for retreats ranging from yoga to healing crystal workshops. For little trips there are beautiful beaches, especially on Koh Nok, and a dreamy lagoon on Koh Hong. Mobile phones operate throughout both the islands.

→PHANGNGA TO KRABI

From Phangnga to Krabi, the road passes mangrove swamps and nipa palm, more dramatic karst formations and impressive stands of tropical forest. For those travelling independently by car or motorbike, there is a lovely detour worth taking for about an hour. Look out for signs to **Tham Raird** or **Ban Bang Toei** and turn left down towards the towering karst formations. The road leads through a pass into a valley in the heart of the karst. It is a little like stepping back in time, and several Thai television commercials idealizing rural life have been filmed here. The backdrop of lush forest on towering karst, with a foreground of rice fields and small villages, is wonderful. Rainy season visitors will be well rewarded with mist and cloud on the peaks and a golden light on the wet paddy. Sadly, behind these wonderful, almost circular limestone crags there are several large limestone concessions blasting the mountains away. To the front there are similar scenes of rice farming against a backdrop of towering mountains, interspersed with the occasional village or temple.

PHANGNGA BAY LISTINGS

WHERE TO STAY

Phangnga Town

$$-$ Phangnga Inn, 2/2 Soi Lohakit, Pet-kasem Rd, T076-411963. A beautiful family house converted into a cosy hotel with immaculately clean en suite rooms. It is off the main road, and clearly marked by a purple sign. Recommended.

Koh Yao Noi

$$$$ Six Senses Yao Noi Beyond Phuket, 56 Moo 5, T076-418500, www.sixsenses. com. Set amid trees – you hardly notice they're there at all – are 56 luxurious wooden villas, all complete with private pool, sunken tubs and sala. Everything is done in natural fabrics and materials, with only a hint of concrete. Six Senses donate a percentage of revenue to carefully selected local projects. Eating here is unforgettable; they have an in-house deli stocking the best cheeses and charcuterie you'll find anywhere in Thailand. Prices are high but you get a lot for your money. Highly recommended.

$$$-$$ Sabai Corner Bungalows, T076-597497, T08-1892 1827 (mob), www.sabai cornerbungalows.com. 10 romantic bungalows are set among cashew and coconut trees with magnificent views over Pasai Beach. Attached toilets. A popular option, often full, ring ahead.

$$-$ Koh Yao Noi Homestay Club, Koh Yao District, Pang Nga Province, 82160, Coordinating Office T076-597244, T08-1968-0877/6942 7999. You'll be housed in any one of several family homes run by this award-winning homestay programme. All monies go directly to the local community with a percentage of income being used to protect the fishing stocks of crab and prawn available locally. Expect reasonably basic accommodation but an unforgettably freindly welcome and some of the best seafood you're ever likely eat. The basic price covers food and accommodation but they can organize an entire programme for you at extra cost that takes in fishing trips, visits to secret islands complete with stunning beaches and cooking courses. One of the most highly recommended places to stay in Thailand. Some details are also available on www.cbt-i.org, a website dedicated to Community Based Tourism.

Koh Yao Yai

$$$-$$ Thiwson Bungalows, 58/2 Moo 4, T08-1956 7582 (mob), www.thiwsonbeach. com. Sweet, clean rooms in the usual bamboo-and-wood style, with bedside lights and Western toilets. Restaurant, deck chairs on the verandas and a pleasant garden overlooking one of the nicest beaches on the island. Recommended.

RESTAURANTS

Phangnga Town

Cafés on Petkasem Rd, near the market, sell the usual array of Thai dishes, including excellent *khaaw man kai* (chicken and rice) and *khaaw mu daeng* (red pork and rice). There is also a good shop selling all manner of rice crackers, nuts and Thai biscuits on Petakasem Rd past **Thaweesuk Hotel**. Try the popular **Kha Muu Restaurant** opposite the **Thaweesuk Hotel**.

There is an early morning market behind **Rattanapong Hotel**. There are a couple very good cafés here that do traditional morning rice soup (*khaaw thom*) to perfection until around about 0900. This soup is a rice porridge with coriander, basil, ginger, spices, onion, lemongrass, pepper and minced pork. You can also get a fix of sweet tea. The market itself, though small, sells an astonishing array of foodstuffs, fish, meat, flowers and lots of sarongs. Recommended.

KRABI AND AROUND

Krabi is a small provincial capital on the banks of the Krabi river. It is fairly touristy and a jumping-off point for Koh Phi Phi (see page 239), Koh Lanta (see page 243), Ao Nang and Rai Leh and smaller islands like Koh Jum, Koh Bubu and Koh Siboya (see page 240). Krabi town itself is a shambling and amiable waterfront port with excellent, easily accessible tourist sites like the Tham Lod cave and Tiger Temple.

In the past, the town acquired the unfortunate reputation of being a haven for junkies and a place where you really shouldn't leave anything in your hotel room. But in recent years Krabi has attempted to cash in on its heritage in an idiosyncratic way. Hence, the kitsch iron statues on Muharat Road of four bearded prehistoric men carrying the traffic signals. This vision, best viewed at twilight with the jungle foliage behind, is meant to remind visitors that big human skulls were found in Tham Phi Hua To Cave, which means Big-Headed Ghost Cave. Aside from anthropological joys, Krabi town is a perfect place to either prepare for, or recuperate from, island-hopping, especially for those who have been on islands with limited electricity and luxuries. Here, you can stock up on bread – Krabi has excellent bakeries – fetch your newspapers and get a decent café latte before heading back to the nature reserve for some more hammock swinging.

Rock climbing, river trips, birdwatching, hiking at national parks and reserves, motorcycle treks and sea canoeing are all available and most tour companies also operate daily and overnight tours around Phangnga Bay (see page 222) often incorporating a visit to Wat Tham Suwan Kuha and other sights.

→ ARRIVING IN KRABI

GETTING THERE AND AROUND

Krabi is well connected with scheduled and charter flights. Krabi International Airport, 17 km from town, offers seven daily flights from Bangkok. The taxi to town from the airport is around ฿400 and to Ao Nang ฿500. *Songthaews* offer a cheaper option. There are also boats to Koh Phi Phi – still worth a day-trip – and Koh Lanta, from the new pier on the outskirts of Krabi town. Free courtesy tuk-tuks from the old pier at Chao Fah to the new one may still be offered, so don't be too keen to flag down a taxi. Meanwhile, Chao Fah Pier continues to operate services to Rai Leh beach and there is a white minibus for ฿50 to Ao Nang from there as well.

From the bus station, around 5 km from the centre in Talat Kao (Old Market), close to the intersection of Uttarakit Road and Route 4, there are regular connections with Phangnga Bay (two hours) as well as with all major towns in the south. For Koh Samui, companies offer combination bus/boat tickets. Motorcycle taxis also wait to ferry bus passengers into town. *Songthaews* are the main form of local transport, they drive through town stopping at various places such as Phattana Road, in front of **Travel & Tour**, for Ao Phra Nang and in front of the foodstalls on Uttarakit Rpad for Noppharat Thara Beach. Red *songthaews* regularly run between the bus station and town, ฿20. Motorbikes are widely available for hire.

MOVING ON

Note that the southwest monsoon months of May to October affect all boat timetables. Klong Jirad Pier on Tharua Road, about 4 km outside town, is now the main ferry departure point, though it's still possible to catch boats at Chao Fah Pier (see Krabi map, below).

During high season (November to April), there is one boat to and from Koh Lanta (two hours, ฿350-400); for further details, see www.phuketferryboats.com or ask at any tour desk. In the wet season (May to October), a minibus runs from Klong Jirad Pier via two short car ferries across Lanta Noi to Ban Sala Dan on Koh Lanta, two hours; contact a tour operator and see Arriving on Koh Lanta, page 243, for details. Tigerline high-speed ferry (www.tigerlinetravel.com) runs a service November to April between Ao Nang and Langkawi in Malaysia, stopping at Koh Lanta, among other places; you can book any leg of this trip separately to do some island-hopping.

TOURIST INFORMATION

Small TAT office ① *Uttarakit Rd, across from Kasikorn Bank, 0830-1630.* For more information on Krabi, Ao Nang, Phra Nang, Rai Leh, Koh Phi Phi and Koh Lanta and some good articles, pick up the free *Krabi Magazine* or Krabi Miniguide, available at various bars and guesthouses. Many other places offer 'tourist information', usually to sell tours, tickets and rooms, which can be either offensive or convenient.

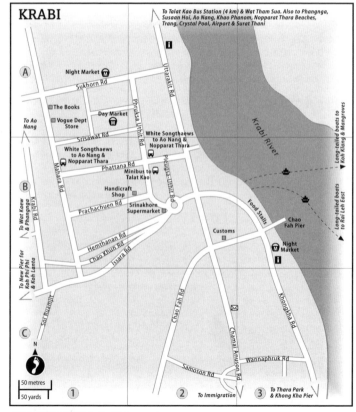

KRABI

To Talat Kao Bus Station (4 km) & Wat Tham Sua. Also to Phangnga, Susaan Hoi, Ao Nang, Khao Phanom, Nopparat Thara Beaches, Trang, Crystal Pool, Airport & Surat Thani

A — Night Market — Sukhorn Rd — Uttarakit Rd

The Books — Day Market — Phruksa Uthit Rd

To Ao Nang — Vogue Dept Store — Srisawat Rd — White Songthaews to Ao Nang & Nopparat Thara

White Songthaews to Ao Nang & Nopparat Thara — Phattana Rd — Minibus to Talat Kao

Krabi River — Long-tailed boats to Koh Klang & Mangroves

B — Handicraft Shop — Prachachuen Rd — Srinakhorn Supermarket — Food Stalls — Chao Fah Pier — Long-tailed boats to Rai Leh East

To Wat Kaew & Phanomga — Mahara Rd — Hemthanan Rd — Chao Khun Rd — Customs — Night Market

To New Pier for Koh Phi Phi & Koh Lanta — Issara Rd

C — Soi Ruamjit — Chao Fah Rd — Chamai Anuson Rd — Khongdha Rd

N

50 metres
50 yards — 1 — 2 — To Immigration — Samoson Rd — Wannaphruk Rd — 3 — To Thara Park & Khong Kha Pier

→KRABI TOWN

There is a **general market** on Srisawat and Sukhon roads, and a **night market** close to the Chao Fah Pier. Chao Fah Pier at night is flooded with foodstalls frequented mainly by locals. The food is highly varied and cheap, although the cooking is quick-fire so you need to make sure everything is properly cooked. However, for a nocturnal nibble alfresco and a promenade walk, the pier is ideal, especially as the streets are thronged with people around twilight. Depending on how you feel about young elephants performing tricks for a cucumber, visitors can pay to feed the gentle beasts. There are also a handful of guesthouses, some shabby but intriguing, along the river and opposite the market if you want to be close to the action.

→AROUND KRABI

WAT THAM SUA (TIGER CAVE TEMPLE)

ⓘ *Wat Tham Sua is east along Route 4. Take a red songthaew from Phattana Rd in town for ฿20 to Route 4 (the songthaew is marked 'Airport/Fossil Beach'). From here either walk along Route 4 to the Cave Temple or take a motorcycle taxi (about ฿25). Walk to the cave from the main road.*
Wat Tham Sua is 8 km northeast of town just past Talat Kao down a track on the left and has dozens of *kutis* (monastic cells) set into the limestone cliff. Here, the monks still meditate in the forest. Tiger Cave is so called because once a tiger apparently lived there and left his pawprints behind as proof, although some visitors have found this a dubious claim and grumble that the pawprints are not at all paw-like. Real wild creatures can be found in the surrounding rocky hillsides and mangrove forest. Here, trees that are hundreds of years old ensconce garrulous macaque monkeys. Walk behind the ridge where the bot is situated to find a network of limestone caves, which eventually lead back to the entrance. There is also a staircase on the left; 1237 steps leading to the top of a 600-m-high karst peak with fantastic views and meditation areas for the monks which are often occupied. This is a demanding climb as it is steep; it is best reserved for cool weather and early morning. Take water and a sunhat.

THAM PHI HUA TO AND THAM LOD

ⓘ *The caves of Tham Phi Hua To and Tham Lod can be reached by boat from a pier just down the road from Hat Nopparat Thara (take the first left as you exit towards Khlong Muang), or you can take one of many tours by boat or canoe to the same caves. It is also possible to visit these areas with companies offering sea canoeing. While generally more expensive than the trips via long-tailed boat (bear in mind that sea canoes cost upwards of US$350 each in Thailand), a more private trip is worth it, particularly when passing through the lush and mysterious limestone canyons. Then you can be assured that the main sounds will be eerie watery echos and the dipping of oars rather than tourist chatter.*
Phi Hua To Cave (Big-Headed Ghost Cave) is famous for the discovery there of ancient and unusually large human skulls as well as 70 paintings in red and black of people and animals, all of which upholds Krabi Province's claim to having hosted the oldest human settlements in Thailand. A large pile of shells was also discovered in the cave. There are two paths in the cave. Take the left for a cathedral-like cavern illuminated by a shaft of light and the right for a hall reputed to have been a shelter for prehistoric people.

Tham Lod Tai is a cavern in the limestone karst through which you can travel by boat along narrow passages filled with stalactites and stalagmites. Tham Lod Nua is a longer and larger cavern with more meandering passages. Both are passable only at low-tide. The boat ride to the caves passes mangroves and limestone karst outcrops.

MANGROVE TRIPS

ⓘ *Long-tailed boats can be hired for a trip into the mangroves at the Chao Fah Pier (rates are negotiable and depend on the time of year, length of time and number of passengers). For this trip it may also be possible to get a rua jaew – the traditional boat used in the Krabi area (including Koh Lanta). Paddles are used instead of a motor (though most now use both).*
Mangroves line the river opposite Krabi. This is a protected area although heavy logging has left most of the forest quite immature. It is worth visiting for the birds and other wildlife including several families of macaques, but ask the boatman to go slowly when in the mangroves so as not to startle the wildlife.

THANBOKE KHORANEE NATIONAL PARK

ⓘ *Entry is ฿400 (the same as for Phanom Bencha National Park and Khao Nor Chu Chi). Take Route 4 towards Phangnga; turn left down Route 4039 for Ao Luk after 45 km. About 2 km down this road there is a sign for the gardens, to the left. By public transport, take a songthaew from Krabi to Ao Luk, and then walk or catch a songthaew.*
Thanboke Khoranee National Park is a beautiful, cool and peaceful forest grove with emerald rock pools, streams and walkways. In the park, swimming is permitted in the upper pool which is near a small nature trail leading up into the limestone cliffs (sturdy shoes are advised).

LAEM SAK

ⓘ *Turn left as you exit Thanboke Khoranee National Park and continue on Route 4039 into the town of Ao Luk and beyond down a small road to the end of the peninsula.*
Laem Sak juts out from the mainland just north of Ao Luk and makes a good trip before or after a visit to the Thanboke Khoranee National Park. Views back towards the mainland are impressive with a wall of limestone karst in the distance fringed by mangroves. Out to sea and to the west are a group of rocky islands. The fishing pier is working with plenty of activity and there are restaurants serving fresh seafood. This is a good place to watch the fishing boats pass by and eat reasonably priced fish.

GAROS ISLAND

ⓘ *A tour leaves from a pier down a rough dirt track which can be reached from Ban Thung. (Turn left at Ban Thung, drive about 500 m and take a right turn down the dirt track. There are signs to the pier after about 5 km, and the pier is about 12 km from the main road). Pre-arrange a tour by calling T076-649149. Mr Mos speaks reasonably good English. His partner (Mr Mudura), can also take the tour but speaks much less English, although he knows more about the area having lived there for most of his 60 years.*
Garos Island lies off the coast of mainland Krabi near Ban Thung (before Ao Luk). A day trip in a small long-tailed fishing boat will take you past mangroves and limestone karst islands to Garos, where you can see somewhat sinister prehistoric wall paintings and several caves used as traditional burial grounds for 'sea gypsies' (Chao Le). It's good for birdwatching and for seeing the traditional lifestyles of fishing communities. The tour, which provides a fantastic lunch cooked on a small island beach where you can also enjoy a swim, is operated by members of the community. Recommended.

KHAO PHANOM BENCHA NATIONAL PARK

ⓘ *Take a motorcycle or other transport out on the main road going towards Trang (past Talat Kao). The turn-off comes before the exit for Wat Tham Sua. Motorcycle theft from the car park at Kho Panom Bencha happens regularly.*

Khao Phanom Bencha National Park provides a magnificent backdrop to the town with a peak rising more than 600 m above the surrounding land. Near the park entrance is the lovely **Huai To Waterfall** best seen between September and December after the monsoon. The drive to the waterfall is pleasant with a distinctly rural feel and the area around the park entrance has some charming trees and open grassland, good for picnics. Park rangers lead treks up to the peak and to a waterfall on the other side. The level of English spoken by rangers can vary – check that you feel comfortable with any potential guide before setting out. The trek takes more than a day as the climb is quite steep.

KHAO NOR CHU CHI FOREST, CRYSTAL POOL AND HOT SPRINGS

ⓘ *Tours can be arranged from most tour offices in town. For self-drive, the turn-off to Khao Nor Chu Chi is just after the major intersection in Khlong Thom town, it's marked. Once you get on to the road to the Crystal Pool and hot springs, you will find clear signposting.*

These sights are all in Khlong Thom district to the south of Krabi province. Khao Nor Chu Chi, which is in the middle of nowhere, is a mere parcel of rainforest surrounded by plantations. It has a forest trail and bungalow-style accommodation (**Morakot Resort**) that was initiated as part of an ecotourism project aimed at conserving the seriously endangered **gurney's pitta**, a bird believed to be extinct; it was re-discovered by the ornithologists Philip Round and Uthai Treesucon. Prince Charles, a keen ornithologist, has also endorsed the fight to save the comically named bird with its flashes of turquoise, red and brown. Gurney's pitta, which favours heavy forest, can be almost impossible to find and visitors have spent two days looking for a glimpse of this jewel-winged bird, which is listed as one of the top 50 endangered birds in the world. The ongoing fear now is that gurney's pitta will become extinct in the next 10 years as deforestation due to rubber and palm-oil plantations continues to dominate over ecological concerns. Tourism could save the day as the Tourism Authority of Thailand gets increasingly involved in the plight of gurney's pitta.

The **Crystal Pool** ⓘ *entrance ฿200*, is visited by the Queen and other royals annually and is so-called because of the exceptional clarity of the water and its emerald colour. The colour derives from mineral deposits that are visible through the water. The pool is shallow and the water buoyant. However, while the pool may look attractive enough, the deposits feel rather crunchy and not particularly pleasant under foot and the slopes are slippery.

A visit to hot springs (฿100) on a hot day may seem rather odd, but the temperature of the water is comfortable and it's a relaxing place to spend some time. The springs have been developed into Thai-style mineral baths with changing rooms, walkway to the original springs and landscaped gardens for the walk through to the river. There are eight of these springs, all with enticing names. They are **Nam Lod** (Water Passing Through), **Cheng Kao** (Valley), **Jorakeh Kao** (White Crocodile), **Nam Tip** (Heavenly Waters) **Nam Krahm** (Indigo Water), **Morakot** (Emerald Water), **Hun Kaeo** (Barking Deer) and **Noi** (Small).

KRABI AND AROUND LISTINGS

WHERE TO STAY

$$ Krabi River Hotel, 73/1 Khongkha Rd, T075-612321, www.krabiriverhotel.com. A 5-storey hotel with a splendid view of the river, the mangroves and the hustle and bustle of the boats. Rooms are bright, if uninspiring. Recommended.

$$-$ Chan Chalay, 55 Uttarakit Rd, T075-620952, www.chanchalay.com. Pleasant white-and-blue building on Uttarakit Rd near the post office. Reasonably priced, clean and airy rooms are set back a little from the road. Serves breakfasts and provides a reliable tour operator service. Recommended.

$ Star Guest House, Khongkha Rd, T075-630234. A charming wooden guesthouse over the top of a small convenience store and tour office, the 7 rooms are tiny, leaving little space for more than a bed, but there is a pleasant balcony with tables and chairs overlooking the night market and the river. Separate bathrooms are downstairs near a small bar in a garden at the back. Recommended.

RESTAURANTS

$$ Chao Sua, on Maharat Rd, along the road from the **Ruen Mai** (the sign, with a leopard on it, is in Thai). Considered by many locals to be one of the best restaurants in Krabi. The restaurant itself has a rambling feel and service is sometimes a little haphazard. Excellent Thai food. Barbecued seafood, crispy duck salad and virtually anything that is fried is especially good.

Foodstalls

A **night market** sets up in the early evening on Khlong Kha Rd, along the Krabi river, and serves good seafood dishes. Halal and Chinese dishes can be found here. Instead of opting for *banana roti* it's worth trying the *mataba* as a savoury dish.

A second **night market** is based in the parking lot near the Provincial Electricity Authority office on the road running between Uttarakit and Maharat roads. This market sells fruit at night, at much cheaper prices than the market by the pier. Keep your eyes peeled for mango and sticky rice.

For a real treat, try the **morning market** on Soi 7 off Maharat Rd. In the middle aisles, are stalls selling extraordinarily complex salads that can be found for around ฿25.

WHAT TO DO

Tour operators

Tour operators are concentrated on Uttarakit and Ruen-Ruedee roads and close to the Chao Fah Pier. There are so many tour and travel agents, and information is so freely and widely available, that it is not necessary to list numerous outfits here. Prices and schedules are all openly posted and a 30-min walk around town will reveal all.

Krabi Full Moon Tours, 66/17 Moo 5 Sai Thai, T08-1606 1916, www.krabifullmoon tours.com. Diving, snorkelling, cultural or adventure tours. Free hotel transfers.

Krabi Somporn Travel and Service, 72 Khongkha Rd, opposite the old pier, T08-1895 7873 (mob). This is run by Mrs Tree. She is friendly and doesn't overcharge.

WEST OF KRABI

The road to the coast from Krabi winds for 15 km past limestone cliffs, a large reclining Buddha, rubber stands and verdant forest. Arriving at the coast in the evening, with the setting sun turning the limestone cliffs of Ao Nang a rich orange and the sea interspersed with precipitous limestone crags, is a beautiful first impression.

The coast west of Krabi consists of the beach areas of Ao Nang and Hat Nopparat Thara (which lie 18 km and 22 km respectively to the west of Krabi town), and also Ao Phra Nang, Ao Rai Leh East, Ao Rai Leh West and Ao Ton Sai.

More than half the native population are now Muslim Thais, discreetly signalled by the absence of pork on restaurant menus, even though you will not hear the call of the muzzein at prayer times. Buying alcohol in public at a beach bar should be disallowed, but in typical Thai-style, bar staff are Buddhist in Muslim-run and owned operations, which nicely gets around that dilemma. It should be remembered that topless sunbathing is very definitely frowned upon. It is rare to see Thai women even in bikinis at the beach – due to modesty and also an abhorrence of tanning. But, while most sun-starved Westerners come to Thailand to sunbathe and indeed are encouraged, with ever-present deckchairs, cold towels and beach masseurs, it is still a good idea to cover up when you leave the beach for restaurants. These establishments will often be staffed by Thai-Muslims even if the bars aren't. If you get too hot and bothered by this option, there's always takeaway.

→AO NANG, NOPPARAT THARA AND KHLONG MUANG

Ao Nang is neither sweeping nor glorious and has coarse dirty yellow sand intermingled with millions of broken shells that are unpleasant to walk on. One end of the beach is filled with kayaks and long-tailed boats for transporting tourists to nearby islands and it is these motorized long-tailed boats that punctuate the quiet with ferocious regularity. The concrete wall behind the beachfront, the construction of which initially excited much antagonism, saved Ao Nang from the greater force of the tsunami and has since been rebuilt. Behind this is the commercial outcrop of Ao Nang itself which has taken up the whole of the beach road and swarmed inland. The town itself is a generic collection of souvenir shops, small resorts and bad restaurants – it is mind-boggling to think that just 20 years ago, Ao Nang was a sleepy fishing hamlet. On the whole, there is little to do in today's Ao Nang, including eating. The food is dreadful; if you don't count the gas-oven pizzerias of which there are far too many, even something simple like a fruit salad or toast is substandard and often served grudgingly. The whole set-up utterly lacks the shameless exuberance of Patong or the charm of Kata Noi and the tourists reflect this. However, there are pleasant features in spite of all this, which makes the current development even more regrettable. The beachfront is lined with coconut palms and mango trees with limestone walls at one end and lovely views of the islands on the horizon. Ao Nang also has good facilities for diving, windsurfing, fishing and tours to the surrounding islands. It is still relatively quiet and the beach water is fine for swimming, out of the monsoon season, with calm waters and beautiful limestone scenery. But it is really the surrounding beaches, coves, caves and grottoes that make the place bearable.

At **Hat Nopparat Thara**, about 3 km northwest of Ao Nang, is a deliciously long stretch of soft, pale beige sand covered in tiny seashells and lined with tall casuarinas at the beachside. To the back are paperbark forests. Locals used to call this place 'Hat Khlong Haeng' or dried canal beach because at low tide the canal dries up, leaving a long beach. Khlong Haeng is also the name of the village closest to the beach – around 900 m away. This 5-km-long beach is divided by a river with the side closest to Ao Nang being the most developed as it is bordered by a main road. The other side, which is lousy with sandflies, can only be accessed by boat or by a dirt track from the road to Khlong Muang.

Khlong Muang, a more remote stretch of average beach, is attracting ever-greater interest from upmarket developers who tout the hotels on the shore as having 'private beaches' (despite these being shallow and rocky) because there is only indirect public access to them once the hotels are up. Many of the bungalows here are closed during the monsoon season and there is little in the way of dining or nightlife outside the resorts.

There are a couple of interesting places on the road in from Ao Nang. The main one, about 8 km before Khlong Muang, is the **Giant Catfish Farm** ① *daily 0800-1800, ฿50*. Set up by Nina, an American expat and her Thai husband, Paichit, a visit here is a genuinely eccentric and fascinating experience. More like an adventure zoo than anything else – there are crocodiles, tarantulas, monitor lizards and ponds of huge catfish – the entire place is set up amid the jungle with gorgeous waterfalls and refreshing pools on hand should you require a dip. They also run a very popular restaurant.

Nopparat Thara has three distinct sections. The first is closest to Ao Nang and is where most of the bungalow and hotel developments have taken place and where most Western tourists wander. This area has limited shade. Further down the beach near the **Hat Nopparat Thara-Mu Ko Phi Phi National Park office** ① *0830-1630*, is the area where most Thai tourists congregate – this area is well shaded with picnic grounds under the casuarina trees. The final section is across the canal, adjacent to the national parks office and by the harbour used by local fishermen. This stretch of beach is home to affordable bungalow resorts, and has a completely different character to Ao Nang and the other parts of Nopparat Thara. These bungalows are accessible by boat across the canal and by road. Although it is a pleasant place to rest with great views and more peace and quiet than in Ao Nang, the water is very shallow, making swimming during anything except high tide next to impossible. Well inhabited with crustaceans and other sea creatures you never know what you might step on, so wear sandals if you decide to paddle in the shallowest waters. Some guests even wear shoes. But there are some sweet sights to be had here – monkeys, kingfishers and sea eagles at the west end of the beach – as well as caves to explore. At low tide it is also possible to walk out to some of the islands in the bay. In these ways, it is an ideal place for children.

In the opposite direction, beyond the limestone crags, is drop-dead gorgeous Phra Nang, see page 235, and the beaches (and accommodation) of boho-chic Rai Leh, which has been visited by the likes of Mick Jagger, Colin Farrell and Fatboy Slim, who gave an impromptu set.

SUSAAN HOI (FOSSIL SHELL BEACH)

① *Take the white songthaews from the corner of Phattana and Maharat Rd in Krabi. ฿50. Coincide your visit with low tide when more pavement is exposed.*

Susaan Hoi, literally 'shell cemetery', lies 20 km southwest of Krabi near the village of Laem Pho (not far from Ao Nang Beach) and 5 km east of Ao Nang. Great slabs of what looks like concrete are littered along the shoreline but on closer inspection turn out to be countless fossilized freshwater shells, laid down 40 million years ago. It is one of only three such cemeteries in the world; the others are in the US and Japan. It is an impressive and curious sight.

KOH BODA AND KOH GAI

Koh Boda is 30 minutes by boat from Ao Nang. It is hugely popular with snorkellers for its wonderfully clear water. Round-trip excursions last five hours. The nearby Koh Gai is also a 30-minute boat trip from Ao Nang. Ao Thalen combines the curious and wonderful shapes of the mangrove, with extraordinary limestone crags, cave paintings, monkey troupes, and an overall sense of mystery in the gorges that is quite magical.

→PHRA NANG AND RAI LEH

Phra Nang is the peninsula to the south of Ao Nang. There are no roads on Phra Nang, which lends it a secret-hideaway ambience – albeit an exclusive one as all the land behind the beach is occupied by the Rayavadee Resort. The point consists of **Rai Leh West** and **Ao Phra Nang** on the west side and **Rai Leh East** on the east. Further west from Rai Leh West is **Ao Ton Sai**. Rai Leh has become something of a mecca for rock climbers, partly because limestone is porous so that the water cuts into it and makes natural grips ideal for climbers. But, equally alluring, say climbers, is the combination of landscape, climate and rock, which rarely come together in such harmonious splendour.

The best beach is on the west side – a truly picture-postcard affair. However, the east coast beach is still amazing at low tide in a sci-fi end-of-the-world way as the landscape transforms into a 300-m stretch of sinister shining mud. When Rai Leh East is not a mudbath, there are still the mangroves lining the beach so that it is fairly impossible to get any swimming in here. Rai Leh East also acts as a pier for taxi boats to and from Krabi and you will often spy tourists slogging across the mud with luggage over their heads. Pretty Rai Leh West, also knows as 'Sunset Beach', is about 10 minutes' walk away from the other beach – this means there is no escaping the daytime noises of the long-tailed boats although the evenings are delightful. There is also good snorkelling and swimming in archetypal crystal-clear water. The limestone rock formations are spectacular, and there are interesting caves with stalagmites and stalactites to explore though they require patience and fortitude as the paths are not always straightforward nor easygoing. At the southern extremity of the bay is a mountain cave (**Outer Princess Cave**) on Phra Nang Beach that is dedicated to the goddess of the area and considered 'her summer palace'. Here, you may be delighted to find an abundance of wooden and stone penises, many in wonderful colours of candy pink, lime green and pillar box red. It is believed local fishermen put the penises there to bribe the goddess into granting them plenty of fish on the sea. Be that as it may, many non-sailors also like to drop by a penis or two and the cave is suitably endowed. Near the penis cave are lots of monkeys that are rather friendly and several beachside stalls selling trinkets, clothes, beer and snacks like barbecued corn on the cob. There is also one outrageously priced bar that looks totally out of place. If you feel you must make an effort, there is Sa Phra Nang (Princess Pool) to explore. This is a pond inside the cliff that can be accessed along a cave trail at the side of the mountain. You can get to the top of the mountain if you keep climbing. There's a walkway to Rai Leh east from Ao Phra Nang if you care to visit the Inner Princess Cave, better known as the Diamond Cave, which is three caverns, one of which has a waterfall of quartz-like frozen amber. Entry is ฿40 or ฿20 for kids.

There are several climbing schools, as the tower karst formations offer some truly outstanding climbing opportunities along with spectacular views.

Rai Leh is suffering from being too popular. The area available for development is small, sandwiched between limestone cliffs and crags, and already the bungalows are cheek-by-jowl in places. It is also going upscale with the recent appearances of superstars, so prices are starting to soar. On the whole, the entertainment here remains coffee houses/bars/bookshops during the day and low-key parties on the east side at night – still more reggae than rave. Electricity, ATMs and high-speed internet have now arrived on Rai Leh but foodies will be seriously disappointed as the closest and most patronized outpost for food is Ao Nang.

Ao Ton Sai, north of Ao Rai Leh West, largely appeals to climbers who can manage far more than five-minute walks. Climbing is the main activity here, followed by frisbee, volleyball and assorted refreshments à la *Big Lebowski*.

WEST OF KRABI LISTINGS

WHERE TO STAY

$$$$ Sheraton Krabi Beach Resort, 155 Moo 2, Nong Thale, T075-628000, www.sheraton.com/krabi. A large and luxurious resort. It's very well planned with nice gardens and good beach access. You can opt for either hotel rooms or bungalows – both are of a very high standard and include all the usual top-end trimmings. 2 large pools, kids play area, elephants and an excellent wood-fired pizza restaurant. Lots of other facilities, including a spa, gym, etc.

$$$$-$$$ Railei Beach Club, Rai Leh West, T08-6685 9359 (mob), www.raileibeachclub.com. Hugging the cliffs at the northern corner of Rai Leh West, these traditional Thai-style teak houses are private holiday homes that the owners let out. Each unique, they range from cute open-plan affairs that sleep 2 up to rambling multi-wing ones that can sleep 8 or more. Kitchens and bathrooms, Wi-Fi, but no a/c. Public amenities are slim – no pool or restaurant – but the quiet natural setting humming with critters is blissful. Bring cooking supplies. Recommended

$$$$-$$$ Royal Nakara, 155/4-7 Moo 3, T075-661441, www.royalnakara.com. Built on the edge of a steep drop, the rooms are reached by descending several flights of stairs. All are very light and spacious, with modern furniture, TV and DVD player. Premium rooms have pantry kitchen and dining area. Infinity pool. Recommended.

$$$ Ao Nang Beach Home, 132 Moo 2, T075-695260, www.aonangbeachhomekrabi.com. Offers large, well appointed a/c rooms, with spacious bathrooms and nice touches such as beach mats in the rooms. Laminate teak furniture, modern and comfortable. Restaurant overlooking the beach. Recommended for price (includes breakfast) and location.

$$$ Jinnie's Place, 101 Moo 3, T075-661 398, www.jinniesplace.com. Red brick a/c bungalows have bags of character and charm. The bathrooms are possibly the largest in Krabi and have baths and even a garden. There's a children's pool and a main pool. Recommended.

$$$ Na-Thai Resort, near Nopparat Thara and Phi Phi Island National Park Headquarters and the Montessori School, T075-637752. It's 5-10 mins by motorbike or car from Hat Phra Ao Nang and Hat Nopparat Thara. Free pick up. Surrounded by oil palms and rubber trees, this is a husband and wife set-up – Gerard and Walee who have more of an eco-friendly approach to running things. There are bungalows and apartments set around a small pool that you can swim in at night and a restaurant. Not the most imaginative place, but great attitude and good for a more isolated getaway. Prices depend on the month. Recommended.

RESTAURANTS

Food in Ao Nang and Rai Leh remains dominated by sloppy Western and tourist Thai restaurants with a silly number of pizzerias. As one would expect, the best food available at Ao Nang is fresh seafood. Almost all the restaurants along the beach-front road, and then lining the path northwest towards the **Krabi Resort**, serve BBQ fish, chilli crab, steamed crab, prawns and so on. There is little to choose between these restaurants – they tend to serve the same dishes, prepared in the same way, in rather lacklustre sauces; food does not come close to the standards set by the better restaurants in Krabi. Most lay their catches out on ice for customers to peruse – snapper, shark, pomfret, tiger prawns and glistening crabs.

WHAT TO DO

Canoeing

Sea Canoe, T076-528839, www.seacanoe.net, hen@seacanoe.net. Offers small-scale sea canoeing trips (self-paddle), exploring the overhanging cliffs and caves and the rocky coastline of Phra Nang, Rai Leh and nearby islands.

Sea Canoe boasts about its strong environmental policies, including restrictions on the number of people per trip, and no foam or plastic-packaged lunches. Some of the other operators have adopted these policies too, particularly in the Ao Thalen area where there is a small group of companies operating in amicable fashion. The best thing is probably to spend some time chatting to your prospective guide to see if you like the way they operate and whether you are happy with the level of English they speak. You should also try to get some guarantees on the number of people on the tour.

Sea Kayak Krabi, on the front, T075-630270/T08-9724 8579 (mob), www.sea kayak-krabi.com. Has been known to promise no more than 10 participants but then take up to 30. Remember too that sea canoes in Thailand are open, so you should either wear a strong waterproof sun block or go for long trousers/sleeves and a hat.

Diving

Ao Nang Divers, 208/2-3 Moo 2, T075-637246, www.aonang-divers.com. Easily the best in town. A 5-star PADI dive centre on the main street.

Poseidon, 23/27 Moo 2, Ban Ao Nang, T075-637 263, www.poseidon-krabi.com.

Rock climbing

Hot Rock Climbing School, East Railay (between Yaya resort and Bhu Nga Thani resort, www.railayadventure.com, T075-662 245. Courses for climbers of all levels.

Shooting

Ao Nang Shooting Range, 99/9 Moo 2, Ao Nang Rd, Ao Nang, T075-695555. You can fire shotguns, Berettas, semi-automatics and Magnums at this well-run shooting range. Prices start at around ฿890 for a full clip.

Therapies

Most luxury hotels are now offering spa facilities.

Pavilion Queen's Bay, www.pavilionhotels.com. Offers the best in-hotel spa. Others offer the services one might expect, but don't have that aura of peace and tranquillity that leads to a truly pampering experience.

Tropical Herbal Spa, 20/1 Moo 2, Ao Nang, www.tropicalherbalspa.com. A glorious day spa, a little away from the beach but set in beautiful gardens and mostly open to the air.

Tour operators

Ao Nang Ban Lae Travel, close to **Krabi Resort**. Runs boat tours to various islands and beaches, including Rai Leh and Phi Phi.

Aonang Travel and Tour, 43 Moo 2, Ao Nang Beach, T075-637152, www.aonang travel.co.th. Specializes in half- and 1-day kayaking and island boat tours.

AP Travel & Tour, Beachfront Rd, T075-637 342, www.aptravelkrabi.com. Offers a range of tours to various islands, temples and short 'jungle tours' – very helpful and friendly though not terribly exciting.

ISLANDS SOUTH OF KRABI

For most arrivals on Koh Phi Phi it seems like you've reached paradise. Anvil-shaped and fringed by sheer limestone cliffs and golden beaches, Koh Phi Phi – the setting for the Leonardo Di Caprio film The Beach – is stunning. However, a quick walk along the beach, heaving with masses of pink, roasting flesh, or through Ton Sai village, which is filled with persistent touts and standardized tourist facilities, soon shatters the illusion of Nirvana; the endless stream of boats spewing diesel into the sea doesn't help either. Ostensibly Phi Phi should be protected by its national park status but this seems to cut little ice with the developers who appear to be doing more irretrievable damage than the Asian tsunami that devastated the island on 26 December 2004. Whether Phi Phi can encourage enough sustainable tourism to survive the future is debatable; what is certain is that it has very quickly reached the same levels of development that existed pre-tsunami.

→KOH PHI PHI

Kho Phi Phi was one of the sites worst-hit by the tsunami – there is a aerial photograph on display in the **Amico** restaurant in Ton Sai village which shows the apocalyptic dimensions of the devastation. Both Ton Sai and Loh Dalem Bay were almost wiped out by the impact of the killer waves overlapping simultaneously on either side of this thin stretch of island. Today, Phi Phi is back to rude health. Tourists are streaming in and the dive shops, hotels, restaurants, shops and bars are now fully up and running. It should also be pointed out that large parts of the island were completely unaffected by the tsunami.

Phi Phi Le is a national park, entirely girdled by sheer cliffs, where swiftlets nest. It found fame as the location for the film *The Beach* starring Leonardo Di Caprio and Tilda Swinton. It is not possible to stay on Phi Phi Le but it can be visited by boat. The best snorkelling off Phi Phi is at **Hat Yao** (Long Beach) or nearby Bamboo Island and most boat excursions include a visit to the **Viking Cave**, which contains prehistoric paintings of what look like Viking longboats, and the cliffs where birds' nests are harvested for bird's nest soup.

Getting there and moving on Phi Phi lies between Krabi and Phuket and can be reached from both, but the only way to get there is by boat. There are daily connections with Krabi, taking one hour on an express boat and 1½ hours on the normal service. Boats also run from the beaches of Ao Nang and Rai Leh close to Krabi (two hours). There are daily boats from Koh Lanta (one hour) and from various spots on Phuket (one to 1½ hours). Note that all arriving visitors must pay a ฿20 'cleaning fee' at the pier – this charge is not included in the ferry ticket price.

Best time to visit It is possible to travel to Koh Phi Phi all year round but during the rainy season (May to October), the boat trip can be very rough and not for the faint-hearted. December to February are the driest months, but hotel rates are ridiculously high and it can be difficult to find an available room.

BEACHES

Koh Phi Phi's beaches include **Loh Dalam**, which faces north and is on the opposite side to **Ton Sai Bay**, so is still under recovery. **Laem Hin** next to Ton Sai Bay, has beautiful fine sand. **Ton Dao** beach is a small and relatively peaceful stretch to the east of Laem Hin, hemmed in with the usual craggy rocks and vegetation.

Hat Yao (Long Beach), post-tsunami, has become a day-trippers' destination as curious folk from the mainland resorts hit Koh Phi Phi to see where everything happened. However, it is gradually starting to attract overnighters. There are other reasons to stay here; the beach has excellent snorkelling offshore. Even before the tsunami, it was touted as having the cleanest water in Koh Phi Phi. Early in the morning (the best time being before 0930) black-tip sharks are a regular fixture here, before they swim further out to sea as the temperature rises. A walk to Hat Yao along the beach from the former Ton Sai Village takes about 30 minutes. You can also get a boat for around ฿100.

Loh Bakao is one of the larger of the minor beaches dotted around this island. **Phi Phi Island Village** is the only resort on this stretch of wide golden sand. **Laem Tong** (Cape of God) boasts a wonderful sweep of white sandy beach that's relatively quiet and empty. There are only a few upper range resorts here, where many guests prefer poolside sunbathing, or the privacy of their own verandas, to the beach. The resorts also offer day trips, diving, snorkelling and cave-exploring expeditions. Increasingly, resorts are also conducting cultural workshops in skills such as Thai cookery, batik-painting and language courses.

AROUND THE ISLAND

Hire a long-tailed boat to take a trip around the island. A six-hour tour costs ฿3000 per boat, maximum four passengers; three-hour tours ฿1500. A day trip snorkelling is well worthwhile (฿600 per person, including lunch, snorkels and fins), with Bamboo Island, Hat Yao and, on Phi Phi Le, Loh Samah and Maya Bay, being particularly good spots. Diving is also possible, with a chance of seeing white-tip sharks. Areas of interest include the Bida Islands, south of Phi Phi Le, where the variety of coral is impressive. There is a 50-m underwater tunnel here for more experienced divers. Wrecks can be found behind Mosquito Island – so-named for its mosquitoes, so do take repellent. The best visibility (25-40 m) is from December to April.

Trips can be taken to see the cliff formations at **Phi Phi Le**, the **Viking Cave**, **Lo Samah Bay** and **Maya Bay** (about ฿300 per person). Maya Bay was used in the filming of *The Beach* starring Leonardo Di Caprio.

→KOH JUM, KOH BUBU AND KOH SIBOYA

These islands, south of Krabi, are places to escape the crowd. The beaches are not as divine as other Andaman Sea spots but they are quiet and somewhat away from the *farang* trail.

KOH JUM (JAM)

ⓘ *The boat from Krabi to Koh Lanta goes via Koh Jum, 1½ hrs, ฿350. There are also connections with Koh Phi Phi and with Laem Kruat, on the mainland.*

The island itself, with its beige-yellow beach and shallow waters, is not one of the most beautiful in the Andaman Sea, although it does have a magnificent pair of sea eagles who make regular appearances on the village side. Its main attraction is as an escape from the crowds on other islands, a slightly rough-hewn edge and enough variety in accommodation and restaurants to keep things interesting. Recently, the island, which only has around a couple of hundred residents – mostly Chao Le and Muslim fishing families – has seen a flourishing of cheap bungalows and there are now over 20 places to choose from. There is a fear that the resort side of the island is quickly running out of space, thus seriously hampering the privacy and quiet that travellers find here. Additionally, there are concerns that high-level developers will step in to create hermetically sealed resorts and drive out the smaller set-ups. But this still seems unlikely as the beach is not particularly attractive and there are no sites of note on the island to visit.

There is also still a sense of being in the jungle, with pythons making slithering debuts in resort kitchens from time to time. Mains electricity has now reached the island but a number of places still remain off the grid, adding a touch of romantic escapism to the experience. The island also has a undeniable quirky charm, both in terms of the locals and expats who have set up semi-permanent base here. There is a working fishing village with a mosque on the other side of the island from the resorts, which protects Koh Jum from being a toy island like the voluptuous Koh Ngai. The village has a superb restaurant with sophisticated seafood dishes that would not be out of place in a metropolis, general stores and clothes shops selling ubiquitous backpacker tat – fishermen trousers, hippy Alice bands and multi-coloured ashram muslin shirts. You can also watch fishermen at work here or have a cool beer away from the resorts. Finally, if you find that Koh Jum is not isolated enough for you, then take a day trip to Koh Bubu or Koh Siboya (see below).

KOH SIBOYA

ⓘ *In high season Nov-Apr, the easiest way to get here is by booking accommodation in advance and catching a Krabi–Lanta ferry. The ferry will stop offshore and the resort will send a long-tail out to pick you up; you'll have to pay full fare, however. Otherwise, take the local bus from Krabi south to Laem Hin Pier (฿100, 1 hr), then catch a long-tail ferry for the 10-min trip. The cost is ฿20-40 and boats depart whenever they're deemed full enough, until about 1500. Long-tail ferry boats also depart infrequently from the pier at Laem Kruad, about 30 km south of Krabi Town. To get to the pier, take the local bus from Krabi Town through Neua Klong town. Or take a private long-tail from Koh Jum.*

Koh Siboya is a speck of an island with a population of about 1000 people, most of whom are Muslim and involved in rubber or fisheries. The beach is really just mud-flats that stretch for an astonishing length and bake and crack in the midday heat. However, it is the isolation of Koh Siboya that attracts returnee visitors – a mixture of hardcore travellers and middle-aged hippies. You will also find expats here who came for a couple weeks years ago and who have stayed on living in idiosyncratic and charming bungalows. There is not a lot to do and, from our reports, the main attraction/activity for visitors remains watching monkeys catch crabs on the beach, and freeform meditation.

ISLANDS SOUTH OF KRABI LISTINGS

WHERE TO STAY

Koh Phi Phi

$$$$ Zeavola, Laem Tong, T075-627000, www.zeavola.com. Set on the beachfront, close to the swimming pool or on the hillside among gardens of the flowering plant after which the resort is named (*Scaevola taccada*, in Thai the flower's name means Love the Sea). Outside living areas are also a feature, although the mosquitoes can be horrific. The food is decidedly average though you can dine on the beach by candle-light. Excellent spa. There's a PADI dive centre and excursions are arranged. Staff are friendly, helpful and courteous.
$$$-$$ Viking Nature Resort, T075-819399, www.vikingnaturesresort.com. These huts have been individually designed with Balinese influences. Most sit on the cliff-side with sea views, all have bags of character. Now operating together with neighbouring Maphrao bungalows, it has direct access to 2 very quiet and secluded sandy beaches between Ton Sai Bay and Hat Yao. Recommended.

Koh Jum

$$$-$ Joy Bungalows, T075-618199, kohjum-joybungalow.com. Best known and most established resort; still the most imaginative in terms of variety, with wooden family beachfront chalets, bamboo huts on stilts, wooden bungalows and treehouses. Tour counter and an average restaurant. Recommended.

RESTAURANTS

Koh Phi Phi

Nearly all the food on the island is aimed at tourists and so few of the culinary delights found in the rest of the country are available here. There are some good Western restaurants though, and Ton Sai is packed with bakeries and all manner of seafood.

$$-$ Jasmine, Laem Tong beach. A tiny little Thai eatery next to the sea gypsy village. Tak (translates as grasshopper), the owner, is a friendly character who serves up excellent Thai seafood. The beachside tables are romantic. Highly recommended.

WHAT TO DO

Diving

There are currently around 15 dive shops operating on Koh Phi Phi. Most of the dive shops charge the same, with 2 local fun dives coming in at around ฿2500. Open Water courses start from ฿13,800. Alternatively, you can book with one of the many dive centres on Phuket. One of the oldest and the best local outfits is **PP Aquanauts**, T075-601213, www.ppaquanauts.com.

Rock climbing

The limestone cliffs here are known internationally, and post-tsunami rebolting efforts have expanded the number of available routes in recent years.

Spidermonkey Climbing, near Tonsai Bay, T075-819 384, www.spidermonkeyclimbing.com. Has several years of Phi Phi experience under its safety belt.

Tour operators

Koh Jum Center Tour, shop on the opposite side of **Koh Jum Seafood** and the pier at 161 Moo 3. Native Koh Jumian Wasana Laemkoh provides tickets for planes, trains, buses and boats. She will also change money, make overseas calls, and arrange 1-day boat trips. Her husband is a local fisherman so you may end up going with him. You can also rent motorbikes here. Honest and reliable.

KOH LANTA

It's not that long ago that Koh Lanta provided a genuine opportunity to get away from it all and have an authentic encounter with a unique local culture. There were no telephones, no electricity and the road that ran the length of the island was unpaved. Step off the boat at Sala Dan Pier today and into the arms of the resort ambushers with their private van service to one of more than 100 resorts and you can see that the island is in the grips of real estate mania.

Not only are new resorts sprouting up, many existing players are busily upgrading and adding swimming pools – hotel pools, we're told, are key in the effort to make Lanta a year-round destination. But while three- to five-star resorts are pushing out bargain shoppers, there are still ฿300 backpacker bungalows towards the national park end of the island. Koh Lanta, with its 85% Muslim population increasingly attracts families and pensioners, mainly here for R&R although superb diving, including the world-famous Hin Daeng (Red Rock) and Hin Muong (Purple Rock), also pull in swashbuckling hardcore divers.

In contrast, Koh Lanta's east coast is still underdeveloped, with villagers dependent on wells and young people rejecting the traditional economy of rubber, cashew and fishing for the tourist industry. And, while it is worth a motorbike ride to see the east coast's rough and tumble hills with giant umbrella trees and the rare python sunning itself in the middle of the unfinished road, there are scant architectural gems apart from the Old Town, site of trade routes for China in the early 1900s and home to an Urak Lawoi (sea gypsy) village. The island was also affected by the tsunami of 2004 when several resorts were swamped and some tourists lost their lives – signs along the main road point to tsunami evacuation routes, though even these have been misplaced, often resulting in conflicting directions.

→ARRIVING ON KOH LANTA

GETTING THERE AND MOVING ON

The main access point to Koh Lanta is from Klong Jirad, around 5 km out of Krabi Town to Sala Dan, via Koh Jum (two hours). The island largely shuts its tourist industry down during the wet season when unpredictable large waves make it too dangerous to cross (May to October). At this time of year, a minibus takes visitors via two short car ferry crossings from Lanta Noi to Sala Dan (two hours). There are boat connections with Ban Hua Hin at the southern end of Koh Klang, and *songthaews* from Krabi to Ban Hua Hin. Minibuses also run from Trang and, during the high-season (November to March), boats run to and from Phi Phi.

GETTING AROUND

Not one bay area accessible from the road has not been developed. To get to the resorts and bungalows, there is a road that stretches the length of the island from Sala Dan Pier to the national park end. It is now fully sealed making exploration of the island easy. However the roads leading to resort land are seriously potholed, steep and after periods of dry weather covered with plumes of chronic red dust. Further down this road, as it approaches the national park and the sealed tarmac ends, accidents are common, it therefore makes sense to wear long trousers and sturdy footwear.

Songthaews are the main form of public transport around the island, though they are few and far between. Motorbikes and mountain bikes are available for hire from guesthouses, some shops and tour companies. Although the rental situation has improved greatly with most places renting out nearly new motorbikes, it is advisable to check the tyres, the brakes and the tank before you set off as most of the rental places expect you to sign a contract before you set off agreeing to pay for any damages incurred. A more reliable solution is to rent a jeep but these are considerably more expensive and there are still only small operators here with no credit-card facilities; thus, you'll be asked to turn over your passport as security. Long-tailed boats can be chartered for coastal trips. There are also a smattering of tuk-tuks in Sala Dan but prices are high – even for the shortest 2-km hop.

→AROUND THE ISLAND

SALA DAN

This dusty two-street town on the northern tip of the island is most arrivees' introduction to Koh Lanta, as the majority of ferries and boats dock here. During the high season it can resemble the Village of the Damned with throngs of blond, blue-eyed Scandinavians mingling with the grumpy locals most of whom seem keen to fleece every dumb *farang* that passes through. To cut to the chase, Sala Dan is geared to emptying the pockets of tourists as quickly as possible. It does provide numerous facilities, including banks, ATMs, internet, bars and restaurants, though most are excessively overpriced, filled with *farang* and serving up weak examples of Thai food.

BAN KOH LANTA YAI

Blink and you miss it; Ban Koh Lanta Yai, the old administrative centre and port on Koh Lanta, usually called 'Old Town' in the brochures, is developing its own tourism niche. With stunning views across to the islands of Koh Bubu, Koh Po, Ko Kum and Koh Tala Beng, and most of its original old wooden shophouse/fishing houses still standing, this micro-town, which is actually only a couple of streets, has buckets of charm. Here, local entrepreneurs have opened galleries and souvenir shops, there are bed and breakfasts and the closest thing to family stays available on the island. Ban Koh Lanta really comprises one main street that doesn't even go on for that long. The end of this road is indicated by an extraordinary ancient tree rather like a banyan and a tiny canal rivulet. There is a distinct Thai-Chinese ambience with rows of busy shophouses, each replete with its own exotically plumed bird in a wooden cage. Trade on this main street is largely fishing tackle shops and general goods stores, indicating the locals' overruling occupations. There are excellent restaurants offering either good working man's fare or more sophisticated seafood dishes.

KOH BUBU

Koh Bubu is a tiny uninhabited island in the Lanta group of Koh Lanta Yai which takes a mere 15 minutes to walk around. There is one resort. People who have stayed here return to the mainland completely relaxed and detached from the world they left behind. There is a very pleasant walk around the island and lots of birdwatching opportunities.

AO KHLONG DAO

Ao Khlong Dao, which starts on the edge of Sala Dan, was one of the first bays to open to tourism in Koh Lanta and as little as eight years ago had only about six small bungalow resorts and a couple of independent restaurants, not to mention the occasional buffalo family going for a paddle in the sea. While it is a lovely bay with soft sand and pleasant views over to Deer Neck Cape, development here has been rapid and unplanned. The bay is now heavily developed with most resorts encroaching onto the beach, some separated by high walls. Khlong Dao itself is a relatively safe place to swim and good for families and with the number of 'proper' hotels, it is often booked via travel agencies offering package tours to Lanta.

AO PHRA-AE (LONG BEACH)

Ao Phra-Ae, also known as Long Beach, is a lovely beach to stroll on with soft white sand and a very long, gently sloping stretch that allows for safe swimming at both low and high tides. In the late evening, as you splash your feet in the waves close to the shore, a magical phospheresence appears as if you are walking on a thin surface of stars. This beach is catering increasingly to well-heeled retirees and families, particularly the Scandinavians, although there are still remnants of its earlier days as a backpacker haven with restaurants and bars like the **Ozone**, which holds big DJ bashes every Thursday. While great for those who like to party all night and sleep all day, the new style of tourists have complained about the noise, although everyone seems to like the by-now standard fire shows. The resorts here are no longer owned by local families and the bungalow resorts make their most lucrative profits through restaurant and bar sales. To encourage their guests to 'stay at home', many of the resorts have created barriers that extend right down to the beach and may use barbed wire or natural borders like strategically planted palms to keep the tourists in. This has resulted in more independently minded travellers feeling trapped and resentful, and has generated an atmosphere of comically poisonous competition between the resorts.

HAT KHLONG KHOANG

Hat Khlong Khoang is advertised by some as the 'most beautiful beach on Lanta'. But the beach is fairly steep down to the sea and the sand not as fine as that at Long Beach. The views along the bay are pleasant, but not spectacular. Behind many bungalow resorts is a canal which is treated as a dump for all sorts of waste from construction debris to coconut husks. In many parts of the beach it smells and is a mosquito trap and consequently best avoided if you are offered a room anywhere near. That said, there are a handful of establishments with real character and charm and, offshore, there are coral reefs that are increasingly attracting snorkellers and divers.

KHLONG TOAB

Khlong Toab, just beyond the Fisherman's Cottage and close to Khlong Toab village, supports two resorts in marked contrast to each other. It is a quiet area and the beach shelves gently and the swimming is safe, so is particularly suitable for families.

AO KHLONG NIN

Ao Khlong Nin is a bit of a mixed bag in terms of accommodation, ranging from basic backpacker places through to the top-of-the-range resorts. There is, as they say, just about something for everyone. The beach itself is picturesque with rocks dotted about and not just a single sweep of sand; the sand is white and fine. The downside is that this means that swimming, in places, can be tricky. Usually, though, it is possible to find a safe place to swim.

AO KANTIANG

Ao Kantiang was once the cheap and secluded hideaway for many Europeans and Scandinavians who spent months resting in bungalows overlooking the bay. With golden sand, steeply sloping hillsides and only a small village, the only accommodation was locally owned and operated and set well back from the local community. All that has changed with the arrival of the **Pimalai Resort**. This luxury resort has completely altered the feel of this bay. Speedboats send guests off to a floating jetty (thus avoiding putting any money into local coffers through the ferry and avoiding the road which was substantially torn up by the construction vehicles building the resort). The Scandinvians still frequent this beach, as do wealthy European retirees.

AO KHLONG JAAK

Ao Khlong Jaak used to be one of the most peaceful bays on Koh Lanta, a relatively small bay with sloping hills to the north and south and coconut plantations and grassland in the middle. However, there is rampant land speculation in this area now, as with all the beaches. In the bay area there is an elephant trekking station (up to the waterfall), and the big beasts are often brought to sea in the late afternoon for a bath. It is important to remember that during the dry season the waterfall turns to a trickle, as this is one of the main selling points of Klong Jark. However, it is still possible to find cheap accommodation and more independently minded tourists here.

AO MAI PHAI

Ao Mai Phai is the last bay before the national park and one of the few on the west coast of Lanta with good snorkelling opportunities. Again, it is a relatively small bay with steeply sloping hills leading down to the bay on the north and south and with a more extensive area of flatter land in the middle.

MOO KOH LANTA MARINE NATIONAL PARK
① ฿400.

The park covers much of the southern part of the island and extends over numerous islands in the area including Koh Rok, Hin Muang and Hin Daeng. The national park headquarters is at Laem Tanod and involves either a boat trip or a long and painful drive. The road to the park is in very bad condition and practically impassable during the rainy season. The peninsula is named after the tanod trees (a type of sugar palm) that grow throughout the area and give it an almost prehistoric atmosphere. There are two bays and in the middle is the lighthouse (navy controlled but the peninsula is accessible to the public). One bay has fine soft sand and is great for swimming. The other, which faces west, bears the full brunt of the monsoons and is rocky and a good place to explore if you like rock pools. Beyond the visitor centre and the toilet and shower block, is a lily pond and the park headquarters. Just beyond this, is a nature trail which takes you up a fairly precipitous path into the forest and then along a contour around the back of the offices in a half loop ending at the road entering the park. It's a well-designed trail though not suitable for children or the elderly because the path is very steep in the early parts and can be slippery. Take plenty of water and some snacks with you. The bay is surrounded by forested hills and filled with forest sounds and the gentle or not so gentle sound of waves crashing on to the rocks or beach (depending on the season). It is a beautiful spot to spend a day swimming and walking, and then watching the sunset from the viewpoint on Laem Tanod.

KOH LANTA NOI

If you take the car ferry route to Lanta Yai, Lanta Noi is the island you cross between the two ferry crossings. Undeveloped for tourism, this island is dominated by mangrove forest and paperbark forest. Few tourists visit the island, but it is worth making a quick visit from Sala Dan using the small long-tailed boats. This will take you to the pier used for the district office (now located on Lanta Noi but once based in Ban Koh Lanta Yai). From here you can walk for at least a couple of hours along a stretch of beach complete with casuarina trees and paperbark forest. With good views to the coast and across to islands, this is a pleasant place from which to escape the noise and dust of the main island. Also on Lanta Noi, but on the main road and in the only village passed en route to Koh Lanta, is a women's group shop that sells the woven matting bags, mats, etc that you may see in souvenir shops on Lanta Yai. Prices here are not much lower than what you'd pay in the shops, but at least all of the money goes to the makers. The quality of the weaving here is very high.

HAD THUNG THALE NON-HUNTING AREA, KOH KLANG

ⓘ *There are few organized tours to this area, but you can self-drive. Signs are reasonably well marked – it's about 17 km off the main road down a couple of turn-offs and through some small villages and plantations.*

Had Thung Thale Non-Hunting Area is on Koh Klang, but you'll have a hard time spotting that fact even if you do drive over to Lanta Yai and take the car ferries. Koh Klang is joined to the mainland by a bridge. The non-hunting area comprises several hundred hectares of beautiful paperbark forest (*pa samet*), coastal grasslands and casuarina forest, and is bordered with some beautiful long stretches of grey/white beaches. Rarely visited, occasionally it is taken over completely with local school trips for their scouting activities and government groups on corporate bonding sessions – the same sort that go to Tarutao. There are several conservation projects sponsored by the king. The paper-bark forests have a bleak but beautiful aspect, are fragrant and present relatively easy walking opportunities.

KOH LANTA LISTINGS

WHERE TO STAY

$$$$ Costa Lanta Moo 3, T02-6623550, www.costalanta.com. Modernism may not be to everyone's taste, but this exclusive resort has succeeded in creating an ambience somewhere between modern urban living and beach hideaway. Designed by Thai architect Duangrit Bunnag, the concrete and wood cabana rooms have huge retractable teak doors that completely open 2 sides to the elements, flooding them with natural light.

$$$$ Pimalai Resort, 99 Moo 5, Ba Kaiang Beach, T075-607999, www.pimalai.com. Huge and very pricey resort; beautifully designed rooms, although there's an awful lot of concrete used in the gardens. The resort also encroaches on the beach – something that undoes its avowed eco-aims in one fell swoop. Extensive facilities.

$$$$-$$$ Cha-Ba Bungalows & Art Gallery, 20 Moo 3, Khlong Dao beach, T075-684118, www.krabidir.com/chababungalows. Walk along Khlong Dao beach and you'll eventually come across a series of giant, brightly coloured, amorphous sea creature sculptures. The rooms and bungalows are not as inspired as the artwork, but it is very friendly. The art gallery holds various exhibitions differing in quality. Good food. Recommended

$$$$-$$$ Sri Lanta, T075-662688, www.srilanta.com. This fairly upmarket resort stars spacious, well-designed bamboo-and-wood bungalows with a/c (but sadly no mosquito screening or ceiling fans) and hot showers. Beautiful spot with access to a sandy beach, massage pavilions and a stylish pool. Recommended.

$$$$-$$ Relax Bay, 111 Moo 2, T075-684194, www.relaxbay.com. 37 large rustic bungalows, some basic, some VIP, raised high off the ground and scattered through a beachside grove. They have unusually angled roofs, comfortable verandas, glass and/or mosquito panels in the windows, fans and showers. Some tented beachfront cabanas are also available. Decent beach bar, restaurant and pool. Recommended.

$$$ Banana Garden Home, 20/2 Moo 3, T08-1634 8799 (mob), www.banana gardenhome.com. Wooden bungalows with a/c, rather tightly packed together but well crafted with natural materials. The manager really goes the extra mile for her guests. Decent restaurant and cushioned beachfront lounging area. No pool but still good value for this location. Recommended.

$$$ Mango House, middle of the main street, T075-697181, www.mangohouses.com. Restored old wooden house overlooking the sea. Was once, allegedly, a government-run opium den. Rooms are nicely decorated, with hardwood floors, kitchenettes and seafront decks. Limited a/c. The owners also have a number of villas for rent (**$$$$**). One of the most original places to stay on the island. Rates halve during the low season (May-Oct). Highly recommended.

$$$-$ Where Else Resort, 149 Moo 2, T075-667024, www.lanta-where-else.com. Bags of character at this budget resort featuring well-designed bamboo and driftwood bungalows half hidden in the coconut grove. All have semi-outdoor bathrooms, mosquito screens and hammocks. The ones at the back are a little cramped together. Recommended.

$ Sea Culture House, 317 Moo 3, T075-684541. Next to Relax Bay on a very quiet stretch of beach with soft sand – the sea here is good for swimming. Basic wooden bungalows which are sturdier than they look. Bathroom inside. Owner also rents out tents for ฿100. Occasional beach parties with live reggae music. For this price and location, recommended.

RESTAURANTS

$$$ Time for Lime, 72/2 Moo 3, Klong Dao Beach, T075-684590, www.timeforlime. net. Popular offshoot restaurant from the Thai fusion cooking school of the same name. Profits go to the owner's local animal welfare centre.

$$$-$$ Golden Leaf, www.goldenbay cottagelanta.com. Beachside restaurant in the bungalow operation of the same name. Excellent Thai and Isaan food on sale here. They also BBQ a fresh catch of seafood daily and offer discounts in low season. Reasonably priced in comparison to other places.

$$ Krue Lanta Yai Restaurant, at the end of 'town', T075-697062. Hours variable. A restaurant on the pier along a walkway filled with plants. Good selection of fresh seafood nicely prepared. Recommended.

$ Green Leaf Café, on the main road, opposite the entrance to the **Where Else Resort**. A warm welcome awaits at this comfy café, which has a rather homely feel. The English and Thai owners offer up real coffees, generous baguettes, served on fresh multi grain bread and healthy salads. For a *farang* food fix, highly recommended.

WHAT TO DO

Diving and snorkelling

There are several schools in Sala Dan (some with German spoken); check equipment before signing on. Snorkelling is known locally as 'snorking'. Most guesthouses hire out equipment for about ฿100 per day, although the quality varies.

Try **Blue Planet Divers**, 3 Moo 1, Ban Saladan, T075-668165, www. blueplanetdivers.net; or **Scuba Fish**, Narima Resort, Klong Nin Beach, T075-665095, www.scuba-fish.com.

Tour operators

Most bungalows can make travel arrangements and offer day trips to Trang's Andaman Islands (see page 252), ฿950-1400 per person (depending on the type of boat), including lunch and snorkelling gear. (Note that it is a long trip – 3 hrs each way – and some people find the noise unbearable for just 1 or 2 hrs' snorkelling.) You can also organize trips from Ban Koh Lanta Yai. For long-tailed boat trips from Ban Koh Lanta, including fishing and camping tours, contact **Sun Island Tours**, 9/1 Sri Raya Rd (main waterfront), Lanta Old Town, T08-7891 6619 (mob),

www.lantalongtail.com. Boats leaving from this side of the island can save a couple of hours from the return trip to Koh Ngai and will take you to explore some of the islands on the east side. There are a couple of small tour shops running these businesses in the old town, and **Khrua Lanta Yai** also runs boat trips. **Freedom Adventures**, T08-4910 9132 (mob), www.freedom-adventures.net, organize various day trips (from ฿1400) and camping adventures (from ฿2600). Encourage your boatman to buoy, rather than use an anchor which damages the coral. Comprehensive island tours are offered by a number of tour agencies based in Sala Dan. **Opal Travel**, www.opalspeedboat.com, has reasonably priced tours and excellent service. **Lanta Paddlesports**, at the Noble House Resort, Ao Khlong Dao, www.lantapaddlesports. com, offers guided paddleboard tours, plus rentals and lessons for surfing and stand-up paddleboarding.

Hire long-tailed boats from bungalows for ฿1200 per person, based on 4 people per trip, per day. This price includes all snorkelling gear and food.

TRANG AND ITS ISLANDS

On first sight, Trang looks like a somewhat drab but industrious Chinese-Thai town, filled with temples and decent schools – in other words – a good place to raise your children. Everything shuts down at around 2230 in the evening and even the traffic signals seem to go to sleep while early morning is filled with bustling tradespeople, eager to make their fortunes and provide for their families. But there is an underlying cranky charm and no-nonsense energy to this town which is famous for its char-grilled pork, sweet cakes and as the birthplace of former Prime Minister Chuan Leekpai. Its unique entertainments include bullfights (bull to bull) and bird-singing competitions (bird to bird) while the people are hugely friendly and exceptionally helpful the minute they realize that you like Trang too.

Finally, Trang has a nine-day Vegetarian Festival in October, similar to that celebrated in Phuket. Vegetarian patriots, dressed all in white, parade the street, dancing through clouds of exploding fireworks, with the revered few shoving various objects through their cheeks. Trang is also an excellent jumping-off point for Koh Lanta, Krabi and the exotic coral islands just off the coast.

→ARRIVING IN TRANG

GETTING THERE AND AROUND
Trang has an airport, 20 minutes from town, and an air-conditioned minibus costs ฿100 and drops you outside the train station. It is possible to charter a tuk-tuk for ฿150, but this depends very much on your bartering skills. Buses arrive at the Thanon Huay Yod terminal. To visit the islands you need to arrange minibuses to Pak meng pier.

MOVING ON
To get to Tarutao National Park, book a minivan from your hotel or via an agency from Trang to Ban Pak Bara (two hours) and then take boat (30 minutes-1½ hours, depending on which island you're going to). Boats only run certain times of the year; see Getting there, page 256. If you want to return to Bangkok from Trang, rather than continuing south to Satun, there are flights from Trang (1½ hours). There are also two overnight trains at 1325 and 1720 (15 hours) to Bangkok which depart from the station on the western end of Thanon Rama VI in Trang.

BEST TIME TO VISIT
The best time to visit is between January and April, out of the monsoon season. In the low season, some of the island resorts close down, so you do need to check availability.

→TRANG

Trang has retained the atmosphere of a Chinese immigrant community, many of whom would be descendents of those who fled the corrupt and oppressive Manchu government. There are good Chinese restaurants and several Chinese shrines dotted throughout the town that hold individual festivals. The **Kwan Tee Hun shrine**, dedicated to a bearded war god, is in Ban Bang Rok, 3 km north of Trang on Route 4. The Vegetarian Festival centres around the **Kiw Ong Eia Chinese Temple** and **Muean Ram**. There is also the **Rajamangkala Aquarium** ① *T075-248201-5, open daily during 'official hours'*, which lies 30 km from the

FESTIVALS
Trang

The **Vegetarian Festival** is held in October (movable) and is a nine-day celebration in which a strict vegetarian diet is observed to purify the body. Mediums pierce their cheeks and tongues with spears and walk on hot coals. On the sixth day a procession makes its way around town, in which everyone dresses in traditional costumes. The same event occurs in Phuket, see page 210.

Bull fighting

Fights between bulls take place at random, depending on whether the farmers have a suitable bull. The only way to find out about whether they are taking place is to ask around. But be warned – this is a very much a local entertainment and you might get some curious looks when you ask, particularly if you are a woman. Scarcely any women attend these events. The fights are usually held during the week and only in the daytime. They occur in a field off Trang-Pattalung Rd near the Praya Ratsadanupradit Monument. The best way to get there is by tuk-tuk, which takes about 20 minutes from the railway station. They are always packed by an excitable betting crowd screaming with dismay or joy and there are plenty of stalls about selling drinks and foods, including noodles and fruit. Dusty and hot but exciting.

city on the road to Pakmeng and is housed in the Fishery Faculty of the Rajamangkala Institute of Technology. The aquarium has 61 tanks of freshwater and marine life. Former **Prime Minister Chuan Leekpai's house** (ask locally for directions) has also become a pilgrimage spot of sorts and is open to visitors.

BEACHES AROUND TRANG

Trang's embryonic tourism industry has so far escaped the hard sell of Phuket and Pattaya – excellent news for nature lovers, reef divers and explorers. The strip of coast running south from Pakmeng (38 km west from Trang) round to Kantang, boasts some of the south's best beaches. Unfortunately, it is also a relatively expensive place to stay with frankly exorbitant rates charged at some of the more popular beaches and islands and very ordinary food. **Pakmeng and Chang Lang** beaches are the most accessible – 40 km west of Trang town. The sea is poor here for swimming but it's a nice place to walk, although scarcely as scenic as the beaches of Koh Lanta or Krabi.

To the north, down the road from Sikao, is **Hua Hin** which has a good beach and is famed for its *hoi tapao* – sweet-fleshed oysters. Unfortunately the oyster season climaxes in November – the peak of the wet season. Hua Hin Bay is dotted with limestone outcrop islets. Other beaches to the south include **Hat San**, **Hat Yong Ling**, **Hat Yao** and **Hat Chao Mai**; private ventures are not permitted at any of the beaches within the national park (ie Hat Chao Mai, Hat Yong Ling and Hat San).

PARKS AROUND TRANG

Hat Chao Mai National Park has some impressive caves near the village, known for their layered curtain stalactites. The beaches and many of the offshore islands fall under the jurisdiction of the 230-sq-km Hat Chao Mai National Park. Accommodation is available at park headquarters (6 km outside Chao Mai). To get to the park, you need to take a minibus from the minibus station on Thaklang Road (฿100).

Khao Chong Forest Park, 20 km from town, off the Trang–Phattalung road, supports one of the few remaining areas of tropical forest in the area and has two waterfalls, Nam Tok Ton Yai and Nam Tok Ton Noi. Government resthouses are available here. To reach the park, you can take a local bus (from the bus station on Huay Yod Road), bound for Phattalung or Hat Yai, ฿15 or a *songthaew* from near the old market on Ratchadumnuen Road, ฿25.

→TRANG'S ANDAMAN ISLANDS

Trang's Andaman Islands number 47 in total and spread out to the south of Koh Lanta. More tourists are visiting the islands, and the beauty, rich birdlife and the clear waters that surround them make more upmarket development highly likely. The islands can be reached from several small ports and fishing villages along the Trang coast, the main ones being Pakmeng (take a minibus from Thaklang Road, ฿60) and Kantang, 24 km from Trang. It is also possible to charter boats with the Muslim fishermen who live on the islands. The best time to visit the area is between January and April. The weather is unsuitable for island-hopping from May to December and although it is sometimes still possible to charter boats out of season, it can be expensive and risky: the seas are rough, the water is cloudy and you may be stranded by a squall or equally by the boatmen's incompetency

and a vessel which was never seaworthy in the first place. There is a also a tendency to overbook these boats and consequent delays as the operators wait for further customers.

KOH NGAI (HAI)

This 5-sq-km island is cloaked in jungle and fringed with glorious beaches. It also enjoys fabulous views of the limestone stacks that pepper the sea around it. A coral reef sweeps down the eastern side, ending in two big rocks, between which rips a strong current – but the coral around these rocks is magnificent. Koh Ngai is the clichéd resort island retreat where you wake up, eat and sleep at the same place. There are just a handful of resorts on this island and no local community. If you like this sort of intense group intimacy, Koh Ngai is perfect but guests have complained of cabin fever setting in after a week. It is more suited to honeymooners or those who will stay here as a base and do day trips to other islands. Although Koh Ngai forms the southernmost part of Krabi province and is most easily reached from Pakmeng in Trang province, 16 km away, it is also possible to get there from Koh Phi Phi and Koh Lanta. Tourists also stop here on island-hopping day trips to eat at one of the resorts and to snorkel in the magnificently clear waters which are rich with marine life.

Koh Chuak and Koh Waen (between Koh Hai and Koh Muk) are also snorkellers' havens – the latter is the best reef for seafan corals.

KOH MUK (MOOK)

On the western side of Koh Muk is the **Emerald Cave** (Tham Morakot) – known locally as Tham Nam – which can only be entered by boat (or fearless swimmers) at low tide, through a narrow opening. After the blackness of the 80-m-long passage it opens into daylight again at an inland beach straight out of Jurassic Park – emerald water ringed with powdery white sand and a backdrop of precipitous cliffs that look as if they are made of black lava frozen over the centuries. The cave was only discovered during a helicopter survey not very long ago and is thought to have been a pirates' lair. **Be warned**, you can only leave the pool at low tide. Unfortunately this is being oversold and there have been groups of Southeast Asian tourists who combine the swimming into the cave with positive reinforcement songs that can be heard up to a mile away as everyone shouts in unison – 'we can do this' and 'we will succeed, onward, onward'. Unless you are in with the crowd, this is unfailingly depressing and destroys the mystique of this one-off place. The only way around the group scene is to hire a long-tailed boat privately and try to go at an early hour although the tide does dictate when it is safe to swim in.

The island's west coast has white beaches backed by high cliffs where swallows nest. There are also beautiful beaches on the east coast facing the craggy mainland.

KOH KRADAN

Koh Kradan, most of which falls within the bounds of the Chao Mai National Park, is regarded as the most beautiful of Trang's islands, with splendid beaches and fine coral, on the east side. Two Japanese warships sunk during the Second World War lie off the shore and are popular dive spots. The area not encompassed by the national park is a mixture of rubber smallholdings and coconut groves. The island – bar the park area – is privately owned, having been bought by tycoon Mon Sakunmethanon in 1985 for ฿5 million. There are just a handful of places to stay here.

KOH TALIBONG (LIBONG)

Koh Talibong (Libong), which is part of the Petra Islands group to the south, is renowned for its oysters and birdlife. The Juhoi Cape and the eastern third of the island is a major stopping-off point for migratory birds, and in March and April the island is an ornithologist's El Dorado. Typical visitors, on their way back to northern latitudes, include brown-headed gulls, crab plovers, four species of terns, waders, curlews, godwits, redshanks, greenshanks, reef egrets and black-necked storks. From October to March the island is famed for its unique Hoi Chakteen oysters. The rare manatee (*Manatus senegalensis*) and the green turtle also inhabit the waters off the island. The best coral reef is off the southwest coast, directly opposite the **Libong Beach Resort**. Snorkelling equipment is available from the resort, which also provides fishing gear. Libong's main town is Ban Hin Kao, where the daily ferry from Kantang docks. Motorcycle taxis take visitors along rough trails to the island's beaches and villages. Just 4 bungalow resorts operate here. The population is almost exclusively Muslim, and alcohol is not widely available, so you would need to stock up in Trang.

KOH SUKORN (MUU), KOH PETRA, KOH LAO LIENG (NUA AND TAI)

Koh Sukorn, Koh Petra, Koh Lao Lieng (Nua and Tai) are also part of the Petra Islands group, off Palien, 47 km south of Trang, and can be reached from there or Kantang. Koh Sukorn (locally known as Koh Muu – or Pig Island) is inhabited by Muslims, who do not seem to mind the name. Apart from its golden powdery beaches, its main claim to fame are the mouth-watering watermelons that are grown here (March/April).

Koh Petra and **Koh Lao Lieng** have sheer cliffs which are the domain of the birds' nest collectors who risk life and limb for swiftlet saliva. The islands have excellent sandy beaches on their east coasts and impressive reefs which are exposed at low tide. Dolphins can often be seen offshore.

TRANG AND ITS ISLANDS LISTINGS

WHERE TO STAY

Trang

$$$$-$$ Wattana Park, 315/7 Huay Yod Rd, T075-216216, www.wattanaparkhotel. com. A little way out from the town centre on the road in from Krabi. A modern hotel with good rooms and friendly service. No pool. Recommended

$ PJ Guesthouse, 25/12 Sathani Rd, T075-217500. Home-like set-up with traveller ambience and attention to detail. Rooms are small but very clean. Helpful owners and both speak good English. Good location about 100 m from the station. Recommended for those on a tight budget.

Trang Beaches

$$-$ Haadyao Nature Resort, Chao Mai Marine Park, Hadyao, T08-1894 6936 (mob), nature-haadyao.weebly.com/index.html. Eco-resort with simple a/c bungalows and dorm rooms. Staff here are well versed about the area and they arrange tours such as dugong tracking and bird watching. Recommended.

Koh Muk

$$$-$$ Rubber Tree Bungalows, T075-215972, www.mookrubbertree.com. Up a long wooden staircase cut into the hill are these marvellous, family-run bungalows. Set in a working rubber tree plantation, so you may be woken early in the morning by rubber tree tappers. You are welcome to observe them at work. The attached restaurant has easily the best food on the island. This is a magical place to have an evening drink, with dozens of twinkling lights providing a dreamy backdrop. Recommended.

$ Mookies, down the lane/dirt path towards the sea gypsy village (there is only one path on from Rubber Tree), T08-72756533 (mob), mookiebrian@yahoo.com. Open all year. Cross over a wooden bridge and follow the disco music to **Mookie's Bar**, where you are likely to find Aussie Mookie reading pulp fiction and drinking in the mid-afternoon. This is a completely eccentric set-up. Rooms are large with spring mattresses and 24-hr electricity with light and fan inside. While the toilet and shower is shared, they are kept clean to military standards. The shower outside also has hot water. Highly recommended.

RESTAURANTS

Trang

Trang's *moo yang* (BBQ pork) is delicious and one of the town's few claims to national fame. It is made from a traditional recipe brought here by the town's immigrant Chinese community and is usually served with rice.

$$ Koh Chai Pla Phrao, Rusda Rd. Look for a bright yellow sign (Thai only) for one of the most popular places in

Trang. Don't be fooled by the cheap plastic furniture, the Thai food here is awesome. Highly recommended.

$ BBQ Pork Shophouse, corner of a small *soi* on Kantang Rd. This tiny Chinese place is often packed to the rafters with families queuing for either takeaway or a table. Only really sells one dish – BBQ pork. You can also get chicken satay if you ask nicely. Highly recommended.

TARUTAO AND THE FAR SOUTH

While some say that Tarutao is merely a mispronunciation of the Malay words ta lo trao, meaning 'plenty of bay', when first spying this ominous humped island rising out of the sea, it is far easier to believe a second interpretation. That is, that Tarutao comes from the Malay word for old, mysterious and primitive. Resonating with a murky history of pirates, prisoners and ancient curses, it is no wonder the island was picked for the reality television series Survivor in 2002. Despite dynamite fishing in some areas, the island waters still have reasonable coral, and provide some of the best dive sites in Thailand – particularly around the stone arch on Koh Khai. Adang Island has magnificent coral reefs. These are part of Thailand's best-preserved marine park, where turtles, leopard sharks, whales and dolphins can be spotted.

Inland, over half of Koh Tarutao is dense dark rainforest with only a single 12-km road cutting through the length of the island and scant paths leading into a potentially lethal jungle filled with poisonous snakes and volatile beasts like the wild boar. Created in 1974, the marine national park comprises 51 islands – the main ones being Tarutao, Adang, Rawi, Lipe, Klang, Dong and Lek. Tarutao Park itself is divided into two main sections– the Tarutao archipelago and the Adang-Rawi archipelago.

In the far south, there is the Muslim town of Satun with its preserved shophouses and the Thale Ban National Park.

→ARRIVING IN TARUTAO NATIONAL PARK

GETTING THERE
Koh Tarutao lies off the coast 30 km south of Pak Bara; Koh Adang, Rawi and Lipe are another 40 km out into the Andaman Sea, while Koh Bulon-Leh is 20 km due west of Pak Bara. Beware of travelling to any of these islands during bad weather; it is dangerous and a number of boats have foundered.

Getting to Tarutao National Park requires some planning. For much of the year, it is not advisable to take a boat to these beautiful islands. Ferries run from October to June, but speedboats or privately hired long-tailed boats can be chartered at other times of year. If you are based on Koh Lipe or Koh Bulon-Leh then hiring private long-tails to other islands is advised as you will otherwise be facing a roundabout route from Satun or **Ban Pak Bara**, thus adding hours to your journey. Ferries depart from Ban Pak Bara and also from Satun's Thammalang pier.

GETTING AROUND
Rented bicycles provide an adequate means of traversing Tarutao's main road which is a gruelling route of steep curves occupied at times by cobras and pythons sunning themselves. The only other road on the island is around 6 km long and was built by the prisoners to link the two jails.

MOVING ON
To get to Satun, you can take a boat from Tarutao National Park. There is a once-daily boat from Koh Tarutao (one hour and 45 minutes) or Koh Lipe, leaving at 1230, to Tammalang Pier in Satun, or take a boat from the islands to Pak Bara and then catch a connecting bus to Satun, 60 km south. To return to Bangkok from Tarutao National Park, you can either travel via Trang (page 250) or Satun (page 261).

BEST TIME TO VISIT

November to April are the best months; the coolest are November and December. The park is officially closed from the end of May to 15 October, but it is still possible to get there. Services run providing the weather is alright. Koh Bulon-Leh is accessible year round, although most resorts are closed for six months of the year so it is wise to ring ahead. The annual Tarutao-Adang Fishing Cup Festival takes place in March.

TOURIST INFORMATION

With limited electricity, basic beach restaurants, simple accommodation and few concessions to mainstream tourism, most of the islands attract hardier, more bohemian travellers in search of an unspoilt paradise. Koh Lipe, however, is rapidly transforming into a mini Koh Phi Phi with most of the area's resorts. Bring plenty of cash, as there are no banks on the islands, and only a few dive shops and resorts accept credit cards. Bring food to Koh Tarutao as the park shop has little choice so you might want to stock up on the basics – including alcohol and even fruit. The entrance fee to Tarutao is ฿200 for adults, ฿100 for children under 14. This charge is not enforced on the other islands. The **national park headquarters** ⓘ *close to the ferry port at Pak Bara, T074-781285*, provides information and books accommodation on Tarutao and Adang (messages are radioed to the islands). There can be a shortage in high season. Camping spaces are usually available. On Koh Tarutao and Koh Adang the accommodation is Forestry Department (ie government) run; Koh Lipe and Koh Bulon-Leh are the only islands where the private sector has a presence, meaning the resorts are better and activities more varied.

→BACKGROUND

Koh Tarutao boasts the remains of the prison that held around 10,000 criminals and political prisoners, some of whom became pirates during the Second World War to stave off starvation. Island rumour also has it that somewhere on Koh Tarutao a tonne of gold dust looted from a French ship still remains buried along with the murdered pirates that attacked the unfortunate vessel. Not all of the prisoners on this island were pirates. Indeed the translator of the English/Thai dictionary – Sor Settabut – completed the T section of the book at Tarutao. Another scholar – Prince Sithiporn Kridaka – continued his study of crop diversification that helped modernize Thailand's agriculture. The prince, who was educated largely in England and was a lifelong Anglophile, had been interned for his involvement in attempts to send railway cars to jam tracks on which tanks were being brought to defend Bangkok during widespread insurrections in 1932. The prince was also known for having invented Thailand's first shorthand – still used today – and for forming a boy scout troop among the youths at a government opium factory that he was sent to manage. Imprisoned for 11 years, the prince fell prey to life-threatening dysentery. Yet, it is now believed that the political prisoners received the best of the treatment on Koh Tarutao, where the general criminals may even have served them. Certainly the two groups did not mix, with the criminals held in the eastern part at the present-day Taloh Wow Cove and the political prisoners detained at Udang Cove in the southern tip. But all suffered during the Second World War when the island was completely cut off – along with essential food supplies. In cahoots with the guards, prisoners took to ambushing passing ships, originally for food and then for anything of value. This only came to an end in 1947 when the British, who had retaken Malaya, sent in the Royal Navy to quell the pirates.

Afterwards, the island was left in total isolation with the prison gradually reduced to the remains of the prison director's house on top of a dune along with a sawmill below and a mysterious hole indicating a torture cellar. Legend has it that, centuries ago, a princess of Langkawi who had been accused of misdeeds declared that the island would never be discovered. Certainly much of Koh Tarutao holds on to its mystery with its brooding interior and inaccessibility throughout the rainy season.

→TARUTAO ARCHIPELAGO

KOH TARUTAO

The mountainous island of Tarutao is the largest of the islands, 26 km long and 11 km wide and covering 151 sq km. A mountainous spine runs north–south down the centre of the island, with its highest point reaching 708 m. The interior remains largely forested, cloaked in dense semi-evergreen rainforest. The main beaches are **Ao Moh Lai**, **Hin Ngam**, **Ao Phante**, **Ao Chak** and **Ao Sone**, mostly on the west of the island which has long sweeps of sand punctuated by headlands and mangrove. Ao Sone, for example, is a 3 km-long stretch of sand fringed with casuarina trees. (Much of the mangrove was cut for charcoal during the early 1960s before the national park was finally gazetted in 1974.) Notorious as the beach where a lone pirate killed a camping tourist in the 1980s, this eerie strip has quite a physical presence, unlike any of the other beaches along the west coast. The water is aggressive and choppy while Tarutao looms out from the water. This haunting beach, while it does have refreshments at one end, is not as busy as the others. Well worth the visit to Tarutao for the feeling that not everything has been tamed. You can also spot the delightfully electric kingfisher here.

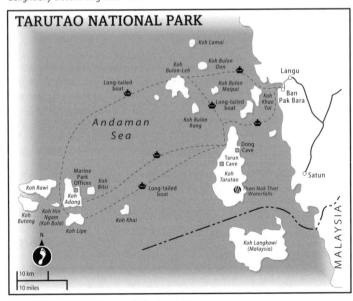

TARUTAO NATIONAL PARK

Koh Lamai
Koh Bulon-Leh
Koh Bulon Don
Langu
Long-tailed boat
Koh Bulon Maipai
Koh Khao Yai
Ban Pak Bara
Andaman Sea
Long-tailed boat
Koh Bulon Rang
Dong Cave
Tarun Cave
Koh Tarutao
Satun
Marine Park Offices
Koh Bitsi
Koh Rawi
Koh Adang
Long-tailed boat
Than Nak That Waterfalls
Koh Butong
Koh Hin Ngam (Koh Bula)
Koh Khai
Koh Lipe
N
Koh Langkawi (Malaysia)
MALAYSIA
10 km
10 miles

Tae Bu cliff, just behind the park headquarters on Ao Phante, has good sunset views. You climb up an imaginative route which includes a path cut into the hill, rickety wooden plank steps and extraordinary rock formations, all the while hearing the sound of monkeys, mouse deer, hornbills and perhaps wild boar. Finally you reach the top and a lookout point over the beach and surrounding forest, which is not as satisfying as the walk itself. You may also find it taken over by groups of young park staff – especially in the early morning.

The prison at Ao Talo U-Dang, in the south, was established in 1939 and was once used as a concentration camp for Thailand's political prisoners; the graveyard, charcoal furnaces and a fish fermentation plant are still there. The other main camp, at Ao Talo Wao on the east side of the island, was used for high-security criminals. During the Second World War, when communications were slow and difficult, the remoteness of the island meant it was cut off from supplies of food. After 700 out of the 3000 prisoners died, the desperate inmates and some of the guards became pirates to stay alive. The prisons have been partially restored as historical monuments. Today the only people living on the island are the park wardens and other staff.

Coconut plantations still exist on Tarutao but the forests have barely been touched, providing a habitat for flying lizards, wild cats, lemur, wild boar, macaques, mouse deer and feral cows, believed to have bred when the prisoners were taken from the island. Crocodiles once inhabited Khlong Phante and there is a large cave on the Choraka (crocodile) water system known as **Crocodile Cave** (bring a torch). The best way to see wildlife on Koh Tarutao is to walk down the 12-km road during the dry season when animals come out in search of water. There are also many species of bird on the islands including colonies of swiftlets found in the numerous limestone caves – mainly on **Koh Lo Tong** (to the south of Tarutao) and **Koh Ta Kieng** (to the northeast). Large tracts of mangrove forest are found here, especially along Khlong Phante Malacca, on Tarutao. The islands are also known for their trilobite fossils, 400 to 500 million years old, found not just on Tarutao but all over the national park.

While the waters around Tarutao are home to four species of turtle (the Pacific Ridleys, green, hawksbill and leatherback), whales and dolphins are also occasionally seen; the sea is clearer further west in the waters of the Adang-Rawi archipelago (see below).

KOH BULON-LEH

ⓘ *Numerous resorts and fishermen operate boat tours around the area, costing about ฿800 for a half-day of swimming, snorkelling and sometimes fishing. Whales, dolphins and turtles are common.*

While Koh Lipe has had an Urak Lawoi (sea gypsy, or Chao Le) population for perhaps centuries, only in the past 50 years or so has Koh Bulon-Leh had year-round residents: a Muslim population of around 50. The reason for this is down to the superstition of the sea gypsy fisher people, who believed the island was cursed and that everyone who lived there met an untimely death. This kept the island uninhabited until after the Second World War; since then it was discovered that the high mortality rate was due to tuberculosis.

The lifestyle here is exceedingly laid-back and in the more expensive resorts – boho-chic. One of the perks to having had few tourists and a rather isolated position, is that visitors will often join simple pleasures like the evening rugby games by the school or fishing trips with the locals. The island has attracted many returnees – many from Italy and France – and of a wide age range. More upmarket than Koh Lipe, it does offer greater comfort to the well-heeled who sometimes stay for months at a time.

Development is still relatively low-key but land speculation has been going on since the 1990s and investors are no doubt hoping that Koh Bulon-Leh will develop, especially as it is relatively near the pier at Pak Bara. Koh Bulon-Leh is less than 20 km north of Koh Tarutao and about the same distance west of Ban Pak Bara. While it is part of the same archipelago as Tarutao, the island is outside the boundaries of the national park. Furthermore, it has two caves of interest: **Bat Cave**, which houses a small colony of fruit bats, and **Nose Cave**, where it's possible to dive in from one side, swim under the rocks and among thousands of little fish (but beware the moray eel) and come up on the other side.

→ADANG-RAWI ARCHIPELAGO

KOH ADANG AND KOH RAWI

Adang and Rawi lie 43 km west of Tarutao and are the main islands in the archipelago of the same name. They offer a stark contrast to Tarutao. While Tarutao is composed of limestone and sandstone, the rugged hills of Adang and Rawi are granite. Adang's highest mountain rises to 703 m while Rawi's is 463 m in height. Koh Adang is almost entirely forested and there is a trail that leads up to the summit, Chado Cliff, for good views over Koh Lipe and the Andaman Sea. There are also a handful of trails through the dense vegetation; to spot the shy inhabitants – including a variety of squirrels, mouse deer and wild pigs – it is best to wait half an hour or so in silence. The main beaches on Adang are Khai, Laem Son, Ao Lo Lae Lae and Lo Lipa, and Sai Khao on Rawi.

KOH LIPE

Koh Lipe, the main tourist destination in this archipelago, is a tropical idyll that is somehow outside the jurisdiction of Tarutao national park despite being located within its bounds. Over the past few years, word of its 600-strong Urak Lawoi sea gypsy populace, its excellent diving and snorkelling in some of the clearest waters in the Andaman Sea, its blindingly white sand beaches and its terrific seafood has spread, particularly among European families with kids in tow. Net result: much of the tiny island, especially the main beach, Pattaya, is now densely populated by bungalows, restaurants and bars, and prices have shot up dramatically. The onslaught hasn't quite reached Koh Lanta or Koh Phi Phi proportions, but signs of environmental strain are everywhere, most glaringly in the form of the smelly barge, overflowing with bags of garbage, that now sits in the middle of Pattaya Beach. Many locals openly lament this rapid development, and its effects were all too obvious on our last visit, when shoddily erected shops were popping up almost overnight along the island's Walking St. While certain resorts have a surface aura of cleanliness and order, this is quickly dispelled by the smell of burning plastic, since rubbish disposal here is largely accomplished on a chaotic and sporadic basis. A rush to push the island upmarket has seen the addition of more energy-sucking amenities, including air-conditioning and swimming pools. Still, though clearly under environmental stress, and pricey, Lipe remains a startlingly beautiful and very mellow island that attracts many returnees.

The Urak Lawoi, who live in a village beside the island's eastern Sunrise Beach, also manage, just, to keep their culture and language intact and hold a traditional ceremony called *pla juk* twice a year. For this, a miniature boat is built out of *rakam* and *teenped* wood by the villagers. Once the boat is completed, offerings are placed in it, and the Chao Le dance until dawn and then launch the boat out to sea, loaded with the village's communal bad luck.

Rampant bungalow expansion on this tiny island means that the resident sea gypsies are hemmed in on both sides by tourist resorts that intrude on their privacy. Some resorts even back directly onto villages, with the unfortunate effect that tourists in bikinis can all too easily stroll into a communal shower occupied by the modest Chao Le, few of whose homes have running water and bathrooms. The Chao Le areas are still at shanty town level, which makes one wonder what benefits they are receiving from unchecked tourism. Indeed, it was only in 1940 that Koh Lipe officially became Thai territory; up to then it was unclear whether the Chao Le here were Malay or Thai. Locals maintain that the Thai authorities encouraged them to plant coconut trees to show that they had settled, presumably on the basis that occupation is as good as ownership.

It's getting harder to do so, but try to seek out and patronize Chao Le-owned businesses wherever possible. More information and tips on being a more eco-conscious visitor are at www.kohlipe.net. Also, bring plenty of cash; as of writing there are still no ATMs on the island, and the resorts and tour desks charge 5-10% for cash advances.

OTHER ISLANDS

Koh Hin Ngam (**Koh Bula**) is southwest of Adang. The name means 'beautiful rocks', and this striking beach is covered in smooth oval stones that appear to have been polished by hand and that twinkle as the waves wash over them. According to legend, these stones should never be removed or the ghost of Hin Ngami will curse you with bad luck. There is excellent snorkelling. **Koh Khai** has the famous stone arch depicted on many postcards, white powdery sand beaches and some excellent diving. *Khai* means 'egg' in Thai, as this island was a popular turtle nesting site in the past. **Chabang**'s sunken reef is home to hundreds of soft corals of many different colours that make for wonderfully rewarding snorkelling.

→THE FAR SOUTH

Approached through towering karst peaks and bordered by limestone hills, Satun is a pleasant town with friendly, mostly Muslim inhabitants. Its only real tourist attraction is old town and the Kuden Mansion – a good example of British colonial architecture built by Penang artisans – which can be seen in a day. Most people use the town as a stopover en route to boats for Koh Tarutao, Koh Lipe and Malaysia. Thale Ban National Park, filled with birds and animals and forest trails is 37 km from Satun.

Satun province, which borders Malaysia on the west coast near the Straits of Malacca in the Indian Ocean, is a relatively peaceful place but it has the misfortune of having some troubled neighbours. The deep south provinces of Narathiwat, Yala and Pattani are hotbeds of an ongoing insurgency that has killed more than 4000 since flaring up in the early 2000s. Blanket travel advisories on the far south have meant that Satun is viewed as a danger zone for terrorist activity, particularly following bombings and attacks over the years in some tourist and transport sites in nearby Hat Yai. Having said that, Satun's majority Muslim population is well integrated with the larger Thai society and has remained largely free of violence.

SATUN

Surrounded by mountains, Satun is cut off from the Malaysian Peninsula and the eastern side of the Kra Isthmus. Few towns in Thailand, particularly provincial capitals, have escaped thoughtless redevelopment. Satun, though, has done better than most. It has an attractive, low-key centre with preserved shophouses and is Malay in feel; 85% of the population are thought to be Muslim. Few tourists include Satun on their itinerary. Instead, they make a beeline for Ban Pak Bara, 60 km or so north of town and catch a boat to the Tarutao islands (see page 256). But perhaps Satun deserves a few more visitors.

The province seems to have spent the last century searching for an identity separate from that of its neighbours. In the early years of the last century it was administered as part of Kedah, in Malaysia. In 1909, following a treaty between Thailand and Britain, it came under the authority of Phuket. Fifteen years later it found itself being administered from Nakhon Si Thammarat, and it was not until 1932 that it managed to carve out an independent niche for itself when it was awarded provincial status by Bangkok.

The town's main mosque, the **Mesjid Bombang**, was built in 1979 after the previous mosque – also in the shape of a pyramid – fell prey to rot and was torn down. The mosque is on Satunthani Road. More interesting perhaps are the preserved **Chinese shophouses** on Buriwanit Road. They are thought to be around 150 years old; fortunately the town's authorities issued a preservation order before they could be torn down. **Ku Den's Mansion**, on Satunthani Road, dates from the 1870s. It was originally the governor's residence. The windows and doors share a Roman motif while the two-storey roof is in Thai Panyi style.

Moving on From Satun to Bangkok, there are several flights daily from Hat Yai (1½ hours), which is accessible by bus or taxi from Satun (two hours).

THALE BAN NATIONAL PARK

ⓘ *Thale Ban National Park Office, Amphoe Khuan Don, Satun Province, T074-797073. Open daily during daylight hours. Take Highway 4, 406 and 4184 to the park. By public transport catch a songthaew from Samantha Prasit Rd (by the pier) to Wang Prajan. From here there are occasional songthaews the last few kilometres, or take a motorcycle taxi.*

Bordering Malaysia, the Thale Ban National Park was gazetted in 1980 after four years of wrangling and threats from local so-called *ithiphon muut*, or 'dark influences'. It is a small park, covering just over 100 sq km, 37 km from Satun and 90 km from Hat Yai. How it got its name is the source of some dispute. Some people believe it is derived from the Malay words *loet roe ban*, meaning sinking ground; others that it comes from the Thai word *thale*, meaning sea.

The best time to visit Thale Ban is between December and April, when rainfall in this wet area (2662 mm per year) is at its minimum.

At the core of the park is a lake that covers some 30 ha, between the mountains Khao Chin to the east at 720 m and Khao Wangpra to the west. The park has a large bird population: hawks, **hornbills**, falcons and many migratory birds. Animals include dusky-leaf monkeys, white-handed gibbon, lesser mousedeer, wild boar and, it is said, the **Sumatran rhinoceros**. Forest trails lead from the headquarters and it is not unusual to see hornbills, langurs, macaques or even wild pigs. The round trip takes about four hours.

A hiking trail leads from the park headquarters to the summit of **Khao Chin** where it is possible to camp. There are also waterfalls and caves; the most frequently visited waterfall is **Ya Roi**, 5 km north of the park headquarters and accessible by vehicles. The falls plunge through nine levels; at the fifth is a good pool for swimming.

TARUTAO AND THE FAR SOUTH LISTINGS

WHERE TO STAY

Koh Tarutao

Book through the National Park office in Bangkok, T02-579052, or the Pak Bara office located next to the pier, T074-783485. Accommodation is in the north and west of Tarutao. There are 3 choices: multi-occupancy bungalows that can accommodate families or groups, longhouses and tents. The 3 main beaches, Ao Pante, Ao Molae and Ao Sone, all offer some or all of these types, with Ao Pante, the one closest to the pier where the park warden offices are, offering the most selection. The rooms may have shared outside toilets. At all beaches the rates are the same: a small, 2-person bungalow costs ฿600, and the larger 4-person, ฿1000. There are big dormitory-type buildings, too, that are usually hired out to large Thai families or students. Tents are on the beach with a public shower and toilet. Check your tent for size and condition, and, if you intend to stay for more than 2 nights, seriously consider buying a tent from the mainland. Hired tents cost ฿100-200; camping in your own tent costs ฿60. Note that the treatment given to tent visitors varies. Best spots for camping are on Ao Jak and Ao Sone. You can also camp on the beach close to the national park bungalows (฿30 per night per person, as in other Thai national parks).

Koh Bulon-Leh

$$$-$$ **Bulone Resort**, T08-1897 9084 (mob), www.bulone-resort.com. Well positioned where the boats dock overlooking a beautiful beach. A wide range of bungalows from pleasant, spacious, almost colonial options to the more basic, single rooms with spotless shared bathrooms. All in good shape and run by friendly and helpful management. Electricity 1800-0200. Good restaurant and the island's best breakfast. Recommended.

$ **Chaolae Food and Bungalows**, up hill further on from **Bulon Viewpoint Resort** (also called Chao Le Homestay). Run by a Chao Le family. 8 raised brick and bamboo bungalows – all adorable. Tucked away, so you might miss it, but it is well worth the hunt. Plenty of personal touches. Sweet restaurant with shell mobiles and lined with cacti and brightly hued flowers in pots. You can choose your fish from the daily catch. Recommended.

Adang and Rawi

Accommodation is all on the southern swathe of Adang island, with longhouses offering $$$-$$ rates, where some rooms accommodate up to 10 people. Tents are available on Adang for ฿200, own tent ฿30 at Laem Son. There is a simple restaurant. The island closes down during the rainy season (mid May-mid Nov).
Laem Son, ฿600 for 2-person bungalow, big tents (8-10 people), ฿300, medium/middle tents (3-5 people), ฿300, small tents (2 people), ฿150.
Rawi Long House, ฿400. 4 people per room. Toilet outside.

Lipe

Accommodation on Lipe is expanding and moving upmarket in rapid order. Electricity is sometimes only available from dusk onwards, mosquito nets are provided but not all places have fans or a/c that work, and, during the dry season, the water pressure can be low or non-existent.

$$$$-$$$ **Andaman Resort**, Sunrise Beach, T074-728017, www.andamanresort kohlipe.com. Next door to Mountain Resort sits this mix of 40 concrete, log and bamboo bungalows generously spaced around Sunrise Beach's pretty northern curve and well shaded by pine trees. Clean, quiet, bright rooms popular with families.

Run by a Chao Le-Chinese-Thai family. Recommended.

$$$$-$$ Mountain Resort, bay to west of Sunrise Beach, T074-750452, www.mountainresortkohlipe.com. Well spaced corrugated-roof bungalows dot a steep, shaded hillside, many with idyllic views across the channel between Koh Lipe and Koh Adang. The fan or a/c rooms have 24-hr electricity, large verandas and basic tiled bathrooms. Steep cliff steps lead down to a gorgeous beach flanked by a row of pricier deluxe bungalows. Recommended.

$$$-$ Varin Beach Resort, Pattaya Beach, T074-750447/T081-598 2225 (mob), www.varinbeachresort.com. 109 clean bungalows,

suites and villas set in a fairly cramped and regimental layout facing each other. Extremely busy in the peak season with a bit of a churning guest-factory feel. The restaurant is a little characterless but service is excellent and attentive. Recommended.

Satun
$$-$ Ang Yee's House, 21/23 Trasatit Rd, T08-0534 0057 (mob), T074-723844, angyeeshouse.com. Colourful place with only 6 a/c and fan rooms with shared bathrooms, centrally located. Bar-restaurant in small garden area. Best to get a room at the back or be content with the street noise and early-morning blasts from the nearby community announcement loudspeaker.

WHAT TO DO

Tarutao National Park
Diving and snorkelling
Some of the best areas for coral are in the waters northwest of Koh Rang Nok, northwest of Tarutao, southeast of Koh Rawi, around Koh Klang between Tarutao and Adang, and off Koh Kra off Koh Lipe's east coast. Equipment is for hire on Adang and Lipe.

Kayaking
There are a few kayak rental shops on each beach and some resorts have free kayaks for guests. These are all sit-on-top crafts, suitable for short excursions only.

Koh Lipe
Diving
Castaway Divers, Sunrise Beach, Castaway Resort, T08-7478 1516, www.kohlipedivers.com. Very professional but approachable outfit.
Sabye Sports, T08-9464 5884 (mob), www.sabye-sports.com. The island's first scuba-diving and sports centre, next to **Porn Bungalows**, offers diving and rents canoes and snorkelling equipment.

Tour operators
Heading further west from Lipe, there are countless islands and coral reefs teeming with a staggering variety of fish – the locals know all the good spots. The best locations, only 1 or 2 hrs away, include Koh Dong, Koh Pung and Koh Tong, Koh Hin Son, Koh Hin Ngam and Koh Chabang.
Dang Dee, next to Sunrise Beach at the end of Walking St, T074-750402, www.dangdeeservice.com. A friendly family-run outfit that arranges all-day snorkelling tours for around ฿2200-2800 per boat for 6 people, as well as boats off the island, visa runs, etc.
KohLipeThailand.com. Well organized tour agency with 2 shops along Walking St. Arranges snorkelling trips, transport and accommodation. There are many more scattered around.

Satun
Tour operators
Charan Tour, 19/6 Satunthani Rd, T074-711453. Runs daily boat tours to the islands Oct-May. Lunch and snorkelling equipment are provided. Has a good reputation.

PRACTICALITIES

266 Ins and outs
   266   Best time to visit Thailand
   266   Getting to Thailand
   267   Transport in Thailand
   270   Where to stay in Thailand
   271   Food and drink in Thailand

274 Essentials A-Z

281 Index

287 Photography credits

288 Credits

INS AND OUTS

→ BEST TIME TO VISIT THAILAND

The hottest time of year is April and May. The wet season runs from May to October in most parts of the country (as you travel south from Bangkok the seasons change). The best time to visit – for most parts of the country – is between December and February. But don't imagine that the wet season means being stuck in your room or bogged down in a tropical storm. Travel to almost all corners of the country is possible at any time of year.

During the rainy season clear skies are interspersed with heavy showers, and it is perfectly sensible to visit Thailand during the monsoon. Flooding is most likely towards the end of the rainy season in September and October. Five to six hours of daily sunshine are normal, even during the rainy season. Visitors will also benefit from lower hotel room rates.

→ GETTING TO THAILAND

AIR

The majority of visitors arrive in Thailand through Bangkok's **Suvarnabhumi International Airport**, see page 35. Chiang Mai in the north and Phuket in the south also have international airports. More than 35 airlines and charter companies fly to Bangkok. THAI is the national carrier. Fares inflate by up to 50% during high season.

Flights from Europe The approximate flight time from London to Bangkok (non-stop) is 12 hours. From London Heathrow, airlines offering non-stop flights include Qantas, British Airways, THAI and Eva Air. You can easily connect to Thailand from the UK via most other European capitals. Finnair flies daily from Helsinki, KLM via Amsterdam and Lufthansa via Frankfurt. SAS flies from Copenhagen and Swiss Air from Zurich. Further afield, Etihad flies via Abu Dhabi, Gulf Air via Bahrain and Qatar via Muscat and Doha. Non-direct flights can work out much cheaper, so if you want a bargain, shop around. Finnair, www.finnair.com, often offers some of the cheapest fares. It is also possible to fly direct to Chiang Mai from Dusseldorf, Frankfurt and Munich in Germany, and to Phuket from Dusseldorf and Munich.

Flights from the USA and Canada The approximate flight time from Los Angeles to Bangkok is 21 hours. There are one-stop flights from Los Angeles on THAI and two-stops on Delta; one-stop flights from San Francisco on Northwest and United and two-stops on Delta; and one-stop flights from Vancouver on Canadian. THAI have now started a non-stop flight from New York to Bangkok, which takes 16 hours.

Flights from Australasia There are flights from Sydney and Melbourne (approximately nine hours) daily with Qantas and THAI. There are also flights with British Airways, Alitalia, Lufthansa and Lauda Air, which are less frequent. There are flights from Perth with THAI and Qantas. From Auckland, Air New Zealand, THAI and British Airways fly to Bangkok.

AIR

The budget airline boom has finally arrived in Thailand with carriers now offering cheap flights all over the country. As routes can change at very short notice, we would recommend travellers check the different airlines' websites; nearly all major towns and cities and tourist destinations are served. **Air Asia** (www.airasia.com), **Bangkok Airways** (T02-265 5678 (ext 1771 for reservations centre), www.bangkokair.com), and **Nok Air** (www.nokair.com) are currently the major players in this market offering dirt cheap flights – but only if you book online and in advance. **Thai Airways** (THAI) (T02-2451000, www.thaiair.com) is the national flag carrier and is also by far the largest domestic airline.

THAI flies to several destinations in Thailand. It is better to book flights through a local office or travel agent displaying the THAI logo. Often THAI domestic fares are cheaper when booked with a credit card over the phone than via their website.

ROAD

Bus Private and state-run buses leave Bangkok for every town in Thailand; it is an extensive network and a cheap way to travel. The government bus company is called Bor Kor Sor, and every town in Thailand will have a BKS terminal. There are small stop-in-every-town local buses plus the faster long-distance buses (*rot duan* – express; or *rot air* – air-conditioned). **Air-conditioned buses** come in two grades: *chan nung* (first class, blue colour) and *chan song* (second class, orange colour). *Chan song* have more seats but less elbow and leg room, and will not offer hostess, food and drink services, or a toilet. *Chan nung* buses will have all of these as well as a maximum of 42 seats (adjustable to 70° recline). For longer/overnight journeys, air-conditioned de luxe (sometimes known as *rot tour*, officially Standard 1A buses, also blue like the *chan rung*) or VIP buses, stewardess service is provided with food and drink supplied en route and more leg room plus constant Thai music or videos. There should be no more than 24 seats (adjustable to 135° recline). The best luxury/VIP bus company in the country is Nakhonchai Air, which operates from its own hub near the Mo Chit main bus terminal, but its routing is limited to Bangkok–Chiang Mai and Bangkok–Khon Kaen. Many fares include meals at roadside restaurants, so keep hold of your ticket. If you're travelling on an overnight air-conditioned bus bring a light sweater and some earplugs – both the volume of the entertainment system and cooling system are likely to be turned up full blast.

The local buses are slower and cramped but worth it for those wishing to sample local life. The seats at the very back are reserved for monks, so be ready to move if necessary.

Private tour buses: Many tour companies operate bus services in Thailand; travel agents in Bangkok will supply information. These buses are seldom more comfortable than the state buses but are usually more expensive. Overnight trips usually involve a meal stop (included in price of ticket) and stewardess service for drinks and snacks. They often leave from outside the company office, which may not be located at the central bus station. Some may also be dangerous, particularly those offered from 'backpacker' areas like Khao San Road. Our recommendation is that travellers take buses from the main bus terminals.

Car There are two schools of thought on car hire in Thailand: one, that under no circumstances should *farangs* (foreigners) drive themselves; and second, that hiring a car is one of the best ways of seeing the country and reaching the more inaccessible sights. Increasing numbers of visitors are hiring their own cars and internationally respected car hire firms are expanding their operations (such as **Hertz** and **Avis**). Roads and service stations are generally excellent. Driving is on the left-hand side of the road.

Car hire: The average cost of hiring a car from a reputable firm is ฿1000-2000 per day, ฿6000-10,000 per week, or ฿20,000-30,000 per month. Some companies automatically include insurance; for others it must be specifically requested and a surcharge is added. An international driver's licence, or a UK, US, French, German, Australian, New Zealand, Singapore or Hong Kong licence is required. The lower age limit is 20 years (higher for some firms). If the mere thought of competing with Thai drivers is terrifying, an option is to hire a chauffeur along with the car. For this service an extra ฿300-500 per day is usually charged, more at weekends and if an overnight stay is included. Note that local car hire firms are cheaper although the cars are likely to be less well maintained and will have tens of thousands of kilometres on the clock.

Safety: There are a few points that should be kept in mind: accidents in Thailand are often horrific. If involved in an accident, and they occur with great frequency, you – as a foreigner – are likely to be found the guilty party and expected to meet the costs. Ensure the cost of hire includes insurance cover. Many local residents recommend that if a foreigner is involved in an accident, they should not stop but drive on to the nearest police station – if possible, of course.

Motorbike Hiring a motorbike has long been a popular way for visitors to explore the local area. Off the main roads and in quieter areas it can be an enjoyable and cheap way to see the country. Some travellers are now not just hiring motorbikes to explore a local area, but are touring the entire country by motorcycle. It is the cheapest way to be independent of public transport, but the risks rise accordingly (see below).

Motorbike hire: Rental is mostly confined to holiday resorts and prices vary from place to place; ฿150-300 per day is usual for a 100-150cc machine. Often licences do not have to be shown and insurance will not be available. Riding in shorts and flip-flops is dangerous – a foot injury is easily acquired even at low speeds and broken toes are a nightmare to heal – always wear shoes. Borrow a helmet or, if you're planning to ride a motorbike on more than one occasion, consider buying one – decent helmets can be found for ฿1500 and are better than the 'salad bowls' usually offered by hire companies.

Motorbike taxi These are becoming increasingly popular, and are the cheapest, quickest and most dangerous way to get from 'A' to 'B'. They are usually used for short rides down *sois* or to better local transport points. Riders wear coloured vests (sometimes numbered) and tend to congregate at key intersections or outside shopping centres for example. Agree a price before boarding – expect to pay ฿10 upwards for a short *soi* hop.

Songthaew ('two rows') *Songthaews* are pick-up trucks fitted with two benches and can be found in many upcountry towns. They normally run fixed routes, with set fares, but can often be hired and used as a taxi service (agree a price before setting out). To let the driver know you want to stop, press the electric buzzers or tap the side of the vehicle with a coin.

Taxi Standard air-conditioned taxis are found in very few Thai towns with the majority in the capital. In Bangkok all taxis have meters. Most Bangkok taxis will also take you on long-distance journeys either for an agreed fee or with the meter running. In the south of Thailand, shared long-distance taxis are common.

Tuk-tuks These come in the form of pedal or motorized machines. Fares should be negotiated and agreed before setting off. It will not take long to discover what is a reasonable price, but don't expect to pay the same as a Thai. Drivers are a useful source of local information and will know most places of interest, plus hotels and restaurants (and sometimes their prices). In Bangkok, and most other towns, these vehicles are a motorized, gas-powered scooter. Pedal-powered *saamlors* (meaning 'three wheels') were outlawed in Bangkok a few years ago and they are now gradually being replaced by the noisier motorized version throughout the country.

BOAT

The waterways of Thailand are extensive. However, most people limit their water travel to trips around Bangkok or to Ayutthaya. *Hang-yaaws* (long-tailed boats) are a common form of water travel and are motorized, fast and fun.

Sea travel There are numerous boats to and from the Gulf Coast Islands of Koh Samui, Koh Phangan and Koh Tao. Principal services run from Chumphon to Koh Tao and from Surat Thani and the port of Don Sak to Koh Samui and then on to Koh Phangan. Fast ferries, slow boats and night boats run services daily. On the Andaman Coast there are services to and from Phuket, Koh Phi Phi, Krabi, Koh Lanta, the islands off Trang and from Ban Pak Bara and Koh Tarutao National Park. The islands off the eastern seaboard are also connected by regular services to the mainland. Note that services become irregular and are suspended during certain times of year because of the wet season and rough seas. Each section details information on the months that will affect regular boat services.

RAIL

The State Railway of Thailand, www.railway.co.th/english, is efficient, clean and comfortable, with five main routes to the north, northeast, west, east and south. It is safer than bus travel but can take longer. The choice is **first-class air-conditioned compartments**, **second-class sleepers**, **second-class air-conditioned sit-ups** with reclining chairs and **third-class sit-ups**. Travelling third class is often cheaper than taking a bus; first and second class are more expensive than the bus but infinitely more comfortable. **Express trains** are known as *rot duan*, **special express trains** as *rot duan phiset* and **rapid trains** as *rot raew*. Express and rapid trains are faster as they make fewer stops; there is a surcharge for the service.

Reservations for sleepers should be made in advance (up to 60 days ahead) at Bangkok's **Hualamphong station** ① *T1690, T02-220 4444, the advance booking office is open daily 0700-0400*. Some travel agencies also book tickets. A queue-by-ticket arrangement works efficiently, and travellers do not have to wait long. If you change a reservation the charge is ฿10. It is advisable to book the bottom sleeper, as lights are bright on top (in second-class compartments) and the ride more uncomfortable. It still may be difficult to get a seat at certain times of year, such as during festivals (like Songkran in April). Personal luggage allowance is 50 kg in first class, 40 kg in second and 30 kg in third class. Children aged three to 12 years old and under 150 cm in height pay half fare; those under three years old and less than 100 cm in height travel free, but do not get a seat. It is possible to pick up timetables at Hualamphong station (from the information booth in the main concourse). There are two types: the 'condensed' timetable (by region) showing all rapid routes, and complete, separate timetables for all classes. Timetables are available from stations and some tourist offices. If travelling north or south during the day, try to get a seat on the side of the carriage out of the sun.

You can buy a 20-day **rail pass** (blue pass) which is valid on all trains, second and third class (supplementary charges are NOT included). A more expensive red pass includes supplementary charges. For further details visit the Advance Booking Office at Hualamphong station in Bangkok, T02-223 3762, T02-224 7788.

→ WHERE TO STAY IN THAILAND

Thailand has a large selection of hotels, including some of the best in the world. Standards outside of the usual tourist areas have improved immensely over recent years and while such places might not be geared to Western tastes they offer some of the best-value accommodation in the country. Due to its popularity with backpackers, Thailand also has many small guesthouses, serving Western food. These are concentrated in the main tourist areas.

HOTELS AND GUESTHOUSES
Few hotels in Thailand provide breakfast in the price of the room. A service charge of 10% and government tax of 7% will usually be added to the bill in the more expensive hotels (categories $$$$-$$). Ask whether the quoted price includes tax when checking in. Prices in Bangkok are inflated.

During the off-season, hotels and guesthouses in tourist destinations may halve their room rates so it is always worthwhile bargaining or asking whether there is a special price. Given the fierce competition among hotels, it is even worth trying during the peak season. Over-building has meant that there is a glut of rooms in some towns and hotels are desperate for business.

Until 10 years ago, most guesthouses offered shared facilities with cold-water showers and squat toilets. Levels of cleanliness were also less than pristine. Nowadays, Western toilet imperialism is making inroads into Thai culture and many of the better-run guesthouses will have good, clean toilets with sit-down facilities and, sometimes, hot water. Some are even quite stylish in their bathroom facilities. Fans are the norm in most guesthouses although, again, to cash in on the buying power of backpackers with more disposable income more and more offer air-conditioned rooms as well. Check that mosquito nets are provided.

Security is a problem, particularly in beach resort areas where flimsy bungalows offer easy access to thieves. Keep valuables with the office for safekeeping (although there are regular cases of people losing valuables that have been left in 'safekeeping') or on your person when you go out. Guesthouses can be tremendous value for money. With limited

PRICE CODES

WHERE TO STAY

$$$$	over US$100	$$$	US$46-100
$$	US$20-45	$	under US$20

Prices include taxes and service charge, but not meals. They are based on a double room, except in the $ range, where prices are almost always per person.

RESTAURANTS

$$$ over US$12	$$ US$6-12	$ under US$6

Prices refer to the cost of a two-course meal, not including drinks.

overheads, family labour and using local foods they can cut their rates in a way that larger hotels with armies of staff, imported food and expensive facilities simply cannot.

CAMPING AND NATIONAL PARK ACCOMMODATION

It is possible to camp in Thailand and **national parks** are becoming much better at providing campsites and associated facilities. Most parks will have public toilets with basic facilities. Some parks also offer bungalows; these fall into our **$$** accommodation category but because they can often accommodate large groups their per person cost is less than this. The more popular parks will often also have privately run accommodation including sophisticated resorts, sometimes within the park boundaries. For reservations at any of the national parks contact: Reservation Office ① *T02-56142923 and the official website, www.dnp.go.th/parkreserve, is excellent for making online bookings*. Alternatively, you can phone the park offices listed in the relevant sections of this guide. **Beaches** are considered public property – anybody can camp on them for free.

If you are camping, remember that while the more popular parks have tents for hire, the rest – and this means most – do not. Bring your own torch, camp stove, fuel and toilet paper.

→ FOOD AND DRINK IN THAILAND

Thai food is an intermingling of Tai, Chinese and, to a lesser extent, Indian cuisines. This helps to explain why restaurants produce dishes that must be some of the (spicy) hottest in the world, as well as others that are rather bland. *Larb* (traditionally raw – but now more frequently cooked – chopped beef mixed with rice, herbs and spices) is a traditional 'Tai' dish; *pla priaw waan* (whole fish with soy and ginger) is Chinese in origin; while *gaeng mussaman* (beef 'Muslim' curry) was brought to Thailand by Muslim immigrants. Even satay, paraded by most restaurants as a Thai dish, was introduced from Malaysia and Indonesia (which themselves adopted it from Arab traders during the Middle Ages).

A Thai meal is based around rice, and many wealthy Bangkokians own farms upcountry where they cultivate their favourite variety. When a Thai asks another Thai whether he has eaten he will ask, literally, whether he has 'eaten rice' (*kin khao*). Similarly, the accompanying dishes are referred to as food 'with the rice'. There are two main types of rice – 'sticky' or glutinous (*khao niaw*) and non-glutinous (*khao jao*). Sticky rice is usually used to make sweets (desserts) although it is the staple in the northeastern region and parts of the north. *Khao jao* is standard white rice.

In addition to rice, a meal usually consists of a soup like *tom yam kung* (prawn soup), *kaeng* (a curry) and *krueng kieng* (a number of side dishes). Thai food is spicy, and aromatic herbs and grasses (like lemongrass, coriander, tamarind and ginger) are used to give a distinctive flavour. *Nam pla* (fish sauce made from fermented fish and used as a condiment) and *nam prik* (*nam pla*, chillies, garlic, sugar, shrimps and lime juice) are two condiments that are taken with almost all meals. Chillies deserve a special mention because most Thais like their food HOT! Some chillies are fairly mild; others – like the tiny, red *prik khii nuu* ('mouse shit pepper') – are fiendishly hot.

Isaan food – from the northeast of Thailand – is also distinctive, very similar to Lao cuisine and very popular. Street stalls sell sticky rice, aromatic *kai yang* (grilled chicken) and fiery *som tam* (papaya salad). *Pla ra* (fermented fish) is one of Isaan's most famous dishes.

Due to Thailand's large Chinese population (or at least Thais with Chinese roots), there are also many Chinese-style restaurants whose cuisine is variously 'Thai-ified'. Many of the snacks available on the streets show this mixture of Thai and Chinese, not to mention Arab and Malay. *Bah jang*, for example, are small pyramids of leaves stuffed with sticky rice, Chinese sausage, salted eggs, pork and dried shrimp.

To sample Thai food it is best to go in a group to a restaurant and order a range of dishes. To eat alone is regarded as slightly strange. However, there are a number of 'one-dish' meals like fried rice and *phat thai* (fried noodles) and restaurants will also usually provide *raat khao* ('over rice'), a curry served on a bed of rice for a single person.

Strict non-fish-eating **vegetarians** and **vegans** are in for a tough time. Nearly every cooked meal you will eat in Thailand will be liberally doused in *nam pla* or cooked with shrimp paste. At more expensive and upmarket international restaurants you'll probably be able to find something suitable – in the rural areas, you'll be eating fruit, fried eggs and rice, though not all at once. There is a network of Taoist restaurants offering more strict veggie fare throughout the country – look out for yellow flags with red Chinese lettering. Also asking for 'mai sai nam pla' (no *nam pla* please)– when ordering what should be veggie food might keep the fish sauce out of harm's reach.

RESTAURANTS

Starting at the top, in pecuniary terms at any rate, the more sophisticated restaurants are usually air-conditioned, and sometimes attached to a hotel. In places like Bangkok and Chiang Mai they may be Western in style and atmosphere. There are a whole range of places from **noodle shops** to **curry houses** and **seafood restaurants**. Many small restaurants have no menus. But often the speciality of the house will be clear – roasted, honeyed ducks hanging in the window, crab and fish laid out on crushed ice outside. Away from the main tourist spots, 'Western' breakfasts are unavailable, so be prepared to eat Thai-style (noodle or rice soup or fried rice). Yet, the quality of much Thai food can be mixed, with many Thai restaurants and street stalls using huge amounts of sugar, MSG and oil in their cooking.

Towards the bottom of the scale are **stalls and food carts**. Stall holders will tend to specialize in either noodles, rice dishes, fruit drinks, sweets and so on. Hot meals are usually prepared to order.

In the north, *khantoke* dining is de rigueur – or so one might imagine from the number of restaurants offering it. It is a northern Thai tradition, when people sit on the floor to eat at low tables, often to the accompaniment of traditional music and dance.

DRINK

Water in nearly every single restaurant and street stall now comes from large bottles of purified water but if you're unsure, buy your own.

Coffee is consumed throughout Thailand. In stalls and restaurants, coffee comes with a glass of Chinese tea. Soft drinks are widely available too. Many roadside stalls prepare fresh fruit juices in liquidizers while hotels produce all the usual cocktails.

Major brands of **spirits** are served in most hotels and bars, although not always off the tourist path. The most popular spirit among Thais is Mekhong – local cane whisky. However, due to its hangover-inducing properties, more sophisticated Thais prefer Johnny Walker or an equivalent brand.

Beer drinking is spreading fast. The most popular local beer is Singha beer brewed by Boon Rawd. Singha, Chang and Heineken are the three most popular beers in Thailand. Leo and Cheers are agreeable budget options although they are seldom sold in restaurants. Beer is relatively expensive in Thai terms as it is heavily taxed by the government. It is a high status drink, so the burgeoning middle class, especially the young, are turning to beer in preference to traditional, local whiskies – which explains why brewers are so keen to set up shop in this traditionally non-beer drinking country. Some pubs and bars also sell beer on tap – which is known as *bier sot*, 'fresh' beer.

Thais are fast developing a penchant for **wine**. Imported wines are expensive by international standards but Thailand now has six wineries, mainly in the northeastern region around Nakhon Ratchasima. For tours around the wine regions (including to a vineyard where the workers use elephants) contact Laurence Civil (laurence@csloxinfo.com).

ESSENTIALS A-Z

Accident and emergency
Emergency services Police: T191, T123. **Tourist police**: T1155. **Fire**: T199. **Ambulance**: T02-2551134-6. **Tourist Assistance Centre**: Rachdamnern Nok Av, Bangkok, T02-356 0655.

Calling one of the emergency numbers will not usually be very productive as few operators speak English. It is better to call the tourist police or have a hotel employee or other English-speaking Thai telephone for you. For more intractable problems contact your embassy or consulate.

Electricity
Voltage is 220 volts (50 cycles). Most first- and tourist-class hotels have outlets for shavers and hairdryers. Adaptors are recommended, as almost all sockets are 2-pronged.

Embassies and consulates
www.thaiembassy.org is a useful resource.

Health
Staying healthy in Thailand is straightforward. With the following advice and precautions you should keep as healthy as you do at home. Most visitors return home having experienced no problems at all beyond an upset stomach. However, in Thailand the health risks, especially in the tropical areas, are different from those encountered in Europe or the USA.

Before you go
Ideally, you should see your GP/practice nurse or travel clinic at least 6 weeks before your departure for general advice on travel risks, malaria and recommended vaccinations. Your local pharmacist can also be a good source of readily accessible advice. Make sure you have travel insurance, get a dental check (especially if you are going to be away for more than a month), know your own blood group and if you suffer a long-term condition such as diabetes or epilepsy make sure someone knows or that you have a **Medic Alert** bracelet/necklace with this information on it.

Recommended vaccinations
No vaccinations are specifically required for Thailand unless coming from an infected area, but tuberculosis, rabies, Japanese B encephalitis and hepatitis B are commonly recommended. A yellow fever certificate is required by visitors who have been in an infected area in the 10 days before arrival. Those without a vaccination certificate will be vaccinated and kept in quarantine for 6 days, or deported.

A-Z of health risks
Dengue fever This is a viral disease spread by mosquitoes that tend to bite during the day. The symptoms are fever and often intense joint pains, also some people develop a rash. Symptoms last about a week but it can take a few weeks to recover fully. Dengue can be difficult to distinguish from malaria as both diseases tend to occur in the same places. There are no effective vaccines or antiviral drugs though, fortunately, travellers rarely develop the more severe form of the disease (which can prove fatal). Rest, plenty of fluids and paracetamol (not aspirin) is the recommended treatment. **Note** The number of cases in Thailand has risen in the last year, consult your GP for further advice.

Diarrhoea and intestinal upset
Symptoms should be relatively short-lived but if they persist beyond 2 weeks medical attention should be sought. Also seek help if there is blood in the stools and/or fever.

Adults can use an anti-diarrhoeal medication such as loperamide to control the symptoms but only for up to 24 hrs. In addition keep well hydrated by drinking plenty of fluids and eat bland foods. Oral rehydration sachets taken after each loose stool are a useful way to keep hydrated.

The standard advice to prevent problems is be careful with water and ice for drinking. If you have any doubts then boil it or filter and treat it. There are many filter/treatment devices now available on the market. Be wary of salads (what were they washed in, who handled them), re-heated foods or food that has been left out in the sun having been cooked earlier in the day. There is a simple adage: wash it, peel it, boil it or forget it. Also be wary of unpasteurized dairy products as these can transmit diseases.

Malaria Malaria can cause death within 24 hrs and can start as something just resembling an attack of flu. You may feel tired, lethargic, headachy, feverish; more seriously you may develop fits, followed by coma and then death. If you have a temperature, visit a doctor as soon as you can and ask for a malaria test. On your return home, if you suffer any of these symptoms, have a test as soon as possible.

To prevent mosquito bites wear clothes that cover arms and legs, use effective insect repellents in areas with known risks of insect-spread disease and use a mosquito net treated with an insecticide. Repellents containing 30-50% DEET (Di-ethyltoluamide) are recommended when visiting malaria-endemic areas; lemon eucalyptus (Mosiguard) is a reasonable alternative. The key advice is to guard against contracting malaria by taking the correct anti-malarials and finishing the recommended course. If you are a popular target for insect bites use antihistamine tablets and apply a cream such as hydrocortisone.

Remember that it is risky to buy medicine, and in particular anti-malarials, in some developing countries. These may be sub-standard or part of a trade in counterfeit drugs.

Rabies Rabies is prevalent in Thailand so be aware of the dangers of the bite from any animal.

Sun The best advice is simply to avoid exposure to the sun by covering exposed skin, wearing a hat and staying out of the sun if possible, particularly between late morning and early afternoon. Apply a high-factor sunscreen (at least SPF15) and also make sure it screens against UVB. A further danger in tropical climates is heat exhaustion or more seriously heatstroke. This can be avoided by good hydration, which means drinking water past the point of simply quenching thirst.

Money
Currency
Exchange rates: for up-to-the-minute exchange rates visit www.xe.com.

The unit of Thai currency is the **baht** (฿), which is divided into 100 **satang**. Notes in circulation include ฿20 (green), ฿50 (blue), ฿100 (red), ฿500 (purple) and ฿1000 (orange and grey). Coins include 25 satang and 50 satang, and ฿1, ฿2, ฿5, and ฿10. The 2 smaller coins are disappearing from circulation and the 25 satang coin, equivalent to the princely sum of US$0.003, is rarely found. The colloquial term for 25 satang is saleng.

Exchange
It is best to change money at banks or money changers which give better rates than hotels. The exchange booths at Bangkok airport have some of the best rates available. There is no black market. First-class hotels have 24-hr money changers. Indonesian rupiah, Nepalese rupees, Burmese kyat, Vietnamese dong, Lao kip and Cambodian riels cannot be exchanged for baht at Thai banks. (Money changers will sometimes exchange kyat, dong, kip and riel and it can be a good idea to buy the currencies in Bangkok before departure

for these countries as the black-market rate often applies.)

Credit and debit cards
Plastic is increasingly used in Thailand and just about every town of any size will have a bank with an ATM. Visa and MasterCard are the most widely taken credit cards, and cash cards with the Cirrus logo can also be used to withdraw cash at many banks. Generally speaking, AMEX can be used at branches of the **Bangkok Bank**; JCB at **Siam Commercial Bank**; MasterCard at **Siam Commercial** and **Bangkok Bank**; and Visa at **Thai Farmers' Bank** and **Bangkok Bank**. Most larger hotels and more expensive restaurants take credit cards as well. Because Thailand has embraced the ATM with such exuberance, many foreign visitors no longer bother with traveller's cheques or cash and rely entirely on plastic. Even so, a small stash of US dollars can come in handy.

Cost of living
One of the key pledges of the Yingluck Shinawatra government elected in 2011 was to increase the minimum wage to ฿300 a day (US$10). By mid-2012, despite complaints by many of the richest individuals and companies in Thailand, this was coming into force. The average salary of a civil servant is around US$250 a month. Of course, Thailand's middle classes – and especially those engaged in business in Bangkok – will earn far more than this. Thailand has appalling wealth distribution yet Thai society is remarkably cohesive. A simple but good meal out will cost ฿60; the rental of a modern house in a provincial city will cost perhaps ฿4000 a month.

Cost of travelling
Visitors staying in the best hotels and eating in hotel restaurants will probably spend at least ฿2000 per day, conceivably much much more. Tourists staying in cheaper a/c accommodation and eating in local restaurants will probably spend about ฿600-900 per day. Backpackers staying in fan-cooled guesthouses and eating cheaply, should be able to live on ฿300 per day. In Bangkok, expect to pay 20-30% more.

Opening hours
Hours of business Banks: Mon-Fri 0830-1530. **Exchange**: daily 0830-2200 in Bangkok, Pattaya, Phuket and Chiang Mai. In other towns opening hours are usually shorter. **Government offices**: Mon-Fri 0830-1200, 1300-1630. **Shops**: 0830-1700, larger shops: 1000-1900 or 2100. **Tourist offices**: 0830-1630.

Safety
In general, Thailand is a safe country to visit. The vast majority of visitors to Thailand will not experience any physical threat. However, there have been some widely publicized murders of foreign tourists in recent years and the country does have a very high murder rate. It is best to avoid any situation where violence can occur – what would be a simple punch-up or pushing bout in the West can quickly escalate in Thailand to extreme violence. This is mostly due to loss of face. Getting drunk with Thais can be a risky business – Westerners visiting the country for short periods won't be versed in the intricacies of Thai social interaction and may commit unwitting and terrible faux pas. A general rule of thumb if confronted with a situation is to appear conciliatory and offer a way for the other party to back out gracefully. It should be noted that even some police officers in Thailand represent a threat – at least 3 young Western travellers have been shot and murdered by drunken Thai policemen in the last few years. Confidence tricksters, touts, all operate, particularly in more popular tourist centres. Robbery is also a threat; it ranges from pick-pocketing to the drugging (and subsequent robbing) of bus and train passengers. Watchfulness and

simple common sense should be employed. Women travelling alone should be careful. Always lock hotel rooms and place valuables in a safe deposit if available (if not, take them with you).

Areas to avoid

The UK Foreign and Commonwealth Office (www.fco.gov.uk/travel) advises against all but essential travel to the 4 provinces of **Yala**, **Pattani**, **Narathiwat** and **Songkhla** on the Thai-Malay border. The US State Department (www.travel.state.gov) does the same. These areas are the main base of Thailand's Muslim minority and are currently home to a slow-burning separatist insurgency. Car bomb explosions, shootings and other acts of politically motivated violence are weekly, often daily occurences.

If you plan to visit the Khmer temple, Preah Vihear, on the Thai-Cambodian border, check all travel warnings before travel; it has been the focus of fighting between troops on several occasions in the last few years. In light of events between Mar and May 2010, when political protests throughout Thailand resulted in the deaths of over 90 people, including several foreigners, and injuries to over 2200 people, it is also recommended that you avoid all political demonstrations, no matter how benign or carnival-like they seem.

If you do get any problems contact the tourist police rather than the ordinary police – they will speak English and are used to helping resolve any disputes, issues, etc. The country's health infrastructure, especially in provincial capitals and tourist destinations, is good.

Foreign and Commonwealth Office (**FCO**), T0845-850 2829, www.fco.gov.uk/travel. The UK Foreign and Commonwealth Office's travel warning section.

US State Department, www.travel.state.gov/travel_warnings.html. The US State Department updates travel advisories on its 'Travel Warnings and Consular Information

Sheets'. It also has a hotline for American travellers, T202-647-5225.

Bribery

The way to make your way in life, for some people in Thailand, is through the strategic offering of gifts. A Chulalongkorn University report recently estimated that it 'costs' ฿10 million to become Bangkok Police Chief. Apparently this can be recouped in just 2 years of hard graft. Although bribing officials is by no means recommended, resident *farangs* report that they often resort to such gifts to avoid the time and hassle involved in filling in the forms and making the requisite visit to a police station for a minor traffic offence. As a visitor, it's best to play it straight.

Drugs and prostitution

Many prostitutes and drug dealers are in league with the police and may find it more profitable to report you than to take your custom (or they may try to do both). They receive a reward from the police, and the police in turn receive a bonus for the detective work. Note that foreigners on buses may be searched for drugs. Sentences for possession of illegal drugs vary from a fine or one year in jail for marijuana up to life imprisonment or execution for possession or smuggling of heroin. The death penalty is usually commuted.

Prisons

Thai prisons are very grim. Most foreigners are held in 2 Bangkok prisons – Khlong Prem and Bangkwang. One resident who visits overseas prisoners in jail wrote to us saying: "You cannot over-estimate the horrors! Khlong Prem has 7000 prisoners, 5 to a cell, with not enough room to stretch out, no recreation, one meal a day (an egg on Sundays) … ". One hundred prisoners in a dormitory is not uncommon, and prisoners on Death Row have waist chains and ankle fetters permanently welded on.

Tourist police

In 1982 the government set up a special arm of the police to deal with the demands of the tourist industry – the tourist police. Now, there is no important tourist destination that doesn't have a tourist police office. The Thai police have come in for a great deal of scrutiny over recent years, although most policemen are honest and only too happy to help the luckless visitor. **Tourist Police**, Bangkok, T02-2815051 or T02-2216206. Daily 0800-2400.

Traffic

Perhaps the greatest danger is from the traffic – especially if you are attempting to drive yourself. More foreign visitors are killed or injured in traffic accidents than in any other way. Thai drivers have a 'devil may care' attitude towards the highway code, and there are many horrific accidents. Be very careful when crossing the road – just because there is a pedestrian crossing, do not expect drivers to stop. Be particularly wary when driving or riding a motorcycle (see page 268).

Telephone → Country code +66.

From Bangkok there is direct dialling to most countries. To call overseas, you first need to dial the international direct dial (IDD) access code, which is 001, followed by the country code. Outside Bangkok, it's best to go to a local telephone exchange if calling internationally.

Local area codes vary according to province. Individual area codes are listed through the book; the code can be found at the front of the telephone directory.

Calls from a telephone box cost ฿1. All telephone numbers marked in the text with a prefix 'B' are Bangkok numbers.

Directory enquiries

For domestic long-distance calls including Malaysia and Vientiane (Laos): T101 (free), Greater Bangkok BMA T183, international

calls T02-2350030-5, although hotel operators will invariably help make the call if asked.

Mobiles

Quite simply the cheapest and most convenient form of telephony in Thailand is the mobile/cell phone. Mobiles are common and increasingly popular – reflecting the difficulties of getting a landline as well as a desire to be contactable at all times and places. Coverage is good except in some border areas.

Sim cards and top-up vouchers for all major networks are available from every single 7-11 store in the country. You will need a sim-free, unlocked phone but you can pick up basic, second-hand phones for ฿600 from most local markets. Unfortunately for smart-phone users, most of Thailand has yet to acquire 3G, although cheap GPRS packages are available from all providers and coverage is pretty good.

AIS and *Happy D Prompt* sim cards and top ups are available throughout the country and cost ฿200 with domestic call charges from ฿3 per min and international calls from ฿8 per min. This is a very good deal and much cheaper than either phone boxes or hotels.

Internet

GPRS data deals are also incredible cheap – the AIS network offers 100 hrs of mobile internet connection for ฿300 per month. Speeds are slow though the network is perfectly adequate for text emails, basic web-browsing and social sites such as Facebook.

Time

GMT plus 7 hrs.

Tourist information

Tourist Authority of Thailand (TAT), 1600 New Phetburi Rd, Makkasan, Ratchathewi, T02-2505500, www.tourism thailand.org; also at 4 Rachdamnern Nok

Av (intersection with Chakrapatdipong Rd), Mon-Fri 0830-1630; in addition there are 2 counters at Suvarnabhumi Airport, in the Arrivals halls of Domestic and International Terminals, T02-134 0040, T02-134 0041, 0800-2400. Local offices are found in most major tourist destinations in the country. Most offices open daily 0830-1630. TAT offices are a useful source of local information, often providing maps of the town, listings of hotels/guesthouses and information on local tourist attractions. The website is a useful first stop and is generally well regarded.

Tourism authorities abroad
Australia, Suite 2002, 2nd floor, 56 Pitt St, Sydney, NSW 2000, T9247-7549, www. thailand.net.au.
France, 90 Ave des Champs Elysées, 75008 Paris, T5353-4700, tatpar@wanadoo.fr.
Germany, Bethmannstr 58, D-60311, Frankfurt/Main 1, T69-1381390, tatfra@t-online.de.
Hong Kong, 401 Fairmont House, 8 Cotton Tree Drive, Central, T2868-0732, tathkg@hk.super.net.
Italy, 4th floor, Via Barberini 68, 00187 Roma, T06-487 3479.
Japan, Yurakucho Denki Building, South Tower 2F, Room 259, 1-7-1, Yurakucho, Chiyoda-ku, Tokyo 100-0006, T03-218 0337, tattky@criss cross.com.
Malaysia, c/o Royal Thai Embassy 206 Jalan Ampang, 50450 Kuala Lumpur, T26-23480, sawatdi@po.jaring.my.
Singapore, c/o Royal Thai Embassy, 370 Orchard Rd, Singapore 238870, T2357901, tatsin@mbox5.singnet.com.sg.
UK, 1st floor, 17-19 Cockspur St, Trafalgar Sq, London SW1Y 5BL, T0870-900 2007, www.tourismthailand.co.uk.
USA, 1st floor, 611 North Larchmont Blvd, Los Angeles, CA 90004, T461-9814, tatla@ix.netcom.com.

Useful websites
www.asiancorrespondent.com
Regional news website featuring guest blogs on Thai politics by writers who dig deep rather than toe the line. A better source of unbiased analysis than either the *Bangkok Post* or *The Nation*.
www.bangkokpost.com Homepage for the country's most widely read English-language daily.
www.bk.asia-city.com The online version of Bangkok's weekly freebie BK Magazine offers instant access to the hipper side of city life, from upcoming events to comment, chat and lifestyle features.
www.fco.gov.uk/travel The UK Foreign and Commonwealth Office's travel warning section.
www.paknamweb.com Umbrella website for the Paknam Network, expat Richard Barrow's assorted websites and blogs covering all facets of Thai culture.
www.thaifolk.com Good site for Thai culture, from folk songs and handicrafts through to festivals like Loi Kratong, and Thai myths and legends. Information posted in both English and Thai – although the Thai version of the site is better.
www.thai-language.com An easy-to-use Thai-English online language resource with an excellent dictionary, thousands of audio clips, lessons and a forum.
www.tourismthailand.org A useful first stop.
www.travel.state.gov/travel The US State Department updates travel advisories on its Travel Warnings & Consular Information Sheets.

Visas and immigration
For the latest information on visas and tourist visa exemptions, see the consular information section of the **Thai Ministry of Foreign Affairs** website, www.mfa. go.th. Having relocated from its central location on Soi Suan Plu, the immigration department that deals with tourists

is now on the outskirts: Immigration Bureau, Government Complex Chaeng Wattana, B Building, Floor 2 (South Zone), Chaengwattana Rd Soi 7, Laksi, Bangkok 10210, T02-141 9889, www.immigration.co.th. Mon-Fri 0830-1200, 1300-1630, closed Sat, Sun, official hols.

For tourists from 41 countries (basically all Western countries, plus some Arabic and other Asian states – see www.mfa.go.th), Thai immigration authorities will issue a 30-day visa-exemption entry permit if you arrive by plane. If you enter at a land crossing from any neighbouring country, the permit is for 15 days.

Visas on arrival

Tourists from 28 countries (most of them developing countries) can apply for a 15-day visa on arrival at immigration checkpoints. Applicants must have an outbound (return) ticket and possess funds to meet living expenses of ฿10,000 per person or ฿20,000 per family. The application fee is ฿1000 and must be accompanied by a passport photo.

Tourist visas

These are valid for 60 days from date of entry and must be obtained from a Thai embassy before arrival in Thailand.

Visa extensions

These are obtainable from the Immigration Bureau (see above) for ฿1900. Applicants must bring 2 photocopies of their passport ID page and the page on which their tourist visa is stamped, together with a passport photograph. It is also advisable to dress neatly. Visas are issued by all Thai embassies and consulates. The length of time a visa is extended varies according to the office and the official.

Weights and measures

Thailand uses the metric system, although there are some traditional measures still in use, in particular the *rai*, which equals 0.16 ha. There are 4 *ngaan* in a *rai*. Other local measures include the krasorp (sack) which equals 25 kg and the *tang* which is 10-11 kg. However, for most purchases (for example fruit) the kg is the norm. Both kg and km are often referred to as lo – as in ki-lo.

INDEX

A

accommodation 270
  national parks 271
Adang-Rawi archipelago
  260
airport transport 35
air travel 267
alcohol 273
ambulance 274
Amulet Market 47
Ancient City 57
Ang thong Marine
  National Park 184
Ao Bang Charu 176
Ao Chalok Ban Kao 171
Ao Chao Lok Lum 178
Ao Chaophao 178
Ao Hat Khom 178
Ao Hat Kuat 178
Ao Hat Yao 178
Ao Hin Kong 178
Ao Hinsong Kon 176
Ao Hin Wong 171
Ao Kantiang 246
Ao Khlong Dao 244
Ao Khlong Jaak 246
Ao Khlong Nin 245
Ao Leuk 171
Ao Mae Hat 178
Ao Mai Phai 246
Ao Nai Wok 178
Ao Nang 233
Ao Phra-Ae (Long Beach),
  Koh Lanta 245
Ao Sri Thanu 178
Ao Ta Not 171
Ao Thian Ok 171
Ao Thong Nai Pan Noi 177
Ao Ton Sai 235
Aranya Prathet 144
ATMs 276
Ayutthaya 72
  background 73
  getting around 72

getting there 72
river tours 78
tourist information 73
transport 72

B

baht 275
Ban Du 129
Bangkok
  24 hrs in the city 40
  Buddhaisawan Chapel 45
  Chao Phaa Sua 47
  Chatuchak weekend
    market 56
  Chinatown 48
  Chulalongkorn University
    53
  Crocodile Farm and Zoo
    57
  Democracy Monument
    46
  Erawan Shrine 54
  floating markets 49, 57
  getting around 36
  getting there 35
  Giant Swing 47
  Golden Buddha 48
  Golden Mount 46
  Grand Palace 41
  Indian Market 48
  Jim Thompson's House 52
  Khaosan Road 45
  Khlongs 49
  Koh Kret 58
  Lak Muang 44
  Loha Prasat 47
  Long-tailed boat tours 49
  Lumpini Park 54
  Muang Boran
    (Ancient City) 57
  Nakhon Kasem 48
  National Art Gallery 45
  National Museum 44
  National Science Museum
    59

National Theatre 45
Old City 39
Pahurat Indian market 48
Pak Khlong market 48
Panthip Plaza 54
Patpong 54
Phra Arthit Road 46
Railway Museum 56
Royal Barges National
  Museum 51
Royal Ploughing
  Ceremony 43
Sampeng Lane 49
Sanaam Luang 43
Santa Cruz 50
shopping 53
Siam Square 52
Silom Road 54
Snake Farm 49
Suan Pakkard Palace 52
Sukhumvit Road 55
Temple of the Emerald
  Buddha 41
Temple of the Golden
  Buddha 49
Thai Red Cross Snake
  Farm 55
Thammasat University 44
Thieves' Market 48
Thonburi 49
tourist information 38
transport 35
Wat Arun 50
Wat Chalerm Phra Kiat 58
Wat Indraviharn 46
Wat Mahannapharam 47
Wat Mahathat 44
Wat Pho 40
Wat Phra Chetuphon
  (Wat Pho) 40
Wat Phra Kaeo 41
Wat Prayoon Wong 50
Wat Rachabophit 48
Wat Rakhang 51

Wat Saket 47
Wat Suthat 47
Wat Suwannaram 51
Wat Traimitr 49
Yaowarat Road 48
Bangkok Airways 267
Bang Pae Waterfall 219
Bang Pa In 59
Bang Po 184
Bang Sai 60
Bang Tao 217
Ban Hua Thanon 186
Ban Khai 177
Ban Koh Lanta Yai,
  Koh Lanta 244
Ban Mae Hat 171
Ban Mai 131
Ban Pak Bara 256
Ban Tai 177
Big Buddha Beach
  (Bang Ruk) 184
boat travel 269
Bophut 184
Bor Sang and San
  Kamphaeng circuit 109
bribery 277
Bridge on the River Kwai 65
Bridge over the River Kwai
  68
bull fighting 251
Bun bang fai 160
Burmese border 98
buses 267

C
camping 271
Cape Panwa 216
car hire 268
Cha-am 165
Chachoengsao 60
Chaliang 95
Chalong Beach 215
Chang Lang Beach 251
Chantaburi 144
Chapel of Phra Buddha
  Sihing 193

Chatuchak weekend market
  56
Chaweng 185
Chiang Dao 111
Chiang Dao Caves 111
Chiang Dao Elephant
  Training Centre 111
Chiang Khong 136
  getting around 136
Chiang Mai 100
  background 101
  Chinatown 107
  Contemporary Art
    Museum 106
  excursions 107
  markets 107
  Museum of World Insects
    and Natural Wonders
    107
  National Museum 106
  tourist information 101
  transport 100
  Tribal Museum 108
Chiang Rai 125
  Hilltribe Education Center
    129
  motorcycle tours 130
  tourist information 125
  transport 125
Chiang Saen 134
Chinatown 48
Chinese Vegetarian Festival
  210
Choeng Mon 185
Chulalongkorn University 53
Chumphon 167
coffee 273
cost of travelling 276
credit cards 276
currency 275

D
Damnoen Saduak 57
dengue fever 274
directory inquiries 278
diving 173, 205, 221, 242,
  249, 264

Chumphon 167
Similan Islands 205
Tarutao national park 264
Doi Pui 108
Doi Sang 110
Doi Suthep 107
Doi Suthep-Pui National
  Park 110
Doi Tung 133
dolphins 60, 254, 259
drink 273
drugs 277

E
electricity 274
Elephant Conservation
  Centre 113
elephant kraals 78
Elephant Training Camp 110
Elephant Training Centre 111
emergency services 274
Erawan National Park 69
Erawan Shrine 54
exchange rate 275

F
farang 76
festivals
  Loi Krathong 92
  Songkran 101
fire 274
flights 267
floating market,
  Damnoen Saduak 57
flying vegetable artistes 97
Fossil Shell Beach
  (Susaan Hoi) 234

G
Garos Island 230
Gibbon Rehabilitation
  Project 219
Golden Triangle 134
Grand Palace, Bangkok 41
guesthouses 270
gurney's pitta 231

H

Had Thung Thale Non-
  Hunting Area 247
Hat Chao Mai National Park
  251
Hat Khlong Khoang 245
Hat Rin 177
Hat Rin Nai 177
Hat Sadet 177
Hat Sai Nuan 171
Hat Salat 178
Hat Sat Rin 171
Hat Som Paen 200
Hat Thien 177
Hat Thung Wua Laen 167
health 274
Hilltribe Education Center,
  Chiang Rai 129
hilltribe villages 136
hornbills 155, 203, 262
hotels 270
Hua Hin 165
Huai To Waterfall 231

I

Irrawaddy dolphins 60

J

Jai Sorn (Chae Sorn)
  National Park 114
James Bond Island 224
Jim Thompson's House,
  Bangkok 52

K

Kamala Beach 217
Kamphaeng Phet 84
Kanchanaburi 65
  background 67
  Death Railway 68
  getting around 65
  getting there 65
  Hellfire Pass 68
  JEATH War Museum 67
  tourist information 67
Karon Beach 214
Kata Beach 214
Khanom Beach 194

Khao Chong Forest Park 252
Khao Lak 204
Khao Luang National Park
  194
Khao Nan National Park 195
Khao Nor Chu Chi forest 231
Khao Phanom Bencha
  National Park 231
Khao Phra Thaeo Wildlife
  Park 218
Khaosan Road 45
Khao Sok National Park 202
Khao Wang 165
Khao Wang Thong Cave 195
Khao Yai National Park 155
Khlong Lan National Park 99
Khlong Muang 233
Khun Yuam 122
Koh Adang 260
Koh Boda 235
Koh Bubu 244
Koh Bulon-Leh 259
Koh Chang 148, 201
Koh Chuak 253
Koh Gai 235
Koh Hin Ngam (Koh Bula)
  261
Koh Jum (Jam) 240
Koh Kaew Pisadarn 215
Koh Kradan 253
Koh Kret 58
Koh Lanta 243
  diving 249
  excursions 244
Koh Lanta Noi 247
Koh Lao Lieng 254
Koh Lipe 260
  activities 264
  tourist information 257
Koh Lone 216
Koh Mai Ton 216
Koh Maprao 216
Koh Matsum 186
Koh Mook 253
Koh Muk 253
Koh Nang Yuan 171
Koh Ngai (Hai) 253

Koh Petra 254
Koh Phangan 174
  Ao Chao Lok Lum 178
  Ao Sri Thanu 178
  Ao Thong Nai Pan Noi 177
  east coast 177
  Hat Rin 177
  Hat Sadet 177
  Hat Thien 177
  north coast 178
  south coast 176
  Thong Nai Pan Yai 177
  Thong Sala 176
  tourist information 175
  west coast 178
Koh Phayam 202
Koh Phing Kan 224
Koh Phi Phi 239
  beaches 240
  diving 240, 242
Koh Rang Yai 217
Koh Rawi 260
Koh Samet 143
Koh Samui 181
  Bang Po 184
  Ban Hua Thanon 186
  best time to visit 183
  Big Buddha Beach 184
  Bophut 184
  Chaweng Beach 185
  Choeng Mon 185
  east coast 185
  Laem Set 186
  Lamai Beach 185
  Mae Nam 184
  Na Khai 186
  Nathon 184
  Samrong Bay 185
  south coast 186
  Thong Krut 186
  tourist information 183
  west coast 187
Koh Siboya 241
Koh Si Chang 141
Koh Similan 205
  diving 205
Koh Sukorn 254

Koh Surin 204
  diving 205
Koh Talibong (Libong) 254
Koh Tan 186
Koh Tao 170
  background 170
  Hat Sai Nuan 171
  Hat Sat Rin 171
  tourist information 170
Koh Tarutao 258
  background 257
  tourist information 257
Koh Waen 253
Koh Yao Noi 224
Koh Yao Yai 224
Korat 154
Krabi 227
  tourist information 228
Krabi town 229
Kuomintang 131
Kuomintang – the Chinese
  Republican Army 133

L
Laem Ka 215
Laem Sak 230
Laem Set 186
Laem Sing 217
Laem Son National Park 200
  beaches and islands 200
Lamai 185
Lampang 111
  Wat Phra That Lampang
  112
Lang Khaai Bay 171
Layan 217
leopard 194
leopard, clouded 155, 203
Lopburi 80
  background 80
  Narai Ratchaniwet Palace
  80
Louta 131
Lumpini Park, Bangkok 54

M
Mae Hong Son 120
  background 121
  excursions 122
  transport 121
Mae Lanna 120
Mae Nam 184
Mae Rim Orchid and
  Butterfly Farm 110
Mae Sa Craft Village 110
Mae Sai 133
Mae Salak 131
Mae Salong 131
  activities 138
  excursions 132
Mae Sariang 122
Mae Sa Valley –
  Samoeng circuit 109
Mae Sa Waterfall 110
Mae Sot 98
  towards the Burmese
  border 98
Mae Yim Falls 110
Mai Khao 218
mangos 60
manta rays 170, 205
mobiles 278
money 275
  exchange rates 275
Moo Koh Lanta Marine
  National Park 246
motorbike hire 268
motorbikes 268
Muang Boran
  (Ancient City) 57
Muang On Caves 109
Muang Pon 122
Muang Singh Historical Park
  69
Museum of World Insects
  and Natural Wonders 107

N
Nai Harn Beach 214
Nai Phlao Beach 194
Nai Thon 217

Nai Yang 218
Nai Yang National Park 218
Na Khai 186
Nakhon 190
Nakhon Pathom 57
Nakhon Ratchasima 154
Nakhon Si Thammarat 190
  background 190
  Hindu temples 193
  National Museum 192
  puppet workshop 192
  Thai Traditional Medicine
  Centre 193
Nan 115
Nang Koi Falls 110
Naresuan the Great of
  Ayutthaya 73
Nathon 184
national parks
  Ang Thong 184
  Doi Inthanon 114
  Doi Suthep-Pui National
  Park 110
  Erawan 69
  Hat Chao Mai 251
  Jai Sorn (Chae Sorn) 114
  Khao Luang 194
  Khao Nan 195
  Khao Phanom Bencha
  231
  Khao Sok 202
  Khlong Lan 99
  Laem Son 201
  Moo Koh Lanta 246
  Nai Yang 218
  Phangnga Bay 223
  Ramkhamhaeng 93
  Sai Yok 69
  Surin 204
  Tarutao 256
  Thale Ban 262
  Tham Than Lot 70
  Thanboke Khoranee 230
Nong Khai 156
Nonthaburi 58
Nopparat Thara 233

O

Opium Museum 134
orchid gardens 110
orchids 110, 155, 203

P

Pai 119
Pakmeng Beach 251
Pansea Beach 217
Panthip Plaza 54
Patong Beach 213
Patpong 54
Pearl Farm 219
Phangnga Bay 222
Phangnga Bay National
  Park 223
Phangnga town 222
Pha Thai caves 113
Phaulcon, Constantine 81
Phetburi 165
Phimai 156
Phi Phi Le 239
Phitsanulok 83
  background 86
  tourist information 83
Phnom Rung 156
Phra Arthit Road 46
Phra Buddha Sihing chapel
  193
Phrae 115
Phra Nakhon Khiri 165
Phra Nang 235
Phra Viharn 159
Phra Viharn Luang 192
Phuket City 210
Phuket Island 208
  Bang Tao 217
  beaches 213
  best time to visit 210
  Cape Panwa 216
  Chalong 215
  diving 221
  Kamala Beach 217
  Karon and Kata beaches
    214

Mai Khao Beach 218
Nai Harn Beach and
  Promthep Cape 214
Nai Thon and Layan
  beaches 217
Nai Yang Beach 218
Pansea Beach 217
Patong Beach 213
Rawai Beach 215
Surin Beach 217
tourist information 210
Phu Phra Caves 69
Phu Ping Palace 108
police 274
Port of Ranong 200
Prachuap Khiri Khan 167
prisons 277
Promthep Cape 214
prostitution 277
puppet workshop
  Nakhon Si Thammarat
    192

Q

Queen Sirikit Botanical
  Gardens 110

R

rafflesia Kerri Meijer 203
Rai Leh 235
Rama V's palace 141
Ramkhamhaeng National
  Park 93
Ranong 199
Rawai Beach 215
restaurants 272
rhinoceros
  Sumatran 262
rice 271
Richelieu Rock 199, 207
road accidents 278
Roong Arun Hot Springs 109
Royal Folk Arts and Crafts
  Centre, Bang Sai 60

S

Saan Chao Mae Thap Thim
  Chinese Pagoda 192
safety 276
Sai Yok National Park 69
Sala Dan 244
Samoeng 110
Samrong Bay 185
Santikhiri 131
Satun 261
Siam Square 52
Similan Islands National Park
  205
Si Satchanalai 94
skyrocket festival 160
Snake Farm, Bangkok 50
Songkran, Chiang Mai 101
songthaew 268
Soppong 120
Sop Ruak 134
Sri Guru Singh Sabha 48
strawberry festival 110
Suan Bua Mae Sa Orchid 110
Suan Pakkard Palace,
  Bangkok 52
Sukhothai 83
  background 87
  best time to visit 87
  getting around 87
  getting there 87
  Old City 89
  park essentials 89
Sukhumvit Road 55
Surat Thani 187
Surin 159
Surin Beach 217
Susaan Hoi (Fossil Shell
  Beach) 234

T

Tad Mok Waterfalls 110
Tahamakeng 131
Takua Pa 202
Tarutao National Park 256
  activities 264
  best time to visit 257
  diving 264

taxis 269
telephone 278
Temple of the Emerald
   Buddha 41
Temple of the Golden
   Buddha 49
Thai Airways 267
Thai Elephant Conservation
   Centre 113
Thai massage 41
Thai Traditional Medicine
   Centre 193
Thale Ban National Park 262
Tham Lod 229
Tham Phi Hua To 229
Tham Suwan Kuha 223
Tham Than Lot National
   Park 70
Thanboke Khoranee
   National Park 230
Tha Rua, Phuket Island 218
Tha Ton 131
therapies 238
Thi Lo Su waterfall 99
Thonburi, Bangkok 49
Thong Krut 186
Thong Sala 176
tiger 70, 194, 203
time 278
Tourism Authority Thailand
   278
   overseas offices 279
tourist police 274, 278

traffic 278
Trang 250
   beaches 251
   best time to visit 250
   parks 251
Trang's Andaman Islands
   252
transport
   air 267
   air travel 266
   boat 269
   bus travel 267
   car hire 268
   flights 266
   motorbike taxi 268
   motorcycles 268
   private tour buses 267
   rail 269
   sea 269
   songthaews 268
   taxis 269
   train travel 269
Trat 145
travel advisories 277
trekking
   Chiang Khong 136
   Khao Yai National Park 155
   Mae Salong 133
   Pai 120
   Soppong 120
   Umphang 99
Tribal Museum 108
turtles 218, 254, 259

U
Ubon Ratchathani 158
Umbrella Festival 109
Umphang 99

V
Vegetarian Festival
   Phuket 210
   Trang 250

W
Wanglao 134
Wat Arun, Bangkok 50
Wat Inthrawat 110
Wat Phra Kaeo 41
Wat Phra Mahathat 191
Wat Phra Sri Ratana
   Mahathat 165
Wat Phra Sri Ratana
   Mahathat, Phitsanulok 86
Wat Phra That Lampang
   Luang 112
Wat Tham Khao Thao 223
Wat Tham Sua 229
Wat That Phanom 158
Wat Wang Tawan Tok 193
weights 280
whale sharks 170, 205
Wiang Kum Kam 108

Y
Yasothon 159

PHOTOGRAPHY CREDITS

Title page: Minyun Zhou/Dreamstime.com.
Page 2: cozyta/Shutterstockstock;
doraclub/Shutterstockstock;
Niti Chuysakul/Shutterstockstock.
Page 3: nofilm2011/Shutterstockstock;
Chaloemkiad/Shutterstock;
defpicture/Shutterstock.
Page 4: Pichugin Dmitry/Shutterstock.
Page 6: blue planet/Shutterstock;
Iakov Kalinin/Shutterstock.
Page 7: Stephane Bidouze/Shutterstock;
Patryk Kosmider/Shutterstock;
Dmitry Pichugin/Dreamstime.com;
topten22photo/Shutterstock.
Page 8: Luciano Mortula/Shutterstock.
Page 9: Donsimon/Dreamstime.com;
Alexey Stiop/Shutterstock;
Palo_ok/Shutterstock. Page
Page 10: Richliy/Dreamstime.com;
BlueOrange Studio/Shutterstock;
Mattbkk/Dreamstime.com;
Naylar/Dreamstime.com.
Page 11: Andy Lim/Shutterstock.
Page 12: Chatchai5172/Dreamstime.com.
Page 13: Elephantopia/Dreamstime.com;
Chaloemkiad/Shutterstock;
Superoke/Dreamstime.com.
Page 14: narokzaad/Shutterstock; 2nix/
Shutterstock; Gudgiie/Dreamstime.com.
Page 15: Kjersti Joergensen/Shutterstock;
Teerawatyai/Shutterstock;
NIRUN NUNMEESRI/Shutterstock.

Page 17: Chollacholla/Dreamstime.com.
Page 18: kongsky/Shutterstock;
freedomman/Shutterstock; Kushch Dmitry/
Shutterstock; Vlad61/Shutterstock.
Page 19: MJ Prototype/Shutterstock;
baitong333/Shutterstock;
isarescheewin/Shutterstock.
Page 20: Shutterstockphotostock/
Shutterstock; Igor Stepovik/Shutterstock.
Page 21: Kushch Dmitry/Shutterstock;
panda3800/Shutterstock.
Page 22: MJ Prototype/Shutterstock.
Page 23: magicinfoto/Shutterstock;
Bule Sky Studio/Shutterstock;
aiaikawa/Shutterstock.
Page 24: Palo_ok/Shutterstock.
Page 26: Stasis Photo/Shutterstock;
Muzhik/Shutterstock;
Patryk Kosmider/Dreamstime.com.
Page 27: Andamanse/Dreamstime.com.
Page 28: Stasis Photo/Shutterstock;
f9photos/Shutterstock.
Page 29: vichie81/Shutterstock;
aiaikawa/Shutterstock;
Petr Malyshev/Dreamstime.com.
Page 31: Zeamonkey Images/Shutterstock.
Page 32: panda3800/Shutterstock

CREDITS

Footprint credits
Editor: Jo Williams
Production and layout: Emma Bryers
Cover: Pepi Bluck
Colour section: Angus Dawson
Maps: Kevin Feeney

Publisher: Patrick Dawson
Managing Editor: Felicity Laughton
Advertising: Elizabeth Taylor
Sales and marketing: Kirsty Holmes

Photography credits
Front cover: Shutterstock.com
Back cover: cesc_assawin/Shutterstock.com;
Iakov Kalinin/Shutterstock.com; Zdorov Kirill
Vladimirovich/Shutterstock.com
Inside front cover: Pigprox/Shutterstock.com
Inside front flap: Kenneth Dedeu/
Shutterstock.com; Charlie Edward/
Shutterstock.com; think4photop/
Shutterstock.com; totophotos/
Shutterstock.com

Printed in Spain by GraphyCems

Every effort has been made to ensure that
the facts in this guidebook are accurate.
However, travellers should still obtain
advice from consulates, airlines etc about
travel and visa requirements before
travelling. The authors and publishers
cannot accept responsibility for any loss,
injury or inconvenience however caused.

Publishing information
Footprint DREAM TRIP Thailand
1st edition
© Footprint Handbooks Ltd
February 2013

ISBN: 978 1 907263 67 5
CIP DATA: A catalogue record for this book
is available from the British Library

® Footprint Handbooks and the Footprint
mark are a registered trademark of
Footprint Handbooks Ltd

Published by Footprint
6 Riverside Court
Lower Bristol Road
Bath BA2 3DZ, UK
T +44 (0)1225 469141
F +44 (0)1225 469461
footprinttravelguides.com

Distributed in the USA by Globe Pequot
Press, Guilford, Connecticut